How to Keep Control
of Your Life after 60

How to Keep Control of Your Life after 60

*A Guide for Your
Legal, Medical, and Financial Well-Being*

TERESA SCHWAB MYERS

Lexington Books

D.C. Heath and Company • Lexington, Massachusetts • Toronto

Library of Congress Cataloging-in-Publication Data

Myers, Teresa Schwab
How to keep control of your life after sixty.

Includes index.
I. Aged—Legal status, laws, etc.—United States.
2. Estate planning—United States. 3. Aged—Medical care—United States. 4. Aged—United States—Finance, Personal. I. Title.
KF390.A4M97 1989   346.7301'3   88-45305
                     347.30613
    ISBN 0-669-19456-5 (alk. paper).

Copyright © 1989 by Lexington Books

All rights reserved. No part of this publication may be reproduced or transmitted in any form or by any means, electronic or mechanical, including photocopy, recording, or any information storage or retrieval system, without permission in writing from the publisher.

Published simultaneously in Canada
Printed in the United States of America
International Standard Book Number: 0-669-19456-5
Library of Congress Catalog Card Number: 88-45305

The paper used in this publication meets the minimum requirements of American National Standard for Information Sciences—Permanence of Paper for Printed Library Materials, ANSI Z39.48-1984.

89 90 91 92 8 7 6 5 4 3 2

Contents

Acknowledgments — xiii

Introduction — xv
  Why Plan Ahead? — xv
  The Consequences of Not Planning Ahead — xvi
  How Best to Use This Book — xvii

PART 1
Planning Ahead

1. Wills, Trusts, and Joint Accounts: Using Them Now — 3
   Overview — 3
   Wills and How They Work — 3
   Advantages and Disadvantages of Wills — 7
   Dying without a Will — 8
   Why Alternatives Are Needed — 8
   Alternatives to Wills — 10
     Tools for Managing Money and Property — 10
     Joint Property Arrangements and Joint Bank Accounts — 11
     Trusts — 14
     Gifts — 17

2. "Medigap" and Long-Term Care Insurance Policies — 19
   Medigap Policies — 19
     Overview — 19
     When Might It Be Necessary to Purchase Medigap Insurance? — 20
     A Word of Caution — 22
     The New Legal Requirements for Medigap Insurance Policies — 23
     Questions to Ask the Insurance Agent — 24

Long-Term Care Insurance Policies	25
Overview	25
When Might It Be Necessary to Purchase Long-Term Care Insurance?	26
What to Look For in Buying Long-Term Care Insurance	27
Legal Requirements for Long-Term Care Insurance Policies	29
Questions to Ask the Insurance Agent	30
What to Do if a Question or Problem Arises	31

3. Paying for Nursing Home Care — 33

   Overview — 33
   Medicare as a Resource — 35
   Medicaid as a Resource — 37
   Veterans' Benefits and Other Resources — 41
   The Importance of Planning Ahead — 42

4. Is a Living Will a Good Idea for You? — 43

   Overview — 43
   What Can Be Put in a Living Will? — 44
   Does a Living Will Constitute Suicide? — 44
   How and When Does a Living Will Work? — 45
   The Problem of Defining *Terminally Ill* — 45
   Writing a Valid Living Will — 46
   How to Make a Living Will Work — 47
   How to Change or Revoke a Living Will — 47
   The Limits of Living Wills — 48
   How Federal Health Care Facilities View Living Wills — 49
   The Issue of Artificial Feeding and Hydration — 50

5. Powers of Attorney and Other Ways to Plan Ahead — 51

   Overview — 51
   Appointing a Guardian to Make Decisions — 52
   Using a Power of Attorney to Transfer Decision-Making Responsibilities — 52
   Durable Powers of Attorney — 53
   Durable Power-of-Attorney Agreements for Health Care — 55
   Why Use a Durable Power of Attorney? — 55
   How to Create a Durable Power of Attorney — 57

Legal Status and Other Points to Remember ... 59
Limits on Decisions and Why a Decision Might Not Be Followed ... 61
Discussing and Registering the Document with Health Care Professionals ... 62

PART 2
Staying in Charge in a Hospital or Nursing Home

6. Saying Yes to Medical Care: What You Should Know First ... 65
    Overview ... 65
    Selecting a Doctor ... 65
    How to Find a Doctor ... 66
    What to Look For in a Doctor ... 67
    Selecting a Hospital ... 69
    How to Get the Most out of the Doctor-Patient Relationship ... 70
    How Patients Can Help ... 71
    Emergency Room Treatment and Hospitalization ... 72
    Surgery ... 73
    Before Entering the Hospital ... 74
    Being Admitted into the Hospital ... 75
    While in the Hospital ... 78
    When Mistakes or Accidents Occur in the Hospital ... 79

7. Patients Have Rights, Too ... 83
    Overview ... 83
    All Relationships Carry a Price ... 84
    The Patient's Rights in the Doctor-Patient Relationship ... 84
    The Patient's Responsibilities ... 85
    The Doctor's Responsibilities ... 86
    The Right of Informed Consent ... 87
    The Right to Information ... 87
    Patients' Rights and Medical Records ... 91
    The Right to Be Free of Restraints and Abuse ... 92
    Patients' Right to Leave a Hospital ... 93
    Rights and More Rights: What They Mean for Patients ... 93
    Making a Complaint ... 95
    Rights Are Not Absolute ... 96

8.	**If the Hospital Tells You to Go Home Too Early**	99
	Overview	99
	The New Medicare System	100
	What the New System Means for Hospitals	101
	What the New System Means for Patients	102
	Helping to Plan Your Own (or a Family Member's) Discharge	104
	What to Do on Admission into a Hospital	105
	When It's Time to Be Discharged	106
	Receiving a Written Discharge Notice	107
	Deciding Whether to Appeal a Discharge Decision to the Medicare Peer Review Organization	108
	Appealing to the Peer Review Organization	108
	Losing an Appeal	109
	Discharge Dates and Supplemental Insurance	109
9.	**What to Do if You Have a Problem or Complaint**	111
	Overview	111
	Nursing Homes and Other Types of Institutions	113
	Choosing a Facility	114
	Types of Problems Occurring in Residential Facilities: Medical, Financial, and Personal	115
	What to Do When There Is a Problem	118
	Pursuing the Matter within the Facility	119
	Complaints about Hospital Care	121
	When to Seek Outside Assistance to Resolve a Complaint	121
	Where to Go for Outside Assistance	123
	The Long Term Care Ombudsman Program	126
	Regulatory and Licensure Agencies for Nursing Homes	129
	Regulatory and Licensure Agencies for Other Health Care Facilities	130
	Regulatory and Licensure Agencies for Health Care Professionals	130
	Getting Help from Law Enforcement Agencies	131
	Getting Help from Lawyers and the Courts	132
	Other Avenues to Pursue	133
10.	**The Medicare/Medicaid Maze**	135
	Overview	135
	Key Components of the Maze	136
	How to Get Through the Maze	138

	Thumbnail Sketches of Each Program and How They Work	139
	Social Security Disability Income (SSDI)	140
	Medicare	141
	Medicaid	142

PART 3
When Someone Can No Longer Make Decisions

11.	Competence and Incompetence: What They Mean	147
	Overview	147
	The Kinds of Decisions That May Need to Be Made for an Individual	148
	Financial Decisions	148
	Decisions about Medical Treatment, Nontreatment, and Experimental Treatment	149
	Personal Decisions	150
	The Concept of Competence	150
	Levels of Competence and Incompetence	151
	Competence to Make Specific Decisions	152
	De Facto Incompetence and De Facto Surrogates	152
	How Health Care Professionals Can Help Determine a Patient's Competence	153
	Policies for Evaluating a Patient's Competence	154
	The Geriatric Mental Status Evaluation	155
12.	Guardians and Conservators: When, If, and How	157
	Overview	157
	What are Guardianship and Conservatorship?	158
	A Few Legal Terms and Their Definitions	159
	The Implications of Guardianship	160
	Full versus Limited Guardianship Arrangements	160
	Public Guardianship Programs	161
	When Is Guardianship Necessary and What Triggers a Petition?	161
	Advantages and Disadvantages of Guardianship	163
	The Duties and Responsibilities of a Guardian	163
	At What Point Is Conservatorship Necessary?	165
	Advantages and Disadvantages of Conservatorship	165
	The Duties and Responsibilities of a Conservator	165

	The Process of Petitioning for Guardianship	166
	The Process of Petitioning for Conservatorship	169
	Removing a Guardian and Terminating a Guardianship Arrangement	169
	The Importance of Considering Alternative Methods	170
13.	When Social Security Payments Go to Someone Else	171
	Overview	171
	When Does the Social Security Administration Designate Representative Payees?	172
	Qualifying to Be a Representative Payee	172
	Institutional Payees: Rules and Regulations	174
	Responsibilities of Payees	174
	Payee Misuse of Funds	175
	Accounting Procedures for Payees	175
	On-Site Review of Federal and State Institutions	176
	Replacing a Payee	177
	A Closing Word	178
14.	Limits on Decisions Made for Someone Else	179
	Overview	179
	Decision-Making Tools: A Review	179
	Decision Makers and De Facto Surrogates	181
	Family Consent Statutes	182
	The Kinds of Medical Care Decisions That Need to Be Made	183
	The Decision to Remove Food and Water	185
	The Decision to Donate Organs	185
	The Decision to Participate in Medical Research	186
	Financial and Personal Decisions	186
	Standards for Making Decisions	187
	What to Do When Decisions Are Challenged or Ignored	187

PART 4
Conclusion

15.	People Will Listen—*If* You Talk	191
	Overview	191
	Getting Involved	191

Getting Involved in the Political Arena		192
Getting Attention and Influencing a Particular Program		193
Involving the Media		195
A Final Word		195

Appendixes

1.	Coverage under Medicare Parts A and B	199
2.	State Insurance Departments	209
3.	Sample Living Will	215
4.	Checklist of State Laws Regarding Living Wills	217
5.	Special Requirements for Creating Durable Powers of Attorney	225
6.	Sample State Power-of-Attorney Form	227
7.	Sample General Power-of-Attorney Form	229
8.	Sample Durable Power-of-Attorney for Health Care Forms	235
9.	Sample Springing (Durable) Power-of-Attorney Form	245
10.	List of Possible Hospital Services	251
11.	The American Hospital Association's Patient's Bill of Rights	257
12.	Sample State Bill of Rights for Patients	259
13.	Sample Federal Bill of Rights for Patients	261
14.	An Important Message from Medicare	263
15.	Guidelines for Hospital Discharge Planning	267
16.	State Peer Review Organizations	271
17.	Model Discharge Notices	277
18.	Medicare Quality Screen	285
19.	State Long Term Care Ombudsman Program Offices	287
20.	State Units on Aging	293
21.	State Public Guardianship Programs	299
22.	State Requirements for Personal Status Reports on Wards	301
23.	State Requirements for Ward Estate Accounting	303
24.	State Requirements for Legal Representation of Wards	305
25.	Sample Petition for Appointment of Conservators (Guardians) of the Person and the Property	307
26.	Sample Conservatorship (Guardianship) Order for the Person and the Property	311
27.	Social Security Payee Application Form	313
28.	Social Security Administration's Order of Preference in Selecting Representative Payee	319

29.	Social Security Payee Report Form	321
30.	Social Security Payee Evaluation Form	325
31.	States with Family Consent Statutes	331
32.	Provisions of Family Consent Laws	333
33.	American Medical Association Statement on Withholding or Withdrawing Life-Prolonging Medical Treatment	335
34.	Health-Related State Agencies and Organizations (Including Licensure Agencies)	337
35.	National Health Care and Self-Help Groups	393

Glossary	401
Additional Reading	409
Index	415
About the Advisory Board	425
About the Author	429

Acknowledgments

THERE is, I think, a certain ineffable excitement that surrounds specific events in our lives. They are events, in this case the writing of this book, that, for lack of a better word, summon up the commitment that lies deep within each one of us. If one is very lucky, then perhaps a few such events will occur in a single life span.

This book seemed blessed from the beginning: the publisher was excited by it; the outline fell together readily enough, waiting to be fleshed into chapters; and, most importantly, top experts in the field agreed to consult on each chapter. Each one, I believe, felt that excitement mentioned earlier—each one was committed to the success of this project. They worked for far less than their usual compensation, made countless excellent suggestions, rearranged already busy schedules, and reviewed all materials quickly and thoroughly. They did so because they care—because this subject, and the offering of clear and usable information to the elderly and their families, is as important to them as it is to me. I have noticed that there are certain topics, and this is one of them, that pull so strongly at the hearts and minds of the people involved that they will outdo themselves in their efforts to make a better world. Anyone who believes that "no one cares about the elderly" has never met these people.

There are a few people who deserve special mention: my mother, who, in addition to giving regular and welcome doses of moral and maternal support, acted as a lay reader of this book and helped to organize the glossary; chapter consultants Susan Pettey, Bill Benson, David Schulke, Tom Jazwiecki, Marshall Kapp, John Fears, John Laster, David Chavkin, Penelope Hommel, Barbara Mishkin, and Cynthia Northrop, who went more than a few "extra miles" to help out; Amy Cohen, who, as my assistant, was industrious, cheerful, and efficient; and Margaret Zusky, of Lexington Books, who without fail remained all that an editor should be—enthusiastic, intelligent, interested, and caring.

Lastly, this book is dedicated to my parents, Joan and Gerald Schwab, who have always urged me to find the best within myself; and to David, who makes all of that worthwhile.

Introduction

Why Plan Ahead?

Why plan ahead? In order to properly use this book, it is necessary to understand why planning ahead is important in the first place. To do that, it is also useful to know why the society we live in makes it vital that we plan ahead for our own illness, infirmities, and death.

In the United States, we have the luxury of holding life to be the most sacred of all things. It is a luxury that does not exist in many poorer, less developed nations, where living is much harder and dying much easier. In those countries, the moral, ethical, and legal questions we face when we make decisions to refuse lifesaving medical treatment simply do not apply. In such countries there are too many other problems to tackle to spend a great deal of time worrying about whether an elderly person should undergo another operation, be put on life-support systems, or be allowed to die.

So life in the United States is a luxury made possible by our standard of living and by our medical and technological knowledge. But it is a luxury that now acts as a double-edged sword. If life is perceived as preeminent, then what about the people who don't want to continue living with illness, or who simply want to be able to control what happens to their bodies?

We are at a crossroads now. Our ability to extend and prolong life has run smack up against our own questions of whether life should always be extended and prolonged. Until society makes some very hard choices, elderly individuals can maintain control over their own life-and-death decisions only by making plans and arrangements before, or shortly after, they become ill—before medicine, technology, doctors, and lawyers take over and decide for them.

The purpose of this book is not to tell anyone to refuse medical treatment, nor is it to tell anyone to demand it. All it sets out to do is simply offer the knowledge and the tools necessary for elderly people to get what they want—in their medical treatment, their finances, and their right to maintain control over their own lives.

Hopefully, it will also help families and friends carry out the wishes of their elderly if they are too ill or frail to do so themselves.

The Consequences of Not Planning Ahead

Some three out of every four Americans die without having written a will. A survey conducted in 1982 by Louis Harris and Associates showed that only about a third of respondents had given instructions to someone about how they would like to be treated if they became too ill to make decisions about health care. Of those who had given instructions, only one-fourth had put those instructions into writing.

By not planning ahead, elderly people who become too ill to decide for themselves place a great burden on their families, their friends, and their caretakers. Few people welcome the responsibility of making such important decisions for others, yet millions of people must make those judgments every year. The decisions these people must make include whether or not to put ailing elderly persons into nursing homes, how to take care of their finances, how they would want to live if ill, and how they would want to die.

If no instructions are left to them and no legal documents are drawn up telling them what to do, those people must try to figure out what their elderly relatives and friends would have wanted. If their religious, moral, and personal beliefs are different from those of the elderly people in their care, they will then have to face the struggle between following their own wishes and following those the elderly individuals may have had. Not only are such decisions difficult; in many cases they could be avoided by a little advance planning.

Planning ahead is also more likely to result in elderly people's wishes being respected. For example, an elderly person may know that a particular friend is more able than a relative to understand and follow his or her wishes. While still healthy, the elderly person can legally plan for that friend to be in charge of making the necessary decisions if the elderly person becomes too sick to do so. If, however, the elderly person becomes very ill before planning ahead, a court might appoint a relative (and not the friend) to make decisions because it is unaware of what the elderly person would have wanted.

Planning ahead by appointing someone to make decisions might also stop a hospital or nursing home from going to court to fight a particular decision.

Why don't we plan ahead? The reasons behind not doing so are understandable: illness and death are not pleasant subjects to think about; many people fear having to go through a complicated (and expensive) legal process; they think their families and their doctors will know what to do; and perhaps most common of all, it's something that just gets put off until it's too late.

Illness and death are frightening for everyone—the patient, the family, and the doctor. The stress and fear and pain that all of us face at these times can be greatly eased by the presence of a few plans and instructions. If an elderly person is already too sick to make decisions for himself or herself, then maybe this book can help his or her family make those decisions. Maybe it will also assist families to plan ahead for themselves.

Enough people have become concerned about these issues that there now exist many ways to plan ahead—some are complicated, expensive, and require a lawyer; some are much simpler, cheaper, and can be done with little if any professional help. Some people don't consult with a lawyer or doctor at all but still manage to do some advance planning. Different ways to plan ahead are described in this book. Hopefully, it will help elderly people or their family members find out what they need to know, who they need to talk to, and what questions to ask.

Patients are not the only ones unfamiliar with the ways to plan ahead. Often, legal and health care professionals are just as ignorant of the options for pre-planning health care. It is important to make sure that the elderly person's doctor, nurse, social worker, and lawyer are aware of the person's plans, and if they are unfamiliar with the planning mechanism chosen by the patient, they will need to be educated. Maybe they should be given this book.

How Best to Use This Book

This book is divided into four parts to help readers easily locate the information they need.

1. Part 1, "Planning Ahead," contains chapters on wills, trusts, and joint accounts; purchasing "Medigap" and long-term care insurance policies; paying for nursing home care; writing a living will; and the various legal tools elderly people can use to appoint someone else to make decisions for them should they become too sick to do so themselves.

2. Part 2, "Staying in Charge in a Hospital or Nursing Home," discusses how elderly people or their families can maintain control of their own medical care in a hospital or nursing home setting. It has chapters on what people should know before they agree to medical care, patient rights, what to do if the hos-

3. Part 3, "When Someone Can No Longer Make Decisions," deals with the problems faced by the families and friends of elderly people who can no longer make decisions for themselves. It has chapters on mental competence and incompetence, guardians and conservators, what to do if Social Security payments should go to a family member or friend, and the limits on the decisions made for someone else.

4. Part 4, the book's conclusion, presents various ways to get results by involving government agencies, the media, and politicians. It also discusses how every individual can help mold and define the important decisions our society must make in how to deal with the problems of the elderly and their families.

Each chapter explains a specific issue and answers the questions and concerns that may be raised by it. Chapters are broken down into individual segments that address particular points of each issue.

The appendixes at the back of this book are designed to accompany each chapter and contain a series of charts, sample forms, additional materials, and addresses that should assist readers in identifying their relevant state laws, understanding what documents they will need to fill out, and locating specific state and national agencies, boards, and commissions from which to request further information or assistance. Also at the end of the book are glossary terms to help readers understand some of the medical and legal language used in the chapters and a list ("Additional Reading") of sources providing more information on specific topics.

This book does not claim to have all the answers, but it does provide the basic information necessary to fight a problem, find an answer, and know where to go for further help. The problems discussed here are among the most important issues facing society today. This book is designed to explain the issues and help the people who need it most—the elderly and their families—to resolve the problems.

Part

1

Planning Ahead

1

Wills, Trusts, and Joint Accounts
Using Them Now

Overview

Writing a will is one of the many ways that an individual can plan ahead. It is an important topic, one that might better be served by a whole book rather than a single chapter. Nevertheless, several legal tools—including wills—that can be used to transfer money and property to others before (as well as after) death deserve to be examined here.

Wills are flexible tools that allow individuals to control all their assets during life and then dispose of them after death. *More important for the purpose of this book, there are alternatives to wills that*

> *greatly assist elderly individuals in transferring their financial responsibilities to friends or family members when they become too ill to manage these things themselves; and*

> *help everybody concerned avoid the cost and trauma of getting court-appointed guardians or conservators to take care of the affairs of an incapacitated elderly individual* (for more information, see chapter 12). In short, they provide another way to plan ahead.

Wills and How They Work

Often, an individual dies without ever having written a will. The reasons for this omission are varied. An individual may

> have little or no property left to give anyone;

> die suddenly and without warning by a stroke or in an accident;

gradually become unable to think for himself or herself and therefore be unable to write a will at a certain point; or

simply not want to think about his or her own death, and avoid writing a will until it's too late.

A will controls the property that an individual owns in his or her own name at the time of death. If a person does not own something when he or she dies, the will normally will have no effect. For example, if Mr. X gives his stock in General Motors to his daughter (so that General Motors thinks the daughter owns it) and then leaves it in his will to his son, there is no stock for the son to inherit.

When an individual dies, it is important to find out if he or she had a will. Wills are supposed to be filed right after someone dies, but certainly within three months after the death. *Anyone who has the will of a deceased person can file it by taking it to the registry of wills (or a similar office) in the local courthouse. It is a crime to hide or destroy someone else's will.* After the will is filed, anyone who might have an interest—such as family members, creditors, or friends who might have been left something—files a petition with the probate court asking that someone be appointed to *administer,* or manage, the estate.

Administering a will or estate involves filing all the appropriate papers with the court; taking charge of all the deceased individual's property, such as bank accounts; and performing such tasks as paying taxes, closing houses, caring for pets, paying creditors, and finding heirs. Usually the person who wrote the will has included the name of an *executor* (male) or *executrix* (female) to administer his or her estate (other terms that mean more or less the same thing are *personal representative* and *administrator*). Usually, the court will appoint the person mentioned in the will. The main reasons a court might not appoint that person are that someone opposes the appointment and the court agrees with his or her reasons or the person is not a resident of a state that requires executors to be residents.

If someone dies with no will or if the person named in the will can't administer the estate because he or she has died or become disabled, the law determines who is entitled to administer. There are set lists of people whom the court prefers to appoint to administer an estate. A typical list would start with the deceased person's spouse (and, if no spouse is available), the person's parents (and, if no parents are available), the person's adult children, and so on.

The will directs much, but not all, of what will happen during the administration of the estate, in a process called *probate*.

During probate, the will's instructions are carried out, and the *bequests*, or gifts listed in the will, are given to the appropriate people or organizations. For example, if Mr. X's will states that $1,000 of his estate should go to his close friend, then the administrator will do that. Or, if Mr. X wants to donate $5,000 to his synagogue, church, or favorite charity, then the administrator will do that. Mr. X might also use his will to "forgive" a debt of $10,000 borrowed by his son, so that the son does not have to pay that amount back into his father's estate.

Other kinds of bequests that an individual might want to make include china, silverware, jewelry, or an autographed baseball. The person writing the will has to decide in advance who will receive those items.

Wills often also include instructions about taxes. For example, in his will Mr. X leaves china and silverware worth $10,000 to his niece, who is both extraordinarily kind and extremely poor. If Mr. X lives in a state that has an inheritance tax, his niece might have to pay a tax for the privilege of inheriting property from Mr. X. If in this state the tax is 10 percent, she would have to pay $1,000. To avoid this situation, Mr. X could request that the tax be paid from money in his estate.

Then, too, Mr. X might prefer *not* to have his estate pay for taxes on the gift to his niece, so as to leave more money for his children, who are inheriting the rest of his estate. Very often, people say that they want their estate to pay all inheritance taxes without thinking through what that means. Of course, if the person receiving the china is the same person receiving the rest of the money, the issue makes much less difference. *All individuals thinking about writing a will should strongly consider consulting a lawyer about taxes and other matters.* Doing so is particularly important if the estate is worth a substantial amount, yet even someone with a smaller estate, who still wants to leave a will, should also consider getting a lawyer's advice. Many lawyers offer a low, set fee to write uncomplicated wills, and it is worth calling several different lawyers or legal clinics to find out what services are offered.

The State Unit on Aging (see appendix 20 for addresses) *should have a legal services developer who can direct callers to the appropriate low-cost legal aid office or clinic. Also, almost all states have an Information and Referral (I&R) hot line for older people or the general public in need of services, and this resource can also provide guidance. Local senior citizens' centers should have the I&R telephone number.*

If Mr. X has young children, he might want to name the person with whom those children should live after he dies. If Mr. X has young children or grandchildren to whom he would like to leave money, he might want to place the money *in trust* for them. This means that some adult would watch over the money and invest it until the children or grandchildren reach a certain age specified in Mr. X's will. There are two reasons to think about a trust for young children or grandchildren: (a) many are unable to manage or spend the money responsibly until they are older, and (b) children cannot sign for the money (even if they have learned to write), because they are minors. When children sign documents, it has less legal effect than when adults do (more information on trusts is included later in this chapter).

A will can also be used to ensure that the intended *beneficiaries,* or heirs, receive as much as possible. For example, Congress allows each individual to give away $600,000 during his or her lifetime (or upon his or her death) without having to pay federal estate taxes. Moreover, people can give unlimited amounts of money to a spouse without being taxed at the time of death or at the time of the gift. A person who has more than $600,000 (including the value of his or her house, life insurance, pension benefits, and so on) will benefit from a will that sets up his or her estate in such a way as to minimize the overall tax. If Mr. and Mrs. X have $900,000 worth of property, all of which is passed to Mrs. X upon her husband's death, there is no federal estate tax, because spouses can give unlimited amounts to each other. However, when Mrs. X dies (assuming that she has not spent the excess over $600,000), there will be a substantial estate tax, thus reducing what ultimately passes to Mr. and Mrs. X's children. Had Mr. and Mrs. X planned ahead, they might have eliminated the tax altogether, thus increasing the amount that passed to their children.

A will can make it easier to administer a person's estate. Some state laws, for example, forbid an administrator from selling real estate without a court order; usually this means that the administrator has to hire a lawyer to get the court order, and the lawyer has to be paid. In other states, however, a person's will can authorize the administrator to sell the real estate without having to go to court. Interested individuals should talk with a lawyer to find out the laws of their state.

Precise definitions in a will can also help the administrator. For example, if

Mr. X wants his adopted grandchild to share in the money given to his children, he should say so.

State laws differ on how a will can be written. For example, it is almost always difficult to omit, or leave out, a spouse, but in most (not all) states, it is possible to omit a child.

States also have varying laws on what makes a will legal. In some states, a will must be signed and witnessed by at least two disinterested people (not heirs). In other states, a will can be in the person's own handwriting and signed by him or her without witnesses. Still other states require three witnesses. Again, interested individuals should check with a lawyer to find out the laws in their state.

Usually, special legal language is unnecessary to the writing of a will. The important thing is to be very clear. In one case, a woman wanted to leave money to her daughter, but if her daughter did not survive her, she wanted her sister to have the money. She wrote, "To my sister, if my daughter does not survive. . . ." While it was clear that she meant for her sister to have the money if her daughter did not survive, several insurance companies thought it was not clear that she wanted her daughter to have the money if the daughter did survive!

Advantages and Disadvantages of Wills

There are many advantages and few disadvantages to making a will. The principal advantage is that individuals can make their wishes known—which itself can be an act of great love for the surviving family members and friends. Moreover, writing a will can save a great deal of money in taxes, as well as aggravation in administration.

The principal disadvantage is that writing a will usually costs money. While it is possible to write one's own will in most states, it is often advisable to go to a lawyer or a legal clinic. Again, the State Unit on Aging's legal services developer can make suggestions (see appendix 20), as can the state's I&R hot line, whose number should be available from local senior citizens' centers. Another option is to purchase computer software to assist in the writing of a will (some recommendations for books and software appear in the "Additional Reading" section at the back of this book). None of these options is right or wrong—it is the individual's personal situation and preferences that should determine which option is used.

Dying without a Will

When people die *intestate,* that means they have died without leaving a will. For people who owned property at the time they died intestate, the state legislature "writes" a will, its structure determined by the state's intestacy law. Frequently, states' intestacy laws divide people's assets somewhat by compromise. Often, the compromise that the state has written into law is exactly what those people wanted anyway. For example, the law might provide that one-half (or one-third) of someone's property go to the surviving spouse, while the other one-half (or two-thirds) go to the surviving children. Particularly in the case of second marriages, one-third may not be enough to support the surviving spouse, although two-thirds would go to any children from the individual's first (and second) marriage.

Intestacy laws often treat the person's spouse and parents equally. If there are no close blood relatives, then distant relatives or the state may inherit the property. Close friends are not included in state intestacy laws. Thus, any individual who has definite ideas about who should inherit what items, should either write a will or take advantage of one of the will substitutes, or alternatives.

The only advantages to intestacy are that it is the least expensive way for people to pass on their estates and that it requires no thought or planning whatsoever. Individuals might choose not to leave a will if they were sure that (a) the state's intestacy law would divide the property in an acceptable way or (b) administration would not be more difficult for survivors than if a will or will substitute had been left.

Why Alternatives Are Needed

Before examining any alternatives, it is important to look at why people might want to do more than leave a will, which simply passes their property to other individuals at the time of death. Death is rarely a neat, quick, uncomplicated event. More often, people become ill, then more ill, sliding slowly toward death. Some may remain alert and mentally healthy throughout this process, but many become confused by pain and painkillers, or illness may rob them of the ability to think clearly (as in Alzheimer's disease). *When people can no longer think for themselves, many personal, medical, and financial decisions have to be made for them while they are still alive. Most people, if given the opportunity, would like to have some way of remaining in control of their own lives even after they are unable to think for themselves, and the only way to do this is to leave advance instructions.*

A great deal of information on these topics is available in the various chapters of this book; however, the thumbnail definitions below should make it a little easier to understand this chapter and determine what alternatives are appropriate in a particular situation.

Competence. A competent individual is one who is able to make informed choices and understand the consequences of his or her decisions. A person who is unable to do so is termed *incompetent* or *incapacitated.* Although mental disability is usually what triggers a guardianship proceeding, physical incapacity can sometimes be grounds for such a proceeding as well.

Guardian or conservator. An individual appointed by the court to make decisions for someone who is incapacitated. Usually a guardian is appointed to make personal and medical decisions, and a conservator to make financial decisions. However, a guardian may be given responsibility for an incapacitated person's finances, just as a conservator may be responsible for an individual's personal and medical decisions.

Ward. An incapacitated individual who has been put under the care and decision-making authority of a guardian or conservator.

Principal. A person who uses a power of authority (defined below) to appoint someone else to take care of his or her affairs and make decisions for him or her.

Agent or attorney-in-fact. A person appointed in a (durable) power of attorney to make decisions for and handle the affairs of the principal before and/or after the principal becomes incapacitated.

Power of attorney. A legal tool to permit decision-making authority by one competent individual (the agent) for another (the principal) while the principal is still competent. There are several varieties—including durable power of attorney and springing durable power of attorney—that allow the agent to start or continue making decisions after the principal becomes incapacitated or even incompetent.

Living will. A document that specifies someone's preferences regarding medical care and treatment decisions. It is most often used when that person is terminally ill and imcompetent, and is unable to express himself or herself, or direct his or her own care and treatment.

For more information on determining whether an individual can make decisions, see chapter 11. To understand who else can make decisions, see chapters 4, 5, and 12. And to understand the restrictions on such decisions, see chapter 14.

Alternatives to Wills

Different legal tools can be used to avoid many of the problems faced by the elderly and their families. The information that follows focuses on alternatives to wills, or will substitutes. *These tools, properly used, may make it possible for an individual to*

avoid the expense of writing a will;

protect his or her family from incurring the cost and trauma of getting a court-appointed guardian or conservator; and

leave behind instructions for someone else to carry out in the event that he or she becomes incompetent.

Among the most common of these alternatives are living wills, which are used to give advance directions for medical decisions, and durable powers of attorney, which appoint an agent who can be left advance instructions on how an incompetent individual's financial and medical decisions should be made. These are important issues, best described in separate chapters (see chapters 4 and 5, respectively). *Both these tools may be useful alternatives or adjuncts to guardianship.*

Tools for Managing Money and Property

If future concerns about an individual's competence revolve primarily around making arrangements for money or property control, there are several alternatives to consider. Any of these might be used with a durable power of attorney.

- Direct-deposit banking of regular income, such as Social Security or pension payments, can usually be arranged with the individual's bank. The check is sent

directly to the bank and credited to the specific account. This arrangement can be extremely helpful for those who tend to forget or misplace their checks or have physical disabilities that prevent them from getting to the bank.
- Some banks have automatic banking services to pay regular bills, such as mortgages or utilities. Again, this service can be very helpful for the person who manages well on a daily basis but can no longer easily handle paperwork. The charge for this service varies from bank to bank.
- A personal money manager or bill-paying service can be hired or is sometimes available through a trust department of a bank, if the individual has adequate income. These services are usually staffed by bonded professionals (often certified public accountants) who keep track of income, pay bills, and may prepare tax returns. Some charge flat fees (such as $40 per month), while others charge a percentage of the individual's monthly income.
- A representative payee can also be appointed to manage an individual's Social Security benefits. (This topic is covered in chapter 13.)

Joint Property Arrangements and Joint Bank Accounts

An elderly individual who is ill or has trouble moving around may also want to add the name of a spouse, adult child, or friends to his or her checking or savings account or other financial asset. In addition to making banking transactions easier, this action can in some cases take the place of a will. By using a special kind of account, the *joint tenant* (joint owner) will receive, on the death of the elderly individual, what is left in the account without having to go to court for it.

It is important to understand the differences between accounts offering *joint tenants with right of survivorship* and those offering only *tenants in common*. Both are joint tenant accounts (that is, two or more names are on a single account), but only the one offering right of survivorship allows one joint tenant to automatically receive the assets after the other joint tenant dies. Some states require that automatic rights of survivorship be specified; however, any bank manager can explain what options are available.

Some joint accounts allow either owner to transact business and sign checks; others require the signature of all joint owners for all transactions; and still others restrict the ability of one or another owner to withdraw funds. Law and local bank practices determine which choices are possible.

The following examples should serve to illustrate some general points about joint tenancies with right of survivorship. If Mr. X puts all his money in an account with his son, who has right of survivorship, and then leaves his daughter $10,000 in his will, there is nothing for the daughter to get. The instant Mr. X dies, his son owns the whole account "by operation of the law."

Another example is if Mr. X opens a checking account by himself, and without any joint tenant with right of survivorship, at his local bank. Under the terms of the account he has opened, the bank will honor only checks with his signature. If there is still money in the account when Mr. X dies, the bank will freeze the account and not release any of the money until a court appoints someone to manage Mr. X's estate.

Even if Mr. X has signed a power-of-attorney card at the bank, allowing his daughter to sign checks as well, her legal authority to do so ends when Mr. X dies (or when she knows he has died). Once again, the bank will freeze the account until the court appoints someone to handle the estate.

Joint ownership arrangements—of bank accounts, certificates of deposit, U.S. savings bonds, stocks, homes, cars, and other assets—are also commonly used tools in estate planning. They avoid the difficulties of transferring power from an incompetent individual to a competent one. State laws differ as to the conditions and consequences of joint property arrangements and the right of survivorship. Interested individuals should have a lawyer verify that joint ownership will provide the desired results.

Joint ownership is an important and useful tool, but it can also be a double-edged sword. Its advantages include the fact that it costs little or nothing to establish for most assets, and can be done quickly and easily. For real estate, the deed must be filed with the recorder or registrar of deeds; for bank accounts, a new bank card or form must be signed; and for stock registered in one name, a transfer must be performed.

If a person is physically ailing, placing funds in a joint account is an easy way for a trusted friend or family member to make deposits and withdrawals for the disabled person. Sometimes joint ownership can avoid the delays and problems of putting an individual's will in probate (the process of carrying out the instructions left in the will, paying creditors from the estate, and so on), should one of the signers die. When the circumstances are right, a joint account can be useful for those people who are mentally or physically unable to handle their own finances.

Still, great care must be taken to choose an honest, responsible joint owner. Remember, while one joint tenant can use funds in an account to take care of the other joint tenant, he or she can also use them for personal gain. A dishonest co-owner could misuse funds in the account at any time. Also, the incompetent owner could withdraw funds and use them unwisely.

Depending on the kind of joint ownership, one person may not be able to withdraw some of the assets without the other person's signature. By the time a problem arises with a joint ownership arrangement, it may be too late to undo it. First, it doesn't do any good to end a joint ownership if the other person has already removed all the money in the account. Second, creditors of one of the joint owners may be able to seize the account, even if the money in it belongs to the other person. Third, it is impossible to undo joint ownership of some assets—U.S. savings bonds, corporate stocks, homes, and other real property—with only one signature. In addition, if one joint owner becomes ill or incompetent, court assistance may be necessary to help the other owner transfer or sell an asset at all.

Finally, in some states, when officials are determining someone's eligibility for Medicaid, the entire joint account is considered part of the individual's property. This stipulation may make someone ineligible, even though the funds in the joint account may belong to the other account owner. (For more information on Medicaid eligibility requirements, see chapters 3 and 10.)

Here is a short list of some of the important estate-planning features of joint ownership:

- Creating a joint asset may mean "giving" a gift that could have gift, estate, and income tax implications.
- Placing real estate into joint ownership or removing it from joint ownership may result in transfer and recordation taxes.
- Placing a home into joint ownership could put an unnecessary income tax burden on survivors. Principal residences, in particular, have special treatment under federal income tax laws.

Although establishment of joint assets might avoid the need for a court-appointed guardian or conservator to manage an incompetent or incapacitated individual's financial matters, joint assets do not completely take the place of a will. Through a will, an individual can plan for many more possibilities than through a joint asset. Once one of the joint tenants dies, the other one owns the asset outright. If that person dies, the asset will be controlled either by that person's will or by the intestacy law if no will exists.

Trusts

A trust is a common legal device used by one person to authorize another person to handle assets. It is the most flexible and versatile tool for arranging assets, and it can be tailored to fit specific needs. During a person's lifetime, a trust can substitute for court guardianship or conservatorship proceedings. If properly written, it can sometimes help an aging or ill person qualify for medical and housing benefits that depend on his or her income and assets. A trust can also act as a will in directing how an individual's assets should be divided upon his or her death. Its principal disadvantages is that it usually costs more to set up than the other options do.

Trusts are good planning tools, and more people ought to think about using them. A trust is like a corporation—a kind of legal entity that can own property; buy, sell, and manage it; invest money or spend it; or use it in whatever way is required to meet someone's living expenses.

Basically, a trust is an arrangement in which property is transferred by one person (the *grantor, settlor,* or *trustor*) to benefit himself or someone else (the *beneficiary*). It is managed by another person (the *trustee*) and is limited by whatever restrictions the grantor (or *testator,* in the case of a testamentary trust) included in the trust agreement. There are two kinds of trusts:

1. A *testamentary* trust, created within a will, which does not take effect until the testator (the person whose will it is) dies.
2. An *inter vivos,* or *living,* trust, which goes into effect while the grantor is still alive. An inter vivos trust can be revocable (changed or canceled by the grantor at a later time) or irrevocable (permanent and unchangeable once the trust has begun).

For the purposes of this book, the information that follows concerns inter vivos, or living, trusts.

To illustrate what happens without one, suppose that Mrs. X goes to her bank to open a checking account. The bank requires that she fill out a signature card. Upon having her signature, the bank will honor Mrs. X's checks for as long as she is able to sign them. If she becomes incapacitated or dies, the bank will not cash her checks signed by anyone else. In either case, the bank will not normally release Mrs. X's money until someone comes forward with the required authority. If Mrs. X becomes incompetent and has asked no one else to act for her under a durable power of attorney, the bank will require that someone be appointed by a court as her guardian or conservator. If Mrs. X dies, the bank will require that someone be appointed by a court as the administrator of her estate.

Now, suppose that Mrs. X has set up the "Mrs. X Trust," in which she is the trustee and beneficiary and her brother is the successor trustee. In this case, Mrs. X opens her bank account in the name of the Mrs. X Trust, and the bank might ask for a copy of the agreement establishing the trust. If Mrs. X becomes unable to sign checks, her brother will show the bank that Mrs. X is incapacitated (for example, by showing the bank a doctor's letter) or dead (by showing the bank a death certificate), and the bank will then honor checks written by the brother. No court papers are needed, and from this point on, the brother can act for the trust as long as necessary.

This example shows two advantages of the living trust: it makes going to court unnecessary if an individual becomes incapacitated, and it can transfer money to the individual's beneficiaries without court action if he or she dies.

Trusts can be set up so that they go into effect only if the grantor becomes incapacitated, in order to ensure that the grantor is well cared for and that his or her finances are handled properly. They are also sometimes combined with a durable power of attorney.

To set up a good living trust, individuals need

one or more beneficiaries;

a trustee, along with a successor or cotrustee;

property and money in the name of the trust; and

a trust agreement that tells the successor or cotrustee what to do with the trust property for the benefit of the beneficiary or beneficiaries.

The individual who sets up the trust might be its lifetime beneficiary, but other beneficiaries (those people Mrs. X wants to provide for during her lifetime) can be listed as well. Mrs. X can also name who would get the trust property after her death. In this way, a trust functions as a will: Mrs. X can specify that the other beneficiaries will receive her money and property as soon as possible after her death, or she can direct that the money be held in trust for them after her death because, for whatever reason, they cannot manage that money themselves.

A trustee can be anyone Mrs. X chooses—herself while she is capable of managing her own affairs, a relative, lawyer, friend, business partner, or even a corporation like a bank or trust company.

The property of the trust is whatever property an individual chooses to put in it. It can be all that is owned or selected property; it can be a home or income-producing property; or it can be bonds or long-term appreciation property.

Like all options, trusts have advantages and disadvantages. *The main advantages are that they provide a relatively seamless plan for dealing with an individual's incapacity, incompetence, or death; avoid court involvement to determine an individual's competence; and avoid the delay and expense associated with estate administration if the individual dies.* Another advantage is that assets can be professionally managed, regardless of whether the grantor becomes ill, dies, or simply finds the problems of management too complex. Also, if a trust is revocable, it allows the grantor control as long as possible, while allowing smooth management when her or she is no longer interested in or able to manage the trust. For the upper-income person, there can be tax advantages to a trust. All interested individuals should consult a lawyer or financial planner when considering setting up a trust.

A trust's primary disadvantage is its cost. Stocks, real estate, and other property may require a great deal of paperwork to put them into trust. If there is a professional trustee (such as a bank), there will be fees. Also, many banks or financial institutions are reluctant to accept responsibility as the professional trustee of a trust that is worth less than $50,000 to $100,000. Moreover, a trust may not be possible unless the grantor has friends or family members who are willing to assume the responsibility of being a trustee for little or no pay. Sometimes, a simple power of attorney may be an equally efficient (and less expensive) way of achieving the same results. A trust does not eliminate the need for either a will or a power of attorney, although these documents can be far simpler when they accompany a trust than when they are the sole means for planning the management of an individual's estate.

Another use of trusts is linked to Medicaid, the federal and state program that pays for long-term care in an Intermediate Care Facility (ICF) nursing home (one that provides some medical care) when people's income and assets are insufficient to meet the costs of nursing home care. Since trusts can legally own property, some people plan to transfer their assets to a trust so that they, individually, can qualify for Medicaid.

When Medicaid officials are considering someone's eligibility, they want to know about any trusts established by him or her or for his or her benefit. Depending on the type of trust and all the relevant dates that show when the trust was set up, they might deny or delay that individual's application. It may be possible for some irrevocable living trusts to allow individuals to qualify for Medicaid if they enter a nursing home, thereby safeguarding the rest of their assets for other beneficiaries; however, *the law changes regularly in this area, and no one should attempt this action without fully exploring its Medicaid* and *tax consequences.*

Trusts also require some expertise with estate and tax planning, as there may be tax disadvantages if a large trust is not carefully set up. If properly established, trusts can achieve all the estate tax savings that a will can, and will have no effect on income tax while the grantor is alive.

If an individual plans to put his or her home into a trust, there are at least two points to remember. First, some banks require that the home be solely owned by that individual, and will not lend money if the house is owned by a trust. Second, some states impose a transfer tax when the home is put into a trust.

Gifts

Giving away assets to one's spouse, children, or others is another way to handle assets. Such giving can be extremely beneficial in estate planning. It also has one obvious serious drawback: once an individual gives away his or her money or assets, he or she no longer has that money or those assets. The individual who gives the gifts (the *donor*) could become dependent on the goodwill of the person or persons to whom the gifts were given (the *donee* or *donees*).

Gifts are not income to the donee. Giving away large amounts, however, may eventually result in higher income taxes for the donee (since the money, once in the donee's hands, will make money). Such giving may also deprive the donor and the donees of important tax benefits.

Giving is easy to do, although sometimes gift tax returns need to be filed. Its principal disadvantage is that it requires an individual to give up control of his or her assets while he or she is still alive. Interested individuals should always consult a lawyer and/or financial planner before choosing this option.

2

"Medigap" and Long-Term Care Insurance Policies

THIS chapter is organized into two parts. The first focuses on "Medigap" and Medicare supplemental insurance policies, designed to cover bills (or parts of bills) left unpaid by Medicare. The second treats long-term care insurance policies, designed to pay policyholders for the long-term care or nursing home services not covered by Medicare. Concluding the chapter is a section—applicable to both parts—on what to do if a problem or complaint arises.

Medigap Policies

Overview

Medicare was not designed to cover all the health care costs of the elderly. Instead, it pays for only those medical services needed by someone suffering from an acute, or serious, illness or accident. As a result, elderly patients still face numerous bills for medical services either not covered by Medicare or covered only in part. These costs, known as out-of-pocket expenses, must be paid by the elderly themselves. In 1986, for example, Medicare paid only 48 percent of the average cost of its beneficiaries' health care bills, leaving the beneficiaries to pay the remaining 52 percent, an average of $17,000, per person that year.

To combat the problem of these out-of-pocket medical expenses, nearly two-thirds of elderly persons have purchased "Medicare supplemental" or "Medigap" insurance policies. These policies are sold by private companies, not the federal government, and are designed to pay for the cost of services not covered by Medicare. Such policies often don't work in an ideal fashion, however, so consumers need to look carefully at whether or not they really need to buy a supplemental policy, and if so, which one best suits their needs.

When Might It Be Necessary to Purchase Medigap Insurance?

The first step in buying Medigap insurance is to understand what Medicare does and does not pay for in the first place (see appendix 1 for a description of services covered by Medicare Part A and Part B). Only by knowing what isn't covered by Medicare can consumers know whether they need another policy, and if so, which one to purchase.

Not everyone needs Medigap insurance, but people without any health care coverage other than Medicare should probably consider buying a supplemental policy. People thinking about buying Medigap insurance should keep the following points in mind.

- *Medicaid.* Elderly persons covered by Medicaid do not need to purchase Medigap policies because Medicaid pays almost all of their health care costs.
- *Employee Group Health Insurance.* Many employed persons may continue to use their group health insurance or, when they reach age sixty-five, convert it to a Medicare supplemental policy. When group coverage is continued, the items it covers are often reduced or the premium to be paid is increased. Some people may have coverage through a working spouse. *These options should be checked with the employer before retirement.* Under a new law, in 1989 and 1990 any employer who currently provides to an employee or a retired former employee health benefits that duplicate at least 50 percent of Medicare's Part A and Part B benefits must provide either (a) additional benefits that are at least equal to the value of the duplicated benefits or (b) a refund to the employee or retired former employee.
- *Health Maintenance Organizations (HMOs).* HMOs offer prepaid health insurance plans that provide all acute medical services that policyholders may need. Medicare is encouraging HMOs to provide services to older people, and more and more HMOs are enrolling people over sixty-five years of age into their

programs. Coverage may be expensive, however, and often subscribers or policyholders must use physicians selected by the HMO.

- *Major medical insurance.* Major medical insurance is supposed to cover large medical bills, and so it may have a high deductible (the out-of-pocket amount that patients spend before the insurance company begins to pay). A major medical insurance policy therefore probably won't cover deductibles and coinsurance for Medicare. If it does cover those costs, its premium, or annual purchase price, is likely to be quite high.

If consumers decide to buy supplemental or Medigap insurance, such policies should cover the gap

of "deductibles," or the out-of-pocket amount that patients spend before Medicare begins to pay;

of "coinsurance," or the balance of the bill after Medicare has paid;

between the amount that Medicare will pay for a specific treatment or health care service and the amount that the doctor, hospital, nurse, or other health care provider will charge for the same treatment or service; and

left by those items which Medicare does not cover at all.

Unfortunately, Medigap policies usually focus only on deductibles and coinsurance, although some policies address the other gaps as well. *Most Medigap policies do not cover services that Medicare doesn't cover, such as*

skilled or specialized nursing home care that is not already covered by Medicare;

intermediate or custodial nursing home care;

private-duty nursing care;

drugs not already covered for hospital or hospice patients (these drugs will be covered by Medicare beginning in 1990);

care received outside the United States, except under certain specific instances in Mexico and Canada; and dental care, routine health care, eye examinations and glasses, hearing aids, and cosmetic surgery such as face-lifts.

A Word of Caution

Elderly consumers need to shop carefully for the Medigap policy that will give them the extra coverage they need; otherwise, they may waste their money. It may not always be possible to get coverage for all out-of-pocket expenses. Many consumers have purchased policies that simply duplicate one another—which doesn't help much—or that cover only one specific disease.

A special note is in order about insurance policies that cover only one illness, also known as *dread disease policies.* Consumers would have to buy many of these single-disease policies to get the same coverage they would receive by purchasing a single, more complete or comprehensive policy. Single-disease policies are usually expensive, often not very valuable to the consumer, and not really designed to fill in the gaps in the Medicare system.

Medigap insurance companies that pretend to represent the federal government or that knowingly sell insurance that duplicates Medicare coverage are breaking the law and are subject to heavy fines. They should be reported to government officials in the state insurance department (see appendix 2 for a state-by-state listing of these departments).

Consumers also should be wary of being sold "replacement" policies to take the place of the policies they already own. New policies often won't pay right away for *preexisting conditions,* illnesses consumers have at the time they buy a replacement policy. Instead, such policies require that the consumers themselves pay the bills for these preexisting conditions for a certain period of time, when the same conditions may already be covered under the first policy. Preexisting conditions might even be excluded completely from a new policy, meaning that the insurance company will never pay for them.

Because insurance agents are licensed by the state, consumers should ask for some proof of an agent's license that also shows the name of the company where the agent is employed. Payment for a policy should be by check, money order, or bank draft and made payable only to the insurance company. Consumers should never pay cash for a policy, nor should they make out a check in the agent's name.

The New Legal Requirements for Medigap Insurance Policies

Although state insurance departments must approve all policies being sold in a state to ensure compliance with specific state laws, those laws do vary from state to state and have different levels of protection for consumers. In recent years, most states have followed the standards set by the National Association of Insurance Commissioners (NAIC), which were also recommended by Congress in 1981.

At the end of 1988, however, the NAIC modified its standards to be consistent with the new expansion of Medicare under the Congressional Medicare Catastrophic Coverage Act. The new NAIC standards require the following:

- Individual and group Medicare supplemental policies are prohibited from containing benefits that duplicate those provided by Medicare.
- Minimum benefit standards in 1989 are to include

   Part A Skilled Nursing Facility (SNF) coinsurance;

   Part A hospital deductible (meaning that policies must pay all of the deductible or none at all; they cannot pay only part of it); and

   the first three units of whole blood.

- Minimum benefit standards in 1990 are also to include

   20 percent copayment of Part B expenses, up to a maximum out-of-pocket amount, not including outpatient prescription drugs;

   coinsurance for immunosuppressive drug therapy; and

   coinsurance for home intravenous drugs, not including the regular drug deductible.

- Duplication of services now covered by Medicare is prohibited. Until 1990, policies must cover 20 percent of Part B expenses, subject to a maximum calendar year out-of-pocket deductible of $200 and to a maximum benefit of at least $5,000 per year.

In its new standards, NAIC also retained several earlier requirements. For example:

- Payment must be made for treatment or services received six months after a policy is issued, whether or not a claim is related to a preexisting condition (one the policyholder already had at the time he or she bought the policy).
- Buyers can cancel policies without penalty for thirty days after purchase.
- The terms of the policy must be disclosed clearly.
- Benefit payments must represent at least 60 percent of the money taken in through premiums. This percentage, called a *loss ratio,* is 60 to 65 percent for individual policies (depending on the state) and 75 percent for group policies. Under a new federal law, insurers offering Medigap policies are required to report to the state insurance commissioners information on the actual ratio of benefits provided to premiums collected.
- After January 1, 1989, companies that issue Medicare supplemental policies must submit their advertising files to the state insurance commissioner to see if their marketing practices comply with state law.

Only policies meeting these standards can be sold as Medigap or Medicare supplemental policies. However, these standards do not apply to major medical, catastrophic, dread disease, or long-term care policies.

By January 1, 1989, companies that have issued Medigap policies must send a letter to their policyholders explaining the improved Medicare benefits in recent legislation, how those improvements affect the benefits in the policy, and the cost of the premium. They must also advise beneficiaries of (a) changes required in existing contracts to avoid duplication of coverage with Medicare and (b) what premium adjustments will be made as a result of eliminating duplicate coverage. Further, insurers must send additional annual notices to policyholders to explain subsequent changes in Medicare supplemental coverage.

Questions to Ask the Insurance Agent

Elderly people buying or thinking about buying a Medigap or supplemental insurance policy might want to ask insurance agents the following questions.

1. Is there a clearly worded and understandable summary or outline of the policy for the buyer to review?
2. What does the policy cover? Does it cover deductibles? coinsurance? services

beyond what Medicare covers? only specific diseases? costs not covered by the amount Medicare would pay were the health provider to charge more than the amount allotted by Medicare?
3. What is the annual premium (yearly price) of the policy?
4. Does the premium increase with age? If so, how often—every year? every five years?
5. Are there exclusions or waiting periods for payments on preexisting conditions?
6. What is the policy's loss ratio, or minimum level of benefits the insurance company expects to pay out?
7. Does the policy offer riders or other optional coverage?
8. Is there a maximum amount of benefits payable under the policy? in dollars? in days covered?
9. Under what circumstances can the company refuse to renew a policy?
10. Is the policy approved by the state insurance department?
11. What is the company's rule regarding prompt delivery of the policy?
12. What is the company's rule regarding refunds?
13. Does the company allow a "free look" for thirty days or longer to review the policy?

Long-Term Care Insurance Policies

Overview

As noted in the first part of this chapter, even Medigap policies may leave large gaps in coverage for health care services. Perhaps the most significant of these gaps is payment for *long-term care,* a phrase that usually refers to a long stay in a nursing home for "intermediate" or "custodial," rather than "acute," care. One example would be patients with Alzheimer's disease who can no longer be cared for in their homes but require almost round-the-clock supervision to make sure they don't wander off or hurt themselves. Another example would be patients who have a stroke and need extensive care and rehabilitation in a nursing home for a period of time before they can return to their homes.

Medicare pays for only about 2 percent of all nursing home care and only 4 percent of home health care in the United States. Fifty percent of all nursing home care costs are paid for, out-of-pocket, by patients or their family members. Most patients who run out of money become eligible for Medicaid, which pays about 42 percent of all nursing home care costs in the United States.

To fill this gap, private insurance companies offer policies to protect consumers against the cost of long-term care. These policies are designed to pay for the care needed by people with a chronic illness or disability that lasts a long time and leaves them unable to care for themselves. Thus, while Medicare and Medigap policies focus on skilled or specialized nursing care, these long-term care policies include intermediate or custodial care and usually also offer more generous home care benefits. Some insurance companies are also beginning to cover such services as "adult day care" and "respite care," both of which offer temporary (half-day or day-long) care up to several times a week for individuals who are being cared for in their homes by family members or friends.

Policy premiums range from about $200 to $1,200 or more per year, depending on age, amount, duration of benefits, and deductible or "elimination periods," such as waiting periods for coverage of a preexisting condition.

When Might It Be Necessary to Purchase Long-Term Care Insurance?

Statistics show that most older people's greatest insurance risk is their need for long term care services not covered by Medicare. Approximately one out of every five elderly people has a chronic illness or disability, and about four out of every ten elderly people will enter a nursing home at some time in their lives. Some 20 percent of older people living in the community rely on friends, neighbors, or family members to help them with some important activity of daily living, such as eating, bathing, or buying groceries.

The cost of nursing home services for these people can be very high—as much as $20,000 to $40,000 a year. Almost two-thirds of elderly people living alone who enter nursing homes run out of money to pay for them after only thirteen weeks of care. More than a third of elderly married couples over age sixty-five will run out of money in thirteen weeks if one of them needs nursing home care.

Obviously, people need financial protection from these expenses. A national policy debate is under way over whether the federal government or private insurance companies should provide more long-term care coverage.

Just like Medigap and Medicare supplemental insurance policies, policies for long-term care should be studied carefully to make sure they meet the needs of the people buying them.

Probably the biggest factor for most people deciding whether to purchase long-term care coverage is the cost of these policies. As coverage increases, so do premium prices, and a number of good policies are likely to be too expensive for many older people living on fixed incomes. Although initially these policies may not have been well designed financially for the people who need them most, they are now improving and may be a better buy for consumers.

For people under sixty years of age, an important element to look for in a long-term care policy is a good inflation adjustment (an increase in the amount paid for benefits that corresponds with the country's rising costs of medical care); otherwise purchasing one may not be worthwhile. For people over age sixty who have a substantial income, a long-term policy may offer good protection of both their health and their assets. People over age sixty who have a modest income and modest assets, however, may not be as interested in this type of insurance, because if they suffered from a long-term illness they would quickly run out of money and would qualify for Medicaid to pay for their care.

What to Look For in Buying Long-Term Care Insurance

Insurance companies use medical and other information in deciding whether or not to issue a long-term care insurance policy. They may refuse to sell coverage, or they may charge higher premiums to high-risk individuals likely to need and use more services. Before buying a policy, consumers need to understand a number of features of long-term care insurance.

- *Index for inflation.* Most policies provide *indemnity benefits,* wherein they pay a fixed amount per day for the illnesses and disabilities they cover. *But because most policies now in effect are not indexed for inflation, the amounts they agree to pay don't rise with the rising costs of medical care. Consumers with policies not indexed for inflation may be paid a smaller percentage of the actual bill for services if the cost of those services has risen due to inflation. Some newer policies now pay a fixed percentage of service costs, or they index benefits for inflation.*
- *Limitations on renewability.* Usually the insurance company has the right to cancel or not renew someone's policy even if the person is paying the premiums. Premiums may have one of four types of renewability provisions:

1. *Optionally renewable.* This means the policy is renewable only by the decision of the insurance company. This kind of policy offers the least amount of protection for the consumer.
2. *Conditionally renewable.* Here, the insurance company can decide not to renew policies for people in certain classes of coverage, or because of where they live, or for a number of reasons other than the policyholder's increased illness.
3. *Guaranteed renewable.* In this type of policy, the insurance company cannot cancel or refuse to renew a policy for any reason, but it can change the amounts of the premiums for similar groups or classes of coverage (for example, requiring substantial increases as groups of subscribers become older).
4. *Noncancelable.* This means the insurance company cannot cancel (or refuse to renew) a policy or increase its premiums. This kind of policy offers the most protection for the consumer.

- *Exclusions of certain conditions.* Most policies exclude, or refuse to pay for, specific conditions or illnesses in their coverage. The most common of these excluded conditions are alcohol and drug-related diseases, treatment received outside the United States, and nervous and mental disorders that cannot be proved to result from an organic, or physical, problem. *Policy exclusions for mental and nervous disorders do not meet the insurance needs of patients with Alzheimer's disease, because there is currently no medical test that can positively diagnose Alzheimer's disease in a living person. Even policies covering mental and nervous disorders or an organic nature may be a problem because the insurance company may require diagnosis by a brain biopsy or autopsy, which can be done only after death.*
- *Exclusions of preexisting conditions.* Many insurance companies have rules against paying for treatments or services related to an illness or condition consumers had before they bought their current insurance policy. This usually means that the insurance companies won't pay for claims from a preexisting condition until a certain amount of time has passed. Insurance companies often define how long policyholders must have had an illness or condition for it to be called preexisting, and how long a policyholder must wait after buying a policy before benefits are paid on that preexisting illness or condition.
- *Prior hospitalization requirement.* Many policies require individuals to stay in a hospital before benefits will be paid for their stay in a nursing home. This requirement severely limits the coverage of these policies and makes them even more restrictive than Medicare,

which does not require prior hospitalization for home health benefits. This restriction has been removed from some of the newer policies being sold.

- *Skilled nursing care.* Many policies follow Medicare's example in paying only for nursing home care and home care that are "skilled," or specialized. Such policies will pay, for example, for home health aide service only if patients need skilled nursing care or another skilled therapy (speech therapy, physical therapy, or occupational therapy). *A policy that defines and covers skilled nursing care the way Medicare does is likely to be of little use. Consumers should seek policies that cover intermediate and custodial or personal care at home or in a nursing home.*
- *Limits on duration of services.* Nearly all policies have a maximum length of time for which they will pay benefits. *True long-term care insurance policies should offer at least twelve consecutive months of benefits.*
- *Waiting periods.* Many policies will not pay benefits to patients until they have waited a specified period of time or have already paid out-of-pocket for a specified number of home care visits or days in a nursing home.

Long-term care policies are still quite new, and the insurance agents themselves may not understand the policies they are selling. Don't rely on what agents say; stick with what is clearly written in the policy summary.

Legal Requirements for Long-Term Care Insurance Policies

While the federal government sets standards for Medigap policies, it does not do so for long-term care policies. Instead, these policies must meet the requirements of state insurance departments, whose rules and regulations vary from state to state.

The National Association of Insurance Commissioners (NAIC) has drafted a model act, or set of proposed standards, that tries to encourage the sale of long-term care policies and still protect the people buying them. Under this act, insurance companies can require policyholders to stay in a hospital before they are eligible for nursing home benefits or can insist that policyholders receive skilled nursing care before they receive intermediate, custodial, or home care benefits. The act also:

- requires clear descriptions of benefits, coverage, major exclusions, restrictions, limitations, and renewal provisions;

- requires a "right to look" provision, allowing policyholders to return a policy and receive a refund within ten days after purchasing it (buyers approached by the insurance company, instead of initiating the purchase themselves, would have thirty days to return the policy for a refund);
- prohibits companies from not covering specific health conditions;
- prohibits companies from offering much greater benefits for skilled nursing care than for intermediate or custodial care;
- requires policies to be of the guaranteed renewable type, although some state insurance commissioners may allow companies to cancel their policies under special circumstances; and
- *prohibits companies from not covering Alzheimer's disease, although policies are not required to specify that the disease is covered.*

By mid-1988, Arizona, Florida, Georgia, Hawaii, Idaho, Indiana, Kansas, Nebraska, North Carolina, North Dakota, Oklahoma, Oregon, South Carolina, Virginia, and Wyoming had adopted the model act, and California, Illinois, Michigan, Ohio, Pennsylvania, and Rhode Island were considering adopting it.

Questions to Ask the Insurance Agent

Elderly people buying or thinking about buying a long-term care insurance policy might want to ask insurance agents the following questions.

1. How much does the policy cost per month? per year?
2. What does the policy cover? Does it cover skilled nursing home care? Intermediate or custodial care in a nursing home? Home health care, including skilled nursing, home health aides, personal care, and other services? Adult day care? Respite care? Other services?
3. How many days or years will the benefits last for each of the services listed above?
4. Does the policy cover nervous or mental disorders such as Alzheimer's disease?
5. Does the policy premium always stay at the same amount? If not, under what circumstances can the insurance company raise it? How often can the premium be increased?

6. Under what circumstances can the insurance company cancel or refuse to renew a policy? Does the company guarantee it will renew the policy as long as the policyholder pays the premium on time?
7. What are the elimination or deductible periods before benefits begin to be paid?
8. What is the waiting period for preexisting conditions?
9. Is a prior hospital stay required for benefits to be paid for nursing home care? If so, how many days of hospitalization are required? Is a prior hospital or nursing home stay required for benefits to be paid for home care or other noninstitutional services?
10. Are there any other limits or exclusions?
11. Will the policy premium be waived if the policyholder is residing in a hospital or nursing home?
12. Are benefits paid on an indemnity basis (a specific dollar amount per day) or as a percentage of the costs of care?
13. Are benefits indexed for inflation? If so, what index is used and how often are benefits adjusted?
14. Will the policy pay even if the policyholder is covered by Medicare or Medigap policies?
15. What is the maximum age at which a person can apply for coverage? Will the premium continue to be based on the age of the person at the time he or she first purchased the policy?
16. Is there a maximum benefit amount a person can receive in his or her lifetime? If so, how much is that maximum amount?
17. Is there a maximum time during which a policyholder can collect benefits? If so, how long is that maximum time?

What to Do if a Question or Problem Arises

The Health Insurance Association of America has a toll-free telephone number for questions about health insurance policies, including long-term care policies. The association can be reached at 1-800-423-8000.

Complaints can be filed with state insurance departments, which are usually responsible for regulating policies sold in their state (see appendix 2, for a list of addresses). These departments should also be contacted if insurance agents claim to represent the government or try to sell Medigap policies that duplicate Medicare coverage.

3

Paying for Nursing Home Care

THIS chapter focuses on patients who will probably live out the rest of their lives in a nursing home. (For patients who need temporary care in a nursing home, see chapter 2; for people who are confused about how to make their way through the Medicare and Medicaid systems, more information can be found in chapter 10.)

Overview

Paying for nursing home care is something most people would rather not think about, much less plan for in the future. Often, it is not the cost that is so frightening as the idea of living out one's life in a nursing home. No one wants to grow old, lose independence, and have a restricted life-style. Yet, for those unfortunate enough to need a nursing home, paying for it can become a confusing and emotional experience for them and their families.

For most people, there may be only two practical options: (a) paying for nursing home services out-of-pocket, from personal savings and resources, or (b) relying on Medicaid for financial assistance. In reality, it is generally a combination of these two options that pays for most nursing home care in the United States today.

The costs of nursing home care vary significantly from state to state and also depend on the amount and type of services needed by the patient. These services define the two main categories of nursing homes:

1. *Skilled Nursing Facilities (SNF)* provide specialized medical and nursing care. SNF residents include those who are more seriously ill or disabled. These patients need frequent medical and intensive skilled nursing services but do not need to stay in a hospital to receive it.

2. *Intermediate Care Facilities (ICF)* provide patients with a limited level of medical and nursing care, as well as custodial, or general, care. ICFs might be used by those patients who need additional time to recover after leaving a hospital but who will eventually be able to return to their own homes. Patients who have broken bones or who have had surgery often fall into this group. Other ICF residents might include elderly people who can no longer care for themselves and have no family members they can live with, or those with Alzheimer's disease who need more constant supervision than can be given them at home.

Daily rates may range from $45 to $75 for ICF residents and may reach $100 or more for SNF residents. Fees can easily exceed $25,000 or $30,000 a year, depending on each patient's care needs and medical services. This is a significant amount, and sadly, most of it has to be paid from the savings of elderly individuals. In 1984, more than $12.5 billion was spent out-of-pocket on nursing home care in the United States.

Many elderly people mistakenly believe that Medicare will protect them from the costs of long-term care or nursing home services. Almost 80 percent of people responding to a 1984 survey conducted by the American Association for Retired Persons (AARP) believed that Medicare would pay for their nursing home care if such care became necessary. Nothing, however, could be further from the truth. *The fact is that Medicare coverage for nursing home fees is almost nonexistent.* Overall, Medicare pays for less than 2 percent of all nursing home costs and, more important, was never intended to pay for general nursing home care at all.

Currently, about 50 percent of all nursing home costs are financed by people's personal resources or savings. Less than 30 percent of nursing home residents, however, are able to pay the full cost of such services solely out-of-pocket. Those who can pay generally cannot afford to do so for more than a year or two. A recent Harvard Medical School study of people age seventy-five or older who live alone concluded that almost half of them would have "spent down," or exhausted their savings, after only thirteen weeks in a nursing home. Only 25 percent of the people studied would not have been impoverished by the end of the first year of living in a nursing home.

Public assistance under Medicaid is available to pay for nursing home care, but this assistance is available only after an individual's personal savings and resources have been spent down to poverty levels. Approximately 70 percent of all nursing home residents depend on Medicaid to help pay for their care.

Private long-term care insurance, while increasing in popularity, still pays only for less than 2 percent of nursing home costs at this time (see chapter 2). Veterans' care and various other public assistance programs pay for the remaining 4 percent of nursing home costs.

Unless someone is independently wealthy, even those who may have planned ahead for their retirement and general health care needs are likely to find the cost of long-term nursing home care to be more than they can afford. In many cases, elderly individuals may face impoverishment or the depletion of most of their available financial resources when having to pay for long-term care needs.

Medicare as a Resource

Medicare, a national health insurance program funded by the federal government, is available to most individuals age sixty-five or older. Although it pays for medical care for the elderly, Medicare is primarily intended to cover hospital care and doctor's services.

Medicare is actually two insurance programs in one: Hospital Insurance (HI) is provided under Part A of Medicare, and Supplemental Medical Insurance (SMI) is provided under Part B. The HI program pays for inpatient and outpatient hospital services, home health care services, and to a limited extent SNF services. The SMI program requires Medicare beneficiaries to pay a monthly premium. (For more information, see chapter 10.)

Medicare's skilled nursing benefit pays for a maximum of 150 days of skilled care in a Medicare-certified nursing home and does not require that patients be hospitalized beforehand. Although Medicare used to have tougher restrictions on patients receiving skilled nursing benefits, those rules were changed at the end of 1988.

To qualify for Medicare SNF coverage, patients must require around-the-clock skilled nursing or have the potential to recover sufficiently to be able to return to the community as a result of receiving this specialized care. It is rare for patients to receive the full 150 days of SNF coverage benefits, as the requirements for skilled nursing and rehabilitation are strictly enforced. In fact, should one ever qualify for Medicare's SNF benefit, the covered length of stay in a nursing home would probably be less than thirty days.

Even if patients are covered, Medicare requires that they pay a *coinsurance* amount—in this case, 20 percent of the average daily fee that Medicare must pay the SNF—for the first eight days of their stay in a nursing home. Estimates of the 1989 coinsurance amount are $20.50 a day; until 1989, patients had to pay considerably more coinsurance ($67.50 a day in 1988) for a much longer time (from the twenty-first to the hundredth day of the patient's stay in the SNF).

Medicare utilization figures show just how restricted the skilled nursing benefit actually is: in 1984, Medicare paid benefits on behalf of more than 18.7 million individuals for doctors' services, 6.2 million individuals for hospitalization, and less than 300,000 individuals for SNF services they received. Depending on how the billing arrangements are set up, Medicare payments can be made directly to the doctor, the hospital, or the patient. To make matters worse, Medicare does not pay for ICF or other nursing home services that are considered primarily custodial (general) in nature.

Limited Part B benefits under Medicare's SMI program pay for such services as doctors' visits, medical supplies, and certain durable medical equipment (like wheelchairs) and prosthetic devices (like artificial limbs) for nursing home residents. Payment under Part B is made either (a) directly to doctors or medical suppliers by assignment or (b) as a direct reimbursement to Medicare beneficiaries after they submit itemized bills for services. *If doctors or suppliers are paid by Medicare under the assignment approach, patients cannot be billed for any amount greater than what Medicare has agreed to pay.*

Local Social Security offices can answer questions about Medicare benefit eligibility (to find local offices, look in the "Government" section of the phone directory). Interviews can be arranged with the local representative for guidance and information on Medicare benefits. In addition, nursing homes should have admissions or social services directors who can assist those nursing home applicants and their families who request information on Medicare eligibility and coverage.

If patients or their families have questions about individual Medicare coverage denials and nursing home claims payments, they should contact the office of the Medicare intermediary handling the claim (that information can be found on the Medicare claim form). They may also wish to contact the health care facility or group that provided the service in the first place. In addition, individuals can contact their local Social Security office for assistance and advice on how to proceed. Other options for "fighting back" include legal services programs for the elderly, funded by the Older Americans Act; legal services programs for the poor, funded by the Legal Services Corporation Act; lawyers willing to work for reduced fees; and some legal clinics or programs associated with law schools. (Also see chapter 10.)

To find appropriate, low-cost legal aid, contact the State Unit on Aging (see appendix 20, for a state-by-state list) and talk with the legal services developer. Also, almost all states have an Information and Referral (I&R) hot line for older people or the general public in need of services, and this resource can provide the same information; local senior citizens' centers should be able to furnish the I&R hot line number.

Medicaid as a Resource

Medicaid is the chief public assistance program that pays for nursing home care. It is a state-administered program, funded by both federal and state government. Medicaid essentially offers financial assistance to certain low-income individuals who cannot pay for their medical care. Most (two out of every three) nursing home residents are dependent on Medicaid to help pay for their care.

Individuals living in long-term care facilities that are not licensed as nursing homes, such as board and care homes and domiciliary care facilities, are not eligible to receive assistance under the Medicaid program. These facilities are not licensed to provide nursing care and instead provide only custodial or domiciliary care services. Personal and residential care facilities may offer limited nursing services, although such services are usually provided and paid for under a separate arrangement between the resident and the facility.

Medicaid programs are administered by each state's government. Each one has its own eligibility and coverage rules, which vary a great deal from state to state. The result is fifty-one different Medicaid programs (all states plus the District of Columbia), all with different standards and a different scope and depth of coverage benefits. People eligible for Medicaid assistance to help pay for nursing home care in one state may not be eligible for such assistance in another state. The same is true of other specific coverage benefits.

Qualifying for medical assistance payments to help pay for nursing home services under Medicaid is a bit more complicated than doing so under Medicare. Medicaid must judge first that individuals applying for assistance actually need nursing home services and second that they are unable to pay for those services themselves. Generally speaking, people who are eligible to recieve Medicaid include

individuals receiving Aid to Families with Dependent children (AFDC);

individuals under the age of twenty-one who receive general relief payments;

individuals age sixty-five or older whose income and financial resources are below the established minimum state resource levels (state Medicaid offices, listed in appendix 34, or nursing home administrators will have this information);

blind adults or children whose income and financial resources are below the established minimum state resource levels; and

residents of nursing homes whose income does not meet the cost of care.

People qualify for Medicaid if they are "categorically needy," or, in many states, "medically needy." Medicaid staff have specific criteria to help them judge who qualifies as categorically needy. These criteria—based on income and financial resource levels—are generally linked to financial limitations for AFDC recipients, federal supplemental security resources, or federal Supplemental Security Income (SSI).

The criteria for being medically needy are based on an individual state's requirements for programs serving the medically needy. Not all states have programs for the medically needy, because such programs are not required by the federal government (again, local Medicaid offices or nursing home administrators can assist individuals interested in this information). Medically needy individuals are people who meet the definition of categorically needy in a somewhat different way—they may have a higher income but also large out-of-pocket medical expenses, such as payments for nursing home care.

This process of contrasting individual income against personal medical expenses to qualify for Medicaid eligibility is called *spend down*. It is through this spend-down process that most middle-income individuals are able to become eligible for Medicaid assistance in paying for nursing home care.

Each state has its own maximum amount of *allowable resources,* that is, the amount of money the state allows individuals to keep. This amount is not large in any state, usually a few thousand dollars. Each state allows individuals a limited amount of personal "protected" income for personal use, such as buying a newspaper or getting a manicure or permanent wave. Although the amount varies by state, it is usually in the range of $25 to $30 per month.

The financial resource and income standards that determine whether people are eligible for Medicaid are quite strict. Medicaid was really intended to serve only those very poor who could not afford basic medical care. While the program has been expanded to help the elderly pay for nursing home care, its requirements often force middle-income individuals to become impoverished in order to qualify for its benefits. *To make matters worse, all joint assets and income from married couples are considered in the eligibility determination if a couple was living together at the time one of them was admitted into a nursing home. This stipulation can have frightening results, in that a spouse who is not ill can also become impoverished and will have to survive on very little money or apply for public assistance as well.* It is also a reason for the elderly to plan ahead, well in advance, with professional legal and financial advisers who can help ward off the financial impact of a serious and long-term illness.

To qualify for Medicaid, individuals should first contact the appropriate local Medicaid office—usually located in the county welfare department, health department, or social services department—and request an appointment to process a Medicaid eligibility application. This application can usually be made by a competent (mentally healthy) family member or by a legal guardian, if applicants have one. While each state has a specific Medicaid agency that determines program requirements and policy guidelines, the application process is generally handled at the local level. The telephone number and address for such offices can usually be found in the telephone book under "Government Offices—County." A county Medicaid claims representative can discuss the application process and provide additional information about local Medicaid requirements. Application forms range in length from just a few pages to many pages, requiring detailed information about financial assets, as well as income and expense statements. Generally, the type of information requested in the application includes:

- proof of income and earnings, including alimony, estate or trust income, annuities, dividends, interest income, capital gains, and retirement or government pensions;
- information on checking accounts, savings accounts, stocks, bonds, individual retirement accounts (including Keogh and 401-K plans), pension funds, trust funds, and other financial assets;
- information on real property, including personal residences and any recent real property transfers;
- information about life insurance policies, including the face value of the insurance policies and their cash surrender values;
- information on burial plots and burial trusts;

- a Social Security card;
- a Medicare card and information about any other health or disability insurance;
- a birth certificate; and
- a driver's license or other proof of identification.

Individuals thinking about admitting a relative into a nursing home should request a copy of the state's application form well in advance of the proposed admission date. Doing so will allow for a review of the type of detailed information required to process a Medicaid application. Gathering all the information in time for the appointment with the local Medicaid office will help hasten the application process.

Most Medicaid application forms will also inquire about or request information on any recent transfers of financial assets and gifts made by the applicant during the previous two to three years. Such transfers or gifts might still be counted as assets for the applicant and could also postpone the person's eligibility for Medicaid. In some cases, states can refuse to grant Medicaid assistance to people who have transferred or given away their assets two to three years prior to applying for Medicaid. States can also refuse to grant Medicaid assistance to people who have sold their assets at less than fair market value, if the real value of those assets would have made the individual ineligible for Medicaid. People facing these issues should talk with a lawyer or financial adviser who is familiar with Medicaid eligibility requirements before they submit their Medicaid applications. When individuals have substantial assets, any property transfers or gifts made as part of their estate and financial planning should be done well in advance of entering a nursing home.

Everyone who applies for Medicaid deserves a polite and complete explanation of his or her eligibility status. Those who do not receive explanations or who disagree with determinations should ask to speak with the claim representative's supervisor. If an issue cannot be resolved, applicants are entitled to a departmental appeal or hearing on the matter (see chapter 10).

People applying for Medicaid either for themselves or for a relative do not have to muddle through this process alone (again, see chapter 10). Most nursing home admissions or social services directors are both qualified and willing to assist family members in the process of applying for Medicaid eligibility. Frequently, nursing home staff have working relationships with Medicaid claim representatives and can be of great help in this process. *It would also be wise to seek the advice of a lawyer if it appears that an appeal will be necessary.*

What Medicaid actually pays to a nursing home will depend on the facility's

Medicaid reimbursement rate and on the eligible individual's income. The eligible individual's income, minus a small amount for personal needs (usually $25 to $30), is paid to the facility; the rest is paid by Medicaid. For example, assume that Mrs. X, an eighty-year-old nursing home resident, has a monthly income of $800 from Social Security and a private insurance annuity. Also assume, in this case, that Medicaid's reimbursement rate for the nursing home is $45 a day and that the state Medicaid allowance for personal needs is $25 a month. The nursing home charges $1,395 each month for caring for Mrs. X ($45 per day for a thirty-one-day month). Mrs. X will pay $775 from her personal income each month ($800 minus $25 for personal needs) and Medicaid will pay the rest—$620 per month—for a total of $1,395.

Nursing homes would prefer to admit only *private-pay patients* (those who have the financial resources to pay for their own care) rather than Medicaid-eligible individuals, because in most states Medicaid nursing home payment rates are significantly below the rates charged to private-pay patients. In several states, Medicaid payment rates are simply not high enough for the nursing home to provide quality services. Most nursing homes use the extra money paid by private-pay patients to offset low Medicaid payment rates. While this practice might seem unfair to the private-pay patients, a negative effect on nursing home quality and care standards could result if the two rates were kept at the same level. At least two states—Minnesota and Connecticut—do restrict private-pay charges to the same amount as Medicaid rates.

While some nursing homes require that financially responsible individuals other than patients sign the admission contracts, such contracts are illegal in some states and generally are not legally enforceable. It is also illegal for a nursing home to request private funds from Medicaid patients or their relatives as a condition of admission and/or of keeping patients. Facilities that attempt any of these actions can be criminally prosecuted under federal law. Those who suspect a facility of engaging in any of these practices should contact their local Medicaid office to complain, or call the office of the Inspector General at the U.S. Department of Health and Human Services. A toll-free number (1-800-368-5779) is available for this purpose.

Veterans' Benefits and Other Resources

Veterans' benefits are available to all eligible veterans, with priority given to veterans with disabilities resulting from their military service. Veterans who require nursing home care may be entitled to receive such care through Veterans Administration (VA) nursing facilities or in private nursing homes. In addition, disabled veterans who are capable of caring for themselves but require minimal medical support in a therapeutic living environment may qualify for domiciliary care.

The VA provides a significant amount of long-term care services, even though those services are limited to veterans. Some 115 nursing homes owned and operated by the VA serve more than 20,000 patients nationwide. The VA also contracts and pays for nursing home and long-term care services in more than 3,000 private community nursing homes throughout the country. In 1985, the VA paid for more than 38,000 veterans to receive care in private nursing homes.

Veterans, their families, or legal representatives can contact the local VA office to discuss eligibility for VA nursing home assistance. Telephone numbers for the local VA office can be found in the "Government" section of the telephone book.

Other ways to finance nursing home care include private long-term care insurance and "Medigap" insurance policies. These options are discussed in chapter 2.

The Importance of Planning Ahead

Overall, America's elderly are fairly well insured against the costs of health care except when it comes to paying for nursing home and other long-term care services. The greatest amount of money spent by the elderly for medical services goes to nursing home care.

Unless people plan ahead, paying for nursing home care can be an upsetting and confusing experience. Hopefully, this problem will never occur, but the older people are, the more likely they are to need long-term care services. By the time individuals become seriously ill, it is probably too late to begin effective financial planning to meet the costs associated with nursing home and long-term care needs. Without insurance, payment for nursing home care is likely to come from either out-of-pocket funds or Medicaid. Serious illness and the cost of nursing home care are as much financial issues as medical ones. Planning to meet the costs of a long-term illness should become an estate- or financial-planning requirement for everyone, not just the elderly.

4

Is a Living Will a Good Idea for You?

Overview

Planning ahead has a simple purpose: it allows individuals to say in advance what they want done regarding their medical treatment and/or estate before they become ill and unable to make those decisions themselves. Without that forethought—that planning ahead—those and many other decisions will be made by other people, people who may not know what the individuals would have wanted (or might disagree with it if they did know). The previous chapters have focused on ways to plan ahead for estate or financial decisions—by writing a will, creating a trust or joint account, purchasing the right kind of health insurance, and considering ways to pay for nursing home care. This chapter, on living wills, examines a way to plan ahead for health care.

Before looking at ways to plan ahead, it is important to understand that "advance directives," like living wills and powers of attorney (the latter are covered in the next chapter), are not new legal rights. The courts have long recognized the rights of individuals to direct their own medical care. *What these advance directives do is extend people's opportunity to direct such care to a time when they may be too ill to make and understand decisions.*

As noted in the Introduction, there are many reasons for planning ahead. Perhaps the two most important ones that individuals have are to

- make sure their wishes are followed; and

- relieve family members and health care professionals of the burden of having to make those difficult decisions for them.

Thinking about illness and death and trying to understand and plan for all the different treatment options can be difficult and confusing, but only the individuals themselves fully know what they want and don't want in the way of medical care. And although such planning might mean making some hard decisions, many people feel that having their wishes followed at a time when they're unable to express themselves makes it all worthwhile. *A living will is a document that gives people the ability to record those treatment decisions so that no one will ever have to guess what they'd want when they are no longer able to speak for themselves.* Unlike a regular will that directs where people's property should go after their death, a living will states what medical care people want while they are still alive but unable to speak for themselves.

What Can Be Put in a Living Will?

Definitional problems can arise over a living will. A particular medical treatment may not be clearly defined as *extraordinary care* (which can be refused) but instead might be seen as *supportive care* (which cannot be refused). Or the patient's doctor might see as supportive a treatment that the patient's family finds extraordinary.

Some examples of what individuals may wish to include in their living wills are

refusal or acceptance of a respirator or mechanical ventilator;

refusal or acceptance of artificial feeding and hydration tubes, depending on state law (this issue is more fully described later in this chapter);

antibiotic therapy, chemotherapy, or radiotherapy; and

invasive surgery.

Does a Living Will Constitute Suicide?

Most state laws that permit the use of living wills also specify that the refusal of life-prolonging treatment does not, for insurance or other purposes, constitute suicide.

People's personal and religious views on suicide may be another matter, but the law does not view as suicide a death that is the result of instructions in a living will. People who have questions about the religious nature of using a living will should consult with a knowledgeable representative of their religious order.

How and When Does a Living Will Work?

Most often, a living will is used to state that if death is near, the patient does not want to prolong the process of dying but does want the care necessary to maintain comfort and dignity until the fatal illness takes it natural course. At the same time, a living will does not *have* to be used to refuse treatment; it can also request medical care or list treatments that the person does want.

The Problem of Defining *Terminally Ill*

Directions contained in a living will do not usually take effect until two doctors have stated, in writing, that the patient is terminally ill (in a few states, only one such opinion is necessary). However, because there is no clear definition of when a patient is "terminally ill," getting that diagnosis is not without problems. *Some doctors believe the label* terminally ill *applies to patients expected to live six months; others feel that patients with only a month or a week left to live are terminally ill; and still others believe that patients are terminally ill* only *when they will die in a few days, no matter what treatment is given.* To put it another way, some doctors may diagnose a patient as terminally ill when certain diseases are first discovered, while others may use the same label only after the disease has spread or a relapse occurs after treatment.

How doctors define terminal illness *is important. Anyone using a living will should interview his or her doctors in advance and find out their definitions of terminal illness and their views on refusing life-supporting treatment.* Once a patient-doctor relationship has formed and a patient's illness has already progressed to a serious stage, it may be too late for the patient (or his or her family members) to comfortably consider switching to another doctor with more compatible views on such matters.

Remember, if a doctor believes that a patient is terminally ill only when death is imminent or around the corner, then directions contained in the patient's living will might not take effect until the last few days or weeks of life. Patients who are victims of serious accidents or strokes and are in an irreversible coma called a *persistent vegetative state* might not be considered terminally ill even if they would not wish to be kept alive were recovery impossible. Family members of a patient in an irreversible coma should know that his or her living will might be accepted anyway; moreover, there are other options available to get life-prolonging treatment halted (see chapters 12 and 14).

Another drawback is that in some states patients can execute and sign a living will only after being diagnosed as terminally ill. For patients in these states who are too ill, too confused by heavy sedatives or painkillers, or too senile by the time they are diagnosed as terminally ill, a living will would not be an option. They would be unable to make the decisions necessary to a living will at the time they most need one.

When terminally ill patients are able to execute a living will, some states permit them to talk about what they want and don't want in the presence of witnesses who then sign a written version.

Writing a Valid Living Will

Different states have different laws surrounding living wills, and so what is legal in one state might not be legal in another. This situation poses several problems. *If individuals execute living wills that are valid for the state in which they live, those same documents may not be valid if those individuals become ill and hospitalized in another state.*

Most states provide a form to make it easier to write a living will, but will accept variations if individual state requirements are met. A sample form for a living will is provided in appendix 3. In addition, organizations like the Society for the Right to Die in New York City, can provide current forms that take state variations into account. (The Society for the Right to Die, 250 West Fifty-seventh Street, New York, N.Y., 10107, [212] 246-6973, will mail the appropriate form on request.)

All states require that living wills be signed in the presence of two adult witnesses. While the rules vary from state to state, most states restrict certain persons from acting as legal witnesses—for example, relatives and potential heirs of the person executing the living wills, anyone paying for that person's health care, and anyone responsible for taking care of him or her. (For a checklist of state laws regarding living wills, see appendix 4.)

Some states require that one witness be the nursing home ombudsman, or patient advocate, when a nursing home resident signs a living will. Others require that living wills be notarized. Still others require that they be filed with a government office, or reviewed and reaffirmed after a certain number of years. The rules and regulations do not stop there: many states limit when a living will can be used, often barring its use by pregnant women, and others prohibit individuals from refusing food and fluids as a part of their living will (see appendix 4 and the section entitled "The Issue of Artificial Feeding and Hydration" in this chapter.)

Living wills written without a lawyer's assistance cost nothing at all. If a lawyer helps to prepare and draw up the document, the cost will usually depend on the lawyer's hourly fees. Although drawing up a living will should not take an excessive amount of time, interested individuals should ask their lawyer in advance how many hours the task is likely to take and how much experience the lawyer has in writing living wills. *A lawyer who is experienced in writing living wills will almost certainly be able to give far better advice, and will probably have more knowledge of state laws surrounding living wills.*

How to Make a Living Will Work

Most state laws require that individuals (or their families) notify their doctors that they have a living will. The doctors are then required to attach a copy of the living will to the appropriate medical records. Ideally, living wills are drawn up by patients before, or soon after, they become ill, thereby allowing sufficient time for discussion and an exchange of opinions before the document goes into effect. Yet even under the best of circumstances, there is no guarantee that everything will proceed smoothly once patients are too ill to speak for themselves.

At the time living wills go into effect, patients might not be under the care of their regular doctors. Patients who are hospitalized in another state, or undergo emergency surgery are likely to experience this problem. Patients and families alike must be alert to this situation and ensure that any new doctors are aware of the existence and contents of their living wills.

Extra copies of living wills should also be kept in a safe place to ensure that if the original is lost, the directions contained in it will still be available to the doctor.

How to Change or Revoke a Living Will

Individuals can change the directions in their living will anytime they want to, as long as they comply with their state's laws about witness requirements. To change directions, they need first to revoke, or cancel, any previously written living wills and then write up new ones, have them witnessed, and file them according to the laws of their state.

A living will can be canceled simply by someone's stating that it is no longer valid; however, to be on the safe side, doctors or nursing administrators in possession of a patient's living will should be told that it has been revoked. The same is true for living wills registered in government offices in compliance with some states' laws. *It is against the law for anyone to produce a fake living will, to lie about a living will's having been revoked when it is still valid, or to hide the fact that an existing living will has been revoked by the patient.*

The Limits of Living Wills

Most states have enacted natural-death legislation that recognizes living wills as legal documents representing a patient's choices. *Even states without such laws, however, do not necessarily ignore the presence of living wills or other advance directives.* Courts in some of these latter states, such as New York and New Jersey, have recognized living wills as evidence of a patient's wishes and have agreed that such instructions may be followed by a doctor. Moreover, all states permit durable powers-of-attorney agreements that can be used for health care purposes and that allow for the same kind of advance planning as living wills do (see chapter 5 for more information). In any event, it is likely that if the question was brought before them, courts in all states would rule that living wills are allowable.

Generally, a doctor or health care provider may accept a living will as evidence of a patient's wishes, and may follow the directions contained in it, unless the patient's family members disagree over whether or not to refuse a particular treatment. When family members do disagree, the patient has far less chance of having his or her wishes obeyed, at least without a court hearing on the matter.

If the patient is terminally ill, if the treatment is considered extraordinary, and if the living will clearly refuses such treatment, the doctor must either comply with the living will or transfer the patient to a doctor who will comply with it. If the treatment is considered ordinary, the doctor has the right to provide it. If the living will is unclear regarding a particular treatment, different people may interpret it differently. In such instances, a hospital or nursing home ethics committee might review the case, or it might go to court so that a judge could decide whether or not a patient should receive a particular treatment.

The biggest barrier to having one's written wishes followed is the doctor's fear of being sued by a family member or some other individual for failing to provide proper care. These fears are very strong, even if they are mistaken.

Sadly, it took only one case—later dismissed by the court—to raise these unrealistic fears. In 1983, two California doctors were charged for removing, with the family's consent, life-support equipment from a terminally ill, comatose patient. One court convicted them, but the doctors appealed and the higher court ruled that the doctors, with the family's consent, had the right to withdraw life-sustaining treatment even if the patient did not have a living will. *Doctors do have the right to discontinue treatment that will not improve the patient's chances for recovery, and no doctor has ever been punished for withholding or withdrawing treatment based on a patient's written, signed directive or on the agreement of next of kin.*

Those facing a situation in which a doctor does not want to follow a terminally ill patient's written wishes or the wishes of the patient's family should keep the following in mind:

- *Doctors who use treatments that prolong life against the patient's or family's wishes can be sued for wrongful treatment and for battery.*
- *Natural-death laws specifically protect health care providers from civil and criminal liability if they withhold or withdraw life-prolonging treatment in accordance with a living will.*
- *In most states, a doctor who doesn't want to conform to a patient's advance directive must try to transfer that patient to another professional who is willing to do so. Failure to conform or to transfer the patient can result in charges of unprofessional conduct or in a misdemeanor.*

How Federal Health Care Facilities View Living Wills

Health care facilities operated by the air force, the navy, the Indian Health Service, and Hansen's Disease Center all recognize living wills as legal documents. These facilities will follow the wishes set forth in living wills as long as those wishes comply with the laws of the state in which the facility is located.

Although the army does not have a policy about living wills, patients who can still speak for themselves always have the right to decide what medical treatment they do or don't want. And while facilities operated by the Veterans Administration don't recognize living wills as legal documents, they will add them to patients' medical records and consider them when deciding what to do.

Further, the Clinical Center at the National Institutes of Health will accept living wills prepared in any state as long as the patient is an adult and the document was witnessed and signed by two other adults; the center does not require that a living will be notarized.

The Issue of Artificial Feeding and Hydration

The issues surrounding the artificial feeding and hydration of patients (the giving of food and water to them) are highly complex and pose special legal, ethical, emotional, and definitional problems for patients with living wills. The question that has raised these problems is, simply, Can artificial nourishment and hydration be withdrawn from a terminally ill or comatose patient?

The reason such food and water are termed *artificial* is that the patients receiving them are unable to eat or drink for themselves. Instead, nasogastric feeding tubes, which enter the stomach through the patient's nose, or gastrostomy tubes, which are inserted directly into the stomach, or intravenous solutions, which are dripped into a patient's veins, are used.

The courts have said that these artificial means of providing food and water are no different from other types of artificial life-support devices, such as the mechanical ventilator or respirator that permits a patient to breathe with the assistance of a machine. Therefore, if a terminally ill patient has specifically requested that food and water be withdrawn, it may be possible to do so.

Yet this is by no means an easy task. Many states do not allow individuals to request in their living wills that food and water be removed (see appendix 4). Also, many doctors and nurses are upset by the request and have occasionally refused to honor it. Such cases, where removal of feeding and hydration is permitted by the state, may end up in court.

The removal of food and water is no trivial matter. Many comatose patients who will never recover can be kept alive for years, even decades, through artificial feeding and hydration. There is no evidence that these patients suffer either hunger or thirst, yet their families can easily use up all their savings paying for this treatment, even if the patient would not have wanted it. If individuals want to refuse artificial feeding and hydration in their living wills, it is probably wise to seek a lawyer's advice on state laws and on how to write their living will to reflect this desire (for more information on this topic, see chapter 14).

5

Powers of Attorney and Other Ways to Plan Ahead

Overview

As discussed in the preceding chapter, a living will is one way to plan ahead for decisions about medical care. But there are other ways to plan ahead for financial, personal, and medical decisions. This chapter considers several ways that mentally healthy elderly people can appoint specific individuals—spouses, adult children, relatives, trusted friends—to make decisions for them.

There may be many reasons why older, mentally healthy individuals might want to give up their rights to make certain decisions and let others make decisions for them now or at some time in the future. These *surrogate decision-makers,* as they are called, can be identified in advance by elderly people or, in cases where those people are already too ill to do so, by a court (see chapter 12). In this chapter, only those surrogate decision-makers who are appointed by mentally healthy elderly people are discussed.

What makes elderly individuals be seen as mentally healthy, or competent to make decisions? This evaluation is often made informally by the family, friends, colleagues, doctors, or lawyers of elderly people (for more information, see chapter 11). It is also a judgment that can be made formally by a court, when there is disagreement about an individual's ability to make rational decisions and appreciate their consequences. A court is *petitioned,* or asked by those concerned with the situation, to decide whether or not an elderly person is competent or incompetent—that is, able or unable to make rational decisions. (Courts may also be asked by concerned individuals to review the authority of family members making decisions for an incompetent person; see chapter 14).

All the laws applying to adult protective services, such as those provided by the county or state departments of aging or social services, require that services be accepted voluntarily if elderly people are competent to make such a decision. Accepting these decision-making services can thus be simply a matter of an elderly person agreeing to receive the services being offered.

Whether or not adult protective services are needed or are being used, older persons may want to give up some or all of their decision-making responsibilities on a temporary or permanent, immediate or future, basis. This action is called a *transfer of decision-making powers.*

Appointing a Guardian to Make Decisions

One way to transfer decision-making powers in advance is for elderly people to appoint guardians. Guardians can also be appointed by a court to take on the decision-making powers of incompetent individuals. (This topic is important and is the subject of chapter 12.)

Using a Power of a Attorney to Transfer Decision-Making Responsibilities

Perhaps the most common way to transfer power or appoint others to make decisions is through a written document called a *power of attorney. Briefly, power-of-attorney documents require two people, a* principal *who wants to appoint someone and an* agent *who is being appointed.* Agents are usually close relatives, lawyers, business associates, or financial advisers who are authorized to sign documents or conduct business for principals. *Principals can decide exactly how much or how little authority to give agents and can end, or revoke, these agreements at any time. These agreements must be canceled in writing. If they are canceled, principals should notify all businesses with which their agents deal on their behalf, even though the businesses have a duty to continually verify the agents' authority, such notification is still a good idea.* (Appendix 6 contains a sample state power-of-attorney form, and appendix 7 a general power-of-attorney form.)

While these agreements can be written by principals and agreed to by agents, it is usually wise to have lawyers draw them up. Doing so can avoid many unforeseen or unintended problems that might arise. Lawyers usually charge by the hour to do such work; however, legal clinics for the elderly often offer these services at a lower cost. These agreements are legal everywhere in the United States.

A power of attorney can be *executed*, or written up, and used only during the period of time that principals are competent. *If at any time a principal becomes incompetent to make decisions, the power-of-attorney agreement is automatically ended. Thus, this agreement is really designed for the convenience of elderly people who could make decisions but for some reason do not want to do so.* If others suspect that a principal is not competent to decide that he or she wants a power of attorney, they can challenge such agreements in court. If the court agrees that the principal was imcompetent when the power of attorney was written or that the principal is no longer competent, the court will revoke the agreement.

Because a power of attorney is useless as soon as the principal dies or becomes incompetent, it also poses another problem: *at the time principals most need agents to make decisions, it is no longer legal for the agents to do so.*

Durable Powers of Attorney

To address the problem outlined above, a different kind of legal tool is available: a *durable power of attorney*. Like the regular power of attorney, this agreement involves principals and agents, and once again the principals can decide how much or how little power they want their agents to have. Principals can also decide to appoint several agents, who must act either unanimously (or by majority vote) or individually but only on specific tasks. *The basic difference between a regular power of attorney and a durable power of attorney is that the durable one doesn't stop being legal when principals become incompetent.* Durable powers of attorney are available in every state in the country and the District of Columbia.

As with the regular power of attorney, agents are usually spouses, adult children, siblings, close friends, or advisers—people who principals believe understand and will act on what they would want. Because these documents may be used for health care decisions, it is not a good idea for principals to appoint as agents their doctors, nurses, home health aides, or other primary paid health care workers. Doing so could cause problems, as it might be considered a conflict of interest.

There are two types of durable power-of-attorney agreements. *First, a* springing durable power of attorney *means that agents are not allowed to make decisions until principals are incompetent to make them on their own.* The advantage of this type of document is that it can be executed by competent principals who still want to make their own decisions but are looking ahead and planning for the time when they might become incompetent. (Appendix 9 contains a sample springing durable power-of-attorney form.) *Second, an* immediate durable power of attorney *means that agents start making decisions as soon as the document is written up, and continue to do so after principals become incompetent.* The advantage of this type of document is that principals can transfer decision-making powers to an agent while they are still competent and do not have to worry about what will happen if they later become incompetent.

Durable powers of attorney can save a lot of lawyers' fees and court costs that might have to be paid if an elderly person becomes incompetent before appointing agents and the court has to do it for the person. (For more information on situations in which a court might need to appoint a surrogate decision-maker, see chapter 14.) *These agreements do not require that the agent be legally supervised, licensed, or bonded, but different states have different witness, agent, and notarization requirements that must be satisfied before the durable power-of-attorney document is considered legal.* Because this is a fast-changing area of the law, it is difficult to compile a complete chart of state requirements for durable power-of-attorney documents. A partial list is included in appendix 5 to illustrate what kinds of rules a state may impose; however, *all interested individuals should consult with a knowledgeable lawyer to find out the laws of their state.*

If people other than the principals or agents are concerned about these agreements or the decisions being made, they can ask a court to review the matter. *A durable power of attorney can be ended or revoked, usually in writing, at any time before the principal becomes incompetent.* Again, to be on the safe side, a principal who cancels such an agreement should notify all businesses with which the agent is doing business on his or her behalf. And again, although these agreements can be written up without a lawyer, it is probably wise to use one; lawyers can structure these agreements to avoid unintended and unanticipated problems.

Lawyers usually charge an hourly fee for these services, but interested individuals should also contact legal clinics that specialize in working for the elderly, as such clinics might do the same thing for a lower cost. To find low-cost legal aid, contact the legal services developer of the State Unit on Aging (see appendix 20 for addresses), who should be able to make some recommendations. Also, almost every state has an Information and Referral (I&R) service for older people or for the general public in need of services. Local senior citizens' centers should be able to provide the area I&R telephone number.

In the past, regular and durable power-of-attorney agreements were normally used by principals who wanted agents to take care of their financial estate and assets. There does not seem to be any legal reason, however, why the durable power of attorney could not also be used by agents to make decisions about the medical care of principals. Indeed, *a few state laws specifically allow durable power-of-attorney agreements to be used for medical care decisions.*

Durable Power-of-Attorney Agreements for Health Care

A few states have special provisions for documents called *durable power of attorney for health care. In actuality, though, the regular durable power-of-attorney documents accomplish the same purpose in almost all cases.* The more specific documents are designed to let principals appoint agents to make health care decisions for them. One advantage such documents might have is to calm the collective worries of doctors, lawyers, hospital administrators, and family members making decisions—especially life-and-death decisions—for incompetent patients.

The durable power of attorney for health care allows principals to state, in detail, what kinds of medical care or life-sustaining treatments are acceptable to them. This kind of advance planning by competent principals can save a great deal of grief and uncertainty on the part of agents.

Like the regular durable power of attorney, these documents can be executed by filling out a standard form and following the laws of one's state. It is probably a good idea for principals to discuss the form with a doctor who can explain the different kinds of medical problems and treatments that principals might want to include in the document. A sample form is provided in appendix 8.

If there are restrictions on the medical care decisions being made, they generally surround life-and-death decisions, such as taking a patient off life-support machines or removing nasogastric feeding and hydration tubes. There is growing support among lawyers, judges, and state legislators to allow durable power-of-attorney agreements to be used by agents to make critical medical care decisions for principals.

Why Use a Durable Power of Attorney?

Durable power-of-attorney agreements are often considered stronger, more flexible documents than living wills because they provide for competent agents who can make and enforce decisions for incompetent principals. There are several advantages to using a durable power of attorney.

- Principals, while still competent, can decide exactly which persons they most trust to make decisions for them. For example, although principals might know that certain friends most clearly understand their wishes, a judge faced with appointing agents might instead select family members.
- Agents will not lose their legal right to make decisions once principals become incompetent.
- Principals can decide whether they want an agent to start making decisions immediately or whether they want the agent to wait until they become incompetent.
- Principals who want agents to start making decisions immediately have only one document to execute, instead of writing up first a power-of-attorney agreement and then a second document to appoint a surrogate decision-maker who could take over if the principal were to become incompetent.
- Durable power-of-attorney documents can save the lawyers' fees and court costs incurred when judges must appoint surrogate decision-makers for incompetent people who have not already done so.
- Because these agreements are available across the country, a durable power of attorney written in one state is likely to be honored in another state if a principal becomes ill and hospitalized outside his or her home state.

Further advantages of durable power-of-attorney documents include the following:

- They apply to many different kinds of health care decisions—such as whether incompetent nursing home residents should have cataract surgery—not just decisions about accepting or refusing life-prolonging treatment.
- They can be used by individuals who want life-prolonging treatment continued, as well as by those who wish to refuse such treatment.
- Unlike living wills, which do not necessarily (but could) appoint agents, durable power-of-attorney agreements always appoint agents who can act as advocates or defenders of principals' wishes. This way, agents can enforce principals' preferences for medical care and ensure that those preferences are not forgotten or ignored by other family members, doctors, hospital administrators, or staff.
- The presence of agents means that principals do not need to anticipate all possible treatment choices. Agents are expected to make decisions for the principal

on the basis of *substituted judgment* (that is, to the best of their ability, agents are to make the same decisions principals would have made).

- Clearly identified agents provide health care facilities with a measure of legal protection and certainty not currently provided by either a living will or the informal consent of unappointed but available family members.
- The presence of appointed agents makes it much less likely that hospital and nursing home administrators—who are afraid of being sued, or doing the wrong thing, when making important medical decisions for incompetent patients—will take cases to court so that judges can review the decisions being made.

How to Create a Durable Power of Attorney

Durable power-of-attorney documents can be created either with or without the help of lawyers. As noted earlier, principals can decide to give their agents many areas of responsibility, only a few areas, or even just one. The document can cover any financial, personal, and health care decisions.

Depending on the state in which principals live, durable power-of-attorney agreements may need to list each specific task to be undertaken by agents. Some states have a *statutory short form power of attorney* that gives broad authority to agents by listing one or more of a number of categories—for example, real estate transactions; chattel and goods transactions; bond, share, and commodity transactions; business operating transactions; banking transactions; insurance transactions; estate transactions; claims and litigation; personal relationships and affairs; benefits from military service; records, reports, and statements; and all other matters.

Following are tasks that, in general, agents may perform for principals under a durable power-of-attorney agreement. In states without the short form described above, principals may have to specify in the agreement each of the tasks agents should perform. (To read more about these tasks, see the first entry for this chapter in the "Additional Reading" section at the back of this book.)

Property Management

To make deposits and withdrawals from checking and savings accounts.

To sell, lease, borrow, and invest assets.

To sign tax returns and represent, or arrange for representation of, the principal in a tax audit. (In these cases, use the IRS's own power-of-attorney forms, and limit the agent's power to specific years.)

To work on retirement plans, pay IRA contributions, handle rollovers, elect payout options, and so on.

To fund a previously created living trust (see chapter 1).

To administer life insurance policies, including buying additional coverage and borrowing against policies when necessary.

To collect or forgive debts, complete charitable pledges, and pay salaried employees.

To redirect mail and to cancel or continue credit cards and charge accounts.

To start, settle, appeal, or dismiss legal proceedings.

To update or reform estate-planning documents other than wills.

To nominate a conservator for estate purposes and a guardian for any minor children.

To resign from public and private offices and positions.

Personal Management

To establish or change residence (for example, when the principal moves into a nursing home).

To arrange transportation, travel, and recreation.

To buy, store, repair, and dispose of clothing, food, household goods, furnishings, and personal items.

To arrange for advance funeral and burial arrangements and for anatomical gifts.

To arrange for the care or disposition of pets.

To employ, pay, or fire paid servants, companions, and other nonmedical personnel.

To arrange for spiritual or religious needs.

To provide for companionship.

To nominate a guardian for any minor children.

Health Care

To have access to and disclose medical records and other personal information.

To employ and discharge health care personnel.

To give or withhold consent regarding medical treatment.

To give or withhold consent regarding psychiatric care.

To authorize relief from pain.

To grant releases to medical personnel and others.

(For more information on making critical care decisions, such as terminating life-support systems or removing artificial feeding and hydration tubes, see chapter 14. This is an important topic, one best dealt with in a separate chapter.)

A durable power-of-attorney agreement can be written by filling out a standard form and checking to see whether all the relevant state laws are followed (see appendixes 5, 6, 7, 8, and 9 for some special state requirements and forms). *Nevertheless, it is a good idea to have all durable power-of-attorney agreements witnessed and notarized, no matter what the relevant state laws may be.* Doing so is particularly important when agreements written in states that do not require notarization end up being used in states that do require it.

It's also a good idea to appoint more than one agent in case the only appointed individual is unavailable. This situation is more likely to occur when couples appoint each other and then are both seriously injured in a single accident. Both partners will then need an agent but may have appointed only each other. Had they each left instructions that, for example, their daughter should become their agent if their spouse could not, then someone would still exist to act on their behalf.

Legal Status and Other Points to Remember

While a great deal can be said in favor of durable power-of-attorney agreements, they are not without a few problems. As mentioned earlier, although these documents are generally accepted for use in health care decisions, their validity for that use can be questioned. *It is essential that the agents' authority to make medical decisions be clearly defined in the durable power of attorney.* However, the tougher the decisions—such as whether to remove life-support systems from an incompetent patient—the more likely are the agreements to be scrutinized, and possibly rejected, by caregivers in favor of receiving "sue-proof" court judgments on those decisions.

Another problem lies with the fact that individuals may not be psychologically ready to execute these documents before, or at the start of, a progressive illness that may afflict them at a relatively early age.

One of the most difficult problems faced by agents, health care facilities, and even courts may be determining when principals are no longer competent to make decisions. This is particularly true when agents have a springing durable power of attorney that goes into effect only when principals become incompetent. (For more information, see chapter 11.) Sometimes this determination seems obvious, but not always. Some elderly people with progressive illnesses may be intermittently competent, with periods of time when they are lucid, rational, and capable of making decisions for themselves. Others may be less competent than they once were, yet still competent enough to make at least some decisions.

Many lawyers recommend that those individuals who have not executed such an agreement but who are stricken with Alzheimer's disease or another illness that slowly robs them of their competence be brought to an attorney for explanations and signatures during times when they are relatively clearheaded and lucid.

Many banks and lending institutions are not familiar with durable powers of attorney and may not accept them as legal proof that principals' finances are now under the control of other individuals, unless the institutions' own forms are used. For those who executed a springing durable power of attorney that took effect when they became incompetent, this poses an impossible situation, as they are no longer competent to sign bank forms.

Yet another problem with these agreements is that their power can potentially be abused. While most elderly people assign these powers to trusted relatives or friends, it is certainly possible that elderly people could be forced or pressured into appointing agents who do not have the people's best interests at heart. For this reason, it is important that the courts be allowed to review decisions being made by agents if other concerned individuals bring the matter to the courts' attention.

Limits on Decisions and Why a Decision Might Not Be Followed

There may be many reasons that agents' decisions are not followed. The reasons may be simple—for example, that doctors don't agree with agents' choices—or more complex. Contributing to the current legal, medical, ethical, and moral confusion over the right of surrogates to make critical care decisions are

the uneasy relationship between law and medicine;

the actual and perceived authority of doctors;

the existence of new life-prolonging technologies;

arguments about the patient's quality of life;

an increasing reliance on and fear of lawsuits;

the public's growing awareness of the individual's right to refuse treatment; and

the growing numbers of incompetent elderly patients.

These problems may also contribute to agents' decisions not being honored without a court battle.

Limits to the rights of agents to make decisions tend to apply on a case-by-case and decision-by-decision basis. As with most things in life, agents' decisions are less likely to be questioned if the other concerned individuals agree with them. Most often, questions and limits arise over end-of-life decisions—decisions made to refuse life-prolonging treatment—and they can be imposed by a number of different people and institutions.

Limits may be imposed by state laws. For instance, if a particular state does not permit patients (or their agents) to refuse food and water supplied through nose or stomach tubes, then agents will be limited by that state law (for a checklist of state laws, see appendix 4; for additional information, see chapter 14). Limits may also be imposed by health care facilities if for religious or policy reasons they do not want to permit patients or agents to refuse treatment (in these cases, facilities should assist agents in finding another facility agreeable to their decision, and should transfer the patients in question). Limits may also be imposed by doctors or nurses who don't agree with agents' decisions and force the issue to be taken to court. The same is true of other friends or family members who do not agree with agents' decisions on behalf of principals.

Discussing and Registering the Document with Health Care Professionals

Doctors and other health care professionals who provide care to competent elderly people can recommend that these patients execute a durable power of attorney. Doctors can also be excellent sources of information in the writing up of these agreements—they can explain medical treatments to principals and help them anticipate and plan for medical decision-making by their agents.

Unfortunately, many health professionals are ignorant of the legal tools—such as living wills and durable power-of-attorney agreements—that can help elderly people and their families plan ahead. They may also feel uncomfortable discussing medical treatments and refusals with patients and their families. *It is important to raise these issues with doctors, nurses, and even administrators so that they become aware of the preferences of patients and their agents.* If these health professionals are unaware of what patients wanted when competent, they may be more reluctant to follow their wishes when expressed by agents.

Once durable power-of-attorney agreements are written, it is important that they be given to, or registered with, the doctors, nurses, hospitals, nursing homes, and other facilities that care for principals. The agreements won't do any good if no one knows about them, and if known about in advance, their mere existence may help to avoid some potential problems. Copies of agreements should be available to these professionals, who will want to know the extent and validity of the agents' powers. Principals or agents should also discuss these documents with each concerned individual. Obviously, others will want to ensure that agents are not making medical decisions when they are authorized only to make financial ones.

Every nursing home should have a written policy about how it views living wills and durable power-of-attorney documents. Some nursing homes even require that competent patients execute a durable power of attorney upon admission, so that in the event patients become incompetent, facilities will know who should be making decisions.

PART

2

Staying in Charge in a Hospital or Nursing Home

6

Saying Yes to Medical Care
What You Should Know First

Overview

When illness strikes, people's everyday lives (and those of their family's) are suddenly thrown into confusion and uncertainty. Terribly important decisions must often be made quickly, and patients and their families may have few chances to really think things through. Medical terms, proposed treatments, and their statistics for patient recovery can be frightening and upsetting. Making a decision to either undergo or refuse surgery, chemotherapy, radiotherapy, or other treatments may have life-or-death results. At the same time, quality-of-life arguments must also be considered. At the very point when people feel the most helpless, they are asked to make some of the most crucial decisions of their lives.

Some steps can be taken in advance—steps that may make the immediate burdens of illness a little lighter when the time comes—and these are of the utmost importance before deciding to say yes to medical care. These steps range from the careful selection of doctors to the questions that should be asked before treatment decisions are made.

Selecting a Doctor

If at all possible, select a doctor before a serious illness develops that requires medical attention or hospitalization. Except in emergencies when people become ill and must be hospitalized while away from home, this is a useful bit of advance planning. In most cases, however, elderly people already have a doctor they regularly see for checkups, minor aches and pains, or problems they had in the past.

A person's regular doctor should be someone who understands the needs of the ill person in particular and the needs of the elderly person in general. Family doctors, internists, and general practitioners may be the best choices. Specialists should be reserved for more complicated needs, such as kidney failure or cancerous growths. Regular doctors can call in specialists as consultants if and when the need arises, and they can also refer patients to those specialists if cases become too complicated for them.

The process of selecting a doctor or of interviewing one's regular doctor to make sure he or she is suitable is important. The last problem patients want to face while gravely ill is finding out that their doctor has a fundamental disagreement with how they want to be treated and how they view their life and death.

How to Find a Doctor

For people who are in the process of selecting a doctor for the first time, a number of steps can be taken to ensure finding one who meets their particular needs. New doctors may have to be found when a person's regular doctor retires or when patients are dissatisfied with a doctor's response to their illness. Also, many elderly people retire to sunnier climates and in so doing lose the services of doctors they have grown used to seeing. When any of these situations occurs, there are several ways to find a new doctor:

- Directories of doctors are available in public libraries, telephone books, and state medical societies.
- Individuals who move to another area can ask their current doctor for recommendations or suggestions about what doctors to use in a new location.
- Friends, family members, nurses, pharmacists, and social workers may all have useful information about and experience with doctors they can recommend.
- Area hospitals and medical centers can suggest individual doctors.
- Individuals who have not yet retired can sometimes tap into the resources of their workplace, such as the company benefits manager.
- Retired individuals who receive pensions can ask their company for lists of doctors and their specialties.

What to Look For in a Doctor

Many factors can go into the choosing of a new doctor. Male patients may feel more comfortable with male doctors, and female patients may prefer female doctors, depending on the types of problems they are experiencing. No one should be embarrassed about interviewing potential doctors, for doctors play an important role in the life of every patient. It's wise to find out in advance whether a particular doctor will suit the needs of an individual patient.

The *American Medical Association's Family Medical Guide* (listed in the "Additional Reading" section at the back of this book) recommends four areas that can act as rough clues to a doctor's performance and a patient's satisfaction with his or her care:

1. *How well organized is the doctor's practice?* A well-organized practice allows for effective follow-up, accurate record-keeping, a minimum of waiting time before appointments, and adequate time for the doctor to spend with each patient.

2. *How does the doctor treat his or her patients?* Does the doctor take enough time to truly examine or evaluate a problem? Are his or her examinations done carefully and with adequate respect for a patient's privacy? Does the doctor explain both what is wrong and what the treatment is in such a way that the patient can understand it? Does the patient feel comfortable asking the doctor questions?

3. *Is the doctor willing to consult with other doctors if a patient's problem is out of his or her area of expertise or appears to be particularly complex?* The doctor should explain why a consultation is needed and should provide the second doctor with adequate information so that he or she can evaluate the patient's situation.

4. *Is the doctor willing to discuss any questions a patient may have about treatment, especially when a disease has been treated for a long time without apparent progress?* The doctor should also discuss other options or different treatments the patient could choose. He or she should tell the patient what choices are available and the advantages and disadvantages of each one.

Other helpful clues can be obtained by asking and observing the following:

- Is the doctor knowledgeable? What are his or her credentials? Has the doctor completed medical school, an internship, and a residency? Is he or she board certified? Has the doctor conducted and published any research?
- Is the doctor experienced in caring for elderly people?
- Has the doctor kept current on new procedures and treatments? How conservative is he or she in recommending treatment? (Individuals will have to decide for themselves whether they want a very conservative, cautious doctor; a more radical one; or someone whose approach is somewhere in between.)
- Is the doctor available for over-the-phone questions? Is he or she willing to make house calls if necessary?
- Does the doctor have someone who will attend to his or her patients if the doctor is out of town or unavailable? Does that second doctor have access to patients' medical records?
- Does the doctor have privileges to practice in one or more area hospitals (*privileges* means that a hospital's medical staff has reviewed the doctor's credentials and abilities and permitted him or her to practice in the facility)? What is the reputation of the hospital(s) in which the doctor has privileges? What services are offered in that hospital(s)?
- What arrangements does the doctor have for being paid? Does he or she accept Medicare or Medicaid payment as payment-in-full for services, or is the patient expected to pay additional money? Individuals should check their health insurance coverage to find out what doctor's services are included.

An excellent book to read on this subject is *How to Choose and Use Your Doctor,* by Marvin Belsky and Leonard Gross (see the "Additional Reading" section at the back of this book). When meeting with a doctor, these authors say that individuals have the following rights:

- To be fully informed. Information and medical terms should be explained in a way that can be understood by patients.
- To expect and receive the doctor's ongoing abilities.
- To be treated with compassion.
- To have their privacy respected and to have their records and medical information be a private and confidential matter between patient and doctor.

- To know everything about a doctor that might influence his or her decisions about treatment.
- To be educated about medical treatments.
- To question the doctor, make suggestions, and be critical when appropriate.
- To have their medical records sent to another doctor on request (whether they are leaving one doctor for another or are receiving a consultation from a second doctor).

Remember, it is always possible for individuals to change doctors if they are unhappy with the care they receive. People who are dissatisfied with a doctor should tell him or her the reasons behind their decision to switch to another doctor. They should also ask that their records be forwarded to the new doctor. (This request may involve signing a release form, although the new doctor's office might be able to handle the process instead.)

Selecting a Hospital

Individuals who select a doctor who has privileges to admit patients into one or more hospitals have in effect already selected (or narrowed down their search for) a hospital. Therefore, it's a good idea to find out where a doctor has privileges and to check out those hospitals before selecting the doctor.

Individuals can arrange to take a look at hospitals in which a doctor they like has privileges. After seeing those facilities, they might also want to check out other hospitals that have good reputations or that seem worth the effort. A hospital's administrator or a member of its community relations department can usually arrange such a visit. When planning to visit a hospital, make a note to ask questions about the food, rooms, personnel, policies, and services offered.

A handy book for such an exercise is Charles Inlander's *Take this Book to the Hospital with You* (see the "Additional Reading" section). It has a complete checklist of questions to ask when visiting a hospital. Other questions to ask are as follows:

- Is the hospital licensed by the state?
- Is it accredited by the Joint Commission on Accreditation of Health Care Organizations?

- Are a wide variety of services available, such as outpatient, surgery, hospice, ambulatory, and home care services? Which services would be available in the individual's particular area? (See appendix 10 for a list of possible hospital services.)
- Does the hospital have ways of evaluating and ensuring quality care?
- Is the hospital affiliated with a university or school?

Also helpful is the American Hospital Association's (AHA) *Guide to the Health Care Field.* This annual directory, which can be found in public libraries, lists AHA-registered hospitals, all U.S. hospitals, U.S. government hospitals located in foreign countries, accredited long-term care or nursing home facilities, and those hospitals accredited by the Joint Commission on Accreditation of Health Care Organizations. Included in every hospital's listing is the name of the administrator, services, facilities, type of hospital, number of beds, number of staff, payroll size, and a great deal of other information. The directory also lists Peer Review Organizations (PROs), state health planning and development agencies, state departments of health and welfare, health care coalitions, and statewide health coordinating councils.

Individuals should also review their insurance policies to identify what hospital services are covered. Some insurance companies require prior permission before they will pay for certain services. Health permitting, individuals should contact their insurance companies to receive permission before agreeing to use such services.

Other health care facilities can be inspected as well. Individuals should find out what is available in their area, such as home care, nursing home, and health maintenance organizations (HMOs). Whenever possible, visit these organizations, ask to speak with their representatives, and review their brochures.

How to Get the Most out of the Doctor-Patient Relationship

Any relationship has to be worked at if it's going to be good. Once a doctor (and a hospital) is chosen, attending to a few matters will help both the doctor and the patient to make the most of their time together.

Patients should make a list of their medical problems or complaints and take it to the doctor's office; trying to remember everything in the doctor's office does not always work. Patients should also have regular appointments and should set a schedule for seeing the doctor based on his or her recommendations.

Patients should be sure to ask the doctor what to do in case of an emergency—should patients call first, go the an emergency room first, or have the doctor call the emergency room in advance? *Because a doctor's privileges are limited to certain hospitals, he or she cannot admit or see patients in just any emergency room. Patients entering the emergency room of a hospital in which their doctors do not have privileges will be assigned another doctor by the hospital.*

Honesty between doctor and patient is essential. Even though some information may be embarrassing to reveal, it is important that the doctor know about it anyway. Appropriate diagnosis and treatment are impossible if the doctor doesn't know all the facts. *The information that a patient gives a doctor is strictly confidential.*

The patient's medical records should be located at the doctor's office, or at the hospital while the patient is hospitalized. Records are also kept by health maintenance organizations, nursing homes, and any other medical services in which the patient is enrolled. These records include previous hospitalizations, previous doctor's records, X-ray and laboratory records, and records of specialists and other consultants who provided the patient with medical care in the past. *A patient has the right to see and copy his or her medical records. The only person who can give permission for these records to be transferred to someone else is the patient. If records need to be sent elsewhere, the doctor or hospital will ask the patient to sign a form agreeing to the transfer.* (For more information, see chapter 7.)

How Patients Can Help

Patients can greatly assist their doctors in helping them to get well by becoming actively involved in the doctor-patient relationship. There are several specific ways for patients to do this:

- Be honest and cooperative. After examining a patient or diagnosing a problem, the doctor will outline a *treatment plan* that may include medications, changes in diet, exercise, medical therapy, or other treatments to improve the patient's condition. Patients should help shape their treatment plan by telling the

doctor if there are parts of it they are unwilling to follow or will find difficult to follow.
- Discuss details or information that may not be clear when first explained by the doctor.
- Discuss medical tests before they are ordered, and find out about any associated risks; ask whether tests are absolutely necessary and what they cost (patients always have the right to refuse tests; for more information, see chapter 7).
- Keep track of test results, and review them with the doctor.
- If hospitalization is recommended for a specific procedure, ask if it can be done outside the hospital (for example, same-day surgery, tests at outpatient departments, or treatment at home or in a hospice).

In some states when doctors prescribe drugs, they can indicate whether pharmacists may use generic substitutes that cost a great deal less than brand-name drugs but have the same effect. Also available in some states are programs that pay for drugs for eligible elderly individuals. Interested persons should check with theit State Unit on Aging, doctor, or pharmacist for this information.

Emergency Room Treatment and Hospitalization

Sometimes hospitalization is inevitable. But whenever possible, it is a good idea for individuals to know some self-care and first-aid skills for dealing with emergencies—for example, knowing how to give cardiopulmonary resuscitation (CPR) for someone who stops breathing suddenly, or how to stop a wound from bleeding. Local American Red Cross organizations and fire departments often offer such courses.

When hospitalization is a necessity, it can be for many different reasons and take several different forms. While emergency rooms (ER) are for emergencies, patients can sometimes get faster medical attention by calling their doctors with urgent requests. Other ER-type alternatives may be available in some communities; independent centers for minor accidents and abrasions or for similarly urgent but nonemergency needs are an example.

When admitted to an emergency room, a patient will be assigned a doctor unless his or her regular doctor is available, can respond, and has privileges to practice in that hospital. Patients should always tell hospitals the name of their doctors in any event.

State and federal laws prohibit hospitals and their emergency personnel from refusing to admit someone in immediate need of hospitalization. Care cannot be denied on the basis of an individual's inability to pay, and hospitals that attempt to do so can be fined and found guilty of a misdemeanor; licensed personnel can be disciplined by the state. Further, a patient can be transferred, rather than admitted to a facility, only if (a) his or her condition is stabilized according to medical opinion, (b) the hospital does not have the proper equipment or personnel, or (c) the hospital does not have any beds available immediately or in the reasonable future.

Individuals may also be hospitalized for nonemergency medical needs, such as the observation and treatment of heart, lungs, kidneys, or other health problems, or to evaluate changes in symptoms or chronic illnesses. Other reasons for hospitalization include treatments such as cardiac care, renal dialysis, and psychiatric and mental health services.

Patients should always ask whether the same results can be achieved at home, through home care. For terminally ill patients, the doctor may recommend pain medications or antibiotic therapy. Once again, patients and their families should ask if this could be done in home care, through a hospice, or at an extended care facility.

Surgery

Being hospitalized for surgery involves a whole new group of medical personnel—a surgeon, an anesthesiologist or nurse anesthetist—and settings, such as a special care unit, an operating room, a recovery room, and possibly the critical care unit of a hospital.

The person who is to undergo surgery is responsible for selecting his or her surgeon. Often a patient's regular doctor can help by recommending several surgeons to contact and interview. Just as important as finding a surgeon, however, is determining whether surgery is really necessary. *Individuals facing surgery should always get a second opinion on the need for surgery.* It has been estimated that about one-quarter of all surgical procedures recommended by one doctor are not recommended by the second doctor.

If surgery is necessary, it is a good idea to find out the surgeon's views and plans depending on what he or she finds while the patient is on the operating table. *Before any surgery takes place, the patient should always make sure that the surgeon knows his or her views on quality of life after surgery, as well as what is and is not wanted. Patient should also ask if the surgeon is board certified in surgery* (two ways to find out without asking the surgeon are to check in the local library for a directory of medical specialists and to write the American College of Surgeons, 55 East Erie Street, Chicago, Illinois 60611). (For more information on what to do before agreeing to surgery, see chapter 7.)

Individuals are also responsible for deciding who will anesthetize them for the surgery. Here, the surgeon may recommend someone whom he or she is familar with and has worked with before. There are two types of specialists educated to give anesthesia: (a) anesthesiologists, who are specially trained doctors, and (b) nurse anesthetists, who are nurses who have taken advanced courses in giving anesthesia. Individuals should always know whether the person giving anesthesia is a doctor or a nurse. *If choosing a nurse anesthetist, individuals should ask if there will be an anesthesiologist (doctor) physically available during surgery in case any problems arise.*

It is also important to ask if the chosen surgeon will be the person actually doing the surgery. In hospitals that act as teaching facilities, a medical resident or intern may be doing the surgery with a surgeon present. *Individuals have the right to know who will be operating on them.*

Patients also have specific legal rights surrounding surgical treatment, including informed consent and refusal. This is an important topic, best dealt with in a separate chapter; see chapter 7.

Before Entering the Hospital

Before agreeing to enter a hospital, individuals should ask several basic questions:

- Why is it necessary to enter a hospital?
- What will be done in the hospital?
- How long is the stay likely to be?
- What will be the result of entering the hospital?
- What will be the result of not entering the hospital?

Upon agreeing to be admitted into a hospital, individuals should take the following items or written information with them:

- Diagnoses the doctor has made.
- Lists of allergies to foods, medicines, and other substances.
- Names and types of medications being taken, doses, directions for their use, and the name of the doctor who prescribed them.
- Special needs, such as eyeglasses, hearing aids, and dentures.
- Valuables (not jewelry) that are needed in the hospital.
- Names and phone numbers of one's regular doctor, family members, and friends.
- A bag of personal items, such as toothbrush, toothpaste, cosmetics, hairbrush, nightgown or pajamas, robe, and slippers. Patients might also want to take along something familiar (and inexpensive).
- A medical insurance card.

(For more information on the above and on entering a hospital in general, see Belsky and Gross, *How to Choose and Use Your Doctor,* listed in the "Additional Reading" section.)

Being Admitted into the Hospital

Entering a hospital usually means a lot of forms to fill out, arrangements to consider, and decisions to make. It also means a frightening upheaval of the daily chores and activities that can sometimes be as familiar and comforting as they are irritating. When people are sick, taken out of their home surroundings, put through upsetting tests on strange equipment, and made to wear hospital gowns and eat unappetizing meals at strange hours of the day, they are likely to feel depressed, anxious, intimidated, and dependent. To make matters worse, hospitals are filled with doctors, medical residents or interns, administrators, and nurses, most of whom seem too busy to explain what is going on with the patients. *It's important for patients and their family members to fight against feeling intimidated or dependent in the face of all this authority and expertise.*

Patients and family members should avoid feeling that they "shouldn't raise a fuss" by asking questions or requesting a certain level of treatment. Although some things, like mealtimes, can't be changed, other matters, such as nonsmokers unhappily sharing rooms with smokers, usually can be corrected. Besides, accidents and mistakes do happen in hospitals from time to time. *The best way for patients to recognize and avoid any of these problems is to ask about—and know—what is supposed to happen: what medication, and how much of it, they are supposed to receive; what time of day they are supposed to be operated on; whether or not they are supposed to receive X-rays or specific treatments; and so on.*

Hospital stays can also be much easier when patients have an advocate, someone (usually a family member or friend) who is looking out for them. Patients who do not feel up to the task of asking questions, getting results, and explaining their needs should choose someone who is willing to do these things for them. Patients with and without their own advocates should, if they need help, ask whether the hospital has patient representatives or patient advocates—that is, people employed by the hospital to act on patients' behalf.

Patients who are dying might not want to stay in a hospital for their last days or weeks. A hospital is a place that focuses on saving lives, and there are many patients who—when death is around the corner and impossible to fight against any longer—would prefer to die without further interference or "help." Some patients may be happier staying at home and using private-duty nurses and home care services as necessary. Other patients may prefer to enter a hospice, a special facility that cares for dying patients and provides them with painkilling medication or assists them in being cared for in their own homes. Medicare and many other health insurance policies now pay for hospice care.

If patients do need or want to stay in a hospital, they will have to make several decisions, including the following:

- Whether to get a private room (which costs more than a shared room) and whether their insurance will pay for it.
- Whether to request private-duty nursing services (those involving nurses who are hired to give the patient additional care) and whether their insurance will pay for them.
- Whether special dietary needs are understood by the hospital. (Such needs include special diets ordered by a doctor, foods that for religious reasons cannot be eaten, and food allergies.)
- Whether or not to get a telephone or television in the room.

Patients will also have to sign admission forms agreeing to enter the hospital and receive the general care provided. *By signing these forms, patients are* not *agreeing to specific medical or surgical treatments; at a later time patients will be asked to sign separate consent forms for such treatments* (for more information, see chapter 7).

Other forms that require a patient's signature include those regarding insurance coverage. The forms signed give the hospital permission to share any information they have about the patient with that patient's insurance company.

Once admitted, patients will then be taken to their rooms or to a laboratory for tests. Because there are so many people working in a hospital, all of them wearing white clothing, the various ranks and titles can be confusing. Here is a list to help patients make sense of it all:

clerks

housekeeping staff

technicians from various hospital departments (the laboratory, X ray, radiation therapy, and so on)

registered nurses (RNs) or staff nurses, who coordinate a patient's nursing care

licensed practical nurses (LPNs), licensed vocational nurses (LVNs), or practical nurses (PNs), all of whom, along with the RNs, monitor and observe the patient, give care, carry out a doctor's orders, and give medication and treatments

charge nurses, nursing supervisors, and nursing administrators, who supervise the nursing staff

nursing assistants, orderlies, and aides, who assist the nurses in carrying out the patient's needs

nursing students (if the hospital is associated with a nursing school), who are there to learn about nursing and who are supervised by nursing instructors

the patient's doctor, who supervises and coordinates that patient's medical care

attending doctors, who supervise interns and residents working on a patient

residents (medical school graduates who have completed their internships in a particular medical specialty), who also examine and work on the patient interns (medical school graduates with one or two years of experience), who may examine and work on the patient

medical school students (especially in teaching hospitals or hospitals associated with a university medical school), who are there to learn

specialists or consultants (doctors trained in a particular specialty), depending on a patient's illness

fellows (doctors in the process of being trained in a particular specialty), depending on a patient's illness

discharge planners and social workers, who work to place the patient in a nursing home, if necessary, or to arrange for home care or other special services that will be needed after a patient leaves the hospital

religious representatives

While in the Hospital

A doctor should visit his or her hospitalized patients daily to evaluate their progress and write medical orders for the nurses. Patients should talk with their doctor, be kept up-to-date on their treatment plans, and understand what the doctor has ordered of the nursing staff. Only by knowing this information will patients or their family members be able to make sure that the various staff members remember to do what is asked of them. Patients can easily call their doctors from the hospital, just as they would from their homes.

If all goes well, patients will recover sufficiently to be discharged (for information on what to do if a patient is being discharged before he or she feels ready, see chapter 8). Surrounding a patient's discharge is a process called a *utilization review,* that includes a Peer Review Organization (PRO) made up of doctors and nurses who review all patients' cases and agree or disagree with the length of time a patient is to stay in the hospital. The PRO must agree to a patient's extended stay in a hospital.

How long a patient stays in the hospital determines how much money the hospital makes or loses in caring for that particular patient. Medicare and other health insurance groups pay a particular amount to the hospital for each patient with a particular disease. Diseases—and the amount paid for their coverage—are categorized into Diagnostic Related Groups (DRGs). Every diagnosis has an average length of hospital stay connected to it. The hospital is paid the same amount of money whether a patient leaves before that average stay is up or after it (under certain circumstances, more will be paid to the hospital if the patient requires a longer stay). Hospitals make money on a patient who leaves early because they stop having to provide the person with expensive space and services, and hospitals lose money on a patient who receives more services than are covered by the insurance money paid to them.

When Mistakes or Accidents Occur in the Hospital

Despite the fact that hospitals are places that treat patients and attempt to return them to a healthy condition, mistakes and accidents do happen that can make a patient worse. These include

falls;

errors in medication (too much or too little of the right medication is given, or the wrong medication is given);

failure to monitor a patient's progress and notice changes in his or her condition;

failure of the doctor or nurse to communicate about a patient's progress;

nosocomial infections (bacteria- or virus-caused infections that develop as a result of the patient's staying in the hospital);

surgical errors, such as sponges being mistakenly left in the site of a patient's operation; and

iatrogenic diseases or disorders (conditions that result from medical personnel, treatment, or diagnostic procedures or simply through the patient's being exposed to the hospital's environment).

Negligence and *malpractice* mean more than that the hospital has made a mistake; they mean that the mistake has led to harm or caused injuries to the patient. The behavior and actions of a doctor, nurse, or hospital are judged on the basis of standards of care. The legal standard of care is that the doctor, nurse, and hospital must be reasonable and prudent under the circumstances; the standard is measured by what other doctors, nurses, and hospitals would do under similar circumstances.

If mistakes do happen, patients should be told about them by their doctor or a hospital administrator. If patients realize a mistake has been made, they should tell a doctor or nurse that they wish to meet with the supervisor and the hospital's patient advocate or representative who should be present at such meetings.

When mistakes occur, patients or their family members might first try to resolve the problem within the facility. If that doesn't work, there is always the option of suing the doctor, nurse, or facility responsible for the problem. Individuals should call a reliable lawyer to discuss their complaint before making any decisions of this kind.

Most hospitals have many different ways of ensuring quality of care and guarding against malpractice and patient injury. Hospitals and their staff don't want to make mistakes, but a mistake does happen occasionally. Hospitals have committees that review the credentials and abilities of the people who practice and have admitting privileges in them. Many also have set procedures for resolving patient grievances or complaints related to injuries, accidents, treatments, or events that may result in the patient suing the hospital.

In some states, hospitals must also educate their staff about

patient safety;

injury prevention;

the legal aspects of patient care;

causes of malpractice claims or lawsuits;

improved communication with patients; and

the responsibility to report professional misconduct.

In addition, licensing authorities in some states oversee hospitals and also require them to report certain incidents, such as

patient's deaths or disabilities due to circumstances other than those related to the natural course of illness, disease, or proper treatment;

fires in the hospital that disrupt patient care services or harm patients and staff;

equipment failures that occurred during treatment or diagnosis of a patient and that harmed or could have harmed a patient or staff member;

poisoning occurring within the hospital;

strikes by hospital staff;

emergency situations outside the hospital that affect the hospital's activities; and

termination of any services necessary to the continued safe running of the hospital or to the health and safety of its patients and staff (including such things as the anticipated or actual termination of telephone, gas, electric, fuel, water, heat, air-conditioning, rodent- or pest-control, laundry, food, or other services).

7

Patients Have Rights, Too

Overview

Our entire society is based on the idea that every person has a number of inherent rights. Children have the right to be protected from abuse, employees have the right to work in a healthy environment, and patients have rights, too. As with all rights, the simple fact that they exist does not mean they are always respected. Rights occasionally have been fought for, and people who abuse those rights may need to be reminded that doing so is illegal.

Explored at length in this chapter are the many rights of patients, as well as the methods for demanding that those rights be observed.

A number of professional associations, hospitals, and nursing homes have come up with their own list of patient rights. The most widely used is the bill of rights of the American Hospital Association (AHA) (see Appendix 11). Under state and federal law, AHA's bill of rights must be posted and made available to patients as a condition of the hospital's being reimbursed under Medicare.

States have also passed laws and regulations on the rights of patients in hospitals and of residents in nursing homes (appendix 12 contains a sample state bill of rights for hospital patients). Further, many states have defined the rights of mentally ill and mentally disabled patients. And even the federal government has its own series of regulations on the rights of patients in health care facilities run by the Veterans Administration (see appendix 13). Moreover, both the federal and the state legal systems have become involved in this issue. Courts make decisions about the rights and responsibilities of patients, doctors, and hospitals. The law views hospitals as corporations that have certain duties to their patients, including the supervision of staff and nonemployee activities.

The extent of laws, rules, regulations, and declarations is not really a surprise. This topic is significant and a formal framework is required to protect patients—often among the most helpless of individuals—from being abused. The importance of the issue has also resulted in a number of excellent books written in language easily understood by any patient or family member. Because these books focus solely on patient rights, they have the luxury of going into much more depth than can be done here. They have been used as the foundation for this chapter and are strongly recommended to all interested individuals. These books are cited throughout this chapter and are listed in the "Additional Reading" section. It may take some effort to become educated on the issues, but doing so is certainly worthwhile.

All Relationships Carry a Price

It must be remembered that patients are not the only ones with rights in a medical situation. Hospitals and doctors have their own rights as well, and they, too, must be respected. The different groups involved in the health care situation each have privileges and responsibilities, all of them intersecting to define the relationships among the various groups.

There is an old saying that cuts to the heart of the matter: "My right to hit you stops at the tip of your nose." In other words, a person's right to do something stops short of violating another person's rights—in this case, the right not be hit.

Hospitals have legal advisers, and doctors are taught the legal boundaries of patient care. Patients are the ones who are most likely to be ignorant of the extent and limits of their rights. In order to enter the doctor-patient relationship on equal footing, individuals must be aware of their own rights and of the responsibilities of doctors to people in their care. (Some excellent information on these issues—explained in brief in the sections that follow—can be found in *How to Talk to Your Doctor: Getting Beyond the Medical Mystique,* by Dr. Janet Maurer; *Take This Book to the Hospital with You,* by Charles Inlander; and *Medical Care Can Be Dangerous to Your Health,* by Eugene Robin.)

The Patient's Rights in the Doctor-Patient Relationship

In the doctor-patient relationship, patients have the right to have as much information as they wish about their illness;

be educated about treatment options and the consequences of refusing treatment;

refuse treatment;

be allowed adequate time to ask questions and state concerns about medical problems;

have privacy and confidentiality;

have continuity of care;

have reasonable access to the doctor;

participate in major decisions about their care;

refuse to participate in research;

know the doctor's availability outside of regular office hours and the provisions the doctor has made for coverage of patients during those hours;

determine who other than the doctor shall have access to information about their health;

know in advance the approximate amount of the bill and possible arrangements for payment;

be seen within a reasonable time of the scheduled appointment;

change doctors if a breakdown in the doctor-patient relationship occurs; and

have medical records permanently transferred to another doctor.

For more information on these issues, see chapter 6.

The Patient's Responsibilities

Rights carry with them certain responsibilities. In the doctor-patient relationship, these responsibilities often aid the doctor in correctly diagnosing an illness or prescribing a treatment. The responsibilities of patients are to

tell the doctor all the information that relates to their illnesses or conditions;

keep office appointments or cancel them well in advance;

plan their visit with the doctor (for example, patients might write down their questions and concerns rather than trying to remember them all in the doctor's office);

stop the doctor when they don't understand his or her explanation of a problem, and ask for a simpler explanation;

ask questions;

follow the doctor's advice;

quickly report to the doctor any adverse reactions to drugs or therapy, as well as any complications from tests or worsening symptoms;

limit phone calls to the doctor between visits except to report the problems listed above or other agreed-upon matters; and

pay agreed-upon bills promptly or in a way that is acceptable to both parties.

The Doctor's Responsibilities

Doctors have specific obligations to people in their care. These obligations are governed by the law and by the doctor's personal code of ethics and good practice. The responsibilities of a doctor are to

thoroughly discuss with the patient his or her diagnoses, laboratory test results, therapy, and prognosis (what is likely to happen in the course of a given disease), in language that the patient can understand;

tell the patient of alternative and generally accepted approaches to therapy or diagnostic procedures, even if the doctor does not agree with them;

recommend to the patient what the doctor considers the best approach and why;

allow adequate time, on at least one occasion, to answer the patient's questions and discuss the patient's concerns;

provide adequate follow-up and emergency care, and make the patient aware of these provisions;

ask a specialist to consult on the patient's case or refer the patient to another doctor for a second opinion if uncertain about a diagnosis;

assist the patient in getting needed social or rehabilitative services;

keep complete patient medical records;

assist in a smooth transition for the patient to another doctor when the relationship has ended; and

make available to the patient a list of charges for the services performed.

The Right of Informed Consent

While all patient rights are important, the right of *informed consent* deserves a close look. *Informed consent simply means that an individual has all the necessary information that he or she needs—in language that he or she understands—to agree to or refuse treatment. Informed consent must be obtained before any medical work can be done. Whoever is actually going to order or perform the treatment or procedure is responsible for giving the patient all necessary information and obtaining his or her informed consent.*

Informed consent applies to medical treatment—from tests to decisions about using life-prolonging technology or treatments. Patients will be asked to sign a consent form agreeing to have surgery or undergo treatment. But before doing anything, patients have the right to understand what they are agreeing to if they sign the form. They should ask the person who will perform the procedure to explain it, along with its risks, benefits, alternatives, and consequences.

Consent forms can be altered to reflect exactly what the patient has agreed to with his or her doctor, surgeon, anesthesiologist, or nurse anesthetist. The form should be correctly dated; it should include the specific procedure that is planned; and the patient's signature should be witnessed (usually by a nurse).

Consent forms should be signed before the patient takes or is given medication to prepare him or her for the operation or procedure in question. The patient should review and sign the form only when thinking clearly.

The Right to Information

The cornerstone of a patient's informed consent is his or her access to information. Without all the necessary knowledge, truly informed consent is impossible. Some excellent books, listed in the "Additional Reading" section, form the basis for the information that follows. Books of particular use in the writing of this chapter were *The Patient's Guide to Medical Tests,* by Cathey and Edward Pinckney;

Medical Care Can Be Dangerous to Your Health, by Eugene Robin; *Take This Book to the Hospital with You,* by Charles Inlander; and *How to Talk to Your Doctor: Getting Beyond the Medical Mystique,* by Dr. Janet Maurer.

A patient's access to information about his or her disease or condition should cover not only the disease itself but all aspects related to it. It is important to use the rights listed below to determine what questions need to be asked of doctors.

Individuals undergoing medical tests have the right to

know the cost of proposed tests;

be accurately tested;

have tests correctly performed by trained and prepared personnel, on properly maintained and precisely calibrated equipment;

know and understand the purpose, need, and rationale for each test;

know how each test is performed;

know and understand each test's dangers and complications;

know what the results of each test will mean;

know how precise each test is;

have tests repeated to ensure accuracy;

know the risks and benefits of each test, including whether it involves an invasion of the patient's body, pain, or a significant risk of harm;

understand the consequences of taking or not taking each test;

know of any alternatives to each test and the consequences of taking or not taking them; and

know and understand all test results.

About the diagnosis, patients have the right to know

how certain the doctor is about his or her diagnosis;

whether there is a possibility that the diagnosis is incorrect;

whether there is any way to confirm the diagnosis; and

whether a second opinion is indicated.

About the cause and nature of the disease, patients have the right to know

what bodily organs are involved in the disease and in what way;

how or why the disease started;

whether the disease will be passed on to, or is likely to be present in, any children; and

how contagious the disease is and what protections to take against other people catching it.

About the course of the disease, patients have the right to know

the prognosis, or likely course the disease will take;

whether the disease is limited to certain organs or whether it will spread;

whether the involved organs will get progressively worse, and if so, how;

what complications may arise and at what stage of the illness;

what symptoms or changes the patient should be concerned about;

whether there are any symptoms that other people should watch for in the patient; and

the names of any organizations that can provide information about the illness or help with problems resulting from it.

About the treatment for the disease, patients have a right to know

what medications are available to control the disease;

how often the doctor has treated this particular illness and with what success;

the risks and benefits of taking the medication at the current stage of the illness;

what the medication is supposed to accomplish;

whether there are alternative therapies if the patient is unable to tolerate the medication or if it proves ineffective;

whether hospitalization will be needed to start the medication;

how to judge whether the treatment is working and how long it will be needed;

whether surgery is an alternative to the treatment, and when or if it would be recommended;

what dietary changes or other measures could lessen the effects of the disease;

how frequently the doctor will have to be seen;

how to contact the doctor in an emergency;

whether any home monitoring of the illness can be done to reduce the need for office visits; and

the cost of the treatment.

About the influence of the disease and treatment on family, social, and work life, patients have the right to

know if they will be able to continue in their jobs;

know if they are likely to have many days when they are too sick to work;

know if the illness will affect their ability to get life or health insurance;

ask if they can continue to be involved in specific hobbies, sports, family, or social activities;

know any limitations on travel, or travel to certain areas;

know if any drugs being prescribed will interact with alcohol or the ability to have sex; and

know if the illness or the treatment will be disfiguring.

About surgery, patients have the right to

get a second opinion on whether the surgery is necessary;

know at what hospital the doctor operates and what kinds of facilities it has to support the operation;

know if the surgeon is board certified in surgery;

know how often the surgeon has performed the operation in question;

know what the usual result of the operation is;

know what will happen during the course of the operation;

know the risks and benefits of the operation;

know if they will be disfigured by the operation, and if so, how;

know what will happen if no surgery is performed;

know how long a recovery period to expect;

know what daily activities, such as cooking, shopping, bathing, and so on, will be more difficult after the operation and for how long;

know how long they will need to be hospitalized after the operation;

know whether they will need any specialized care after surgery, and if so, for how long;

know whether the necessary care can be provided at home.

Knowing one's rights to information but not asking any questions to get it is useless. Patients have the right to know because they need to know. Ask questions—it is the doctor's responsibility to answer them in a way that is understandable to the patient.

Patients' Rights and Medical Records

According to state law and hospital policies, a patient has the right to see and copy his or her medical records. Specific rules on this issue vary, but generally a patient can see his or her own record by notifying the appropriate doctor or hospital. The hospital may ask to see the request in writing, or it may require a patient to be with his or her doctor or a medical records staff member when reviewing records.

Rarely, a doctor will decide that it will harm a particular patient to know what is contained in his or her record. This judgment is known as the doctor's *therapeutic privilege.* In such instances, the patient might instead be offered a summary of his or her record or be asked to identify someone else who could see the record.

In some states, a patient who doesn't agree with what is said in the record can amend it by inserting his or her own statements. Usually the patient is charged a reasonable fee to copy a chart, but if he or she is unable to pay the fee, the hospital must make the chart available anyway.

A hospital record is a legal document kept by a business (the hospital). It has many uses, including ensuring continuity of care, recording a patient's response to treatment, and creating a history of what treatments have been tried and their outcomes.

Hospitals do audits of their records to ensure quality of care, and researchers use the records to study particular diseases, drugs, and treatments. A patient's permission must be obtained before his or her record can be seen by a researcher, unless all identifying information (name, address, social security number, and so on) is removed from it and the patient's privacy is ensured. Insurance companies review records as a basis of paying for health services rendered; government agencies review records to ensure that standards are met. Lastly, a patient's medical record has legal applications as well—it can be used as evidence of care in a malpractice lawsuit or as evidence of a patient's mental status in a lawsuit over a patient's estate or will.

In cases in which a patient changes to another doctor, seeks a second opinion, or consults with a specialist, he or she will be asked to sign a form agreeing to release the record to that other person. A patient can limit the permission on the release of his or her records by requesting that only certain information be released (such as only those records which pertain to a patient's most recent heart attack). A patient can also require that his or her records be sent to a specific person, to be used only for a specific purpose.

The Right to Be Free of Restraints and Abuse

Patients have the right to be free of restraints and abuse. There are very specific state laws and regulations governing patient abuse. Health care providers, including doctors and nurses, are required to report patient abuse to the state. Under no circumstances does anyone have the right to abuse a patient.

A patient can be restrained, but only if his or her safety (or the safety of others) requires doing so. This means that the use of restraints must be related to a patient's specific therapeutic needs and be an essential part of his or her treatment plan.

Restraints are not allowed to be applied as a punishment or for the convenience of the staff or facility. The least restrictive methods of restraining a patient must be tried first. Only if less restrictive measures are inadequate to protect the safety of the patient, or of others around the patient, can more restrictive methods be applied.

Restraints can be ordered only by the patient's doctor, except in emergency cases wherein a registered nurse can temporarily order the use of physical restraints.

Hospitals have written policies that must be followed by staff members when they apply restraints. These policies include written doctor's orders specifying the length of time restraints should be applied and the type of restraints to be used (some types, such as leather straps, are prohibited). When restraints are applied, the nursing staff has a duty to closely monitor the patient, remove the restraints periodically (some policies require that they be removed at least once every two hours), and remove them completely when they are no longer needed.

Patients' Right to Leave a Hospital

A competent (mentally healthy) patient has the right to leave the hospital, even if doing so goes against his or her doctor's opinions and wishes (for more information, see chapter 11). Similarly, any patient who disagrees with his or her doctor or with the proposed treatment plan can leave the hospital. A patient may be asked to sign a form stating that he or she is being discharged against medical advice, but the patient is not legally required to do so. *If a patient is kept against his or her will, the hospital can be sued for false imprisonment. A patient may leave even if his or her bill is not paid.*

Hospitals are not allowed to keep patients against their will unless a patient is thought to be a danger to himself or herself or others. If that is the medical opinion and the patient wants to leave anyway, the hospital and the doctor must institute an involuntary commitment proceeding.

State laws specify rules about involuntary commitment (such as requiring that two doctors state that a patient should be held for up to seventy-two hours for observation and evaluation). A patient is entitled to legal representation and due process (a notice and a hearing on the case) in these instances. When this happens, a patient's health status and situation are reviewed by a court, which decides whether the patient should be committed for treatment or released.

Even patients who are involuntarily committed have the right to refuse certain treatments, such as medications.

Rights and More Rights: What They Mean for Patients

Many people may understand that they have specific rights but are unsure how those rights translate into particular situations (some excellent material on this matter—illustrated briefly below—can be found in *Take This Book to the Hospital with You,* by Charles Inlander; *The Rights of the Critically Ill,* by John Robertson; and *The Rights of Hospital Patients,* by George Annas, all of which are listed in the "Additional Reading" section). A quick guide to other patient rights is as follows:

- *Contrary to popular belief, most individuals do not have a legal right to medical care.* (Prisoners and the involuntarily committed mentally ill, however, do have a legal right to health care.)
- *An individual has the right to hear the truth about his or her illness or condition.* A doctor is required to give an honest diagnosis and prognosis to every patient. A doctor who fails to do so in cases in which such failure leads to patient injury can be sued for malpractice. A doctor who fails to tell a patient the whole truth—particularly if asked—can be sued for breach of contract. And a doctor who withholds information that affects the medical, financial, or personal decisions made by a patient can be held liable for any damages. (Two exceptions to this right exist when a patient asks not to be told the truth and when a doctor has a reason to believe that the patient would be harmed by hearing the truth.)
- *A competent (mentally healthy) patient has the right to full information about his or her condition, even if his or her family members object to the patient's hearing the truth.*
- *An individual has the right to keep his or her condition a secret from family members.* A doctor must go along with the decision made by the patient in this matter. (An exception exists in cases in which the information is necessary to prevent harm or to protect others from catching a contagious disease.)
- *A competent patient has a right to continued treatment if he or she can pay for it.* This is true whether or not the patient's family members want the care continued. If a patient is terminally ill and unconscious or comatose, then the family members are more likely to be consulted about the patient's wishes.
- *A competent adult patient has the right to refuse medical care, even when it is life prolonging.*
- *A patient has the right to consent to (or refuse) the donation of his or her organs or tissues.* The hospital must ask if the patient would like to be a donor, not just assume that he or she intends to be one. In some cases, the patient's family members may be able to consent to or refuse the donation on a patient's behalf.

- *In some instances, a patient may be asked if he or she wants life-sustaining treatment, such as cardiopulmonary resuscitation (CPR).* Usually, what is being asked is whether the patient wants to be revived if his or her heart fails. Patients do have the right to make these decisions.
- *A doctor can refuse to treat a patient who is unable to pay but cannot stop treating a patient who can't pay.* Once treatment has started, the doctor must continue it for as long as the patient wants it, benefits from it, or decides to stop receiving it. (An exception to this right exists if the doctor has told the patient in advance that he or she must pay for treatment in order to receive it.)
- *A patient cannot be thrown out of a hospital if he or she can no longer pay for care or treatment.* A patient whose condition has stabilized can be transferred out of one hospital and into another. If a patient is discharged because of his or her inability to pay and then gets worse or suffers additional problems, the patient can sue the hospital for abandonment.
- *If a patient asks to be referred to another doctor for a second opinion or expert consultation, his or her doctor is not legally required to make the referral.* Making the referral is, however, commonly regarded as a good and ethical practice. If a doctor refuses to do so and incorrectly treats and harms the patient, the doctor can be sued for negligence.
- The relationship between the doctor and the patient can end only if both individuals want it to end, the doctor is no longer needed, or the doctor gives the patient sufficient notice that he or she will no longer handle the patient's case. A doctor who does not give the patient sufficient notice can be sued for abandonment.
- *A patient can refuse to be examined by a medical student, intern, resident, or anyone else in a hospital setting.*
- A cancer patient does not have the right to demand to be treated with laetrile (a controversial anticancer drug), even in those states in which laetrile is legal. If a patient wants to try laetrile but his or her doctor refuses to prescribe it, the patient can always seek another doctor who is willing to use it.

Making a Complaint

A patient can complain about the violation of his or her rights. In most instances, the problem can be taken up with the doctor or hospital staff and be resolved that way. In other cases, a patient may feel more comfortable taking a complaint to authorities outside the hospital (see chapter 9).

Two places outside the hospital that may be of help are the medical and nursing licensing agencies and the hospital licensing agencies (see appendix 34 for addresses). These agencies can receive and investigate confidential or anonymous reports about doctors', nurses', or hospitals' care of patients.

Rights Are Not Absolute

Patient rights are not absolute. The right to refuse treatment, for example, can, under very few circumstances, be overridden by important state interests, including the following:

- The protection of innocent third parties. For example, patients may not be allowed to refuse treatment of contagious diseases that threaten the health of the public. Similarly, individuals may be required to receive vaccinations if the danger to the community is severe. This exception applies even if the treatment goes against the wishes or religious convictions of the patients involved.

- The preservation of life. For example, a woman who wishes to refuse a blood transfusion may be overruled if the transfusion is the only way to save her life and she has an infant to look after. Cases to which this exception might apply are decided on a case-by-case basis, and patients (or their family members) should always seek the advice of a lawyer if a refusal of treatment is not honored by the hospital.

- The prevention of suicide. This exception does not include terminally ill or comatose patients; *in those cases, the courts have determined that the refusal of treatment is not the same as suicide.* Insurance companies must follow the court in these matters and are prohibited from classifying as suicide cases those terminal or comatose patients who refuse treatment.

- The maintenance of the ethical integrity of the medical profession. For example, in one case a Massachusetts court decided that a hospital did not have to honor a patient's refusal of treatment but did have to assist the patient in transferring to another hospital that would honor the refusal. In New Jersey, however, a court upheld a patient's right to refuse treatment but refused to order the patient's transfer; in that case, the original hospital had to comply with the patient's decision to refuse treatment.

When patients refuse treatment, complex ethical, legal, and practical problems can arise. Hospitals should have specific policies to guide them in these areas. Ethics committees, case conferences, and careful medical and legal evaluations can usually provide an answer on how to proceed. Equally important, patients themselves can avoid many of the potential complications that surround their refusal of treatment by preparing in advance written documents that specify their wishes (for more information, see chapters 4 and 5).

8

If the Hospital Tells You to Go Home Too Early

*L*IKE *many other chapters in this book, the information here is addressed both to patients and the family members of those patients who may be too ill to speak for themselves. This chapter details the necessary steps in fighting an early discharge from the hospital; and patients who may or may not be able to carry out the suggestions herein should try to arrange for their family members or friends to read this material. Nevertheless, as in most situations in which the patient is too sick to take charge personally, it is always useful to have a written document—such as a durable power of attorney with health care decision-making authority—from the patient that appoints a family member or friend to act on the patient's behalf if and when the patient is unable to do so (see chapter 5 for more information).*

Patients and family members should also be prepared to discuss with the doctor whether or not a patient wants to receive life-sustaining treatment (including resuscitation). These discussions, held in advance, can save much trauma and hurt during emergency situations.

Overview

Recent stories in newspapers, in magazines, and on television about patients being "dumped," or released from hospitals too early to fend for themselves, have raised new fears among patients and their family members. Entering a hospital for treatment can be frightening, and the possibility of not being allowed to stay can make the prospect even worse. These fears are particularly pronounced for the elderly, who even when healthy may face a host of day-to-day problems. If forced to leave a hospital before they can return home to their normal routine, elderly patients must either temporarily enter another health care facility (such as a nursing home) or be cared for at home by friends, family members, or hired professionals.

Why are stories of patients being released too early surfacing now? Were we simply unaware of a practice that always existed, or is the problem a new one? In fact, it is a new problem. And in order to understand how to combat it, patients and their families should first understand why it is happening in the first place.

Individual patients and their families are not the only ones feeling the pinch of rising hospital care costs. For a number of years now, the federal government, which pays specific medical bills for individuals eligible for Medicare, has also found itself paying out more and more money for hospital care. The government (like its individual taxpayers) cannot easily afford to pay ever-increasing hospital care costs.

However, the problem was, and is, bigger than the government's money woes. While medical costs rose higher and higher, reports began to surface that hospitals were running unessential (and sometimes risky) tests on patients and keeping them longer than necessary. These extra tests represented extra income, because Medicare used to pay for each additional day of hospital care. At the same time, many hospitals threatened to close down unless they were adequately paid for their services. The question was how to contain costs without hospitals either shutting down—which would be a disastrous public health problem—or recommending more services to make up for less funding.

By 1983, the government decided what to do about the situation. That year, Medicare instituted a new payment system for hospitals. It was part of a series of reforms designed to keep Medicare itself from going bankrupt.

The New Medicare System

Under the new system, Medicare categorized all health problems into Diagnostic Related Groups (DRGs). It then decided to pay hospitals a fixed amount of money for each Medicare patient in a particular DRG. *The amount of money paid by Medicare for each DRG is based on the average cost of care of treating a patient for a specific (or similar) disease, condition, or problem.*

To discourage hospitals from keeping patients too long so as to receive more federal funds, Medicare does not pay for a certain number of days of care per patient; rather, it pays only that one fixed amount associated with a specific disease or condition. The hospital, in return, must keep caring for patients as long as they need acute, or specialized, hospital care.

Medicare pays higher DRG rates across the board to hospitals with unavoidably higher costs, such as teaching hospitals and those serving large numbers of poor and elderly patients, those in urban areas, and those with higher labor costs. These higher DRG payments apply to all Medicare patients treated by a hospital that meets government criteria as a high-cost institution.

Medicare has several safety-valve mechanisms for recognizing extraordinary situations in which an individual needs more hospital care than the average patient does. Medicare will make additional payments to a hospital, beyond the regular DRG payment, for the continuing care of an individual patient under the following conditions:

- *The patient needs continued hospital care for much longer than the average stay of a person with a similar diagnosis, and care for the patient at another kind of institution would be inadequate.*
- *The patient needs such expensive hospital treatment that it costs the hospital more to treat him or her than it does to treat the average patient with a similar diagnosis.*
- *The patient needs skilled nursing home care, but no skilled nursing home will accept him or her.*

What the New System Means for Hospitals

Under the old system, hospitals had a good reason to give patients the kind of care that could have been provided at home or in a nursing home—they generally could get Medicare to pay for it. As a result, both patients and health care professionals began to rely on hospitals for services that could have been provided more cheaply somewhere else.

The new system gives hospitals a strong incentive to provide no more services than are medically necessary, because for most patients the average payment is all the hospital will receive from Medicare. The hospital can lose money on patients whose care costs more than the fixed payment.

What does all this mean for hospitals? They can respond to the new system with good management that cuts costs while preserving quality care, or they can cut corners that result in poor quality care. *In the end, the most effective way for hospitals to reduce services and costs is to reduce the amount of time a patient spends in the hospital.*

There are two legitimate ways for hospitals to cut a patient's length of stay:

1. Hospitals can ask doctors to perform some or all diagnostic tests and other treatments before admitting a patient into the hospital, and to wait until it is medically necessary to admit him or her.
2. Hospitals can discharge a patient as soon as he or she no longer requires special equipment and around-the-clock medical care.

While these cost-cutting strategies could cause various problems for patients and their families, the most serious problems occur because patients are discharged too early. There are two ways in which this problem shows up:

1. Patients are discharged while their condition is so unstable that hospital care and supervision by doctors and nurses are still needed. Medicare program managers report that this problem occurred in about 1 percent of all Medicare hospital cases in late 1984 and early 1985. Congress has created a national network of Peer Review Organizations to catch hospitals that discharge patients prematurely. (The role of these organizations is described more fully later in this chapter.)
2. Patients who do not require continued hospital care but still need continued nursing care are discharged before preparations are completed for their necessary after-hospital nursing care or supportive services. This problem seems to be more common than the early discharge of patients who still require hospital care, although there are no figures to show just how common—or rare—it may be. Congress has imposed strict new requirements on hospitals to ensure that discharge planning is improved to correct this problem.

While the government has taken action to prevent these problems from occurring, they still do happen. Patients (and their family members) can protect themselves by understanding the system and by knowing whom to call for help.

What the New System Means for Patients

It's not always easy, even for doctors and nurses, to know the right time to discharge a patient. *The decision of when to release a patient is a judgment call that involves both the medical situation and the social situation of each patient. Patients and families can influence this decision.*

Patients who still feel ill and weak may wonder whether they should be discharged at the time the hospital wants them to leave. Many patients think they should stay in the hospital until they are fully recovered; however, Medicare and private insurance companies see the matter differently.

Medicare views hospital care as only one part of a patient's medical treatment. Medicare wants to move patients—as soon as it is safe to do so—to less costly settings in which a lower level of care can be provided (for example, patients' homes or nursing homes). Even dying patients may have little need for hospital care and may be moved back into their homes, nursing homes, or hospices.

Yet, just because patients or family members do not understand Medicare's rules does not mean they should always leave the discharge decision up to the professionals. Remember, the professionals, too, are often making a judgment call. For example, while doctors and hospitals usually agree on a date of discharge, they may also disagree. And patients, family members, and friends can certainly disagree with the decision being made as well.

Medicare has contracts with Peer Review Organizations (PROs). These organizations are made up of groups of doctors and nurses who are asked to resolve disagreements and ensure that patients receive all the hospital care they require (but no more than is medically necessary).

In cases in which the doctor and hospital disagree, a hospital may ask the PRO to decide whether the patient should be discharged over the objection of the patient's doctor. By law, if the hospital asks the PRO to review the case to overrule the attending physician, the hospital must inform the patient that it has done so. Because hospitals are often reluctant to upset the doctor and patient, they rarely ask the PRO to overrule a patient's doctor. For this reason, having one's doctor on one's side of the argument can be crucial.

Patients and their families may also argue against a proposed discharge by appealing to the PRO. If successful, a patient may be allowed to stay longer in the hospital or may receive a better discharge plan from the hospital (see appendix 16 for a list of state PROs).

In any event, there is no substitute for the patient having an advocate—someone on the patient's side of the argument, such as a doctor, friend, or family member—who can help argue the case. Some hospitals employ patient advocates or representatives to work on behalf of patients that need their help. A call to the hospital switchboard or its social services department can determine whether a given hospital offers this service.

Helping to Plan Your Own
(or a Family Member's) Discharge

The time to prepare for a patient's discharge is before his or her admission into the hospital. Since emergencies do happen, certain steps should be taken before any hospital care is needed. The following steps can help.

- Patients should talk with reliable friends and family members who would be willing and able to assist them in getting to and from the hospital, if someday they should need care.

- Patients should share this book with family members or friends who are willing to help; such persons may need to use it to assist patients who are feeling too ill to handle matters themselves.

- Patients should consider executing a durable power of attorney that authorizes someone to make health care decisions if patients are unable to do so themselves. This way, patients can make sure that a trusted friend or relative will be in charge either temporarily or permanently. (For more information, see chapter 5.)

- Patients who discuss their upcoming treatment with friends who have had similar treatments or procedures should also find out from their own doctor whether their experience is likely to be the same as or different from their friends'.

- Before entering a hospital for a scheduled (nonemergency) treatment or procedure, patients should talk with their doctor to find out how their lives might be temporarily or permanently changed as a result of the upcoming surgery or medical care. This includes asking what daily activities, such as cooking, walking, climbing stairs, eating, dressing, and bathing, might be more difficult after leaving the hospital and for how long those tasks would be more difficult to perform.

- Patients should also ask their doctors which agencies will provide them with formal medical or nursing care following discharge from the hospital. If patients will need nursing home care, they should check the institutions' reputations with the Long Term Care Ombudsman Program (see appendix 19 for the addresses of state ombudsman program offices; for more information about the program itself, see chapter 9).

What to Do on Admission into a Hospital

Upon admission to the hospital, eligible patients should be given a copy of *An Important Message from Medicare*. (This document is reprinted in appendix 14.) Patients should then put this message in a safe place where they and their family members or friends can find it. (Patients who do not receive a copy or who lose the one they have should request one from the hospital admissions department. *Under federal law, patients have the right to have this information.* The message from Medicare briefly describes some, but not all, of the rights of patients under Medicare. It also lists the name and telephone number of the local Medicare PRO. *The PRO will investigate immediately if told that the patient is being discharged too early or lacks proper arrangements for posthospital nursing care.*

As soon as possible after being admitted into the hospital, patients or family members should ask to speak with a hospital discharge planner. This person may be a social worker or a nurse; he or she should meet with patients (or family members) and doctors to determine whether a patient should have a formal discharge plan. *Under federal law, patients have the right to have the hospital, upon request, formally evaluate their need for a discharge plan.*

- *Patients should not* assume *that a discharge plan is being prepared; if they don't request one, the hospital may decide they don't need one.*
- Preparing a discharge plan can take a few hours or a few days, depending on how busy the discharge planner is and how long patients are expected to stay in the hospital. *Although discharge planners are usually very busy, patients who need a discharge plan should not leave the hospital without one.*

The best discharge plan is developed with patients and, if possible, the people (spouses, siblings, adult children) who will care for them after they leave the hospital. Everyone involved with the care of patients leaving the hospital should arrange to be available at the same time and place to talk with the discharge planner, if he or she feels that would be helpful. Questions to raise when meeting with the discharge planner should be the same ones that were asked of the doctor—for example, the ease or difficulty with which the patient will be able to perform daily tasks after discharge from the hospital, and who or what will be available to assist the patient on a day-to-day basis.

Organizations such as the American Association of Retired Persons, the American Hospital Association, and the National Association for Home Care have developed complete guidelines for good discharge planning (see appendix 15 for guidelines written by the American Hospital Association).

When It's Time to Be Discharged

How a discharge is handled by both hospitals and patients is important. Often a doctor or hospital representative will tell patients—or family members, if patients are unable to understand—the date they are to be discharged. Because patients or family members might not be given a written notice, they should write down the name of the person who informs them of the discharge, the date and time of the conversation, and the date and time of the proposed discharge.

A hospital may bill Medicare patients who stay past the date of their scheduled discharge; at the customary rate, this fee could amount to $500 a day or more. *However, it is against federal law for a hospital to bill Medicare patients for services provided past their date of discharge unless the hospital has given patients a written notice of their discharge date and of their right to appeal the discharge.* It is also important to remember that under federal law,

- *it is the hospital's responsibility to give the patient a written discharge notice, not the patient's responsibility to ask for one;*
- *the hospital cannot bill the patient for care provided before the third day after giving the patient a written discharge notice (except, of course, for the annual Medicare hospital deductible); and*
- *the patient must receive the written discharge notice before he or she can appeal the proposed date to the PRO.*

By law, the hospital's written discharge notice must contain certain information and must not mislead patients into thinking that Medicare will pay only for a certain number of days in the hospital. Patients will be asked to sign a form indicating that they have received the written notice.

Model discharge notices for situations in which (a) the doctor and hospital agreed with the proposed discharge and (b) the PRO overruled the patient's objections to the proposed discharge can be found in appendix 17.

Receiving a Written Discharge Notice

Once patients receive a written discharge notice, they have until noon of the following working day (weekends are excluded) to decide whether they want to appeal it. There are several ways patients and their family members and friends can respond to the written notice.

First, they must decide if they want to fight the proposed discharge. In deciding this issue, patients should consider whether they are recovering as the doctor expected, whether the doctor and discharge planner have answered all their questions, and whether all their necessary posthospital care has been arranged for in the discharge plan.

If patients do not feel ready to be discharged, they should discuss it as soon as possible with their doctor and the discharge planner. *Remember, if patients and family members are assertive and have good reasons for objecting to the discharge date, they can be very effective in getting it changed without any formal or legal process.*

Some patients and family members have also gotten discharge dates changed with what might be considered extreme behavior. Family members have been known to refuse to leave a doctor's offices and have even threatened to barricade themselves in the patient's room until the doctor approved a necessary extra day or two. This sort of action may not be for everyone, but if the situation is severe, it might be worth a try as a last-resort tactic.

Another way of working with doctors and discharge planners to change a discharge date involves a useful tool known as a *quality screen*, a device developed by Medicare to identify possible cases of premature discharge. A quality screen poses a series of medical questions, the answers to which can help determine whether or not patients should be released.

One difficulty with using a quality screen is that patients would need to read and understand their medical records. Also, the screen asks for information that the doctor may not yet have at the time a patient is first notified of an impending discharge, such as the pulse or blood pressure of the patient twenty-four hours before discharge. Because quality screens were designed for use by doctors and nurses, the best way to use one is to make it available to one's doctor or discharge planner and to discuss it with them item by item (a copy of a Medicare quality screen can be found in appendix 18).

Remember, the quality screen is only a tool that can help patients or family members discuss the situation with a doctor or discharge planner. It is not the final word on whether or not patients should be discharged on a particular day.

Deciding Whether to Appeal a Discharge Decision to the Medicare Peer Review Organization

If the doctor and the discharge planner continue to believe that a patient should be released when the patient or the patient's family continue to disagree with that proposal, the case can be appealed to the PRO. Here, some simple dos and don'ts can help the patient or family member who is considering an appeal to the PRO.

- *Do call the PRO and appeal the decision if the doctor or discharge planner will not agree to discuss the case with the patient by the morning of the next working day after the patient has received a written discharge notice. The PRO must be called by noon of that day to ensure that patients will not to be charged by the hospital for extra days if the appeal is turned down.*

- *Do call the PRO and appeal if the discharge plan fails to address a patient's serious problem or personal need; if the hospital does not provide convincing evidence that the problem is resolved; or if the discharge plan does not meet the standards of the discharge-planning guidelines listed in appendix 15.*

- *Do call the PRO and appeal if the patient's medical condition is unstable. The Medicare quality screen can assist individuals in recognizing possible problems (see appendix 18). Remember, try to discuss these issues with the doctor before assuming they mean trouble.*

- *Don't call and appeal unless a patient's health and safety will be jeopardized by the proposed discharge. If the PRO decides that the appeal is unnecessary and that the patient or family member knew it was unnecessary when they appealed, the PRO may let the hospital bill the patient for any delay in the scheduled discharge.*

Appealing to the Peer Review Organization

Once patients have decided to appeal to the PRO, received a written discharge notice from the hospital, and called the PRO by noon of the working day after receiving the notice, the appeal process is set in motion.

The PRO representative, who is usually a registered nurse, will ask patients why they think the discharge date is unsafe or inappropriate. *Patients (or the people appealing a discharge) should be ready to answer these questions when the initial telephone call is made.* Thus, it's a good idea before making the call to compose a written list of reasons that the discharge is being appealed.

The PRO will try to complete its work quickly and decide on the appeal so that even if patients lose, they will still have time to leave without being billed for noncovered hospital days or services.

Losing an Appeal

Hospitals may bill a patient for staying beyond a proposed discharge date beginning with services provided on the third day after they have given the patient a written discharge notice and a notice of his or her right to appeal. *If, however, the PRO takes longer than two days to decide the appeal and the patient receives the answer on, or later than, the third day after receiving the written discharge notice, the patient is not liable for the cost of the continued stay until noon of the day after he or she has been informed that the appeal was turned down. This extra time at no charge is allowed only if (a) patients filed their appeals by noon of the working day after they received their written discharge notice and (b) the PRO believes that patients were unaware that their continued stay was not medically necessary.*

Oddly enough, Medicare instructions indicate that the PRO may decide that written discharge notices are sufficient evidence that patients knew that any further stay was not medically necessary; however, if patients agreed with the decision, they obviously would not be appealing it. Therefore, until the rules change, patients should be prepared to convince the PRO that their continued stay is medically necessary.

If patients lose their appeals, it is up to the hospitals to collect any money owed. *Patients or family members might be able to convince a hospital to waive the charges if they leave promptly after receiving notice of the PRO's decision.*

Lost appeals can also be taken a step further. Patients can ask the PRO for instructions on how to file a further appeal. This next level of appeal, however, will take too long for patients to remain in the hospital while it is being decided.

Discharge Dates and Supplemental Insurance

Patients should not assume that any "Medigap" or Medicare supplemental insurance policies they carry will pay for their continued stay in a hospital after the discharge date. Many patients wrongly believe that these policies will pay for any continued hospitalization that Medicare won't cover. In fact, all insurance companies use standards similar to those of Medicare to decide whether patients require additional hospitalization. Like Medicare, they will not cover days in the hospital that are not medically necessary. (For more information, see chapter 2.)

Hospital managers are aware that these supplemental policies will not cover continued hospitalization that is not medically necessary. They are reluctant to accept patients' offering them as evidence of upcoming payment because they generally find they cannot collect on these accounts. Patients should be prepared to pay if they stay long after their appeal is lost.

9

What to Do if You Have a Problem or Complaint

LIKE many chapters in this book, this one is worthwhile reading for residents of nursing homes and other facilities, their families, and their friends. When residents are unable to effectively resolve a complaint by themselves, it is often these other people who become involved in trying to correct the situation. Although this chapter primarily addresses problems and complaints that arise in nursing homes, it also discusses what to do when similar difficulties occur with or in other types of health care facilities.

The picture painted here of nursing homes is not always pretty, but it should be remembered that nursing homes range in quality from very poor to excellent, and not all nursing homes treat their residents in such a way that problems and complaints arise frequently. Whether a nursing home or other health care facility is good, bad, or in between, this chapter should give readers an idea of how to get their problems and complaints taken care of—which should make for a more comfortable stay in any health care facility.

Overview

It is probably unnecessary to say that the nursing home industry has been plagued by scandals, horror stories, abuses, and poor quality. These are not private problems, they have been splashed across everybody's television screens, newspapers, magazines, and—thankfully—government agendas.

Numerous studies and reports were commissioned that basically said the same thing: many nursing homes do not give appropriate or sufficient care to their residents, abuses do exist, and the systems of inspection and enforcement of standards are inadequate to solve the problem. The bad publicity surrounding nursing homes in the late 1960s and early 1970s resulted in many laws being passed, and supervisory programs started, at both federal and state levels of government. These laws and programs have dealt with quality-of-care issues, enforcement of standards, and nursing home complaint resolution. As a result, there has been considerable improvement in the quality of care that residents receive in nursing homes.

People who are residents of a nursing home—either for a temporary stay or for the rest of their lives—may face a lot of potential concerns, disputes, and problems. These problems can be trivial and are frequently a matter of residents preferring one thing over another. But they can also be serious and affect the quality of care residents receive or their basic rights. Problems can affect one particular resident, all residents, or even the entire population of nursing home residents in a single state.

Many of the problems experienced by nursing home residents, their families, and their friends are for the most part due to the nature of life in an institution. The typical nursing home is large (a hundred residents or more) and may have only one nurse's aide to take care of fifteen to twenty residents or more. As a result, nursing homes usually make decisions based on how they can most easily deal with a large number of residents and limited staff. These decisions include when and what meals are served, when residents must sleep, when residents must bathe, and so on. Nursing homes try to treat everyone the same, and have them follow the same routine, even though the residents themselves may be very, very different from one another. This is a real problem all by itself, because some residents may be much younger than others, some may be extremely confused while others are still mentally alert, and some may be severely disabled while others are quite physically fit.

Nursing home staffs usually have a heavy work load. Few facilities have a registered nurse on duty around the clock, and it is extremely rare to have a doctor present on a regular basis. Nursing homes also rarely have enough employees, and those they do have are usually underpaid, overworked, and too often lacking in the skills needed to do their jobs. Almost 80 percent of all direct resident care is provided by nursing assistants who have no medical background and often receive little if any training.

Recently, federal laws were passed that will require all nursing assistants in the approximately 15,000 federally certified facilities to complete a training program and skills evaluation.

Demands on the existing staff's time mean that a minimal amount of attention is paid to an individual resident's preferences and interests; his or her concerns can easily be overlooked, ignored, or denied. This situation may also mean poor-quality care and, worse, inappropriate or inadequate care. When this happens, it's important to remember the old saying "The squeaky wheel gets the grease." *Residents, their family members, and their friends have to be aware that the best way to receive needed care or desired attention is to ask for it and, if necessary, to insist on it.* If that fails, it may be necessary to take those concerns elsewhere to insist that they be handled.

The best way to ensure that residents receive appropriate care and attention is to make sure they are visited frequently by people outside the facility. Unfortunately, a great many residents do not have any visitors—many have outlived their families and friends—and may have to depend on the more formal mechanisms available to residents as a way to handle their complaints.

Nursing Homes and Other Types of Institutions

As mentioned earlier, the focus of this chapter is on residents of nursing homes, but many of the options are applicable to other health care institutions, such as hospitals and related settings, for example, board and care homes.

The phrase *nursing home* is used to cover almost all health care facilities that provide services related to health care in a residential or long-term care setting. They may be licensed or categorized as *Skilled Nursing Facilities (SNF)*, which provide extensive medical and skilled nursing services; *Intermediate Care Facilities (ICF)*, which provide some medical services; or other names, depending on the state in which they are located.

Board and care homes include a number of different types of facilities, such as those which provide "residential care," "domiciliary care," and "assisted-living care." These facilities don't provide medical care but do house many chronically ill or frail elderly people who may require supervision and assistance with things like bathing, grooming, and eating.

It is important that residents of a particular facility, as well as their family members, know and understand the category into which their facility falls. Wherever possible, this chapter will note which issues, options, and programs for resolving complaints apply to which type of facility.

Choosing a Facility

There are many fine nursing homes whose top priorities include high-quality medical care and respect for the wishes of residents. Careful shopping for a facility is probably the best way to avoid problems in the first place, but unfortunately, such shopping is not always possible.

Where shopping for a nursing home or other residential care facility is possible, family members (and, health permitting, the people who are going to reside in the nursing home) should do the following:

- Visit a number of facilities. Many federal, state, and local agencies and organizations publish excellent guides on how to select a nursing home. These guides offer sound, practical advice on what to look for while visiting a nursing home and what factors to consider in choosing a facility. A good place to start in obtaining a guide is the state department of health or aging (see appendix 34 for a list of addresses by state).
- Talk with residents, staff, and any available visitors.
- Request and examine the following information, most of which is public information, available on nursing homes:

    Medicare and Medicaid certification inspection or survey reports

    state licensure inspection reports

    "statement of deficiencies" reports

    "plans of correction" for problems

    complaint investigation reports (depending on state laws)

    cost reports showing what money is spent on food, nursing, and other key categories

    This kind of information is available to people who request it from state medical and nursing licensure and certification agencies, which are generally part of a state's department of health (see appendix 34); some local Social Security offices; and the Health Care Financing Administration (HCFA). HCFA is preparing to publicly distribute information on facility deficiencies or problems noted during annual surveys.

- Speak with people who visit facilities on a regular basis, including those who serve as patient advocates. In particular, speak with representatives of state and local offices of the Long Term Care Ombudsman Program, which was established and authorized under the federal Older Americans Act to "investigate and resolve complaints made by or on behalf of older individuals who are residents of long-term care facilities." Ombudsman program offices should have copies of inspection reports or be able to direct people on how to get them (see appendix 19 for the addresses of ombudsman program offices by state).
- Speak with community advocacy and citizen action committees or organizations; they are often very knowledgeable about the nursing homes and other health care facilities in their area.
- For facilities that do not participate in the Medicare or Medicaid programs, check with the state licensure agency, usually located in the state department of health, or with the local groups mentioned above to see what information must by law be made available and where to get it (see appendix 34 for a listing of state addresses).

Obtaining information about individual facilities requires determination and some legwork, but it's worth it. If individuals know about deficiencies identified by federal, state, and local agencies, such knowledge can provide helpful clout when dealing with problems arising in a particular facility. Nonetheless, no matter how much information is available, residents may still encounter problems.

Types of Problems Occurring in Residential Facilities: Medical, Financial, and Personal

In many cases, the need to enter a nursing home may be a sudden event that doesn't allow residents or family members the time to visit and compare many facilities. A common problem is that many nursing homes don't have enough beds for the residents who want to fill them. This problem is worse for residents who must rely on Medicaid to pay their bills, since not all facilities accept Medicaid residents and many don't accept them very willingly (for more information, see chapters 3 and 10). Too often, people who need to find a nursing home in a hurry have to accept the first bed in the first institution that has an opening.

For the frail and ill elderly people who lack family and friends to assist them in looking for a nursing home—and who are therefore dependent on busy strangers to place them in a facility—this problem is particularly severe.

Yet even residents who have the funds to pay for their care, as well as those who rely on Medicaid, may still face problems or have complaints, even in the best of facilities. Although the types of problems that occur in a residential facility vary tremendously, the following indicates the kinds of medical, financial, and personal problems that may arise:

Medical problems

- *Inappropriate use of restraints and chemical sedatives.* Residents are "tied up" or "doped up" for the convenience of other residents and staff; restraints are too restrictive or are left on for too long; doctors don't order restraints for residents who need them; residents are restrained without doctor's orders.
- *Inappropriate medical care.* Residents develop decubitus ulcers (that is, bedsores and pressure sores); insufficient care is given for decubitus ulcers, severe bowel impactions, or extreme constipation; sudden and significant losses of weight are not acknowledged or treated; overdrugging occurs; potential drug reactions and interactions are not taken into account (for example, the impact of a particular dosage of a drug may differ greatly in a frail eighty-two-year-old woman and in a healthy sixty-year-old man); infections develop or spread; contractures (permanent shortenings of muscle, tendon, or tissue that produce deformity or distortion and are caused by lack of exercise, therapy, or movement) form and are inadequately treated.
- *Inattention.* Residents are left for too long on the toilet or in the bath, resulting in falls, broken bones, and other injuries; residents are left in one position too long or not turned often enough, resulting in bedsores and pressure sores; residents are left sitting or lying in their own feces or urine for extended periods of time.
- *Therapy.* Therapy, such as speech and physical therapy, is not provided regularly or is not provided at all.

Financial problems

- *Coverage of care and eligibility for care.* Residents are bumped from one level of care to another; residents are denied certain forms of therapy, care, or treatment; residents are denied coverage under Medicare or Medicaid.

- *Billing.* Residents and families are charged for services not received or are charged for services that should be paid by insurance or health care coverage (such as hospital gowns); families are not refunded for services not received if a resident is discharged or dies early in a month for which they have already paid.
- *Financial discrimination.* Residents who cannot pay for themselves but who are covered by Medicaid are discriminated against in admission procedures; residents are discriminated against in the types of care received and where it is received (such as in a separate "Medicaid wing" of the facility).
- *Mishandling of funds.* Facilities use inappropriate accounting, combine resident funds with facility funds, misuse funds, or occasionally steal funds from residents.

Personal problems
- *Food* (probably the most common category of complaints in long-term care facilities). Inappropriate diets are given to diabetic and hypoglycemic residents (or those with other conditions); food given lacks in choice, variety, or amount; food is unappetizing or cold when served; the facility is insensitive to patients' cultural and religious preferences.
- *Privacy.* Residents are exposed to view while on the toilet, in the bath, and being cared for in bed; residents experience lack of privacy while making personal calls or receiving personal visits from spouses, relatives, friends, and patient advocates.
- *Roommates.* Personality conflicts occur between roommates; mentally incompetent residents share rooms with alert residents; residents are put in rooms with abusive or noisy roommates.
- *Recreation and education.* Residents have inadequate recreational and educational activities—or none at all.
- *Abuse.* Residents suffer from physical, verbal, and mental abuse; they are yelled at or struck by staff or other residents; residents are ignored, belittled, and even sexually assaulted.
- *Transfers.* Residents are moved from one room to another or from one floor to another; residents are sometimes required to leave the facility as a form of retaliation.
- *Disability discrimination.* Residents are discriminated against in admission proce-

dures when they require a great deal of care or could be disruptive to other residents and staff.
- *Racial discrimination.* Residents are discriminated against in admission and care procedures because of their race.
- *Theft* (a severe problem in many facilities). Residents have personal items, such as TVs, radios, clothes, and mementos, stolen from their rooms.
- *Patient rights.* Many resident rights, as stated in the "Federal Patients' Bill of Rights" and in numerous states' resident rights laws, are violated, as shown by this list of problems (see chapter 7 for more information). Residents are denied the right to share a room with their spouses; to meet with and participate in social, religious, and community group activities; to organize and participate in resident groups in the facility; and to express grievances about the facility's quality of care or lack of care provided.

What to Do When There Is a Problem

Problems are most easily pursued by people who have organized and factual information on the issue(s) of concern. The following checklist should provide some ideas about the kind of information that will be helpful in pursuing a complaint.

- How serious is the problem, how important is the problem, and how far is the person raising the complaint willing to go to get it resolved?
- Will complaining about the problem make future communications more difficult, cause retaliation against a resident, or result in the individual and resident concerned being labeled troublemakers?
- Decide what remedy or resolution would solve the problem, what would be an ideal solution, and what would be a reasonable one—know one's "bottom line."
- Be as specific as possible about the problem, determining what specific incident or issue is the subject of the complaint.
- Gather the facts, including the date and time the problem occurred (or did not occur, as in when a resident did not receive therapy), who was involved, if there were any witnesses who can corroborate what happened, why the incident was inappropriate, and any evidence or other information that can support the existence of a problem or basis for a complaint.

- Determine whether the matter was an isolated incident or has happened before to this particular resident or other residents; whether there is a pattern to the problem; whether it has been raised before (by oneself or others); whether anything was done or promised when the problem occurred at other times, and if so, what was done or promised; and whether the situation or a recurrence of it could adversely affect other residents.
- Determine why the situation occurred and whether there were any unusual or mitigating circumstances.
- Determine whether there is any legal basis for concern or any patient rights' that were violated, whether any terms of the resident's admission agreement were breached, whether a specific patient right was violated, whether the incident breached federal or state laws or facility policies, and whether it involved a potential criminal violation.
- Determine who would be helpful, or even necessary, in order to involve others in getting assistance.
- Identify who is the most appropriate person to resolve the problem, who is likely to resolve it most quickly, who is likely to find a long-term solution, and who is most likely to permit individuals to comfortably express their complaints (the answers to these questions do not all necessarily lead to the same person).

In other words, know as much as possible about the complaint or incident before bringing it to the attention of the authorities. It is particularly useful to know whether any legal, procedural, or contractual rights have been violated or are at stake. It is also important to decide how far one is willing to go in resolving the complaint.

The nursing home industry is large, complex, and highly regulated by policies, laws, and government agencies. There are a considerable number of things that can go wrong in nursing homes—and an equally large number of places to take a complaint.

Pursuing the Matter within the Facility

Most people wish to resolve their problems in the quickest manner possible, with the least amount of conflict. This can usually be done by expressing the grievance to facility employees—the staff person directly involved with the problem, the one who oversees it (such as the food services director, if the problem is about food, or the head nurse, regarding a care problem), or the facility's administrator. If this doesn't work, the next step may be to go to the facility's owners or governing board. If the facility is part of a large chain, there may be regional staff who can be approached. At least one national chain established its own toll-free telephone line for consumer complaints. Many facilities have specific grievance procedures; in most instances, it is appropriate to follow the suggested procedures until the problem is solved or the options in it exhausted. Then take the problem elsewhere.

It may be useful to work with a facility's social services staff member or social worker, if it has one. A new federal law will require that facilities with more than 120 beds employ at least one full-time social worker with at least a bachelor's degree or similar professional qualifications to either provide social services or direct residents and families in getting them (individual states may have a similar requirement). The role, training, and orientation of such workers are to solve problems, and they could be very helpful. They may not always be effective in tackling problems that are not the fault or responsibility of the nursing home (such as denials of eligibility, or coverage of medical devices under the state's Medicaid program). Another facility employee who can be of use is the activities director. Again, it all depends on the type of problem.

Many facilities have residents' councils that may participate in the grievance procedure. A council may be a place to express a problem and provide a way to solve it—particularly if the problem is experienced by other residents as well. It may be worthwhile finding out what kinds of authority and independence the council actually has, before taking the problem to its members. Positive signs are

its ability to meet without facility staff being present;

the presence of individuals from outside the facility who may participate at meetings and advise the council; and

the presence of individuals from outside the facility who may act as members of the council.

Other vehicles for resolving complaints are family councils, or committees made up of the families and friends of the facility's residents. Such councils can be very useful in dealing with resident problems. If a council is not reasonably independent or open to outside participation, there is a danger (as with some residents' councils) that it may be a time-consuming dead end for the airing of complaints.

Some facilities, usually good ones, have established community advisory committees made up of knowledgeable and concerned citizens from the local area. Again, depending on the makeup of the community council and the loyalty and dedication of its members, this group could be an effective ally in pursuing a grievance.

Federal law gives people the right to express grievances about treatment and care that are or are not received, without discrimination or retaliation for doing so. It also gives people the right to urge the facility to solve the problem, even if the problem has to do with the behavior of other residents. Further, the law insists on the rights of residents to organize and participate in resident councils, and of family members to meet in the facility with the families of other residents in the facility.

Complaints about Hospital Care

For complaints about hospital care, many of the same principles apply, especially with regard to speaking with appropriate staff, following the facility's suggested grievance procedures, and working one's way up the chain of command.

In addition, hospitals usually have patient advocate or patient relations offices that are intended to respond to patient-related problems and grievances. Growing numbers of hospitals are beginning to provide long-term care by buying or building nursing homes, converting empty hospital beds into nursing home beds, or converting whole sections of hospitals into nursing facilities. If the nursing home part of a hospital is not a separate facility, it is important to find out what state nursing home laws apply to it. The existence of a hospital patient relations office or staff could be helpful in dealing with problems related to the nursing home part of the operation.

When to Seek Outside Assistance to Resolve a Complaint

Sometimes, residents, friends, or family members voicing a complaint are dissatisfied with a facility's response to it. There also are times when taking grievances to facility personnel is not desirable or even appropriate. When either of these two circumstances arises, it is probably best to take the problem outside the facility.

Taking the complaint to the facility's management may not be wise if past complaints have been ignored or have been met with hostility. Doing so may also be inappropriate in situations in which the administrator, key personnel, or owners are the subject of the complaint—for example, when there is possible misuse of funds or suspected fraudulent billing, or when essential medications were not provided and harmful results occurred. In the latter case, if the matter were brought to the facility authorities, they could change resident medical charts to indicate that the medication had been given.

In matters that may involve a serious risk to the resident's health, safety, or welfare, or that may involve possible fraud or other criminal behavior, individuals must consider the possibility that discussing the matter with facility personnel could lead to destruction of evidence or some other form of cover-up. This is not to say that all nursing home personnel act in an unethical or criminal manner; however, for unscrupulous people, the prospect of civil fines, suspension or loss of professional licenses, suspension or termination from Medicare or Medicaid, facility closure or a forced sale, loss of business, civil litigation, criminal indictments, and related bad press and community relations can provide a powerful incentive to alter the facts.

Individuals raising problems should strongly consider seeking the advice of an attorney or other knowledgeable authority if the matter

is serious;

involves violations of the law;

is symptomatic of other serious problems; or

adversely affects the health, safety, or welfare of the resident involved (or has the potential to do so).

Typically, however, individuals are likely to seek outside assistance for the following reasons:

- To obtain objective guidance and advice.
- To find out more about the issue of concern and the options available to resolve it.
- To find a witness to meetings with facility administrators.
- To get moral support (for example, arguing with a tough, seasoned head nurse can be an intimidating experience).
- To mediate a dispute.

- To argue the case and negotiate on behalf of the resident or the person raising the complaint.
- If the issue reflects a violation of public law or regulation, is contrary to public policy, or should be noted in the public record to spur change or help ensure that fewer similar incidents happen in the future. (For example, persistent staff shortages not only violate the law and are harmful to all the facility's residents; they may also reflect significant underlying problems with the facility, its corporate management, and public policies regarding nurse shortages and inadequate reimbursements in public financing programs).

If the problem is a minor one—such as a resident's being cold and needing another blanket—then the options chosen should be simple ones, such as asking the nursing assistant or aide for a blanket. If the problem is serious and could affect a resident's health, safety, and rights; if it is a recurring problem; or if the specific problem is just a symptom of other major difficulties, then solving it might require some real creativity and persistence. Problem solving is often much easier when people other than residents are involved, for complaints expressed by residents are frequently dismissed as confusion, imagination, or hostility.

Options for seeking outside assistance are varied, and which one is used can be strongly influenced by the nature of the problem.

Where to Go for Outside Assistance

There are a wide variety of options, available in nearly every community, to help people resolve complaints. The subject and severity of the complaint will often determine what measures are appropriate. In some cases, a variety of actions may be necessary to appropriately resolve a complaint. The range of actions taken is limited only by the determination, resources, and creativity of the person trying to solve the problem. The following list does not include all the options that may be available in a specific community, but it does give ideas of where to go for assistance.

Private resources
- Facility administration, board of directors, or owners, if necessary.
- Facility-based grievance committees, including residents' councils and family councils.

- Nursing home industry-based grievance mechanisms.
- Private attorneys for pro bono or free services, or attorneys paid by the hour or on a contingency-fee basis. Often used in malpractice and personal injury cases, *contingency fees* mean that lawyers don't charge the client unless they win the case; if they do win the case, they are paid a predetermined percentage of the settlement.
- Small-claims courts.
- Unions representing facility personnel.
- The media. This is probably the option that facilities fear most, as negative stories in newspapers, in magazines, and on television can greatly harm their reputations and, as a result, their profits. (For more information, see chapter 15.)

Public resources
- Ombudsman programs (for more information, see the next section, entitled "The Long Term Care Ombudsman Program," and see appendix 19 for a list of ombudsman program offices).
- Citizen or community-based advocacy programs, typically operating under such names as the Bay Area Advocates for Nursing Home Reform (in San Francisco) and Kansans for the Improvement of Nursing Homes.
- State and local organizations and agencies that deal with issues affecting older Americans, such as the Gray Panthers, the Older Women's League, and the local Area Agency on Aging. The State Unit on Aging (see appendix 20) can also direct interested individuals to their nearest resources.
- State nursing home licensure and certification officials, who have responsibilities for licensing, certifying, and regulating nursing homes, as well as for investigating problems that arise in them (see appendix 34 for addresses).
- Officials with licensure and certification responsibilities over various professionals who provide care in nursing homes, such as nursing home administrators, doctors, hospitals, nurses, nursing assistants, psychologists, and therapists (check with the licensing and certification division or the consumer affairs department of the area agency on aging for this information).
- Federally funded Peer Review Organizations (PROs) that can evaluate care being provided in a facility (see appendix 16 for a list of state addresses).

- Law enforcement agencies, such as the police, district attorneys, and state offices of the attorney general (including their Medicaid fraud and abuse divisions).
- The U.S. Department of Health and Human Services' Office of the Inspector General and Office of Civil Rights, located in Washington, D.C.
- State civil rights investigative authorities.
- Publicly funded legal aid offices, including legal programs for the elderly—often funded by the Older Americans Act. (To find low-cost legal aid, contact the State Unit on Aging, whose addresses are listed in appendix 20, and talk to the legal services developer.) Also, almost every state has an Information and Referral (I&R) hot line for the elderly or the general public in need of services; local senior citizens' centers should have the telephone number of this resource.
- Judges or other officials, such as public guardians, who have authority over guardianship and conservatorship proceedings and practices (it is strongly recommended that interested individuals consult with an ombudsman or lawyer in these instances).
- State or local consumer protection agencies (look under "Consumer Protection" or "Consumer Affairs" in the telephone directory, or check with the Area Agency on Aging or the State Unit on Aging, whose addresses are listed in appendix 20).
- State and local mediation and dispute resolution agencies (again, check with the Area Agency on Aging or the State Unit on Aging).
- Special state or local commissions and investigative groups, particularly those with experience in examining nursing home and other elder-individual issues (to find these groups, check with the area ombudsman; addresses are listed in appendix 19).
- Officials in state or local welfare agencies and protective services agencies with responsibility for investigating elder-abuse complaints. (Check "Social Services Agencies" under the "State Agencies" or "County Agencies" section of the telephone directory. Or ask the area ombudsman; see appendix 19 for addresses.)
- Financing sources for nursing home coverage, such as insurance companies, Medicare intermediaries, and state Medicaid agencies (check with the area ombudsman for these listings).

- Local agencies and organizations that place or help to place elderly people into long-term care facilities. These would include home health care agencies, visiting nurse associations, family services agencies, hospital discharge planners, and county welfare and protective services workers (again, check with the area ombudsman for these listings).
- Federal, state, and local elected officials and legislative committees such as the committees on aging in the U.S. Senate and House of Representatives and their state equivalents.

The Long Term Care Ombudsman Program

One of the best and most widely available resources to call upon when faced with a problem in a nursing home is the Long Term Care Ombudsman Program (LTCOP). Under the Older Americans Act, each state is required to have an ombudsman program (see appendix 19 for addresses of each state's program).

The program is free of charge. It is responsible for investigating and resolving complaints made by or on behalf of older individuals who are residents of long-term care facilities. It also permits the ombudsmen themselves to raise concerns or initiate complaints on behalf of residents. Specifically, the problems they investigate are those which may adversely affect the health, safety, welfare, or rights of residents relating to the action, inaction, or decisions of (a) providers of long-term care or their representatives, (b) long-term care services, (c) social services agencies, or (d) public agencies. Examples of problems ombudsmen would normally investigate include the following:

- Denial of home health care or adult day care that would allow residents to move out of the nursing home into a less restrictive setting.
- Failure of a nursing home licensing agency to fully or quickly investigate problems in a facility or to only minimally penalize them when stronger sanctions would seem more appropriate.
- Failure of guardians to provide appropriate resources or clothing to their wards in nursing homes.
- A Medicaid agency determination that residents are not eligible for coverage or should be moved out of a facility.
- A Medicaid agency denial of Skilled Nursing Facility (SNF) coverage.

- Inappropriate placement of residents by a community social services agency, such as into a facility with a poor record or into one that is too restrictive for the particular needs of the residents in question.

The program was designed to provide a way to respond to residents' complaints, both on an individual basis and as a way to bring about changes in the entire nursing home system. Many states have very strong programs, with solid state laws governing them. *The programs are generally statewide, and their services should be available to residents in all nursing homes and in certain board and care or residential facilities.*

The state ombudsman program is usually a part of the State Unit on Aging, often known as the state department or Agency on Aging. Some states, however, have the program located elsewhere.

Most state ombudsman programs have local program offices, known as substate programs. Most of the activity related to investigating and solving complaints is done at the substate level. There are now nearly seven hundred substate programs throughout the country, located in such places as legal services offices, area agencies on aging, social services agencies, community nursing home reform groups, county departments, and various senior citizens' organizations. To find the nearest substate ombudsman office, contact the state ombudsman program office (see appendix 19 for addresses); nursing homes should also be able to provide this information.

Ombudsmen can be invited by residents to visit a facility, investigate a particular complaint, or speak at a residents' or family council meeting. Most ombudsmen programs, particularly the substate ones, depend on volunteers to visit facilities and investigate complaints. Volunteer ombudsmen are usually older individuals with diverse backgrounds who are trained before they begin responding to problems.

Ombudsmen frequently get to know local facilities and their personnel, residents, family members, and other visitors. This kind of familiarity often makes residents and family members feel easier about discussing problems or filing complaints. The regular presence of the ombudsman in a facility is also important because most residents would be reluctant to use the facility's pay phone—often located by the nurse's station—to make a long-distance or even a toll-free call to the state's nursing home regulatory agency or the attorney general's office.

Ombudsmen are allowed to see residents' medical and social records, if they receive written permission from residents or their legal guardians. Many states already have strong laws to enforce the ombudsman's right to see such records.

Ombudsmen rarely have any power to punish facilities—they cannot levy fines, suspend Medicaid funds, issue citations, or otherwise force actions to be taken. For the most part, ombudsmen must rely on their knowledge, credibility, persistence, negotiating skills, and other tactics to solve a problem or, if necessary, bring it to the public's attention.

Ombudsmen are also effective in advising residents and other concerned individuals on the most appropriate and desirable strategy to solve a problem. They are knowledgeable about the realities, limitations, and consequences of taking a particular problem to any of the public and private resources listed earlier in this chapter.

The ombudsman's only purpose is to work on behalf of the rights and interests of current and potential nursing home residents. Ombudsmen are not dependent on or under the authority of any other groups having conflicting interests. They will also not reveal the identity of people making complaints unless they receive written permission to do so (or are so ordered by a court).

It is against the law for nursing homes to retaliate or punish residents or employees who file complaints or provide information to an ombudsman. Some states have passed other laws involving ombudsmen, including requiring them to act as witnesses when residents sell or transfer property at less than fair market value to anyone related to the nursing home, or when residents write a living will (see appendix 4 for a checklist of state laws regarding living wills). In Minnesota and California, for example, ombudsmen may provide services to hospital patients under certain conditions.

Ombudsman programs, particularly at the substate level, are often understaffed and underfunded. Ombudsman services are available to people who need them, however, and ombudsmen are obligated to respond to complaints. People have a right to go to ombudsmen for their services and to expect them to act quickly and effectively. Once again, the old saying "the squeaky wheel gets the grease" may come in handy. Insist on their assistance.

While the ombudsman program is certainly not the only place to go for help, it's often a good place to start. If ombudsmen can't help directly, they can offer reliable advice and guidance on where to go next or concurrently. Ombudsmen act as brokers of problems, leading concerned individuals everywhere they need to go to correct a situation. If indi-

viduals are going to go to only one place to make a complaint, it ought to be the ombudsman program or the state licensing authority (see appendixes 19 and 34 for state addresses for these groups).

Regulatory and Licensure Agencies for Nursing Homes

In each state are a variety of state regulatory and licensure agencies and boards that address concerns related to health care. The most widely known among them is the state health department's licensure and certification agency (or division). Another commonly used group, the Peer Review Organization (PRO), is also responsible for examining complaints about quality of care provided to Medicare patients in nursing homes (for more information on PROs, see chapter 8).

The federal government and state governments are both responsible for making sure that nursing homes comply with their requirements and for overseeing nursing home quality. States are also responsible for licensing nursing homes. Nursing homes are inspected at least once every fifteen months, more often if the state believes circumstances warrant it. These inspection surveys specifically include interviews with residents and others to elicit their comments about their care and treatment in the facility.

More typically, however, complaints would be made directly to the regulatory agency when an incident occurs (rather than waiting for the inspection). The actual procedures used to investigate complaints vary from state to state. To find out the procedures for a particular state, interested individuals can consult the area ombudsman. Also, each nursing home should have posted information about the filing of complaints with the licensing and certification agency.

As previously stated, only complaints that involve violations of federal and state laws and standards governing nursing home care—particularly those which have adversely affected or may adversely affect, the health, safety, welfare, and rights of residents—are appropriately brought before the state's nursing home regulatory agency. These regulatory and licensing agencies can penalize nursing homes in a variety of ways, such as removing a facility's license to operate or decertifying a facility from participating in Medicare and Medicaid programs. Such penalties are not often invoked, however, as they are severe, and too many individuals need nursing home beds to easily close a facility. Instead, less severe penalties, such as levying fines or requiring new management of a facility, may be used. (See appendix 34 for a list of state medical and nursing licensure agencies.)

Regulatory and Licensure Agencies for Other Health Care Facilities

In addition to regulating nursing homes, a wide range of other facilities related to health care are regulated by the states or are required to meet federal and/or state standards. Hospitals are typically licensed by the state's health department—usually the same entity that licenses nursing homes.

As mentioned earlier, long-term care facilities for the elderly and disabled that do not provide health or medical services are generally known as board and care homes. Some states regulate these homes, and some do not. Some states also regulate clinical laboratories that conduct a wide variety of tests, while others provide minimal oversight at best.

Increasing numbers of states are not only licensing home health care agencies but also taking seriously the need to investigate problems associated with this kind of care. Nevertheless, when problems arise with these types of facilities and others, it is essential to find out who has reponsibility for overseeing quality in them and what the appropriate procedures are for filing complaints. Again, the area ombudsman should be helpful in this regard.

Regulatory and Licensure Agencies for Health Care Professsionals

States provide for licensure of a wide variety of professionals, a number of whom may interact with nursing home residents. These include, but are not limited to, nursing home administrators, nurses, doctors, pharmacists, social workers, psychiatrists, psychologists, and physical therapists. Inevitably, certain types of problems that arise in the nursing home (or hospital or health care setting) will involve questions about the quality of care or treatment by various health care professionals.

For example, if a nursing home resident develops severe decubitus ulcers (bedsores) that become infected, it raises questions not only about the nursing home's compliance with federal and state standards but also about the competence or professionalism of the following: the nursing home administrator (for not selecting appropriate staff or for not taking appropriate action if the problem is brought to his or her attention), the facility's medical director and/or the resident's doctor (for not adequately supervising the care or treatment of the resident), the nursing staff (for allowing the sores to develop and become infected and possibly for not quickly alerting the doctor to the problem), and the nursing assistants or aides (for possibly failing to turn the resident appropriately or provide other preventive measures, or for failing to bring the problem to the attention of other staff on a timely basis). Depending on the circumstances, each of these professionals could merit a complaint about the care given.

Generally, the agencies that license and regulate health care professionals have few ways to penalize professionals short of suspending or revoking their licenses, reprimanding professionals for the public record, and making their licenses conditional. Few of these agencies have the staffing or resources to conduct extensive investigations, and most people do not file complaints with them anyway. Even when complaints are filed, many of these agencies are run by professionals who are reluctant to police their own.

Nonetheless, a threat to the license of an administrator, doctor, nurse, or other health care professional is a serious threat to his or her professional standing and economic well-being. Federal law requires that nursing home administrators meet certain standards under Medicare and Medicaid. As a result, each state has a licensure agency for nursing home administrators (see appendix 34 for a list of addresses). Typically, complaints can be brought to the attention of these agencies for investigation and the imposition of standards, as appropriate.

Getting Help from Law Enforcement Agencies

The role that law enforcement agencies can play in dealing with certain nursing home or other complaints related to health care can be considerable. Local police can, and should, be brought in anytime there is a potential violation of criminal law. Although theft of residents' personal goods is a large problem in some nursing homes, the police are rarely brought in to investigate such events. Nursing home personnel often hate the idea of police in their facilities, but police are the people best equipped to investigate theft and other criminal acts. The mere presence of police can also act as a deterrent for future acts of theft. Assaults on residents and other forms of physical abuse against residents are criminal acts, and it is certainly appropriate to involve police in these matters.

District attorneys have an important role to play in investigating and prosecuting criminal acts. It is important to remember that district attorneys do more than address traditional criminal acts (such as theft, assault, and possible drug misuse by facility personnel). They also address violations of civil law, including enforcing consumer protection laws and fair business practices statutes. Facility practices that limit admissions to a nursing home, price-fixing, billing fraud, overcharging for services, and many other practices could be matters that a local district attorney's office would be interested in investigating.

At the state level, the attorney general can and should play an important role in taking on a wide variety of matters related to nursing homes, including situations that may have broad or statewide implications. Also, under federal law, states establish Medicaid fraud and abuse units to investigate and prosecute a range of activities that can occur in nursing homes (they can also investigate Medicaid providers, such as doctors, nurses, hospitals, and other groups). These units would investigate, for example, fraudulent billing of families and the government, as well as instances in which nursing homes seek or receive additional amounts in the form of "donations" or "gifts" to consider individuals for admission.

Getting Help from Lawyers and the Courts

Residents and their families can also seek the assistance of lawyers. To find low-cost legal aid, interested individuals should contact the legal services developer within the State Unit on Aging (see appendix 20 for addresses). Also, nearly all states have an Information and Referral (I&R) hot line for the elderly or for the general population in need of services; local senior citizens' centers should have the telephone number of this resource.

The most typical types of cases that legal services programs deal with are public entitlement cases involving disputes and problems concerning Medicare and Medicaid eligibility and coverage (for more information, see chapter 10). Other cases, more rarely, may involve personal injury and malpractice, as well as class action suits.

Small-claims courts are another option to pursue. These courts are inexpensive, conduct cases quite quickly, and do not use lawyers to represent either side. They are primarily used to settle disputes involving limited amounts of money, and the disputes are settled by the presiding judge (juries are not involved). These courts are especially effective in recovering the cost of residents' personal items that have been stolen or lost in a facility, but they can also be useful in recovering funds from billing disputes and other problems.

Other Avenues to Pursue

Other avenues to pursue in resolving problems and complaints are outlined below.

- Community advocacy and consumer organizations that focus on nursing homes and other matters related to senior citizens can be of great help. Each state and region should have at least one group that can either directly assist or make referrals to other appropriate bodies.
- Federal, state, and local government agencies that may be able to assist with certain types of problems are too numerous and diverse to discuss here. When consulting knowledgeable individuals about particular problems, ask what agencies might be useful to involve.
- Mediation and arbitration services are also a possibility for resolving complaints. These programs typically use an objective third party to try to help resolve disputes. The mediator, or arbitrator, will usually propose a settlement that may or may not (depending on the kind of mediation) be accepted by either or both individuals or groups involved in the dispute.
- Each state has a protection and advocacy system designed to protect the developmentally disabled and the mentally ill. Such programs typically operate at the state level and respond to complaints made by or on behalf of their constituencies, many of whom reside in nursing homes and other long-term care facilities. A great many nursing home residents have significant mental health problems and therefore qualify for these services. Protection and advocacy groups generally address problems that affect many of their clients, rather than solve individual problems.
- Finally, the media and elected officials are two other options that may be useful in resolving disputes. For more information see chapter 15.

10

The Medicare/Medicaid Maze

IT would be impossible to provide a clear understanding of everything that Medicare and Medicaid programs do and do not pay for in the confines of this chapter. Entire books have been written to explain the details of these programs' eligibility and reimbursement policies. To answer specific questions about specific claims, interested individuals will have to do some necessary extra reading and work on the telephone. This chapter has a different purpose—to outline the most basic services and intentions of each program and, more important, to discuss where to go for help when there is a problem.

Several excellent books have formed the basis for much of the information that follows. Specifically, they are *Understanding Alzheimer's Disease: What It Is, How to Cope with It, Future Directions,* by Miriam Aronson, and *Losing a Million Minds: Confronting the Tragedy of Alzheimer's Disease and Other Dementias,* by the Office of Technology Assessment. Highly recommended to interested individuals, both works are listed in the "Additional Reading" section at the back of this book, as are other publications that are useful aids in explaining the rules and regulations of Medicare and Medicaid. In addition more information on these programs can be found in chapters 2 and 3.

Overview

Anytime a bureaucracy as large as Medicare or Medicaid is responsible for matching millions of claims against an enormous number of rules and regulations, there's bound to be trouble. And while few people enjoy the challenge of "fighting City Hall" when healthy, most people really dislike doing so when ill. Often, the process of applying for eligibility or of arguing over a denied claim can seem like an endless series of false starts, closed doors, and mysterious answers. In short, it seems like a maze with no directions about how to get out.

Medicare and Medicaid both have a vast number of restrictions, limitations, and requirements that must be met before any medical costs are paid or reimbursed. To start with, there are complex eligibility requirements and puzzling service coverages. Public misconceptions about each program and the sometimes inept and often overworked employees who work in them exacerbate the situation.

Bluntly put, the multiple rules and regulations can be as confusing to Medicare and Medicaid employees—who often misinterpret them and unfairly deny people their benefits—as they are to applicants and beneficiaries. To make matters worse, program administrators have no real reason to grant claims or applications, because they are often penalized for giving benefits to ineligible individuals but are not penalized for denying benefits to eligible ones.

Key Components of the Maze

When faced with the problem of looking for available benefits, it is helpful to understand what programs exist, who funds or administers them, what they are meant to do, and a few other key words or phrases that can help individuals make order out of chaos:

Medicare. A government-funded health insurance program for individuals usually over the age of sixty-five or those who have been entitled to Social Security disability benefits for twenty-four months. It pays for certain medical care costs of the people who are eligible to receive it, but it usually does not pay for long-term care or nursing home services. Eligibility is administered through the Social Security Administration; services and reimbursement issues are handled by the Health Care Financing Administration of the U.S. Department of Health and Human Services (HHS).

Medicaid. A federal- and state-funded social welfare program that pays for certain medical care costs of the people who are eligible to receive it. In most states, eligible individuals include elderly persons who either receive Supplemental Security Income (SSI) or need nursing home care. Medicaid will often pay for long-term care or nursing home services.

General Public Assistance (GPA), general assistance or *home relief.* A social welfare program funded only by states or counties, not by the federal government. It gives financial aid to indigents, that is, poor people who have no other income.

Social Security Disability Income (SSDI). A social insurance program that provides financial assistance to people who, because of a physical or mental disability, can no longer work. It is administered by the Social Security Administration of HHS.

Supplemental Security Income (SSI). A social welfare program that provides financial aid to poor people over the age of sixty-five and those who are blind or totally and permanently disabled. This program is also administered by the Social Security Administration of HHS.

Entitlement program. Any program that provides financial or other kinds of assistance to all persons who meet specific eligibility requirements.

Health care providers. Any persons or organizations that provide health care—doctors, hospitals, home care services, "meals on wheels," and so on. The services they provide may or may not be covered by entitlement programs, depending on specific program rules and regulations.

Benefits. The money paid by an entitlement program to reimburse patients or pay doctors, hospitals, or other health care providers.

Beneficiary or recipient. A person who is eligible for the benefits paid by any of the entitlement programs.

Claim. The bill for the medical care or service that the beneficiary wants reimbursed by an entitlement program.

Case manager. An individual whose job it is to manage, plan for, and arrange continuing health care services for ill individuals. Case managers are employed by hospitals, social service agencies, local health departments, and other agencies and occasionally by families directly.

Food stamp program. A social welfare program for low-income persons that provides vouchers redeemable for food items at grocery stores. The program is administered by the U.S. Department of Agriculture through state or county welfare offices.

How to Get Through the Maze

As is the case with most mazes, people who persist despite the dead ends will eventually get through. Some initial frustrations can be avoided by doing a little background research. Choosing the appropriate entitlement program is one way to start. When evaluating any of the entitlement programs listed on page 137, it is important to ask a series of questions to find out who would be eligible in the first place:

- Who is eligible for the program?
- What are the requirements for eligibility?
- What benefits do recipients receive?
- Does the program make cash payments, offer services, or reimburse health care providers?
- What government agencies pay the benefits to recipients?
- Is the program administered by the federal, state, or county government or by some other group?
- What are the program's requirements for continued eligibility?

All entitlement programs have printed information about who is eligible. To receive this information, individuals should contact the programs themselves. The district Social Security Administration office should have information on SSI, SSDI, and Medicare. Other program information should be available through the county welfare agency. Look under the "Government" section of the telephone directory.

Once individuals know which program or programs they might be eligible for, the next step is to apply. *If turned down, individuals should not automatically assume they are ineligible.* Remember, all mazes have a way out; finding it requires a little persistence, determination, and stubbornness. Sadly, elderly ill people often don't have the energy to keep battling a bureaucracy and may have to depend on the efforts of a social worker or case manager. Those with family members or friends may be lucky enough to have someone who is willing to do it for them. Whoever does the work, the reward for making a successful effort can be substantial and worth all the effort involved.

Many applicants for benefits are initially turned down, even if they deserve the benefits.

A recent study of federal welfare benefits showed that of the people who are wrongfully turned down, less than 5 percent ever challenge the denial. In light of rising costs, increased claims, and tighter budgets, there is no motivation for these programs to initially grant benefits. If people successfully appeal negative decisions, then the agency only ends up giving out money it was required by law to pay in the first place. If negative claims are not appealed, the agency saves money.

Persons denied eligibility can appeal the decision within the program itself. Each program has set procedures for this, as well as numerous employees who generally do nothing but review appeals. Usually, the notice sent to individuals informing them that they have been denied eligibility will include information on how to appeal the decision.

A skilled guide is always useful in an appeal. *Happily, there are many ways individuals and their family members can get assistance in pursuing or appealing claims that are wrongfully denied:*

- *The Older Americans Act funds legal services programs for the elderly.*
- *The Legal Services Corporation funds legal services programs for the poor.*
- *Some lawyers will pursue such claims for less than their regular fee.*
- *Some legal clinics or programs associated with law schools may also provide such services for little or no cost.*

There are several ways to locate low-cost legal help. Interested individuals can contact the State Unit on Aging (see appendix 20 for addresses); the legal services developer there should be able to recommend where to get assistance. Also, almost all states have an Information and Referral (I&R) hot line for older people or for the general public in need of services; local senior citizens' centers should have the area INR telephone number. Finally, each state's legal system has a bar association whose referral service can provide this information as well.

Thumbnail Sketches of Each Program and How They Work

As previously mentioned, each program has its own criteria for determining eligibility, along with its own set of procedures for individuals to appeal either a refusal of eligibility or a denied claim. Thumbnail sketches of the programs and their procedures are provided below.

Social Security Disability Income (SSDI)

This social insurance program is designed to protect wage earners who can no longer be gainfully employed. It is the major program available to people under the age of sixty-two who are disabled by dementia (such as those who have Alzheimer's disease). Applicants must have worked a certain amount of time before becoming disabled and must not wait too long before applying for disability benefits after becoming disabled. Applicants must also be prevented from being gainfully employed because of a "medically determinable physical or mental impairment" that can be expected to last for at least a year.

If turned down after reviewing all the eligibility requirements and making an application, individuals have the options listed below. *First, though, they should remember that many applicants for SSDI benefits are turned down the first time they apply. Benefits may never be granted unless the applicant*

files a request for reconsideration and, if that also denies eligibility,

requests a hearing before an administrative law judge and, if that also yields the same negative result,

requests an Appeals Council review and, if that is unfavorable,

petitions for judicial review.

A *reconsideration* consists of a review of existing paperwork and applications by someone not previously involved in denying eligibility. During the reconsideration, applicants can submit additional medical documentation to support their cases.

The *hearing* provides another opportunity for someone not previously involved in denying eligibility to review appealed cases. Oral and written testimony can be presented at this stage of the appeals process, and the applicants can be assisted by family members, friends, lawyers, or paralegals.

The *Appeals Council* and the *judicial review* are two more levels of review. They allow less participation by applicants and other interested individuals.

It is important to note that about half of all denials are overturned, and benefits granted, at the administrative hearings stage. However, less than 10 percent of the people denied benefits at the earlier stages ever appeal in the first place.

Medicare

Since Medicare almost automatically covers individuals age sixty-five and older, there are fewer problems with people being refused eligibility (coverage often depends on an individual's eligibility for Social Security old-age and disability benefits). Once eligible for Medicare, a beneficiary is eligible for benefits under Parts A and B of the program. (For more information on Medicare, see appendix 1.)

- Part A's major benefit is that it pays for all hospitalization costs of Medicare beneficiaries after the patient pays a single annual deductible ($560 in 1989). In 1989, under the recently passed congressional catastrophic care bill, a supplemental premium is imposed based on a beneficiary's federal income tax liability, up to $800 per enrollee. Under very limited circumstances, Part A benefits will also pay part of the cost for a patient to stay in a Skilled Nursing Facility (SNF), a special nursing home that provides a substantial amount of medical care, for up to 150 days. The SNF coinsurance amount a patient is required to pay is 20 percent of the nationwide average per-day cost for eight days ($25.50 a day in 1989). (For more information on using Medicare to cover SNF costs, see chapter 3 and appendix 1.)

  Under certain conditions, Part A also pays for home health care, including physical and speech therapy, and hospice care for terminally ill beneficiaries.

- Part B's major benefit is that it pays for 80 percent of the approved fee for doctors' services. If a doctor charges more than the amount set aside by Medicare for the service, the beneficiary must pay the remaining 20 percent of the approved fee and the rest of the full amount charged by the doctor. However, Medicare will pay for covered Part B expenses after the first $1,370 of out-of-pocket costs in 1990. The monthly premium for Part B is $27.90 in 1989 and will increase thereafter.

  Part B also covers outpatient hospital services, home health visits under certain conditions, and other medical and health services, such as ambulance transportation, home dialysis equipment, independent laboratory tests, and oral surgery.

Neither Part A nor Part B covers custodial (general) nursing home care, personal care, day care, respite service (except for eighty hours per year), or less specialized nursing care. Medicare beneficiaries do, however, have the opportunity to appeal denials of other specific claims in Part A or Part B. If claims are denied and then appealed, many beneficiaries do end up receiving coverage for at least a portion of the service (or bill) that was originally denied. Once again, all it takes is determination.

An individual who disagrees with a decision regarding his or her eligibility for Medicare has the same appeal rights as under the SSDI program. These rights include the opportunity for an appeal to an administrative law judge (ALJ) and the right to judicial review of an ALJ decision.

A beneficiary who disagrees with a denial, in whole or in part, of a claim submitted under Part A of Medicare can request reconsideration by the fiscal intermediary. If the amount in question is $100 or more, the beneficiary is entitled to a hearing before an ALJ. The beneficiary can also seek judicial review of the ALJ's decision, if the amount in question is $1,000 or more.

A beneficiary who disagrees with a denial, in whole or in part, of a claim submitted under Part B of Medicare can request reconsideration by the carrier. If the amount in controversy is $500 or more, the beneficiary is entitled to a hearing before an ALJ. The beneficiary can also seek judicial review of the ALJ's decision if the amount in controversy is $1,000 or more.

It is important to refer to the Medicare denial notices for each claim, as they will indicate a time limit for appealing decisions. These time limits are ordinarily strictly enforced.

Medicaid

Most people become eligible for Medicaid in one of three ways. First, many people establish eligibility for Medicaid through receipt of Supplemental Security Income (SSI) benefits. Another group of people establish eligibility when they enter a nursing home and have insufficient income and resources to pay for their costs of care. These first two classes of recipients are referred to as *mandatory* and *optional categorically needy,* respectively.

The third group of recipients is referred to as the *medically needy.* Approximately two-thirds of the states have a program for the medically needy that assists at least some persons whose high medical care costs offset a higher than usual amount of allowable income. Resources may still not ordinarily exceed approximately $2,000.

Being determined eligible for Medicaid does not mean that the services people need are covered under each state's program. States have wide discretion in deciding which services will be reimbursed. Most states provide a mix of inpatient and outpatient services, however, including hospital care, nursing home care, physician services, and prescribed drugs.

It is nearly impossible to give any hard-and-fast rules about appealing eligibility and services under Medicaid, because each state runs its own program and has its own rules. There are some common characteristics, however, since all states must comply with federal law.

Medicaid recipients have a right to appeal decisions by requesting an administrative hearing (called a *fair hearing*). This hearing is requested from the agency administering the Medicaid program in that state. Ordinarily, a decision must be rendered within ninety days of the date of the request for a hearing. Dissatisfied recipients may then seek further administrative review, in some states, or may seek judicial review.

Several years ago, statistics showed that fewer than 5 percent of all recipients appealed to Medicaid in cases in which their coverage was wrongfully withheld, ended, or denied. Sadly, a state can be penalized by the federal government for paying too much or for paying for an uncovered service but not for wrongfully paying too little or denying service in the first place. The system does not provide any motivation for Medicaid program employees to grant benefits.

PART

3

When Someone Can No Longer Make Decisions

11

Competence and Incompetence
What They Mean

Overview

People must make decisions almost from the time they are born. They start out simply—what game to play, what to eat for lunch, what to wear—and then progress to much harder decisions about marriage, career, and finances. The one constant that ties all these things together is that they are decisions that have to be made. Normally, people are able to make their own decisions, choosing the personal or professional options that make them happiest. But what happens when people are no longer able to make decisions? And who is qualified to decide that people can no longer make decisions?

These are not simple questions. And in most cases, there are no simple answers. Adult children may have witnessed their parents' increased senility or inability to understand decisions that need to be made. They may instinctively know that their parents are incapable of making decisions, but that does not mean the adult children have an instant legal right to make decisions for them (in some states, certain family members are given an automatic right to make certain medical decisions for incompetent relatives; for more information, see chapter 14). Besides, who is to say that the parents aren't still able to make some decisions? Or that they are able to make decisions but in a less sophisticated manner than their children expect? Also, people are often less willing to accept the same "silly" or "foolish" decision from elderly people that they would from younger adults. The problem is that elderly people are faced with some of the most difficult decisions of all, decisions of life and death, and they need to be competent to make those decisions—or have guardians or other representatives to make decisions for them.

Competence and *incompetence* are legal terms for someone's ability—or inability—to make informed, rational decisions. Elderly individuals are more likely than the rest of the adult population to become incompetent to make decisions. They may become so because of depression, grief, loneliness, the effects of prescribed drugs or painkillers, or a particular disease. *Dementia,* a medical term for the slow loss of brain function that gradually makes people incompetent, affects up to 10 percent of people over age sixty-five, and 20 percent of people over age eighty. Dementia can be caused by more than seventy illnesses (the most common of which is Alzheimer's disease); its symptoms include memory loss, inability to remember words, inability to care for oneself, personality and behavioral changes, and a confusion over time and place. There is no cure for Alzheimer's disease or for some other illnesses that cause dementia, and often no available drugs that work without making patients confused and incompetent. Despite that, problems keep presenting themselves, and decisions must be made, whether people are competent to make them or not.

When individuals are no longer able to make decisions, there are a number of legal tools that can give their decision-making power to other people. These tools, including living wills, durable powers of attorney, guardianships, conservatorships, and representative payee appointments, are explained in other chapters in this book. To know when these tools should go into effect, however, it is important to understand competence and incompetence and the situations in which they are likely to matter.

The Kinds of Decisions That May Need to Be Made for an Individual

Financial, medical, and personal decisions are the three most important categories of decisions that may need to be made for an individual. These categories are briefly discussed below. It is difficult to give any hard-and-fast rules, or even suggestions, for making decisions about them, because each case is unique. Other problems arise because different patients may have different levels of ability to make decisions, or different levels of incompetence, as discussed later in this chapter.

Financial Decisions

Bills don't stop arriving when people become too ill or confused to pay them. Car payments, monthly rent checks or mortgage payments, insurance premiums, and credit card debts still need to be paid. When people become incompetent to manage their own finances, the surest and least complicated way to have other people take over is to have planned ahead. Obviously, such planning should be done before an individual becomes incompetent (for more information, see chapters 5 and 12).

When no advance planning has been done, putting others in charge can be more difficult and more expensive. The reasons for the difficulty (and the expense) are simple: the law tries to protect people from being taken advantage of, or from having their money stolen by corrupt or unethical people. Often, when people who have not planned ahead become incompetent, their closest relatives or friends start to make decisions for them on an informal basis. Patients' Social Security checks can be assigned to others under the representative payee system (see chapter 13). Bankers, lawyers, and stockbrokers, however, may be less willing to simply accept that people other than their original clients are now in charge (see chapter 14).

Decisions about Medical Treatment, Nontreatment, and Experimental Treatment

Obviously, the most important decisions that can be made for other persons are those affecting their life and death. Usually, in the case of sick and elderly individuals, these decisions must be made in hospitals or nursing homes. One possible treatment decision is *nontreatment,* or a decision not to treat patients, a decision often resulting in death.

Deciding not to treat patients can frighten and upset everybody: family members, friends, doctors, nurses, lawyers, judges, and hospital and nursing home administrators. Such decisions may also pose serious legal problems, and individual states, courts, hospitals, and nursing homes often have their own rules about accepting a request for nontreatment. Too, individual state laws must be consulted. Some states have family consent laws that automatically allow family members of incompetent patients to make certain medical decisions for them (see chapter 14).

Another highly personal medical decision that may have to be faced is whether or not patients should participate in scientific research experiments that may eventually lead doctors to find a cure for their illnesses. This is a difficult decision, particularly because it's unlikely that any cure, if eventually found, will arrive in time for patients to benefit from it. *By law, only competent patients or patients with guardians or other legally authorized representatives can make the decision to be part of a research experiment, and both federal and state laws must be consulted on this matter* (interested individuals should discuss this issue with their lawyers). Many states, however, do not have laws prohibiting people from making decisions about someone else's research participation, and so it is a difficult question for both the decision makers and the research groups. Like most decisions, this one is best made while patients are still competent.

Many people believe that patients who cannot themselves weigh the risks and benefits of research should probably not participate in it. Yet research is vital to finding cures. If research participation is a possibility and patients are incompetent to agree to it, the following questions need to be answered:

- Is the research dangerous, painful, or physically difficult?
- What are the benefits to patients if they participate?
- Are the possible benefits, either to patients or to society, important enough for others to agree to it on behalf of patients?
- Is it what the patients would have wanted?

For more information, see chapter 14.

Personal Decisions

Personal decisions that need to be made are as varied as the people making them. Briefly, they include where to live, what to wear, whom to befriend or associate with, whether to vote, whom to marry, whether to drive a car, what activities or groups to join, whether to donate one's bodily organs after death, and so on.

The Concept of Competence

If people are considered mentally competent, they are assumed to have a particular set of mental skills and abilities. In a strictly legal sense, people are presumed competent unless they are legally declared incompetent, in the same way that those accused of a crime are presumed innocent until proven guilty.

Basically, doctors and judges call patients *competent* if they are

aware of who they are (their name);

aware of time (what day and year it is);

aware of place (where they are);

capable of understanding the diagnosis of their illness;

capable of understanding how their illness is likely to progress;

capable of making a choice between real options;

able to make reasonable, thoughtful decisions based on rational reasons and to appreciate the consequences of those decisions.

Levels of Competence and Incompetence

Competence to make decisions is not like a light switch that turns on or off. Many elderly people may be partially competent, that is, able to make some decisions but not others. Or they may be intermittently competent—more lucid or clearheaded on some days than on others.

In making medical decisions, the competence of patients to agree to (or refuse) treatment could be evaluated in terms of how fully they understand the information about their treatment options. Here, patients fall roughly into three categories in their abilities to agree to or refuse treatment:

1. *Some patients are completely incompetent to consent to or refuse treatment. The most obvious case would be patients in a coma or those who are otherwise unaware of their surroundings.* Some patients may be able to recognize certain people or things but still be unable to make or communicate decisions. If treatments were suggested, patients either could not answer at all or would not make sense when they did answer.

2. *Other patients are partially competent. They may be able to answer some simple questions but probably not any complex ones.* They may understand that they are being asked a question, and they may answer it, but they aren't likely to fully understand their treatment options and thus cannot give an informed opinion or answer to the question. Good examples of this state would be patients who cannot repeat back much of the information given them about their treatment options and patients who refuse all treatment but have no understanding that they are ill.

3. *Still other patients are competent to agree to or refuse treatment. They understand and appreciate the possible risks and benefits of various treatment options, as well as how*

the information applies to them. Simply understanding (or repeating back) the information is not enough; they must also grasp the realities of their situation.

It is important to remember that competence is not a simple matter of patients agreeing with proposed treatments, nor is incompetence the same as a difference of opinion. *Patients are much more likely to have their competence questioned if they disagree with what their doctors or families want to do, and it is important to keep this factor in mind. Just because patients disagree does not automatically mean they are incompetent to make decisions.*

Finally, out of respect for patients and their dignity, they should be encouraged and allowed to make as many decisions as possible, for as long as possible.

Competence to Make Specific Decisions

Another way of looking at competence is to make it *decision-specific,* or to ask the question, Is this person competent to make this specific decision? In this way, decisions can be roughly broken down into the following categories:

- *Trivial decisions,* such as what to eat, what to wear, and what to do.
- *Minor decisions,* such as what clothing to buy, whether to agree to less important treatments, and whether to participate in certain activities.
- *Important decisions,* such as whether to have surgery, whether to take medications that may have strong side effects, whether to take part in research experiments, whether to make large financial investments, and whether to sell property.
- *Major decisions,* such as whether to enter or leave a nursing home or other health care facility and whether to appoint a guardian or other decision maker.
- *Life-and-death decisions,* such as whether to agree to risky surgery, medications, or other treatments and whether to refuse treatment or discontinue life-prolonging treatments.

De Facto Incompetence and De Facto Surrogates

Ideally, everyone should be allowed to stay in control and make the decisions he or she is capable of making until the time he or she dies. Partially competent people, for instance, would make those decisions they are competent to make, and intermittently competent people would make decisions when they were capable of making them. But real life does not always follow the ideal, or even the rules of the court, and many people are judged and treated as incompetent by their doctors, family members, and friends without ever having been examined by a psychiatrist or declared legally incompetent.

Most clearly incompetent patients never go through a court hearing for a formal determination of their incompetence. Instead, their doctors and family members decide they are incompetent and the family begins making decisions for them. These patients are called *de facto incompetent,* and their family members become *de facto surrogates.* Court guardianship hearings that determine whether patients are incompetent—and if so, appoint guardians for them—can be expensive, upsetting, and time-consuming for both families and patients. Such hearings are therefore often avoided. (For more information on guardianship hearings, see chapter 12.) The nonlegal alternative explained above works well in many cases, and disagreements between the family and the health care facility can usually be resolved without anyone's needing to go to court.

De facto surrogates can, however, run into problems if courts have not declared patients incompetent, or appointed individuals to make their decisions. Problems are more likely to arise if de facto surrogates want patients taken off life-support systems or if they refuse life-prolonging treatments. *In other words, the more controversial the decisions, the more likely that hospitals, nursing homes, and family members who disagree with the proposed decisions will insist that decision makers be formally appointed by a court or that a court formally agree with the decision being made.* The reverse is also true, and family members can take health care facilities to court over decisions with which they disagree.

How Health Care Professionals Can Help Determine a Patient's Competence

Health care professionals taking care of elderly patients can and should be involved with determining whether those patients are competent to make decisions or are incompetent and in need of a guardian or some other type of surrogate decisionmaker. Although such involvement regularly occurs as a practical matter, only the courts can legally declare people incompetent. Because health care professionals work with many patients, they are often able to use their experience to help them decide if patients are competent or not. Often, questions about the competence of patients first arise when discussing a proposed treatment.

When health care professionals and family members fear that patients are incompetent, they should remember that competence and incompetence are not divided by a definite line. Patients may be more or less competent depending on the time or day, where they are, temporary medical problems, their reaction to medication they are receiving, and the presence or absence of people who may be trying to pressure them into making a particular decision. *Giving patients the same information under different circumstances—such as in their own homes instead of doctors' offices or during different times of the day—may help. Changing or temporarily lessening their medication may also make a difference. Also, patients who take a long time to decide should not automatically be viewed as incompetent; it may simply take them a while to come to a decision.*

If patients are thought to be incompetent and there are strong disagreements about how to treat them, then guardians for them may have to be appointed by a court. This is particularly true if family members and health care professionals cannot agree on how to proceed.

When courts are asked to appoint a guardian, health care professionals are often asked to evaluate the patient in question and to give information and opinions on whether or not the patient is incompetent and in need of a guardian. Courts may also ask other experts to evaluate patients. Normally, experts would be doctors or psychiatrists, although nurses may also have a great deal of information and insight based on their contact with patients.

Policies for Evaluating a Patient's Competence

There is no precise medical test that proves patients are competent or incompetent. When patients are called *incompetent,* that label is really based on the personal and expert opinions of the family, the doctor, and other individuals. Many nursing homes and hospitals, however, have general guidelines or written policies to help them evaluate patients' abilities to make decisions. Those guidelines or policies should include

  who in the institution has the responsibility for deciding if patients are competent or incompetent;

Competence and Incompetence 155

how such decisions should be made; and

what kinds of questions patients should be asked.

An institution's policy should require that several different kinds of experts participate in the decision. Although the patients' doctors are usually the ones in charge of such an evaluation, other health professionals and family members can and should help them in making the decision. Nurses or nurse's aides, for instance, may have noticed behavior changes, and family members and friends can tell if patients are acting strangely or are making decisions that don't match their lifelong opinions.

The use of family members, friends, doctors, and other experts to decide whether patients are incompetent is also important in other ways—it gives institutions a justification for deciding whether patients are competent or incompetent without going to court for a formal decision.

The Geriatric Mental Status Examination

The evaluation of patients by medical experts should begin with a complete *geriatric mental status examination*. This examination should include observations about the patients and answers to the types of questions listed below. (Much of the following information is taken from Marshall Kapp's *Preventing Malpractice in Long Term Care: Strategies for Risk Management,* listed in the "Additional Reading" section.)

1. How does the patient dress?
2. Is the patient clean?
3. Does he or she make eye contact?
4. How does the patient talk?
5. How does he or she move or walk?
6. Does the patient make any unusual movements?
7. What is the mood of the patient?
8. Is the patient's mood normal for his or her situation?
9. Does the patient's ability to think match his or her level of education?
10. Does the patient's knowledge match his or her career or work experience?

11. Can the patient remember things that just happened?

12. Does he or she remember things that happened a short time ago?

13. Does he or she remember things that happened a long time ago?

14. Is the patient acting in a dangerous or self-destructive way?

15. Does the patient understand his or her problems?

16. Does the patient know the date?

17. Is the patient aware of where he or she is?

18. Does the patient know who he or she is?

19. Does the patient recognize specific people?

20. Does the patient have any delusions, hallucinations, or illusions?

When trying to decide if patients are competent to agree to or refuse particular medical treatments, still more questions need to be asked. In these cases, patients should be asked what they think will happen if they decide to accept or refuse treatment, and whether they understand. (Much of the information that follows is based on the article "Competence to Refuse Medical Treatment: Autonomy vs. Paternalism," by George Annas and Joan Densberger, listed in the "Additional Reading" section.)

1. What is their present physical condition?

2. What treatment is being suggested?

3. What does the doctor think will happen if treatment is refused?

4. What does the doctor think will happen if treatment is accepted?

5. What are the other available treatments?

6. What is likely to happen if those other treatments are accepted?

Competence and incompetence are, as shown in this chapter, not always clear-cut; and the people involved with determining an individual's ability to make decisions should proceed with all the care and caution necessary to taking such a grave, and usually irrevocable, step.

12

Guardians and Conservators
When, If, and How

Overview

One of the most significant concerns of older people is the potential need for others to make financial and personal decisions for them in the event they become unable to make such decisions themselves. Some elderly individuals reach a point when, because of either disease or accident, they experience mental confusion or physical limitations that prevent them from attending to everyday needs, such as paying bills, shopping, or cooking.

The court's appointment of guardians or conservators is the most common legal mechanism for putting in place the needed surrogate decision-makers, or people who make decisions on behalf of other individuals. It is also, however, the most dramatic and restrictive form of legal intervention that can be imposed on aged individuals.

The state statutes and court decisions governing guardianship vary significantly from state to state. Even within each state, practices may vary greatly depending on the statute under which a guardianship proceeding is begun. In some states, different guardianship statutes exist for incapacitated adults, minors, and developmentally disabled or retarded individuals. Other variables include the beliefs and practices of individual judges that influence the nature and results of the proceedings. Because of all these variations and uncertainties, this chapter does not attempt to describe the laws or procedures as they apply to any one region or courthouse. Rather, it describes, in general terms, the process and consequences of having a guardianship or conservatorship imposed.

No one likes the idea of not having the capacity or right to make the decisions that shape his or her life. Even so, by understanding the purpose and uses of guardianship and alternatives to it, older individuals and their family members can often plan ahead to keep as much of their individual autonomy, or freedom to make their own decisions, as possible. Sometimes individuals may be able to use legal tools other than guardianship that still provide for their personal and property management. Better yet, with a little advance planning, elderly people can arrange for these surrogate decisions to be made according to directions they have written in the event they become incapacitated (these legal alternatives are best described in separate chapters; see chapters 4 and 5).

What Are Guardianship and Conservatorship?

Guardianship and conservatorship are really just two sides of the same coin; the two words are often used interchangeably. The term *guardianship* generally refers to the court's appointment of someone (the *guardian*) to make decisions for and handle the affairs of another person (the *ward*) whom the court has found to be incapacitated or incompetent, that is, unable to make rational decisions and understand their consequences. (For more information, see chapter 11.) Although the formal terms vary from state to state, generally speaking there are two forms of guardianship:

1. *The term* guardian *refers to someone with the legal authority to make decisions regarding the ward's "person."* For example, the guardian has the power to determine where the ward will live, what medical treatment he or she may receive, and other life-style matters. A guardian is appointed only after the court has decided that a person is incompetent.

2. *The term* conservator *generally refers to someone with the legal authority to make decisions regarding the ward's property.* For example, the conservator has the power to manage property, make investments, and pay bills. In some states, the appointment of a conservator does not depend on the court deciding that someone is incompetent. Similarly, in some states a conservatorship can be requested by the individual in need of assistance as well as by other interested persons.

Other terms used to describe the two types of guardians include *guardian of the person, guardian of the estate, conservator of the person, conservator of the estate, curator, and committee. For the purposes of this chapter, unless otherwise stated the term* guardian *or* guardianship *is used to refer to legal decision-making authority over another individual's "person."* Conservator *or* conservatorship *is used to refer to legal decision-making authority over another individual's property and estate.*

A Few Legal Terms and Their Definitions

Because this chapter concerns legal issues, there is no way to get around using legal terms. Thus, some additional terms and definitions are included here to help the reader fully understand the chapter's content. (These terms are also listed in the Glossary.)

Competence; capacity. Terms referring to an individual's ability to think clearly, make rational decisions, and understand their consequences. People who are unable to do so may be termed *incompetent* or *incapacitated* (see chapter 11 for a more complete explanation.)

Probate court. The court involved in handling guardianship and conservatorship petitions in most states (although the name does vary). There is usually a probate court and a probate judge in each county.

Guardian ad litem. A court-appointed individual (not necessarily a lawyer) authorized to represent the ward in a specific matter being heard by the court (or by another official forum that can make decisions affecting the rights of the ward). A guardian *ad litem* has a very limited function and should not be confused with an individual's legal representation by a lawyer.

Hearing. The proceeding in which a judge reviews a petition, hears the evidence, and decides whether someone is competent or incompetent and in need of a guardian or conservator.

Petition. A legal form that must be obtained from a court to start proceedings requesting the appointment of a guardian or conservator. The petition must be completed by stating why a guardian or conservator may be needed and by giving facts about the incapacity or incompetence of the person in question.

Petitioner. The individual who files a petition and requests that a guardianship or conservatorship hearing be held by the court. The petitioner is usually a family member or another person who wants to become the ward's guardian, but it can also be a hospital, nursing home, or social service agency that is asking the court to determine who is responsible for the person in question. Most states allow "any interested party" to act as petitioner.

Ward or respondent. The individual who either has a guardian or is the subject of a guardianship hearing. The term *ward* is typically used after a guardian has been appointed; *respondent* is used during the court process to determine the need for guardianship.

The Implications of Guardianship

Guardianship takes away from wards many important and basic civil rights. Depending on the state, such rights may include the loss of the right to marry, to sue and be sued, to hold licenses (such as a driver's license), to decide where to live, and—in some states—to vote. (In most states, guardians have the same rights and duties toward wards that parents have to minor children.) *Perhaps the most important and basic right that wards lose is the right to self-determination, that is, the ability to make choices about their lives and determine where their own interests lie. In light of these serious losses, guardianship is a drastic action that may be an emotionally painful experience for everyone involved.*

Before initiating guardianship proceedings, one should be convinced that they are truly necessary. Considering the extreme nature of guardianship, it is essential before filing a petition to first explore alternatives, such as trusts, living wills, and durable powers of attorney (see chapters 1, 4, and 5).

Full versus Limited Guardianship Arrangements

Guardianship typically refers to *full,* or *plenary, guardianship,* wherein the guardian has very broad and general powers (the right to make almost all decisions) over the ward.

Some states now allow *limited guardianships,* which means that if a judge finds the respondent to be totally incapacitated, a full/plenary guardianship will be imposed; however, if the judge finds that the respondent can partially take care of himself or herself, a limited guardianship may be imposed. Under a limited guardianship, the powers and duties of the guardian are expressly limited by the court and the ward keeps all the rights and powers that are not turned over to the guardian.

Most states also have even more limited forms of guardianship, such as *temporary* or *emergency guardianship,* when a particular situation requires someone other than the person in question to be able to make immediate decisions. *Single-transaction guardianship,* for one event only (such as the sale of the ward's home), is also possible depending on the state. Sometimes these more limited forms of guardianship may be all that are necessary.

Public Guardianship Programs

The phrase *public guardian* is used very loosely. It often means a guardian of last resort who is paid by public funds, whether that guardian is a government employee or simply some person or organization known to the court to be available to provide such services for a fee.

Some state agencies have public guardianship programs that serve as guardians for people who have no one else able or willing to fill that role (see appendix 21 for a list of states with limited or statewide programs). Public guardians have the same responsibilities as other court-appointed guardians—they decide where wards will live, agree to or refuse medical treatment, determine how wards' assets are used, and so on. In these instances, public guardians are state or county employees who are paid a salary and therefore do not need to charge a fee for services; however, some programs do charge a fee, which is taken out of the ward's estate.

Public guardianship programs, generally understaffed and overworked, are not without problems. Some have been criticized for neglecting wards, sending wards to nursing homes for the sake of convenience, and occasionally misusing funds. Yet they also fill an important need, as incompetent people without guardians must have someone reviewing their cases and making decisions for them.

Recently, a few private nonprofit organizations under state contract have been established to perform the same duties as those of the state-administered programs. Some churches and other nonprofit groups offer these services as well, on a case-by-case basis, generally being paid on an hourly basis. There are also private for-profit agencies that offer, for a fee paid out of the ward's estate, to act as guardians; they take a fee or percentage of assets as payment for services.

When Is Guardianship Necessary and What Triggers a Petition?

Unless an individual has done advance planning and established a durable power of attorney, a trust, or some other mechanism for handling personal affairs and property, a guardianship becomes necessary only when the person is no longer competent.

It is difficult to generalize about the many situations that may result in the filing of a petition for guardianship. Sometimes an individual has lost all capacity to function or communicate (for example, following a severe stroke or a serious accident). Perhaps more typically, an individual experiences no sudden or severe medical problem and retains some ability to function and communicate but may still need someone to help make decisions for him or her.

Four factors usually trigger the filing of a petition for guardianship:

1. *The petitioner believes that the individual is behaving in an unreasonable manner.*
2. *The individual is unwilling or unable to change the behavior that the petitioner sees as unreasonable.*
3. *The unreasonable behavior threatens some facet of the person's life that the petitioner thinks is important.*
4. *The unreasonable behavior is apparent to the outside world.*

For purposes of guardianship, the term *incompetence* has a precise legal meaning. While specific legal standards defining incompetence differ from state to state, they basically involve a two-part test. First, the person must be mentally incapable of giving *informed consent* (that is, be unable to understand the consequences of his or her decisions). Second, as a result of the inability to give informed consent, the person must be incapable of handling his or her own affairs.

When thinking about legal incompetence and the need for guardianship, one must separate the idea of informed consent from subjective terms like *rational* and *reasonable* (for more information on informed consent, see chapter 11). To assess someone's competence based on one's personal views can lead to inappropriate guardianship and the loss of individual rights. After all, what is a rational or reasonable decision for one person with one set of values could be an irrational or unreasonable decision for another person with another set of values.

Before guardianship can be imposed, legal incompetence or incapacity must be proved in court; however, with some of the other alternatives, such as durable powers of attorney, it may not be necessary to go before a judge at all.

Advantages and Disadvantages of Guardianship

The primary advantage of guardianship is that at its best, it appoints an honest and concerned individual to make decisions for an incapacitated person and provides some court oversight. The amount of actual court supervision available to oversee this protection, however, is often limited. For a well-meaning family with a totally incapacitated member, guardianship may be the best solution to an unhappy situation.

There are a number of disadvantages to guardianship. One is the social stigma that some people attach to the phrase *legally incompetent.* If a person's condition is temporary and he or she is able to recover from an illness, accident, or stroke, it may be traumatic to have been previously declared legally incompetent.

Then too, guardianship does not have many practical means of protecting the ward from a corrupt or unethical guardian. Once the ward is declared legally incompetent, he or she is often denied the right to hire a lawyer to get the guardianship order overturned. Decisions to appoint a guardian are often made quickly and without a great deal of evidence being presented. In short, it is not a process designed to give maximum protection to the rights of the ward.

Guardianship is sometimes a last-ditch solution occurring because there has been no adequate advance planning. The incapacitated person's wishes may be better served by one or more of the alternatives listed in chapters 4 and 5.

Although most guardians and conservators do a good job, there is the possibility for abuse if the person appointed does not really have the ward's best interests at heart. Even when states require that financial accountings and personal status reports be provided, abuse or neglect of the ward can and does occur because the overburdened court system does not have the time or the personnel to carefully review these reports. Depending on state laws, guardians may have to file a report each year.

The Duties and Responsibilities of a Guardian

The general boundaries of a guardian's authority to make decisions are set out in state law, case law, and court rules. For any particular case, obligations and/or limitations are spelled out in the court's *order of appointment,* the judge's ruling of how much authority the guardian shall have. (See appendix 26 for a sample order.) In some states, the guardian has only those powers specifically noted in the order. In others, the guardian may be given almost unrestricted authority (though even in these cases, a guardian may have to seek the court's approval for certain serious decisions that strongly influence the life and death of the ward).

In general, a guardian must keep enough contact with the ward to be aware of his or her current condition and needs. Specifically, a guardian may have any or all of the following powers, rights, or duties:

- To determine where and with whom the ward will reside.
- To see to the care, comfort, and maintenance of the ward. (This may include the duty to obtain services for the ward and seeing to the care of the ward's belongings.)
- To consent to medical and professional treatment of the ward. (Such decisions run the gamut from physical examinations, dental examinations, and vaccinations to surgery, after-death organ donation, experimental treatments, and withholding or withdrawing of life-supporting treatment. Depending on state laws and the individual case, guardians may need to get prior court approval to make some of these decisions.)
- To maintain a lawsuit on behalf of the ward.
- To receive and apply any of the ward's money or property to his or her current needs for support and care. (In some places, the guardian must get the court's approval before spending any money. While this arrangement is meant to protect the ward, it can backfire, as when a nursing home demands payment and threatens to discharge the ward before the court gets around to approving the expense.)
- To conserve any of the ward's excess money for his or her future needs.
- To report the condition of the ward and his or her estate to the court.

Some states have additional duties, responsibilities, and restrictions for guardians. *For example, depending on state law and the court orders in a particular case, a guardian may or may not be allowed to place a ward in a nursing home against his or her wishes; in order to do so, the guardian may have to get the court's prior approval.* Some states also require that guardians provide reports on the personal status of wards (see appendix 22 for a list of states that have this requirement).

At What Point Is Conservatorship Necessary?

When an individual becomes incapable of caring for or managing his or her own property and estate, a court-appointed conservator may be necessary if alternatives have not been established through advance planning. As previously noted, in some states conservatorship is not linked to a formal ruling on a person's incompetence. (Sometimes the term *conservatee* is used instead of *ward,* but for the purposes of this chapter, *ward* will be used.)

Also, some states allow an individual in need of assistance to petition the court for conservatorship on his or her own behalf and to nominate the person he or she would like to have serve as conservator.

Advantages and Disadvantages of Conservatorship

The primary advantage of conservatorship is that at its best, it protects the ward from an inexperienced, foolish, or dishonest conservator by imposing court supervision and review of reports and financial accountings.

Unfortunately, many courts do not have the time or staff necessary to monitor conservators and to review their reports as carefully as they should. There are some serious problems with conservators misusing their ward's assets, as was shown recently in a study done by the Associated Press.

Legally, a conservator does not have any power over the ward's "person." However, in having control over a ward's funds, the real powers of a conservator over the ward are substantial.

The Duties and Responsibilities of a Conservator

A conservator is entrusted with the duty to protect, preserve, and wisely invest the ward's property. Most states also require conservators to post a bond (put up their own money) as a financial guarantee that the duties will be performed faithfully. *A conservator is not permitted to gain any personal profit or advantage from dealing with the ward's property or estate.* Some states also require conservators to provide annual or periodic accountings of wards' estates (see appendix 23 for a list of states that have these requirements).

Like the duties of a guardian, the duties of a conservator vary from state to state and depend on the exact amount of authority granted by the court (see appendix 26 for a sample of a court order for conservatorship). In general, a conservator may have the powers, rights, and duties to

invest funds of the estate;

collect, hold, retain, or dispose of assets;

continue or participate in the operation of a business;

handle banking transactions on behalf of the ward;

make ordinary or extraordinary repairs, alterations, or improvements to real estate;

enter into leases either as the lessee or the lessor;

engage in securities transactions on behalf of the ward;

pay the expenses and debts of the ward;

settle or contest a claim;

pay taxes owed by the ward or the ward's estate;

employ persons to assist in the administration of the ward's estate; and

use funds for the support of dependents of the ward.

The Process of Petitioning for Guardianship

The guardianship process begins with the filing of a petition for guardianship in the appropriate court (see appendix 25 for a sample petition). Who can petition a court to hold a guardianship hearing depends on individual state laws, and concerned individuals should ask a lawyer to explain the guardianship statutes in their state. In many states, anyone can file such a petition. Most of the time, however, petitioners are the people who want to become guardians.

Petitioners are usually relatives. About 75 percent of the time a family member serves as the ward's guardian, although the petitioner also can be a social service agency, such as a county health department, Catholic Charities, a senior citizens' center, the visiting nurse association, or "meals on wheels." Social service agencies act as petitioners when they discover people in the community who they believe can't take care of themselves and who refuse offered services. Social service agencies, both because their role is to protect people and because of their own fears of liability if they don't, will often initiate proceedings. Hospitals and nursing homes may also file guardianship petitions (a) just because a patient is old, (b) to determine who is legally responsible for paying an individual's bills, and (c) to find out who is legally authorized to agree to or refuse treatment on behalf of a patient.

Some, but not all, states have preprinted forms that must be completed to petition for guardianship. These forms can usually be found by contacting an organization listed under "Legal Forms" or "Legal Stationers" in the telephone directory.

No matter who files for a hearing or why, all petitions for guardianship must allege (state that the petitioner believes) that the proposed ward is incapable of properly caring for himself or herself or of managing his or her estate. Once the petition has been filed with the appropriate court, a date for a hearing will be set. In many states, a guardian *ad litem* must be appointed by the court to protect the potential ward's interests throughout the legal proceedings.

The court will then send a notice to various individuals, depending on the state. All states except Alabama, Louisiana, and Mississippi require that the proposed ward receive notice of the time and place of the hearing, regardless of his or her mental state. Generally, the guardianship statutes also require that notice be given to a third person, usually a relative. This requirement is to help protect the ward both from his or her own confusion and from a possibly dishonest or unethical petitioner. If the ward is too confused to understand the notice, the third person might ensure that the ward's interests are protected. If the proposed ward wishes to protest the petition, then the notice allows him or her to begin to take steps to fight the proceeding.

Unfortunately, the notices are often inadequate, in that they do not convey what is at stake, what defenses may be raised, or that the proposed ward has the right to be present, hire a lawyer, present evidence, and cross-examine witnesses. Whatever rights prospective wards do have are meaningful only if they are asserted.

When individuals receive such a notice, they should seek the assistance of a lawyer or a trusted friend, insist on being present at the hearing, and make arrangements to do so. Even if people want a guardian or know they need one, they may still want a say in who that person will be and in what areas that person will be authorized to make decisions. Their presence at the hearing will ensure that they can express their opinions and their preferences.

The right to a lawyer, or counsel, at a guardianship hearing depends on the laws of each individual state (see appendix 24 for a list of state requirements for the legal representation of wards). If an individual can afford to personally pay for and hire a lawyer, he or she can always have one. If the individual does not have the money or the mental ability to enter into a lawyer-client relationship, then it is up to state law as to whether the court has to appoint a lawyer for that individual and as to how the lawyer will be paid. *There is no constitutional right to have a court-appointed lawyer at a guardianship hearing. A potential ward should always ask the court to appoint a lawyer if he or she is without one and wishes to contest the need for guardianship.*

Hearings are frequently held very quickly after a petition is filed. Most statutes do not specify the amount of time that must pass between the notice and the hearing, but it is often less than ten days. This short period does not allow much time for the proposed ward to plan a defense.

Hearings are usually held in the absence of the proposed ward. While proposed wards have the right to attend, they may not realize they do or may not understand the importance of attending. They may even believe that a guardian cannot be appointed in their absence. Although some states do require that proposed wards be present at these hearings, even in those states many courts routinely waive the requirement in the belief that it will not help the wards and might aggravate their condition to attend. *The specific rules and regulations surrounding such hearings vary; however, most hearings are held without the proposed ward unless he or she insists on being present.*

Often, no witnesses are called and the court thus makes its decision based on affidavits (sworn statements by individuals) and written doctors' reports. In 1987 the Associated Press conducted a study of 2,200 guardianship hearings, finding that approximately 30 percent of them did not require that medical evidence be presented.

Decisions in these hearings are usually made by a judge, not a jury, in a probate court. In some cases, a jury is allowed only on request. Each state has a different *standard of proof,* that is, type of evidence required before a judge can decide that someone is incompetent and in need of a guardian. In some states, the standard is simply what the judge feels has a 51 percent weight, or likelihood of being true—legally called *preponderance of evidence.* Other states have more restrictive laws that demand clear and convincing evidence. *Ordinarily, a decision is made at the end of the hearing.*

Guardians (and conservators) are paid according to state law. It is not unusual for them to receive, each year, a certain percentage of disbursements (the amount the guardian or conservator has paid out of the ward's estate on the ward's behalf). They also may receive a percentage of the remaining estate when the guardianship or conservatorship ends, usually on the death of the ward.

The cost of a guardianship proceeding is generally taken out of the estate of the proposed ward—whether guardianship is granted or not and whether the proposed ward wants it or not. The cost will vary from case to case but will almost always include fees for the petitioner's lawyer and the guardian *ad litem,* bond costs, court costs, and, depending on the case, the lawyer for the proposed ward. It is not unusual to pay $2,000 to $4,000 for a normal guardianship hearing. In contested cases, in which disagreements are expressed by the ward or other individuals, the fees can run very high indeed. If no estate exists, then the cost is paid for out of public funds or by the petitioner.

The Process of Petitioning for Conservatorship

The process of petitioning for conservatorship is similar to that for guardianship. It typically requires the filing of a petition with the probate court in the county in which the potential ward lives. In some states, the court process, notice requirements, and so on, are the same as those for guardianship. In other states, the law does not require that a person be declared incompetent in order to appoint a conservator; rather, the court must find that the person is in need of protection because he or she cannot manage his or her own financial matters. Because this latter situation is considered less serious than being declared incompetent is, many of these states have fewer notice requirements and other procedural protections for wards for conservatorship than for wards for guardianship.

As with guardianships, some states have preprinted forms that need to be completed to petition for conservatorship. These forms can be found by contacting an organization listed under "Legal Forms" or "Legal Stationers" in the telephone directory.

Finally, some states allow for *voluntary conservatorship,* in which the individual who wants assistance petitions the court for the appointment of a conservator.

Removing a Guardian and Terminating a Guardianship Arrangement

At any point during a guardianship or conservatorship, most states allow any interested person to ask the court for an order removing a guardian or conservator. In some cases, the court itself may initiate action to dismiss a guardian.

A guardian may be dismissed for several reasons, such as the mismanagement or waste of the ward's assets, or the fact that the guardian has become physically or mentally unable to continue serving as guardian. Similarly, guardians (and conservators) can always petition the court if it is no longer possible for them to continue in that position; in such cases, the court will appoint a new guardian. A guardianship may also be completely ended if a ward recovers sufficiently to handle his or her own affairs.

To fully understand the seriousness of imposing a guardianship, one needs to examine the restoration process required for the courts to find a ward healthy enough not to need a guardian. This process usually has to be initiated by formal procedures, involving petitioning the court that granted the guardianship in the first place. Although notice to interested individuals is usually required, the ward has even fewer legal safeguards in this process than during the appointment of a guardian. As previously noted, once the ward is declared legally incompetent, he or she may lose the ability to hire a lawyer. The restoration hearing is generally considered more of a review of current medical judgment than a fight between the guardian and the ward.

Some statutes allow for partial as well as complete restoration of the rights of the ward. Many statutes barely address the restoration process at all, probably because of the unfounded belief that individuals rarely recover enough to be considered competent. As a result, the statutes generally do not specify the period that must pass between additional petitions for restoration if the first petition is denied. In addition, the appeals procedure is not clearly defined. Finally, it should be noted that even where the restoration petition is successful, there is usually no way to erase the social or professional stigma of the ward's having been declared incompetent in the first place. In short, a guardianship is not an easy matter to undo.

The Importance of Considering Alternative Methods

With advance planning, there are a number of alternatives for handling the affairs of a mentally or physically incapacitated person. Without such planning, the choices are few, and guardianship may be the only real option. For more information on options that can be used instead of guardianship, see chapters 1, 4, and 5.

13

When Social Security Payments Go to Someone Else

Overview

Most people who receive Social Security payments are able to manage and spend their money as they see fit. However, when disease or confusion makes it impossible for an individual to handle a bank account, pay bills, or make financial decisions, someone else usually takes over those responsibilities for him or her. In the case of Social Security benefits, there is a specific term for people who are appointed to manage and supervise money paid to Social Security recipients—they are called *representative payees,* or just *payees.*

Payees have a very important position, and their honesty is perhaps the most crucial aspect of it. Payees are in charge of other people's money at a time when those people are unable to make their own financial decisions or even to protect themselves from a payee's misuse of their money. There are laws surrounding how these funds can and should be used, but in order to understand them, it is necessary first to understand the system.

A payee is an individual or an institution, such as a nursing home, board and care home, or mental hospital, that is *designated* or appointed, to receive Social Security payments on behalf of the *beneficiary,* or the person who would ordinarily receive them. Once designated, the payee is the only person (or institution) who has the legal right to spend the beneficiary's money.

While this situation works well most of the time, it is not without problems. A 1983 study evaluating payees showed that nearly 20 percent of them performed unsatisfactorily and/or misused the benefit checks they received. The study, conducted by the Social Security Administration (SSA), did not evaluate parents or spouses who acted as payees, and so it is possible that the real number of problems could be even greater than 20 percent.

Among other protections designed to combat the misuse of funds is that payees are now required to submit a report every year showing how they have spent beneficiaries' money. This reporting requirement was instituted in 1987, after a court forced SSA to review how beneficiaries' monies were being spent.

This chapter focuses on when individuals may need a payee, how to get one appointed, and how payees should handle beneficiaries' money.

When Does the Social Security Administration Designate Representative Payees?

The SSA has the right to designate a payee whenever it appears that a beneficiary would be helped by having one. *A beneficiary does not have to be legally declared incompetent, that is, unable to make rational decisions and understand their consequences, before a payee can be appointed* (for more information, see chapter 11), *and by law, the SSA must appoint a payee for any beneficiary who is diagnosed as an alcoholic or a drug addict.*

SSA has guidelines for determining whether or not to designate a payee. SSA believes that payees are needed for

individuals who are legally incompetent or mentally incapabable of managing their benefits;

individuals who are physically incapable of managing their benefits; and

beneficiaries under the age of eighteen, unless they receive Social Security benefits in their own name, are serving in the military, are living alone and supporting themselves, are parents and are capable of supporting themselves, or are four months away from being age eighteen.

Qualifying to Be a Representative Payee

When the SSA designates a payee, it certifies benefit payments to that individual. It is important that a payee be carefully investigated because the beneficiary must depend on him or her for the purchase of food, clothing, and shelter. Although the investigation should be completed before the payee is certified, the law requires that the investigation be completed no later than forty-five days after certification. Information used in selecting a payee, as well as SSA's preferred order of selection, can be found in appendix 28.

The SSA assigns a high preference to guardians to act as payees, although in rare instances it will appoint someone other than the guardian. A few states have public guardianship programs that fulfill the same purpose as payees (see appendix 21 for a list of states with public guardianship programs).

Under SSA policy, the person who wants to be considered for the position of payee must complete an application that covers his or her qualifications to be a payee, his or her relationship to the beneficiary, the availability of other potential payees, and how he or she would spend the benefits if appointed payee. The application also requires the potential payee to state that he or she is aware of reporting requirements and understands his or her legal liability for the deliberate misuse of funds. A copy of the application appears in appendix 27.

Once the application is completed, the potential payee must be interviewed by an SSA field office. This interview, which usually takes place in person, is a way for the SSA to evaluate an applicant's qualifications and explain the responsibilities of being a payee. *Sometimes the SSA will decide to contact other individuals who know the beneficiary and who are aware of the situation. This is likely to happen when there is more than one applicant, when the beneficiary does not live with the applicant, or when the SSA thinks that other individuals may have important information about the beneficiary or the applicant.*

The SSA prefers to appoint as a payee someone who lives with or has responsibility for the beneficiary. If more than one person qualifies as payee, the SSA will try to appoint the person who demonstrates the most concern and responsibility for the beneficiary's health and well-being.

In most instances, the SSA will contact the beneficiary directly, which allows the beneficiary to state a preference for who should be his or her payee. The SSA is required to contact the beneficiary if he or she lives alone, is in a facility that is not approved by either Medicare or Medicaid, and is not in close contact with the potential payee. These requirements allow the SSA to better determine the applicant's qualifications.

When an application is submitted, the SSA sends a written notice about the proceedings to the beneficiary (and his or her legal representative, if one exists). One notice is sent before the SSA appoints a potential payee, thereby giving the beneficiary a chance to object or to submit more information. A second notice is sent after the appointment has been made. *The beneficiary (or his or her legal representative) has the right to appeal both the SSA's decision that a payee is needed and the appointment of a specific payee.* Only a beneficiary who is declared legally incompetent, is diagnosed as an alcoholic or drug addict, or is a minor is not allowed to appeal the need for a payee.

If the SSA believes that a payee's use of funds needs to be carefully tracked, it will review the payee's performance within four months. A special review also takes place if the payee receives a large lump-sum payment, which may happen when a beneficiary wins an appeal for disability payments or waits a long time before filing a disability claim. In such instances, special payee evaluation procedures go into effect and the SSA field office monitors the payee's performance more closely than usual.

Institutional Payees: Rules and Regulations

A federal, state, or private institution can also be appointed as the payee for a patient in its care. Obviously, this situation can pose problems, since the institution is in charge of deciding what care to provide, providing it, and then paying itself for it. Federal and state institutions, such as nursing homes or mental hospitals, are investigated and monitored by the SSA through its on-site review program. Private institutions, such as room and board homes, are investigated and monitored by the SSA in the same way as individual applicants for payee positions are; however, because many room and board homes are not regulated by any federal or state law, it may not be wise to designate one as a payee.

An institutional payee must deduct its normal fee from the benefit check it receives on behalf of a particular patient. This fee must go toward only the care of the patient who is the beneficiary and must be written down in an *earnings record* or statement of how the patient's money is being used. The earnings record is then submitted to the SSA for review every year. An institution that receives Medicaid funds and Social Security checks for a specific patient is allowed to use the latter only for that patient's personal needs.

Responsibilities of Payees

Payees can easily be confused by all the possible uses for a beneficiary's Social Security checks. *Generally, the SSA believes that benefits should be spent on a beneficiary's maintenance care, such as rent, food, clothing, and medical treatment.* Payees should not use benefit checks to pay for any of a patient's old debts; under federal law, money from benefit checks is exempt from collection agencies or any of the patient's creditors.

If any money from the benefit checks is left over after the patient's current care needs are paid for, it should be kept in a separate account that is held in trust for the beneficiary.

Payee Misuse of Funds

Before 1987, the SSA was not responsible for requiring or reviewing a payee's accounting statements of how a beneficiary's money was spent. In the past, such monitoring was done only in special circumstances. *However, a lawsuit over the possible misuse of funds resulted in the Supreme Court's requiring all individual payees to submit annual accounting statements to the SSA. To comply with the court, the SSA now sends out accounting forms to be filled out by each payee.*

The Social Security Disability Benefits Reform Act of 1984 used to exempt parents and spouses of beneficiaries from submitting accounting statements. As a result of court actions, however, they, too, must now submit annual accounting statements. By law, the SSA must request these accounting statements from all payees except for those federal and state institutions which are reviewed under the SSA's on-site review program.

The SSA's internal studies show that these annual accounting statements are useful not only for finding and investigating the misuse of funds but also for educating and monitoring payees on their use of beneficiaries' funds. Payees who do not submit accounting statements are usually those who misuse benefit checks. While the misuse of funds can be investigated and proved through reports submitted by people other than payees, the annual signed accounting form is helpful to the SSA in successfully prosecuting payees for fraud.

Payees are legally liable for any intentional misuse of benefit funds. Punishment for the misuse of funds can include large fines and even prison sentences. Payees who are first-time offenders in misusing funds may receive one-year prison sentences and be fined $5,000; second-time offenders may face five years in prison and $25,000 in fines. In addition, offenders may have to repay beneficiaries all the money that was misused.

Accounting Procedures for Payees

At least once a year, payees are asked to complete a "representative payee report," an accounting form (see appendix 29 for a sample form). This relatively short accounting form comes with the SSA's full instructions on how to complete it. It asks payees for information on beneficiary custody, how much involvement payees have with beneficiaries, the use of benefits, the amount spent on beneficiaries' personal needs, and the amount and investment of any money left over from benefit checks. The SSA then reviews the report and checks it against SSA guidelines for how payees should use benefit funds. If the report is accepted, nothing more happens until payees fill out the next report (which, in turn, is also reviewed).

If payees don't seem to understand how to complete the form or if they leave out some of the more important information, the SSA will try to contact them directly to resolve the problem. If the SSA is unable to get in touch with these payees or cannot resolve the problem by discussing it with them, then the SSA field office will fill out a "representative payee evaluation report" (see appendix 30 for a sample evaluation form). This report is also used if the regular short accounting form is missing important information or if payees do not submit the regular accounting forms.

Evaluation reports request a much more detailed accounting of the use of all benefit funds and also include an SSA interview with the payee in question. The SSA field office is then responsible for checking and evaluating in writing all the information obtained in these reports. The field office is also responsible for initiating any follow-up actions that may be necessary. For example, the field office may directly contact beneficiaries or their custodians in order to verify all payee statements.

On-Site Review of Federal and State Institutions

The law requires that all state institutions covered by the SSA's on-site review program be audited at least once every three years. The review program is designed to evaluate the performance of state institutions that serve as payees. The SSA's general policies and procedures for on-site reviews are as follows:

- The ten SSA regional offices are responsible for conducting on-site reviews in states that fall under their region. In conducting reviews, the SSA staff must discuss specific payee procedures with institutional staff, audit patient accounts, interview the caretaking staff, and observe beneficiaries in the institution.

- The SSA conducts an in-depth review of how an institution uses patient benefits and checks to see whether SSA policies for the use of funds are being followed. Institutions under the on-site review program do not need to complete individual accounting forms for each patient, which minimizes their paperwork.
- Once the review is completed, a report on the SSA's findings is given to state health officials. During the review process, officials from the institution or the state may ask SSA staff to meet with them and discuss SSA recommendations.

Information obtained from the accounting process or other sources may lead the SSA to conduct a more thorough investigation of an institutional payee's performance. It may also lead the SSA to question whether or not the institution is suited to be a payee. These investigations may result in the SSA's replacing the payee or prosecuting the institution for the misuse of funds.

Replacing a Payee

Replacing a payee is always an alternative, and a new payee may be appointed even if no misuse of beneficiary funds has occurred. Payees may be replaced when

they do not comply with SSA guidelines for the use of beneficiary funds;

there is sufficient evidence that they have misused funds;

they die or are unable to fulfill the responsibilities of a payee; or

they fail to cooperate with the SSA or do not provide accounting statements, evidence, or other information.

Whenever a payee is replaced, the SSA tries to get back any savings left over from a beneficiary's checks, as well as any misused funds from the former payee. All funds that the SSA gets back are then given to the new payee for use on behalf of the beneficiary. In cases in which funds have been misused, a payee is almost always replaced.

If the SSA decides that funds have been misused, it notifies the Office of the Inspector General (OIG) of the U.S. Department of Health and Human Services. The OIG then reviews all misuse cases. If after reviewing a case the OIG believes it does not have enough evidence to prove the misuse of funds (or doubts it will be able to find enough evidence to prove misuse), it closes the case. If there is sufficient evidence, the OIG conducts another investigation before deciding whether to pass the case to the Justice Department for prosecution of the payee. If the OIG or the Justice Department does not recommend prosecution, the OIG tries to get back all misused funds from the payee.

If the Justice Department does prosecute, it tries to get back any misused funds or court-ordered fines directly from the payee. It also works to enforce prison sentences. When payees are prosecuted, the OIG acts as the go-between for the Department of Health and Human Services and the Justice Department.

A Closing Word

Because of the vulnerability of beneficiaries, it is obvious that a fair, efficient, and carefully monitored program is needed when Social Security checks go to someone else.

Beneficiaries who are unable to manage their own money are at the mercy of the people who handle it for them. Most payees are conscientious and do a good job for the beneficiaries they represent. Still, inasmuch as nearly $2 billion is paid each year to some five million payees of beneficiaries, precise monitoring, investigation, and accounting procedures are extremely important.

14

Limits on Decisions Made for Someone Else

Overview

Up to this point, this book has focused on how individuals can maintain control over their own lives and continue to make the decisions important to them even after they have become too ill or confused to speak for themselves. It has also dealt with how, when necessary, other people can step in and take over the making of decisions for seriously ill or senile individuals.

Whether decisions are made in advance by individuals who later become ill or by people with the responsibility of making decisions for others, there may be limits on the decisions being made. Some of the limits are legal ones, imposed by the state. Some are emotional ones, imposed by doctors and by hospital or nursing home administrators who either fear being sued or simply disagree with the decisions being made and decide to fight them.

Much of the information about the limits on decisions is contained in chapters that deal with decision-making tools or decision makers. Interested individuals should read chapters 4, 5, and 12. A short review of the issue of limits on decisions, however, is worthwhile.

Decision-Making Tools: A Review

As discussed in earlier chapters, there are legal tools available to individuals who want to leave directions about how they should be treated in the event they become incompetent, that is, unable to make rational decisions and understand their consequences.

One of the more common tools is a *living will,* a document that can be written by individuals on their own (and witnessed by a number of other people) or with the assistance of a lawyer. *Living wills provide elderly individuals with a way to make their medical decisions in advance.* Basically, they allow individuals to express their preferences on the kinds of medical treatments they do or do not want to have in the future. By stating these desires in advance, individuals who become too ill to speak for themselves still have written instructions that their doctors can follow. For example, individuals may decide that they do not want to be revived if they suffer a bad heart attack on top of an already serious illness. Or they may not want to be put on a respirator to be kept alive if they are already terminally ill. Or they may want to be given only painkilling drugs, and not antibiotics or chemotherapy, once they reach a certain point of illness. All these contingencies could be written into a living will.

Living wills are not automatically enforceable—doctors do not have to follow their instructions without question. But if doctors do not wish to comply with the directions in living wills, judges petitioned to review these cases will almost certainly use living wills as strong evidence of what patients wanted. Since patients have the right to determine the outcome of their own lives, courts will usually decide that the choices expressed in living wills should be followed. Doctors and health care institutions, such as hopsitals or nursing homes, can be sued for refusing to follow the wishes of their patients. Doctors can safely rely on living wills without having to go to court.

Living wills have to be written carefully. Sometimes states will have already written into law certain decisions that they believe cannot be made in advance by patients. It is important to find out any state limitations on directions that can be left in living wills. For more information, see chapter 4.

Another common legal tool is the *durable power of attorney,* which permits individuals to authorize other people to make decisions for them after they have become incompetent or too ill to speak for themselves (see chapter 11). Unlike living wills, durable powers of attorney are not limited to medical decisions.

One of the advantages of durable powers of attorney over living wills is that the ill individuals have left behind more than just a set of written instructions; they have put into place people who are authorized to make decisions and argue that those decisions be followed. Some, but not all, states permit living wills to appoint such a person (a *proxy*). Often, people with durable power-of-attorney documents will discuss their preferences and future instructions with the individuals they appoint. This way, not only are their wishes known, but their rights to make those decisions in advance can be protected by the authorized individuals.

As with living wills, decisions made (or instructions followed) by the authorized individuals still have to comply with state laws. Once again, interested individuals must take the time to find out the limits imposed by their state legislatures and courts. For more information on powers of attorney, see chapter 5.

Decision Makers and De Facto Surrogates

There are a number of different ways people can be authorized or appointed to become *surrogate decision makers*—people who make decisions for those unable to do so for themselves. These surrogates can go by various names, depending on how they were appointed to their positions of authority.

Surrogates appointed by judges are called *guardians* or *conservators*. They are appointed after the individuals in question are declared incompetent and in need of a surrogate decision-maker (see chapter 12). Guardians have the most legal authority to make decisions for others, but even they may have to seek court approval to make certain serious decisions.

Surrogates appointed by a durable power-of-attorney document are called *agents* or *attorneys-in-fact*. Their decisions are limited to whatever categories (medical, financial, personal) are listed in the documents. *While durable power-of-attorney documents are not guarantees against agents having to go to court to enforce the wishes of principals (those who execute durable power-of-attorney agreements), the existence of such documents can certainly lessen those risks and give added weight to the decisions made by agents.*

Still others become *de facto surrogates,* people, usually family members, who are not formally appointed or authorized to make decisions but are the only ones available to do so. Many people become de facto surrogates when individuals around them become ill. They begin taking over those individuals' personal care and making decisions and arrangements for it. They begin monitoring an individual's finances, making sure that bills get paid and checks get deposited into the correct accounts. Finally, they are looked to for instructions and decisions by doctors taking care of the individuals in question. This arrangement is commonplace, particularly between spouses and between elderly parents and their adult children.

De facto surrogates are the people to whom the decisions fall either when individuals have not planned ahead and authorized someone to be their agent or when no court hearing takes place to formally appoint guardians for them. *Often, this system works well enough—if there are no disagreements with the decisions being made.*

If family members disagree over the use of finances or about what kind of medical treatment the people in question should receive, then there can be trouble for de facto surrogates. Because they have no legal standing—no formal appointment or authorization—their decisions can easily be challenged both in courts and in hospitals and nursing homes. *Actually, de facto surrogates have only as much decision-making power as is allowed them by other interested parties (doctors, lawyers, bankers, other family members, and so on).*

The more controversial the decisions being made, the more likely it is that people may have to go to court to get them approved or enforced. This is true whether or not ill individuals have authorized agents, the courts have authorized guardians, or de facto surrogates have simply stepped in to make decisions that must be made; *however, those with legal authority to make decisions are far less likely to have their decisions challenged.*

All decisions made by all surrogates must comply with the laws of their states. These laws usually surround the making of critical care decisions—those which can directly result in the death of the ill people in question.

Family Consent Statutes

Several states have provided another way for families to make decisions on behalf of individuals who become incompetent without having appointed a surrogate. Instead of requiring families to petition a court to select a guardian, or letting them become de facto surrogates, these states have automatically authorized them to make health care decisions for incompetent patients (see appendix 31 for a list of states). In six of these states, family members are allowed to make all health decisions for incompetent patients; in the other nine, they are allowed to make decisions if patients are diagnosed as terminally ill (for more information on doctors' views of when patients are considered terminally ill, see chapter 4).

These *family consent statutes*, as they are called, vary somewhat from state to state. Some states have their own order of preference for which family members should be allowed to make decisions, while others list no priority at all. Some specifically authorize family members to make critical care decisions, including the withholding or withdrawing of life-prolonging treatment, for terminally ill or comatose patients. Others name specific conditions for which consent is not valid, such as abortion, sterilization, and mental health care (see appendix 32 for specific provisions included in family consent laws). If the incompetent individuals have already authorized agents or been given court-appointed guardians, they—not the family member named in the statute—would have the legal priority to make decisions in these states.

In states without family consent laws, doctors and hospitals usually decide to rely on the informal consent of families or require families to have formal guardians appointed for the individuals in question.

The Kinds of Medical Care Decisions That Need to Be Made

A number of different kinds of medical care decisions may need to be made for incompetent patients—ranging from routine care to critical care, or life-and-death, decisions. Each kind of decision is accompanied by different requirements in the decision-making process. The categories and their requirements, discussed briefly below, are taken from the American Health Care Association's statement on health care decision making in long-term care facilities.

1. *Routine treatment decisions.* These decisions include changing medications for such chronic problems as blood pressure and diet or prescribing more exercise or physical therapy. Often, the general consent form signed by patients (or their family members) when they enter hospitals or nursing homes is enough to authorize these kinds of decisions. Such facilities should, however, try to inform agents, guardians, or family members of every routine decision to give them the opportunity to consent or object. Often, nurses can do this communicating after discussing treatment decisions with doctors.

2. *Nonroutine treatment decisions.* These decisions include surgery and invasive tests. In these cases, doctors should be the ones to get consent from agents, guardians, or family members. In some instances, doctors can simply note on a patient's chart that they have received consent; in other instances (depending on state law), doctors will need written consent.

3. *Life-and-death treatment decisions.* Life-and-death decisions include whether or not to take patients off respirators when they aren't expected to be able to

breathe for themselves, agreeing to or refusing surgery or chemotherapy needed to keep patients alive, and removing or retaining equipment for artificial feeding and hydration.

Facilities should, but are not likely to, have set procedures that allow surrogates to have treatments withheld (not started) or withdrawn (taken away). *It should be noted that both the courts and other professional groups have stated that there is no real difference between withholding and withdrawing treatment, and that legally authorized surrogates have the right to make either of those kinds of decisions on behalf of the patients they represent.* Once again, de facto surrogates may be able to make such decisions as well, as long as the decisions are agreed to by the doctors, hospitals, or nursing homes involved in the case. (See appendix 33 for the American Medical Association's statement on withholding or withdrawing life-prolonging medical treatment.)

Procedures and guidelines used by facilities to help them through the decision-making process include the following:

- Doctors of incompetent patients will usually be the ones to explain life-and-death situations and the need for medical decisions to family members, agents, guardians, and so on. They will also obtain informed consent or refusal of treatment from the surrogate decision-maker(s). (For more on informed consent, see chapter 7.)

- *Facilities may require that patients be diagnosed as terminally ill before such decisions can be made, or that the expected burdens (pain, nausea, weakness) of the treatments be greater than the expected benefits (improvement, longer life, less pain) before surrogates can refuse such treatment.*

- *When facilities (and family members) evaluate decisions, they should pay attention to how the burdens of proposed treatments compare with the benefits.* For example, if surgery is not expected to prolong life but is expected to relieve great pain, it may be appropriate, but if surgery will prolong life a little for people who will remain in great pain, then it might not be appropriate. This kind of comparison can help put some perspective into making life-and-death decisions.

- A review of prior decisions made by patients while still competent is also of great value. Such decisions can give considerable insight into what patients would have wanted. The existence of living wills, durable powers of attorney, and other legal documents that show patients' wishes is also important.

The Decision to Remove Food and Water

One kind of life-and-death decision merits special notice: the removal of food and/or water from incompetent patients who are comatose or terminally ill. The crux of the issue is whether or not food and water, supplied by tubes that enter through patients' noses, esophagi, or stomachs, are considered medical treatment or ordinary care. (These patients are unable to eat either by themselves or with assistance by the normal spoon-to-mouth technique.)

If these tubes are considered medical treatment, then surrogates have a greater legal right to refuse them. If, however, they are considered ordinary care, then surrogates cannot refuse them on behalf of patients. Some surrogates who refuse the use of life-support systems will also want to refuse feeding and hydration tubes. When writing a living will or a durable power-of-attorney document, interested individuals should discuss this issue with their lawyers to find out whether refusal is permitted in their states. All surrogates, including guardians, may have to go to court to have these kinds of decisions enforced.

This issue is highly controversial, and individuals must be prepared to face the emotional and legal toll of making it. Many doctors, hospitals, and nursing homes are opposed to the removal of food and water and may be willing to challenge in court a decision to refuse such treatment or care.

The Decision to Donate Organs

Individuals may decide, while still competent, that they wish to donate their organs for use after they die. They may express this wish by filling out organ donation cards or by writing the request into their living wills or durable powers of attorney.

When no cards or documents have been signed, family members of a deceased individual may authorize organ donations on his or her behalf. The order of preference in which family members may make such decisions is

the spouse;

any adult child;

either parent;

any adult sibling;

the guardian; and

other authorized agents.

No family members are allowed to authorize organ donations if they are aware that the deceased patient (or other individuals with a higher priority in the decision-making process) would not have wanted them to do so.

The Decision to Participate in Medical Research

Generally, the only individuals allowed to make the decision to participate in research experiments are patients themselves. Such participation is something they should decide and arrange to do while still competent. They may include these wishes in their living wills or durable powers of attorney. Guardians can probably consent to research participation as well. It is possible that family members, too, can make these arrangements in cases in which patients have said that they wished to participate in research experiments but did not document those statements. This is a sensitive subject, however, and the decision is probably best left to still-competent patients.

Financial and Personal Decisions

Medical decisions are not the only ones that carry restrictions and limitations, but they are probably the most common ones. Financial and personal decisions can be limited as well, either by the terms of a durable power of attorney or guardianship order or by other interested individuals who challenge such decisions in court.

Once again, formally appointed or authorized conservators and agents are less likely to be challenged in their decisions than de facto surrogates are. Conservators have their decision-making limits set by the courts, which, if asked, will review the decisions being made to ensure that they are appropriate. The same is true of agents, whose decision-making powers are determined in durable power-of-attorney documents. Challenges to agents may also be brought to court by other interested persons.

Standards for Making Decisions

Two standards are involved in making decisions on behalf of others.

1. *When individuals write durable power-of-attorney documents authorizing specific agents to make decisions for them, those agents are expected to use the* standard of substituted judgment, *which means they are to make, to the best of their ability, the same decisions as they think the incompetent patient in question would have made (even if they disagree with those decisions).*
2. *Guardians may use either the standard of substituted judgment or the* best-interests standard. *This second standard means that the decisions made by a guardian should serve, in the guardian's opinion, the best interests of the incompetent patient.*

What to Do When Decisions Are Challenged or Ignored

When guardians, conservators, agents, or de facto surrogates make decisions that are challenged or ignored, they have four basic responses available to them. They can

review and change a decision that seems inappropriate on second thought;

go to the doctor or individual disputing the decision;

go to the facility disputing the decision; or

go to court.

Whenever possible, it is probably best for decision makers to try to resolve their problems with the family members, friends, doctors, or nurses raising the complaints. If problems concern medical decisions and cannot be resolved by the people involved, decision makers can always go a step further—to hospital or nursing home administrators. Often health care facilities have their own sets of procedures for resolving problems, and it is usually worthwhile following them to see if the problems can't be worked out through the normal channels. Such facilities may also have special groups of people that review controversial medical decisions and may be helpful in the solving of problems; an example is an institutional ethics committee, made up of health care professionals, religious representatives, philosophers, and ethicists.

The fourth possibility, usually a last resort, is to go to court. Courts can resolve disputes over medical, personal, and financial decisions. They are also more expensive than the other options, as they involve lawyers' fees and court costs. Anyone can take cases to court. For example, if a hospital disagrees with a guardian's decision to remove a patient from a respirator, the hospital can petition the court to review the decision. Similarly, the guardian (or the agent or the de facto surrogate) could also take the case to court to get the court's approval to remove the patient from the respirator.

There are several places individuals can go for legal assistance in resolving problems:

- *The Older Americans Act funds legal services programs for the elderly.*
- *The Legal Services Corporation funds legal services programs for the poor.*
- *Some lawyers will pursue such claims for less than their regular fee.*
- *Some legal clinics or programs associated with law schools provide such services for little or no cost.*

Making important decisions is never easy, and it can be doubly painful if those decisions are challenged or ignored. While surrogates need to make the best decisions possible for the people they represent, *surrogates' responsibilities are greater than just the making of decisions—they include working to make sure those decisions are enforced or approved. People who can no longer speak for themselves depend on surrogates to speak for them, and there is perhaps no greater gift or sign of respect that can be given to elderly individuals than to stand up for their rights, their wishes, and their choices when they are unable to do so themselves.* (For more information on resolving problems, see chapters 7 and 9.)

Part 4

Conclusion

15

People Will Listen—*If* You Talk

Overview

This book examines a great many issues and, hopefully, answers a great many questions. If it has served its purpose, it will provide both the reasons and the incentive for readers to plan ahead and avoid potential medical, financial, and legal problems. If nothing else, this book should have given enough information and ideas to its readers that they will know where to go next for help in dealing with a particular problem.

But what happens when an issue can't easily be solved or when individuals become so immersed in a situation that they want to make a difference not only in their own lives but also in the lives of others? Our very system of government depends on professional advocates and on individuals who see a problem to call it to the attention of their community, their state, and their nation.

If a problem can't be resolved by working directly with a hospital, a nursing home, a lawyer, or a federal or state agency, there are other options. Individuals can always take additional steps by going to the media; to local, state, or national advocacy groups and government bodies; and even to elected officials.

Getting Involved

Individuals who are dissatisfied with the results of working directly with a health facility or other group may wish to continue their fight. One way to do so is to become an advocate or activist on a particular issue. There is not only a place but also a tremendous need for community, state, and national involvement by people who have firsthand experience with the problems of the elderly.

Individuals who really know and understand these problems are valuable assets to many organizations and coalitions seeking change. Their involvement opens the door not only to providing advice based on personal experience but also to providing services. Many people frustrated by the care and advice received by their elderly relatives or friends have become volunteer ombudsmen, "Medigap" insurance counselors, and members of family councils or committees working with nursing homes to improve conditions. Accountants who have had problems with a parent in a nursing home would be welcomed into any number of groups that need financial advice not only for their own organizations but also for evaluating how money is spent by nursing homes or other groups they are in charge of monitoring. The same is true for people who have experience in fund-raising, public relations, secretarial work, and any number of other occupations.

It is also possible to participate on boards, commissions, committees, and groups such as the county or regional advisory committee on aging or the board of examiners for nursing homes. Many of the people sitting on these boards are political appointees, not professionals who have specialized in this kind of work—get appointed. In any particular state or community, both individuals and groups are working to improve a given problem or situation—find them, join them, and get involved.

Getting involved has several benefits: it is one of the best ways to force change within the system, it is an avenue into which frustrations can be channeled in a positive way, and it is an excellent link to the people who can sometimes do the most good—legislative authorities. Those who are putting on federal, state, or public hearings of one kind or another are usually eager to find people with personal experiences they're willing to share. Regular citizens *can* change national policy.

Getting Involved in the Political Arena

Opportunities for involvement and change exist at all levels of local, state, and federal government. In choosing which way to go, individuals should figure out which level is likely to have the most power and authority to address the particular problem they want to attack. If a problem involves a single nursing home, then it is probably better to deal with state and local officials. If the problem is wider reaching and involves federal law or policy, then federal officials are likely to be able to do the most good. Whatever the problem, having the support of local and state officials is likely to result in more people taking notice of the problem and more changes being made.

There's sometimes a tendency on the part of the public to believe that politicians and elected officials don't accomplish much or work very hard. The fact of the matter is that whether these people work hard or not, individuals who want to get their attention will have to be persistent and intelligent about getting it. Officials should be told that a particular situation is not the only one of its kind—that there are other people who are experiencing the same problem and who will also get involved if the problem is not solved.

Many officials at all levels are grateful to have bright, capable people to work with them on a particular problem. It's likely that individuals trying to get something done will have to do a lot of the work themselves. For example, if individuals need to have a letter from an official sent on their behalf, they should provide the official with a draft of that letter. Chances are it will get done faster that way anyway, and it's likely that the letter will be used word for word. If individuals are capable of working and fighting for something, they allow officials to free up their time to do the work for people who can't do it themselves.

Getting Attention and Influencing a Particular Problem

When approaching officials about a particular problem, explain it to them in *specific* terms. Don't drop in on elected or appointed officials unannounced, unless doing so is a deliberate tactic or a last resort. They are busy, too. Treat them as professionals, make appointments, insist on meeting with a particular person who is knowledgeable about—or at least familiar with—the problem to be presented. Individuals should send the person they are going to meet a history of the problem, as well as any other available background material. This kind of competent and determined display of action will let people know that the problems (and the individuals providing the information) are not going to go away.

When calling an official or staff member for the first time, understand that the person may not have much time to talk. If the subject requires a long time to explain, let the person know and offer to make an appointment at a time convenient to him or her. Ask what he or she would prefer. All people are entitled to the services of elected officials and government workers; they are elected, appointed, or employed to work on problems. It is reasonable to expect good service and if necessary, to insist on it.

If more than one official needs to be approached at the same time, do so directly and in a personalized fashion. If one letter is sent to six individuals, they may all think that someone else is going to take care of the problem. Write or call each one individually. Do any necessary homework before approaching a government official. For example, if one of the two senators in a state concentrates only on defense issues and is not known for dealing with human services, calling him or her might not do much good (unless the senator is a friend or relative). But if the second senator in the state is better known for his or her involvement with elder issues, then that is the person to contact. Find out the official's committee assignments and what legislation he or she has proposed—it's a matter of public record.

Be brief but clear, and prepare information in advance. Well-organized presentations of specific problems are going to get faster results. Offer to provide more detailed information if the person wants it, and set up an appointment to do so. Above all, have a sense of what changes are appropriate and necessary. Giving officials a sense of what can actually be done will save them a lot of time.

Don't underestimate the importance of working with an official's staff members—it's often an important part of getting changes made. The more important officials are, the less time they have to get directly involved. Senators and representatives have a great many issues to work on, so talk with their staff and get them interested and involved with specific problems. Don't dismiss the influence of the official's staff members; they are likely to have much more time, energy, and even expertise to devote to the subject and will be advising the official on what to do. Persistence and determination do pay off, as long as the problem is presented in an intelligent, thoughtful way.

Individuals should not expect that public officials or their staff know a great deal about a particular issue. That may be frustrating, but it is important to remember that they have a lot of subjects to deal with and may not be up-to-date on a particular problem. Take the opportunity to educate them.

When approaching an official, individuals can do more than simply explain the problem. They can offer to be a witness at a hearing or can suggest that the official hold a hearing on a particular subject. Offer to work with the official's staff on holding that hearing by supplying witnesses and background information. Above all, be professional when approaching officials—they are wary of people who seem to have an axe to grind or a chip on their shoulder. It's both necessary and important to be tenacious, tough, and determined—but individuals should use their anger to motivate what they do, not how they do it.

Involving the Media

Another option that can be used to get results is to involve the media. This can be done instead of or in addition to getting involved with an advocacy group or official body. Television and newspaper journalists are interested in getting stories; if individuals have a story to tell, they should do so. There are several advantages to getting the media involved. First of all, it can produce quick results. Media involvement is often what a health care facility or public agency fears most; exposure and bad publicity are both embarrassing and bad for business.

The problems of the elderly are often tailor-made for human interest stories and news—people who are fighting guardianship, people who are released too early from hospitals or abused in nursing homes, people whose money has been misused by their representative payees, and other stories can all attract the interest of the media. Sometimes just the threat of going to the media or of having a reporter come to a meeting can have immediate positive effects.

Letters to the editor and newspaper editorials can also force positive solutions to particular problems. Locate other people facing the same problem and try to get an appointment with the editorial board of a newspaper. Ask the board to consider writing an editorial or publishing a feature story on the problem.

Remember that many groups and individuals are as eager to get good publicity as they are to avoid bad publicity. When talking with officials or staff members who have been particularly helpful, make sure they know that their name (or their boss's name) will be mentioned to the press. Elected officials and their staffs, particularly, will respond to this gesture, as it is important to their ability to get reelected.

Whether approaching low- or high-ranking officials, the media, or bureaucrats, it is important to let them know, in a professional and polite way, that this problem is not going to go away. Individuals should be clear and firm that they are not going to give up, that they know what they're talking about, and that they know what they want done about it.

A Final Word

Many elderly people feel they have to accept what's been given to them—that they shouldn't make a fuss or upset the applecart. However, arguing for one's rights and the rights of others is an important part of the democratic process.

Forcing a particular problem into the spotlight and demanding that it be changed are not only okay; they're often the only way to get things done.

Above all, remember that there are many ways to get things done. Direct contacts with health facilities, lawyers, advocacy groups, elected officials, and the media are options to be considered. Wherever possible, however, it's wise to plan ahead and avoid the problem in the first place.

APPENDIXES

Appendix 1
Coverage under Medicare Parts A and B

What Is Medicare?

Medicare is a Federal health insurance program for people 65 or older, people of any age with permanent kidney failure, and certain disabled people. It is administered by the Health Care Financing Administration. Local Social Security Administration offices take applications for Medicare, assist beneficiaries in claiming Medicare payments, and provide information about the program.

Medicare has two parts—hospital insurance and medical insurance. Hospital insurance helps pay for inpatient hospital care and certain follow-up care. Medical insurance helps pay for your doctor's services and many other medical services and items.

Hospital insurance is financed through part of the payroll (FICA) tax that also pays for Social Security. Voluntary medical insurance is financed from the monthly premiums paid by people who have enrolled for it and from general Federal revenues.

Who Is Eligible for Hospital Insurance

You are eligible for Medicare hospital insurance at 65 if:

- you are entitled to monthly Social Security or railroad retirement benefits, or

- you have worked long enough to be insured under Social Security or the railroad retirement system, or

- you have worked long enough in Federal, State, or local government employment to be insured for Medicare purposes.

Source: Adapted from *Medicare,* U.S. Dept. of Health and Human Services, Social Security Administration, SSA Publication No.: 05-10043, January 1988.

You are eligible before age 65 if:

you have been entitled to Social Security disability benefits for 24 months, or

you have worked long enough in government employment and meet the requirements of the Social Security disability program.

Under certain conditions, your spouse, divorced spouse, widow or widower, or dependent parents may be eligible for hospital insurance at age 65. Also, disabled widows and widowers under 65, disabled surviving divorced spouses under 65, and disabled children 18 or older may be eligible. For more information, contact a Social Security office.

You are eligible at any age if you need maintenance dialysis or a kidney transplant for permanent kidney failure and:

you are insured or are getting monthly benefits under Social Security or the railroad retirement system, or

you have worked long enough in government employment.

Your wife, husband, or child may be eligible if she or he needs maintenance dialysis or a transplant. Only the family member who has permanent kidney failure is eligible for Medicare protection.

If you are entitled to a railroad disability annuity or railroad retirement benefit based on disability, contact a railroad retirement office to find out if you are eligible for hospital insurance.

How You Get Hospital Insurance Protection

Some people have to apply for hospital insurance protection before it can start. For others, hospital insurance protection starts automatically.

If You Are Nearing 65

You do not have to retire to have hospital insurance protection at 65. But if you plan to keep working, you will have to file an application for hospital insurance in order for your protection to begin. You should apply at a Social Security office about 3 months before you reach 65.

If you are receiving Social Security or railroad retirement checks, your hospital insurance protection will start automatically at 65.

If you are a government retiree who is eligible for Medicare on the basis of government employment, you will have to apply for hospital insurance in order for it to begin at 65. Contact a Social Security office about 3 months before your 65th birthday to file your application.

If you aren't eligible for hospital insurance at 65, you can buy it. The basic premium is estimated to be $156 a month for 1989. To buy hospital insurance, you also have to enroll and pay the monthly premium for medical insurance. If you are an alien, you must be a permanent resident and must reside in the U.S. for 5 years before you can buy Medicare. You can apply at any Social Security office.

If You Are Disabled

If you are under 65 and disabled, you will have hospital insurance protection automatically when you have been entitled to Social Security disability benefits for 24 months.

If you are a widow or widower between 50 and 65 and have been disabled at least 2 years but haven't applied for disability benefits because you are already getting other Social Security benefits, you may be eligible for hospital insurance. Contact a Social Security office for more information.

If you are a government employee and you become disabled before age 65, you may be eligible for Medicare on the basis of your government employment. Generally, there is a 29-month waiting period before your hospital insurance protection can start. But, you should contact a Social Security office as soon as you become disabled.

If You Have Permanent Kidney Failure

If you, your spouse, or your dependent child needs kidney dialysis or a kidney transplant, contact a Social Security office to apply for Medicare. You can apply by phone, or a representative can visit you to take an application if you are unable to go to the office.

If you are eligible for Medicare, your protection will start with the 3rd month after the month you actually begin maintenance dialysis treatments. Under certain conditions, your coverage can start earlier. The people in the Social Security office can tell you exactly when your protection will begin.

Who Is Eligible for Medical Insurance

Almost anyone who is 65 or older or who is eligible for hospital insurance can enroll for Medicare medical insurance. You don't need any Social Security or government work credits to get medical insurance.

Aliens 65 or older who are not eligible for hospital insurance must be permanent residents and must reside in the U.S. for 5 years before they can enroll in medical insurance.

How You Can Get Medical Insurance Protection

If you want medical insurance protection, you pay a monthly premium for it. The basic premium is $27.90 a month in 1989.

Some people are automatically enrolled in medical insurance. Others must apply for it.

Automatic Medical Insurance Enrollment

If you are receiving Social Security benefits or retirement benefits under the railroad retirement system, you will be automatically enrolled for medical insurance—unless you say you don't want it—at the same time you become entitled to hospital insurance.

People Who Must Apply for Medical Insurance

You will have to apply for medical insurance if you:

plan to continue working past 65,

are 65 but aren't eligible for hospital insurance,

have permanent kidney failure,

are a disabled widow or widower between 50 and 65 who isn't getting disability benefits,

are eligible for Medicare on the basis of government employment, or

live in Puerto Rico or outside the U.S.

Contact your local Social Security or railroad retirement office for detailed information about medical insurance enrollment.

Your Medical Insurance Enrollment Period

There is a 7-month initial enrollment period for medical insurance. This period begins 3 months before the month you first become eligible for medical insurance and ends 3 months after that month.

If you enroll during the first 3 months of your enrollment period, your medical insurance protection will start with the month you are eligible. If you enroll during the last 4 months, your protection will start 1 to 3 months after you enroll.

If you don't take medical insurance during your initial enrollment period, you can sign up during a general enrollment period—January 1 through March 31 of each year. But if you enroll during a general enrollment period, your protection won't start until the following July. Also, your monthly premium will be 10 percent higher than the basic premium for each 12-month period you could have been enrolled but were not.

Special rules apply to workers and their spouses age 65 or older and to disabled people under 65 who have employer group health coverage. (See Employer Group Health Plans.)

Hospital Insurance Benefits

Medicare hospital insurance can help pay for inpatient hospital care, inpatient care in a skilled nursing facility, home health care, and hospice care.

Inpatient Hospital Care

If you need inpatient care, hospital insurance pays for up to the entire year of hospital coverage except for the first $560 in 1989.

If you ever need more than 90 days of hospital care in any benefit period, you can use some or all of your 60 non-renewable "reserve days." For each reserve day you use, hospital insurance pays for all covered services except $270 a day.

Covered services include semiprivate room, all meals, regular nursing services, operating and recovery room costs, hospital costs for anesthesia services, intensive care and coronary care, drugs, lab tests, X rays, medical supplies and appliances, rehabilitation services, and preparatory services related to kidney transplant surgery.

Skilled Nursing Facility Care

If you need inpatient skilled nursing or rehabilitation services and meet certain other conditions, hospital insurance helps pay for up to 150 days in a participating skilled nursing facility in each benefit period. In 1989, patients must pay a coinsurance amount, estimated at $25.50 per day, for the first eight days of their stay in a skilled nursing facility.

Covered services include semiprivate room, all meals, regular nursing services, rehabilitation services, drugs, medical supplies, and appliances.

Home Health Care

If you are confined to your home and meet certain other conditions, hospital insurance can pay the full approved cost of home health visits from a participating home health agency. There is no limit to the number of covered visits you can have.

Covered services include part-time skilled nursing care, physical therapy, and speech therapy. If you need one or more of those services, hospital insurance also covers part-time services of home health aides, occupational therapy, medical social services, and medical supplies and equipment.

Hospice Care

Under certain conditions, hospital insurance can help pay for hospice care for terminally ill beneficiaries, if the care is provided by a Medicare-certified hospice.

Special benefit periods apply to hospice care. Hospital insurance can pay for a maximum of two 90-day periods and one 30-day period. There is no limit to the amount of time hospital insurance will pay for hospice services, as long as the patient's need for such services is certified by a doctor.

Covered services include doctors' services, nursing services, medical appliances and supplies including outpatient drugs for pain relief, home health aide and homemaker services, therapies, medical social services, short-term inpatient care including respite care, and counseling.

Hospital insurance pays part of the cost of outpatient drugs and inpatient respite care. For all other covered services, hospital insurance pays the full cost.

Medical Insurance Benefits

Medicare medical insurance helps pay for your doctor's services and a variety of other medical services and supplies that are not covered by hospital insurance. Most of the services needed by people with permanent kidney failure are covered only by medical insurance.

Each year, as soon as you meet the annual medical insurance deductible, medical insurance generally will pay 80 percent of the approved charges for covered services you receive during the rest of the year. In 1989, the annual deductible is $75.

Doctors' Services

Medical insurance covers doctors' services no matter where you receive them in the United States. Covered doctors' services include surgical services, diagnostic tests and X rays that are part of your treatment, medical supplies furnished in a doctor's office, services of the office nurse, and drugs which are administered as part of your treatment and cannot be self-administered.

Outpatient Hospital Services

Medical insurance covers outpatient hospital services you receive for diagnosis and treatment, such as care in an emergency room or outpatient clinic of a hospital.

Home Health Visits

Medical insurance can cover an unlimited number of home health visits if all required conditions are met.

Other Medical and Health Services

Under certain conditions or limitations, medical insurance covers other medical services and supplies. Some examples are: ambulance transportation; home dialysis equipment, supplies, and periodic support services; independent laboratory tests; oral surgery; outpatient physical therapy and speech pathology services; and X rays and radiation treatments.

What Medicare Does Not Cover

Medicare provides basic protection against the high cost of illness, but it will not pay all of your health care expenses. Some of the services and supplies Medicare cannot pay for are: custodial care, such as help with bathing, eating, and taking medicine; dentures and routine dental care; eyeglasses, hearing aids, and examinations to prescribe or fit them; long-term care (nursing homes); personal comfort items, such as a phone or TV in your hospital room; prescription drugs and patent medicines; and routine physical checkups and related tests.

In certain situations, Medicare can help pay for care in qualified Canadian and Mexican hospitals. Otherwise Medicare cannot pay for hospital or medical services you receive outside the U.S. (Puerto Rico, Guam, American Samoa, the Virgin Islands, and the Northern Mariana islands are considered part of the U.S.)

If You Have Other Health Insurance

Many private health insurance companies point out that their policies for people who have Medicare are designed to coordinate their coverage with Medicare. They recommend that their policy holders sign up for Medicare medical insurance to have full protection.

If you have other health insurance, it may not pay for some of the services that are covered by Medicare medical insurance. You should get in touch with your insurer or agent to discuss your health insurance needs in relation to Medicare protection. This is particularly important if you have family members who are covered under your present policy. Also, in planning your health insurance coverage, remember that long-term care (or nursing home care) is not usually covered by medicare or most private health insurance policies.

If you have health care protection from the Veterans Administration (VA) or under the CHAMPUS or CHAMPVA program, your health benefits may change or end when you become eligible for Medicare. You should contact the VA, the Department of Defense, or a military health benefits advisor for information before you decide not to enroll in Medicare medical insurance.

If you have health care protection from the Indian Health Service, a Federal employees' health plan, or a State medical assistance program, the people there probably can help you decide whether it is to your advantage to have Medicare medical insurance.

For your own protection, be sure not to cancel any health insurance you now have until the month your Medicare coverage begins.

Buying Supplemental Health Insurance

If you are thinking about buying private insurance to supplement Medicare, please make sure it does not simply duplicate your Medicare coverage. If you want help in deciding whether to buy private supplemental insurance, ask at any Social Security office for the pamphlet, "Guide to Health Insurance for People with Medicare." This free pamphlet describes the various types of supplemental insurance available.

Employer Group Health Plans

Employers with 20 or more employees are required to offer their workers age 65 or older the same health benefits that are provided to younger employees. They also must offer the spouses age 65 or older of workers of any age the same health benefits given younger employees.

If you are 65 or older and continue working or are the spouse 65 or older of a worker and you accept the employer's health plan, Medicare will be the secondary health insurance payer. If you reject the employer's health plan, Medicare will be the primary health insurance payer. The employer is not allowed to offer you Medicare supplemental coverage if you reject his or her health plan.

Coverage under Medicare Parts A and B

Also, if you work past 65 or are a spouse 65 or older and are covered under an employer health plan, you can wait to enroll in Medicare medical insurance during a special enrollment period. You won't have to pay the 10 percent premium surcharge for late enrollment, if you meet certain requirements.

If you are under 65 and disabled, Medicare will be the secondary payer if you choose coverage under your employer's health plan or a family member's employer health plan. This provision applies only to large group health plans. A large group health plan is any plan that covers employees of at least one employer that has 100 or more workers. But, you have the same special enrollment period and premium rights under Medicare medical insurance that workers 65 or older have. For more information about these special rules, contact your employer.

If you are under 65, are entitled to Medicare solely on the basis of permanent kidney failure, and have an employer group health plan, Medicare will be the secondary payer for an initial period of up to 12 months. At the end of the 12-month period, Medicare becomes the primary payer.

Any Questions

If you have any questions about Medicare, please call your local Social Security office. The phone number is listed in your telephone book under "Social Security Administration" or "U.S. Government."

Appendix 2
State Insurance Departments

Alabama
Insurance Commissioner
135 South Union Street #160
Montgomery 36130–3401
205/269–3550

Alaska
Director of Insurance
P.O. Box D
Juneau 99811
907/465–2515

American Samoa
Insurance Commissioner
Office of the Governor
Pago Pago 96797
684/633–4116

Arizona
Director of Insurance
801 E. Jefferson, 2nd Floor
Phoenix 85034
602/255–5400

Arkansas
Insurance Commissioner
400 University Tower Building
12th and University Streets
Little Rock 72204
501/371–1325

California
Commissioner of Insurance
100 Van Ness Avenue
San Francisco 94102
415/557–9624

Colorado
Commissioner of Insurance
303 West Colfax Avenue
5th Floor
Denver 80204
303/620–4300

Connecticut
Insurance Commissioner
165 Capitol Avenue
State Office Building
Room 425
Hartford 06106
203/566–5275

Source: National Association of Insurance Commissioners, 1988.

Delaware
Insurance Commissioner
841 Silverlake Boulevard
Dover 19901
302/736-4251

District of Columbia
Superintendent of Insurance
613 G Street, NW
6th Floor
Washington 20001
202/783-3190

Florida
Insurance Commissioner
State Capitol
Plaza Level 11
Tallahassee 32399-0300
904/488-3440

Georgia
Insurance Commissioner
2 Martin L. King, Jr. Drive
Floyd Memorial Building
704 West Tower
Atlanta 30334
404/656-2056

Guam
Acting Insurance Commissioner
P.O. Box 2796
or
855 West Marine Drive
Agana 96910
011-671/477-1040

Hawaii
Insurance Commissioner
P.O. Box 3614

Honolulu 96811
808/548-5450

Idaho
Director of Insurance
500 South 10th Street
Boise 83720
208/334-2250

Illinois
Director of Insurance
320 West Washington Street
4th Floor
Springfield 62767
217/782-4515

Indiana
Commissioner of Insurance
311 West Washington Street
Suite 300
Indianapolis 46204-2787
317/232-2386

Iowa
Insurance Commissioner
Lucas State Office Building
6th Floor
Des Moines 50319
515/281-5705

Kansas
Commissioner of Insurance
420 S.W. 9th Street
Topeka 66612
913/296-7801

Kentucky
Insurance Commissioner
229 West Main Street

P.O. Box 517
Frankfort 40602
502/564-3630

Louisiana
Commissioner of Insurance
P.O. Box 44214
Baton Rouge 70804
or
950 North 5th Street
Baton Rouge 70801
504/342-5328

Maine
Superintendent of Insurance
State Office Building
State House, Station 34
Augusta 04333
207/582-8707

Maryland
Insurance Commissioner
501 St. Paul Place
(Stanbalt Building)
7th Floor South
Baltimore 21202
301/333-2520

Massachusetts
Commissioner of Insurance
280 Friend Street
Boston 02114
617/727-7189

Michigan
Insurance Commissioner
P.O. Box 30220
Lansing 48909
or

611 West Ottawa Street
2nd Floor North
Lansing 48933
517/373-9273

Minnesota
Commissioner of Commerce
500 Metro Square Building
5th Floor
St. Paul 55101
612/296-6848

Mississippi
Commissioner of Insurance
1804 Walter Sillers Building
P.O. Box 79
Jackson 39205
601/359-3569

Missouri
Director of Insurance
301 West High Street 6 North
P.O. Box 690
Jefferson City 65102-0690
314/751-2451

Montana
Commissioner of Insurance
126 North Sanders
Mitchell Building
Room 270, P.O. Box 4009
Helena 59601
406/444-2040

Nebraska
Director of Insurance
Terminal Building
941 O Street, Suite 400

Nebraska (continued)
Lincoln 68508
402/471-2201

Nevada
Commissioner of Insurance
Nye Building
201 South Fall Street
Carson City 89701
702/885-4270

New Hampshire
Insurance Commissioner
169 Manchester Street
P.O. Box 2005
Concord 03301
603/271-2261

New Jersey
Commissioner of Insurance
20 West State Street CN325
Trenton 08625
609/292-5363

New Mexico
Superintendent of Insurance
PERA Building
P.O. Drawer 1269
Santa Fe 87504-1269
505/827-4500

New York
Superintendent of Insurance
160 West Broadway
New York 10013
212/602-0429

North Carolina
Commissioner of Insurance
Dobbs Building
P.O. Box 26387
Raleigh 27611
919/733-7343

North Dakota
Commissioner of Insurance
Capitol Building
Fifth Floor
Bismarck 58505
701/224-2440

Ohio
Director of Insurance
2100 Stella Court
Columbus 43266-0566
614/644-2658

Oklahoma
Insurance Commissioner
P.O. Box 53408
Oklahoma City 73152-3408
or
1901 North Walnut
Oklahoma City 73105
405/521-2828

Oregon
Insurance Commissioner
21 Labor and Industries Building
Salem 97310
503/378-4271

Pennsylvania
Insurance Commissioner
Strawberry Square
13th Floor
Harrisburg 17120
717/787-5173

State Insurance Departments

Puerto Rico
Commissioner of Insurance
Fernandez Juncos Station
P.O. Box 8330
Santurce, PR 00910
809/722-8686

Rhode Island
Insurance Commissioner
233 Richmond Street, Suite 237
Providence 02903-4237
401/277-2246

South Carolina
Chief Insurance Commissioner
1612 Marion Street—29201
P.O. Box 100105
Columbia 29202-3105
803/737-6117

South Dakota
Director of Insurance
Insurance Building
910 E. Sioux Avenue
Pierre 57501
605/773-3563

Tennessee
Commissioner of Insurance
Volunteer Plaza
500 James Robertson Parkway
Nashville 37219
615/741-2241

Texas
Chairman—State Board of Insurance
1110 San Jacinto Boulevard
Austin 78701-1998
512/463-9979

Member—State Board of Insurance
1110 San Jacinto Boulevard
Austin 78701-1998
512/463-6330

Member—State Board of Insurance
1110 San Jacinto Boulevard
Austin 78701-1998
512/463-6332

Commissioner of Insurance
1110 San Jacinto Boulevard
Austin 78701-1998
512/463-6464

Utah
Commissioner of Insurance
P.O. Box 45803
Salt Lake City 84145
801/530-6400

Vermont
Commissioner of Insurance
State Office Building
Montpelier 05602
802/828-3301

Virginia
Commissioner of Insurance
700 Jefferson Building
P.O. Box 1157
Richmond 23209
804/786-3741

Virgin Islands
Commissioner of Insurance
Kongens Garde #18
St. Thomas 00801
809/774-2991

Washington
Insurance Commissioner
Insurance Building AQ21
Olympia 98504
206/753-7301

West Virginia
Insurance Commissioner
2100 Washington Street East
Charleston 25305
304/348-3394

Wisconsin
Commissioner of Insurance
P.O. Box 7873
Madison 53707
or
123 West Washington Avenue
Madison 53702
608/266-0102

Wyoming
Commissioner of Insurance
Herschler Building
122 West 25th Street
Cheyenne 82002
307/777-7401

Appendix 3
Sample Living Will

**Society for the
Right to Die**
250 West 57th Street
New York, NY 10107

Living Will Declaration

*INSTRUCTIONS
Consult this column for help
and guidance.*

To my Family, Doctors, and All Those Concerned with My Care

This declaration sets forth your directions regarding medical treatment.

I, _____, being of sound mind, make this statement as a directive to be followed if I become unable to participate in decisions regarding my medical care.

If I should be in an incurable or irreversible mental or physical condition with no reasonable expectation of recovery, I direct my attending physician to withhold or withdraw treatment that merely prolongs my dying. I further direct that treatment be limited to measures to keep me comfortable and to relieve pain.

You have the right to refuse treatment you do not want, and you may request the care you do want.

These directions express my legal right to refuse treatment. Therefore I expect my family, doctors, and everyone concerned with my care to regard themselves as legally and morally bound to act in accord with my wishes, and in so doing to be free of any legal liability for having followed my directions.

You may list specific treatment you do not *want. For example:*

  Cardiac resuscitation
  Mechanical respiration
  Artificial feeding/fluids
    by tubes

Otherwise, your general statement, top right, will stand for your wishes.

I especially do not want: _____
_____
_____
_____
_____
_____
_____
_____

You may want to add instructions for care you do *want— for example, pain medication; or that you prefer to die at home if possible.*

Other instructions/comments: _____
_____
_____
_____
_____

If you want, you can name someone to see that your wishes are carried out, but you do not have to do this.

Proxy Designation Clause: Should I become unable to communicate my instructions as stated above, I designate the following person to act in my behalf:

Name _____
Address _____

If the person I have named above is unable to act in my behalf, I authorize the following person to do so:

Name _____
Address _____

Sign and date here in the presence of two adult witnesses, who should also sign.

Signed: _____ Date: _____
Witness: _____ Witness: _____

Keep the signed original with your personal papers at home. Give signed copies to doctors, family, and proxy. Review your declaration from time to time; initial and date it to show it still expresses your intent.

Appendix 4
Checklist of State Laws Regarding Living Wills

THE chart that follows gives a rough outline of the provisions required by each state's living will law. It is impossible, within the context of this book, to include all the important details of each state's law. Therefore, this chart should be used only as a guide. Interested individuals should consult with a reliable lawyer who is familiar with the individual provisions of their state's living will law. Remember, these provisions are important and may mean the difference between a living will's being considered valid or invalid at the time it is most needed. Additional information can be obtained by writing the Society for the Right to Die, 250 West Fifty-seventh Street, New York, New York 10107, or by calling (212) 246-6973.

The information that follows is from a chart, copyrighted by and reprinted with permission from the Society for the Right to Die.

Chart definitions:

Declaration. A living will.

Declarant. The person writing, or executing, the living will.

Statute. The state law authorizing the use of living wills.

A number of common provisions are not noted on the chart:

- Living will declarations must be executed voluntarily by an adult of "sound mind" to express treatment choices in the event of that adult's terminal condition and inability to participate in decision making.

Source: Society for the Right to Die.

- A *qualified patient* is typically one who is in a terminal condition with no prospect of recovery (some states specifically include patients in a persistent vegetative state (PVS), or permanent coma, although the absence of this provision does not necessarily exclude PVS patients from being qualified).
- *Terminal condition* may be a condition that will cause death "imminently," or "within a short time," if life-sustaining procedures are not used. It may also be a condition in which death will occur with or without life-sustaining procedures.
- *Life-sustaining procedures* that can be withheld or withdrawn are defined as mechanisms that only prolong dying; may specifically include or exclude artificial feeding and hydration; may not specifically mention and may therefore permit withdrawal of this kind of treatment; or may be unclear about withdrawing such treatment if not needed for a patient's comfort.
- Revocation (cancellation) procedures are simple, often merely requiring a patient to state that the living will is no longer valid.
- A qualified patient's expressed wishes take precedence over any prior declaration.
- People who are not allowed to act as witnesses to a living will declaration include any *interested party* such as any of the patient's relations by blood or marriage, any heirs to the patient's estate, and anyone professionally or financially responsible for the patient's medical care. Where a special witness is required for a living will declaration made by a nursing home patient, that person is usually, but not always, a state-appointed ombudsman or patient advocate.
- A living will declaration has no effect on a patient's life insurance or medical benefits.
- There are penalties for hiding, forging, or intentionally destroying a living will declaration or its revocation.
- A living will declaration is presumed valid.
- A state's living will law does not condone suicide, aided suicide, euthanasia, or homicide.

Checklist of State Laws Regarding Living Wills

	ALABAMA	ALASKA	ARIZONA	ARKANSAS	CALIFORNIA	COLORADO	CONNECTICUT	DELAWARE	DISTRICT OF COLUMBIA	FLORIDA
1. Declaration may include personalized instructions	✓	✓	✓	✓		✓	✓	✓	✓	✓
2. State statute authorizes appointment of a representative				✓		✓		✓		✓
3. Declarant can direct someone else to sign declaration	✓	✓		✓		✓		✓	✓	✓
4. Statute authorizes oral declarations										✓
5. Statute provides decision-making procedures for patients with no declaration				✓			✓			✓
6. Doctor notified of patient's declaration shall make it part of patient's medical record	✓	✓	✓	✓	✓	✓		✓	✓	✓
7. Statute provides immunity from liability to health professionals complying with declaration	✓	✓	✓	✓	✓	✓	✓	✓	✓	✓
8. Terminal condition must be certified before declaration is used	✓	✓	✓	✓	✓	✓	✓	✓	✓	✓
9. Doctor must implement declaration or make reasonable effort to transfer patient to another doctor	✓	✓	✓	✓	✓	✓			✓	✓
10. Statute has penalties for doctors failure to comply with declaration		✓		✓	✓	✓			✓	
11. Declaration must be signed in presence of two witnesses	✓	✓	✓	✓	✓	✓	✓	✓	✓	✓
12. Special witnessing is required for nursing home patients					✓			✓	✓	
13. Other requirements for execution are required								✓		
14. Statute permits (A), could be interpreted to permit (B), or prohibits (C) the withholding or withdrawing of artificial feeding and hydration	A	A	B	A	A	C	C	A	A	C
15. Statute recognizes validity of out-of-state declarations		✓		✓						
16. Statute does not impair or restrict other rights	✓	✓		✓		✓			✓	✓
17. Statute includes other provisions worth noting		✓		✓	✓					

Checklist of State Laws Regarding Living Wills (continued)

	GEORGIA	HAWAII	IDAHO	ILLINOIS	INDIANA	IOWA	KANSAS	KENTUCKY	LOUISIANA	MAINE
1. Declaration may include personalized instructions	✓	✓		✓	✓	✓	✓		✓	✓
2. State statute authorizes appointment of a representative		✓	✓		✓	✓			✓	
3. Declarant can direct someone else to sign declaration			✓			✓	✓	✓		✓
4. Statute authorizes oral declarations									✓	
5. Statute provides decision-making procedures for patients with no declaration						✓			✓	
6. Doctor notified of patient's declaration shall make it part of patient's medical record	✓	✓		✓	✓		✓		✓	✓
7. Statute provides immunity from liability to health professionals complying with declaration	✓	✓	✓	✓	✓	✓	✓		✓	✓
8. Terminal condition must be certified before declaration is used	✓	✓	✓	✓	✓	✓	✓		✓	✓
9. Doctor must implement declaration or make reasonable effort to transfer patient to another doctor	✓	✓		✓	✓	✓	✓		✓	✓
10. Statute has penalties for doctors failure to comply with declaration		✓			✓		✓			✓
11. Declaration must be signed in presence of two witnesses	✓	✓	✓	✓	✓	✓	✓		✓	✓
12. Special witnessing is required for nursing home patients	✓				✓					
13. Other requirements for execution are required	✓	✓	✓	✓						
14. Statute permits (A), could be interpreted to permit (B), or prohibits (C) the withholding or withdrawing of artificial feeding and hydration	C	B	A	A	B	B	A		A	A
15. Statute recognizes validity of out-of-state declarations		✓								✓
16. Statute does not impair or restrict other rights		✓	✓	✓	✓	✓	✓		✓	✓
17. Statute includes other provisions worth noting	✓	✓			✓				✓	

Checklist of State Laws Regarding Living Wills (continued)

	MARYLAND	MASSACHUSETTS	MICHIGAN	MINNESOTA	MISSISSIPPI	MISSOURI	MONTANA	NEBRASKA	NEVADA	NEW HAMPSHIRE
1. Declaration may include personalized instructions	✔				✔	✔	✔		✔	✔
2. State statute authorizes appointment of a representative										
3. Declarant can direct someone else to sign declaration	✔				✔	✔	✔			
4. Statute authorizes oral declarations										
5. Statute provides decision-making procedures for patients with no declaration										
6. Doctor notified of patient's declaration shall make it part of patient's medical record	✔					✔	✔		✔	✔
7. Statute provides immunity from liability to health professionals complying with declaration	✔				✔	✔	✔		✔	✔
8. Terminal condition must be certified before declaration is used	✔				✔	✔	✔			✔
9. Doctor must implement declaration or make reasonable effort to transfer patient to another doctor	✔				✔	✔	✔		✔	✔
10. Statute has penalties for doctors failure to comply with declaration	✔					✔	✔			
11. Declaration must be signed in presence of two witnesses	✔				✔	✔	✔		✔	✔
12. Special witnessing is required for nursing home patients										✔
13. Other requirements for execution are required					✔				✔	✔
14. Statute permits (A), could be interpreted to permit (B), or prohibits (C) the withholding or withdrawing of artificial feeding and hydration	B				A	C	A		A	B
15. Statute recognizes validity of out-of-state declarations	✔					✔				
16. Statute does not impair or restrict other rights	✔					✔	✔		✔	✔
17. Statute includes other provisions worth noting	✔				✔	✔				

Checklist of State Laws Regarding Living Wills (continued)

	NEW JERSEY	NEW MEXICO	NEW YORK	NORTH CAROLINA	NORTH DAKOTA	OHIO	OKLAHOMA	OREGON	PENNSYLVANIA	RHODE ISLAND
1. Declaration may include personalized instructions		✓		✓			✓			
2. State statute authorizes appointment of a representative										
3. Declarant can direct someone else to sign declaration										
4. Statute authorizes oral declarations										
5. Statute provides decision-making procedures for patients with no declaration		✓		✓					✓	
6. Doctor notified of patient's declaration shall make it part of patient's medical record								✓		✓
7. Statute provides immunity from liability to health professionals complying with declaration		✓		✓				✓		✓
8. Terminal condition must be certified before declaration is used		✓		✓				✓		✓
9. Doctor must implement declaration or make reasonable effort to transfer patient to another doctor		✓						✓		✓
10. Statute has penalties for doctors failure to comply with declaration								✓		✓
11. Declaration must be signed in presence of two witnesses		✓		✓				✓		✓
12. Special witnessing is required for nursing home patients										✓
13. Other requirements for execution are required		✓		✓				✓		
14. Statute permits (A), could be interpreted to permit (B), or prohibits (C) the withholding or withdrawing of artificial feeding and hydration		A		A				B		A
15. Statute recognizes validity of out-of-state declarations										
16. Statute does not impair or restrict other rights		✓		✓					✓	
17. Statute includes other provisions worth noting				✓						

Checklist of State Laws Regarding Living Wills (continued)

	SOUTH CAROLINA	SOUTH DAKOTA	TENNESSEE	TEXAS	UTAH	VERMONT	VIRGINIA	WASHINGTON	WEST VIRGINIA	WISCONSIN	WYOMING
1. Declaration may include personalized instructions	✓		✓	✓	✓	✓	✓	✓	✓	✓	✓
2. State statute authorizes appointment of a representative				✓	✓		✓				✓
3. Declarant can direct someone else to sign declaration				✓	✓				✓	✓	✓
4. Statute authorizes oral declarations							✓				
5. Statute provides decision-making procedures for patients with no declaration				✓	✓		✓				
6. Doctor notified of patient's declaration shall make it part of patient's medical record			✓	✓	✓			✓	✓	✓	✓
7. Statute provides immunity from liability to health professionals complying with declaration	✓		✓	✓	✓	✓	✓	✓	✓	✓	✓
8. Terminal condition must be certified before declaration is used	✓		✓	✓	✓		✓	✓	✓	✓	✓
9. Doctor must implement declaration or make reasonable effort to transfer patient to another doctor	✓		✓	✓	✓	✓	✓	✓	✓	✓	✓
10. Statute has penalties for doctors failure to comply with declaration	✓		✓							✓	
11. Declaration must be signed in presence of two witnesses	✓		✓	✓	✓	✓	✓	✓	✓	✓	✓
12. Special witnessing is required for nursing home patients	✓										
13. Other requirements for execution are required	✓		✓		✓			✓			
14. Statute permits (A), could be interpreted to permit (B), or prohibits (C) the withholding or withdrawing of artificial feeding and hydration	B		A	A	B	A	A	A	B	C	B
15. Statute recognizes validity of out-of-state declarations											
16. Statute does not impair or restrict other rights			✓	✓	✓		✓		✓	✓	✓
17. Statute includes other provisions worth noting	✓		✓	✓	✓	✓			✓		

Appendix 5
Special Requirements for Creating Durable Powers of Attorney

Special Requirements for Creating Durable Powers of Attorney

State	Notary Required	Filing Required	Other
Arkansas	Yes (or approval of Probate Court)	Probate Court	
California*	Yes (or signed by two witnesses)		If patient is in nursing home, one witness must be patient advocate or ombudsman.
			Must be accompanied by statutory notice or signed by an attorney.
Connecticut	Yes		Must be accompanied by statutory notice.
Florida	No		Only a spouse, parent, adult child, sibling, niece or nephew may be appointed.
Minnesota	Yes		
Missouri	Yes	Recorder of deeds	
New York	Yes		Must be accompanied by statutory notice.
North Carolina	Yes	Register of deeds (copy with clerk of Superior Court)	
Oklahoma	No	Clerk of State District Court	Must be approved by judge of state District Court.

Source: B. Mishkin, *A Matter of Choice: Planning Ahead for Health Care Decisions,* Senate Special Committee on Aging, 1986.

Special Requirements for Creating Durable Powers of Attorney

State	Notary Required	Filing Required	Other
Rhode Island*	No		At least one witness must not be related by blood, marriage or adoption and must not be entitled to any part of the maker's estate.
South Carolina	Yes	Register of Mesne Conveyance	Requires three witnesses.
Wyoming	No	Clerk of District Court (copy with clerk of county court where principal resides)	Must be approved by judge of state District Court

*California and Rhode Island have statutory forms for durable powers of attorney for health care which include a notice or warning to persons executing the document.

Appendix 6
Sample State Power-of-Attorney Form

Statutory Form of Power of Attorney
(Minnesota)

§523.23. Statutory short form of general power of attorney; formal requirements; joints agents.

Subdivision 1. Form.

The use of the following form in the creation of a power of attorney is lawful, and, when used, it shall be construed in accordance with the provisions of sections 523.23 and 523.24:

Notice: The powers granted by this document are broad and sweeping. They are defined in section 523.24. If you have any questions about these powers, obtain competent advice. The use of any other or different form of power of attorney desired by the parties is also permitted. This power of attorney may be revoked by you if you later wish to do so. This power of attorney authorizes the attorney-in-fact to act for you but does not require that he or she do so.

Know All Men by These Presents, which are intended to constitute a Statutory Short Form Power of Attorney pursuant to Minnesota Statutes, section 523.23:

That I

(insert name and address of the principal) do hereby appoint

(insert name and address of the attorney-in-fact, or each attorney-in-fact, if more than one is designated) my attorney(s)-in-fact to act (jointly):

Note: If more than one attorney-in-fact is designated and the principal wishes each attorney-in-fact alone to be able to exercise the power conferred, delete the word "jointly." Failure to delete the word "jointly" will require the attorneys-in-fact to act unanimously.)

First: In my name, place, and stead in any way which I myself could do, if I were personally present, with respect to the following matters as each of them is defined in section 523.24:

[To grant to the attorney-in-fact any of the following powers, make a check or "x" in the line in front of each power being granted. To delete any of the following powers, do not make a check or "x" in the line in front of the power. You may, but need not, cross out each power being deleted with a line drawn through it (or in similar fashion). Failure to make a check or "x" in the line in front of the power will have the effect of deleting the power unless the line in front of the power of (O) is checked or x-ed.] Check or "x"

(A) real property transactions;
(B) tangible personal property transactions;
(C) bond, share, and commodity transactions;
(D) banking transactions;
(E) business operating transactions;
(F) insurance transactions;
(G) beneficiary transactions;
(H) gift transactions;
(I) fiduciary transactions;
(J) claims and litigation;
(K) family maintenance;
(L) benefits from military service;
(M) records, reports, and statements;
(N) all other matters;
(O) all of the powers listed in (A) through (N) above.

Second: [You must indicate below whether or not this power of attorney will be effective if you become incompetent. Make a check or "x" in the line in front of the statement that expresses your intent.]

This power of attorney shall continue to be effective if I become incompetent. It shall not be affected by my later disability or incompetency.

This power of attorney shall not be effective if I become incompetent.

Third: [You must indicate below whether or not this power of attorney authorizes the attorney-in-fact to transfer your property directly to himself or herself. Make a check or "x" in the line in front of the statement that expresses your intent.]

This power of attorney authorizes the attorney-in-fact to transfer property directly to himself or herself.

This power of attorney does not authorize the attorney-in-fact to transfer property directly to himself or herself.

In Witness Whereof I have hereunto signed my name this _____ day of _____, 19____.

(Signature of Principal)

(Acknowledgment)

Specimen Signature of Attorney(s)-in-Fact

Appendix 7
Sample General Power-of-Attorney Form

KNOW ALL PEOPLE by these presents that I, (name of principal), Social Security Number _____, permanently domiciled in (residence of principal—city and state), do hereby make, constitute, and appoint my (relationship of attorney-in-fact to principal), (name of agent or attorney-in-fact), presently of (residence—city and state only—of attorney-in-fact), as my true and lawful attorney-in-fact to act in my name, place and stead, for my use and benefit, and to exercise or perform any act, power, duty, right or obligation whatsoever that I now have or may hereafter acquire relating to any person, matter, transaction or property, real or personal, tangible or intangible, now owned or hereafter acquired by me, including, by way of example and not by way of limitation, the powers set out in this power of attorney. If (s)he cannot or will not so serve, then I appoint my (relationship of substitute attorney-in-fact), (name of substitute attorney-in-fact), presently of (residence—city and state—of substitute attorney-in-fact), to serve in his/her stead.

Article I—Powers

My [agent or] attorney-in-fact shall have, by way of illustration and not by way of limitation, the following powers:

Section 1. To ask, demand, sue for, collect and receive each and every sum of money, including, but not limited to, wages, checking or savings account(s), debts, legacies, bequests, money-market accounts, Treasury bills, interest, dividends, certificates of

---

Source: *Guardianship and Alternative Legal Interventions: A Compendium for Training and Practice,* The Center for Social Gerontology, Inc.

deposit, annuities, demands, pensions or government benefits, now or hereafter due, owing, or payable, to which I have a claim; to take any lawful means for the recovery of the same; to execute and deliver a satisfaction or release, together with the right and power to compromise or compound any claim or demand;

Section 2. To perform any and all banking business including, by way of example and not by way of limitation: to draw, make, sign in my name, accept or deliver notes, checks, drafts, orders, receipts and to otherwise make withdrawals from any checking or savings account in which I may have any interest, solely or jointly with any other persons, in any financial institution; to endorse, negotiate and deliver checks, certificates of deposit, notes, drafts, money-market instruments or any other instrument for the payment of money and to deposit same as check or for collection and cash into any savings or checking account in which I may have an interest, solely or jointly with other persons, in any financial institution; to have access to any safe deposit box of which I am tenant or co-tenant and to exercise any rights I might have with regard to that safety deposit box and the contents thereof.

Section 3. To contract for, buy, sell, exchange, transfer, and in any legal manner deal with personal property, tangible or intangible, including but not limited to goods, wares and merchandise, choses in action and all other property in possession or in action; and to mortgage, transfer in trust, or otherwise encumber the same to secure payment of a negotiable or non-negotiable note or the performance of any obligation or agreement;

Section 4. To contract for, purchase, receive and take possession of real property, or any interest in or building on real property, and of evidence of title thereto; to lease the same for any term and for any lawful purpose; to sell, exchange, grant or convey the same with or without warranty; and to mortgage, transfer in trust, or otherwise encumber the same to secure payment of a negotiable or non-negotiable note for the performance of any obligation or agreement; it being expressly intended to permit my attorney-in-fact to act on my behalf with respect to all transactions related to my residence at [*], and any such other real property as I may own or acquire; it being further intended that my attorney-in-fact may record or cause to be recorded upon public land records any such act or transaction authorized above;

Section 5. To borrow or lend money, and to execute and deliver or receive negotiable or non-negotiable notes, with or without security as my attorney-in-fact shall deem proper;

Section 6. At my attorney-in-fact's sole discretion, to make such gifts as my attorney-in-fact may deem proper, either outright or in trust, including charitable gifts and

---

*It is appropriate to insert the address *and* legal description of any real property so that it is clear that the attorney-in-fact has authority to act with regard to that property. This also facilitates recording the power of attorney with the register of deeds.

pledges; provided, however, that no gifts to a single donee shall in any one calendar year exceed the amount of Ten Thousand Dollars ($10,000.00);

Section 7. To prepare, execute and file, by way of illustration and not by limitation, reports, returns, declarations, forms and statements of all and any kinds for tax purposes including, but not limited to, federal, state, local, income, gift, real estate, personal property, business, and intangibles taxes and any other kind of tax whatsoever; to receive any and all information whatsoever bearing upon my obligations to pay taxes, to adjust, settle, pay and compromise any and all claims regarding my tax liabilities; to appear for me and represent me in connection with any tax matter; and to receive any tax refunds due me;

Article II—Durability

Section 1. This power of attorney shall not be affected by my subsequent disability or incapacity, and all acts done pursuant to its terms shall be as fully effective as if I were competent and were myself so acting or causing others to act. This declaration of durability is made as an expression of my intent, and I ask that my intent be honored, if necessary, pursuant to any law of any other jurisdiction that may have an interest in the proceeding in question, whether the law is now in effect or later enacted to authorize powers of attorney which survive the incompetence of the principal.

Section 2. If for any reason this power is determined not to be legally binding, I ask that it be honored to the fullest extent possible.

Section 3. In executing this general durable power of attorney, it is my intent to avoid the necessity of ever having to seek judicial appointment of a guardian of my person and/or for my estate; however, should I ever be adjudged incapacitated or incompetent by a court, I hereby nominate my attorney-in-fact to be appointed as the guardian of my person and/or my estate.

Article III—Discretion in the Exercise of Duties

Section 1. I give and grant to my attorney-in-fact full power and authority to do and perform all and every act and thing whatsoever required, necessary or appropriate, to be determined solely in his/her discretion, to be done as fully to all intents and purposes as I might or could do if personally present, hereby ratifying all that my attorney-in-fact shall do or cause to be done by virtue of this power of attorney. The power and authority hereby conferred upon my attorney-in-fact shall be applicable to all matters relating to my financial and business matters, as well as to other matters, as fully as I may decide such matters myself if competent and present.

Section 2. My attorney-in-fact may retain, compensate, and make such use of agents to assist in acting under this power as my attorney-in-fact may deem advisable; and my attorney-in-fact may designate another person as the joint or successor attorney-in-fact either temporarily or permanently, under this power of attorney if for any reason my attorney-in-fact is unable or unwilling to act individually pursuant to the other provisions of this power of attorney but my attorney-in-fact has no duty to appoint a joint or successor attorney-in-fact and it would be contrary to my wishes and intent for any person to require that my attorney-in-fact do so or to require that my attorney-in-fact obtain the consent of any other person for any determination which my attorney-in-fact makes.

Section 3. My attorney-in-fact has sole discretion to determine the time when, purpose for, and manner in which any power herein conferred upon my attorney-in-fact shall be exercised, and the conditions to be accepted or waivers to be granted incident thereto.

Section 4. The powers delegated under this power of attorney are separable, so that the invalidity of one or more powers shall not affect any others.

Article IV—Revocation

Section 1. This general durable power of attorney revokes any previous powers of attorney granted by me.

Section 2. This general durable power of attorney may be voluntarily revoked by me at any time, either by my written revocation delivered to the last known address of my attorney-in-fact or by my written revocation entered of record in the deed of records of _____ County, _____ (State).

Article V—Third Party Reliance

Section 1. Third parties may rely upon the representation of my attorney-in-fact as to all matters relating to any power granted herein.

Section 2. For the purpose of inducing any third party to act in accordance with the grant of powers in this Power of Attorney, I and my successors, assignees, heirs and legal representatives agree to indemnify and hold harmless from any loss suffered or liability incurred by said third party by it acting in good faith in accordance with the Power of Attorney prior to said third party's receipt of written notice of termination of this Power of Attorney.

I have signed and delivered this Durable Power of Attorney consisting of _____ pages this _____ day of _____, 19_____.

_____
(name of principal)

Sample General Power-of-Attorney Form

(name of principal), the Principal named in the foregoing instrument, signed this instrument, on the _____ day of _____, 19_____. At that time, (s)he declared that the instrument reflects his/her will and intent with respect to his/her financial affairs and all other matters contained herein. At the request of (name of principal), in the presence of (name of principal) and in the presence of each other, each of us believing (name of principal) to be now competent, we have signed our names as witnesses. [Note: The attorney-in-fact should not act as a witness, as that may cause third parties to question the authenticity of the document.]

Witnesses:

_____

_____

State of _____)SS.
_____)
County of _____

On the _____ day of _____, 19_____, before me, the undersigned, a Notary Public in and for (jurisdication of signing), personally appeared (name of principal), known to me to be the person whose name is subscribed to the within instrument, and acknowledged that (s)he executed the same. Witness my hand and official seal.

            (Seal) _____
                Notary public in and for
                (jurisdiction of signing)

My Commission expires _____

Drafted by:
(Name of attorney
address
telephone number)

Appendix 8
Sample Durable Power of Attorney for Health Care Forms

Generic Short Form

I, _____ hereby appoint:

_____
name

_____
home address

_____

_____
home telephone number

_____
work telephone number

as my agent to make health care decisions for me if and when I am unable to make my own health care decisions. This gives my agent the power to consent to giving, withholding or stopping any health care, treatment, service, or diagnostic procedure. My agent also has the authority to talk with health care personnel, get information, and sign forms necessary to carry out those decisions.

If the person named as my agent is not available or is unable to act as my agent, then I appoint the following person(s) to serve in the order listed below:

1. _____
   name

   _____
   home address

   _____

   _____

   _____
   home telephone number

   _____
   work telephone number

Source: Barbara Mishkin, Hogan and Hartson, Washington, D.C.

2. _____
   name

   _____
   home address

   _____

   _____

   _____
   home telephone number

   _____
   work telephone number

By this document I intend to create a power of attorney for health care which shall take effect upon my incapacity to make my own health care decisions and shall continue during that incapacity.

My agent shall make health care decisions as I direct below or as I make known to him or her in some other way.

(a) Statement of desires concerning life-prolonging care, treatment, services, and procedures:

_____

_____

_____

_____

_____

(b) Special provisions and limitations:

_____

_____

_____

_____

_____

_____

_____

Appendix 8 (continued)

Sample State Durable Power of Attorney
for Health Care Decisions Form

(California Civil Code Sections 2410–2443)

Warning to Person Executing This Document

This is an important legal document. It creates a durable power of attorney for health care. Before executing this document, you should know these important facts:

1. This document gives the person you designate as your attorney-in-fact the power to make health care decisions for you. This power is subject to any limitations or statement of your desires that you include in this document. The power to make health care decisions for you may include consent, refusal of consent, or withdrawal of consent to any care, treatment, service, or procedure to maintain, diagnose, or treat a physical or mental condition. You may state in this document any types of treatment or placements that you do not desire.

2. The person you designate in this document has a duty to act consistent with your desires as stated in this document or otherwise made known or, if your desires are unknown, to act in your best interests.

3. Except as you otherwise specify in this document, the power of the person you designate to make health care decisions for you may include the power to consent to your doctor not giving treatment or stopping treatment which would keep you alive.

4. Unless you specify a shorter period in this document, this power will exist for seven years from the date you execute this document and, if you are unable to make health care decisions for yourself at the time when this seven-year period ends, this power will continue to exist until the time when you become able to make health care decisions for yourself.

5. Notwithstanding this document, you have the right to make medical and other health care decisions for yourself so long as you can give informed consent with respect to the particular decision. In addition, no treatment may be given to you over your objections, and health care necessary to keep you alive may not be stopped if you object.

6. You have the right to revoke the appointment of the person designated in this document to make health care decisions for you by notifying that person of the revocation orally or in writing.

Source: *A Matter of Choice: Planning Ahead for Health Care Decisions,* AARP, Washington, D.C.

7. You have the right to revoke the authority granted to the person designated in this document to make health care decisions for you by notifying the treating physician, hospital, or other health care provider orally or in writing.

8. The person designated in this document to make health care decisions for you has the right to examine your medical records and to consent to their disclosure unless you limit the right in this document.

9. This document revokes any prior durable power of attorney for health care.

10. *If there is anything in this document that you do not understand, you should ask a lawyer to explain it to you.*

1. Designation of Health Care Agent

I, _____

_____
(Insert your name)

do hereby designate and appoint:
Name: _____
Address: _____

_____

Telephone Number: _____
as my attorney-in-fact to make health care decisions for me as authorized in this document.

(Insert the name and address of the person you wish to designate as your attorney-in-fact to make health care decisions for you. None of the following may be designated as your attorney-in-fact: (1) your treating health care provider, (2) an employee of your treating health care provider, (3) an operator of a community care facility, or (4) an employee of an operator of a community care facility.)

2. Creation of Durable Power of Attorney for Health Care

By this document I intend to create a durable power of attorney by appointing the person designated above to make health care decisions for me as allowed by Sections 2410 to 2443, inclusive, of the California Civil Code. This power of attorney shall not be affected by my subsequent incapacity.

3. General Statement of Authority Granted

In the event that I am incapable of giving informed consent with respect to health care decisions, I hereby grant to the attorney-in-fact named above full power and authority to make health care decisions for me before, or after my death, including: Consent, refusal of consent, or withdrawal of consent to any care, treatment, service, or procedure to maintain, diagnose, or treat a physical or mental condition, subject only to the limitations and special provisions, if any, set forth in Paragraph 4 or 6.

4. Special Provisions and Limitations

(By law, your attorney-in-fact is not permitted to consent to any of the following: Commitment to or placement in mental health treatment facility, convulsive treatment, psycho-surgery, sterilization, or abortion. If there are any other types of treatment or placement that you

Sample Durable Power of Attorney for Health Care Form 239

do not want your attorney-in-fact to have authority to give consent for or other restriction you wish to place on his or her attorney-in-fact's authority, you should list them in the space below. If you do not write in any limitations, your attorney-in-fact will have the broad powers to make health care decisions on your behalf which are set forth in Paragraph 3, except to the extent that there are limits provided by law.)

In exercising the authority under this durable power of attorney for health care, the authority of my attorney-in-fact is subject to the following special provisions and limitations:

_____
_____
_____
_____
_____
_____
_____

5. Duration

I understand that this power of attorney will exist for seven years from the date I execute this document unless I establish a shorter time. If I am unable to make health care decisions for myself when this power of attorney expires, the authority I have granted my attorney-in-fact will continue to exist until the time when I become able to make health care decisions for myself.

I wish to have this power of attorney end before seven years on the following date: _____.

6. Statement of Desires

(With respect to decisions to withhold or withdraw life sustaining treatment, your attorney-in-fact must make health care decisions that are consistent with your known desires. You can, but are not required to, indicate your desires below. If your desires are unknown, your attorney-in-fact has the duty to act in your best interests; and, under some circumstances, a judicial proceeding may be necessary so that a court can determine the health care decision that is in your best interests. If you wish to indicate your desires, you may initial the statement or statements that reflect your desires and/or write your own statements in the space below.)

(If the statement reflects your desires, initial the box next to the statement.)

1. I desire that my life be prolonged to the greatest extent possible, without regard to my condition, the chances I have for recovery or long-term survival, or the cost of the procedures. (_____)

2. If I am in a coma which my doctors have reasonably concluded is irreversible, I desire that life sustaining or prolonging treatments or procedures *not* be used. (_____)

3. If I have an incurable or terminal condition or illness and no reasonable hope of long-term recovery or survival, I desire that life sustaining or prolonging treatments *not* be used. (_____)

4. I do not desire treatment to be provided and/or continued if the burdens of the treatment outweigh the expected benefits. My attorney-in-fact is to consider the relief of suffering, the preservation or restoration of functioning, and the quality as well as the extent of the possible extension of my life. (_____)

(If you wish to change your answer, you may do so by *drawing* an "X" through the answer you do not want, and circling the answer you prefer.)

Other or additional statements of desires:

_____
_____
_____
_____
_____
_____
_____
_____
_____

7. Designation of Alternate Attorney-in-Fact

(You are not required to designate any alternative attorney-in-fact but you may do so. Any alternative attorney-in-fact you designate will be able to make the same health care decisions as the attorney-in-fact designated in Paragraph 1 above in the event that he or she is unable or unwilling to act as your attorney-in-fact. Also, if the attorney-in-fact designated in Paragraph 1 is your spouse, his or her designation as your attorney-in-fact is automatically revoked by law if your marriage is dissolved.)

If the person designated in Paragraph 1 as my attorney-in-fact is unable to make health care decisions for me, then I designate the following persons to serve as my attorney-in-fact to make health care decisions for me as authorized in this document, such persons to serve in the order listed below:

Sample Durable Power of Attorney for Health Care Form

A. **First Alternative Attorney-in-fact**

Name: _____

Address: _____

_____

Telephone Number: _____

B. **Second alternate Attorney-in-fact**

Name: _____

Address: _____

_____

Telephone Number: _____

8. Prior Designations Revoked

I revoke any prior durable power of attorney for health care.

(You must date and sign this power of attorney).

I sign my name to this Statutory Short Form Durable Power of Attorney for Health Care on _____

_____ at
(Date)

_____,
(City)

_____.
(State)

_____
(Signature)

(This power of attorney will not be valid for making health care decisions unless it is either (1) signed by at least two qualified witnesses who are personally known to you and who are present when you sign or acknowledge your signature or (2) acknowledged before a notary public in California.)

Certificate of Acknowledgment of Notary Public

(You may use acknowledgment before a notary public instead of the statement of witnesses.)

State of California _____)

_____)SS.

County _____) of

On this _____ day of _____, in the year _____, before me,

_____
(here insert name of notary public)
personally appeared

_____
(here insert name of principal)

personally known to me (or proved to me on the basis of satisfactory evidence) to be the person whose name is subscribed to this instrument, and acknowledged that he or she executed it. I declare under penalty of perjury that the person whose name is subscribed to this instrument appears to be of sound mind and under no duress, fraud, or undue influence.

Notary Seal _____

(Signature of Notary Public)

Statement of Witnesses

(You should carefully read and follow this witnessing procedure. This document will not be valid unless you comply with the witnessing procedure. If you elect to use witnesses instead of having this document notarized, you must use two qualified adult witnesses. None of the following may be used as a witness:

(1) A person you designate as the attorney-in-fact,
(2) A health care provider,
(3) An employee of a health care provider,
(4) The operator of a community care facility,
(5) An employee of an operator of a community care facility.

At least one of the witnesses must make the additional declaration set out following the place where the witnesses sign.)

I declare under penalty of perjury under the laws of California that the principal is personally known to me, that the principal signed or acknowledged this durable power of attorney in my presence, that the principal appears to be of sound mind and under no duress, fraud, or undue influence, that I am not the person appointed as attorney-in-fact by this document, and that I am not a health care provider, an employee of a health care provider, the operator of a community care facility, nor an employee of an operator of a community care facility.

Signature: _____
Print Name: _____
Residence Address: _____
Date: _____

Signature: _____
Print Name: _____
Residence Address: _____
_____
_____
Date: _____

(At least one of the above witnesses must also sign the following declaration.)

I declare under penalty of perjury under the laws of California that I am not related to the principal by blood, marriage, or adoption, and to the best of my knowledge I am not entitled to any part of the estate of the principal upon the death of the principal under a will now existing or by operation of law.

Signature: _____
Signature: _____

Special Requirements

(Special additional requirements must be satisfied for this document to be valid if (1) you are a patient in a skilled nursing facility or (2) you are a conservatee under the Lanterman-Petris-Short Act and you are appointing the conservator as your agent to make health care decisions for you.)

1. If you are a patient in a skilled nursing facility (as defined in Health and Safety Code Section 1250(c)) at least one witness must be a patient advocate or ombudsman. The patient advocate or ombudsman must sign the witness state-

Sample Durable Power of Attorney for Health Care Form

ment *and* must also sign the following declaration.

I declare under penalty of perjury under the laws of California that I am a patient advocate or ombudsman as designated by the State Department of Aging and am serving as a witness as required by subdivision (a) (2)A of Civil Code 2432.

Signature: _____

Print Name: _____

Residence Address: _____

_____

_____

Date: _____

2. If you are a conservatee under the Lanterman-Petris-Short Act (of Division 5 of the Welfare and Institutions Code) and you wish to designate your conservator as your agent to make health care decisions, you must be represented by legal counsel. Your lawyer must sign the following statement:

I have advised my client _____
                                 (Name)
concerning his or her rights in connection with this matter and the consequences of signing or not signing this durable power of attorney and my client, after being so advised, has executed this durable power of attorney.

Signature: _____

Print Name: _____

Residence Address: _____

_____

Date: _____

Copies: You should retain an executed copy of this document and give one to your attorney-in-fact. The power of attorney should be available so a copy may be given to your health care providers.

Appendix 9
Sample Springing (Durable) Power-of-Attorney Form

A springing power of attorney should be carefully drafted to ensure that the power does not take effect either too early or too late. One possible version is presented below. Any definition and test of disability may be used so long as they provide the principal with adequate protections considering the facts of his or her particular situation.

KNOW ALL PEOPLE by these presents that I, (name of principal), Social Security Number _____, permanently domiciled in (residence of principal—city and state), do hereby make, constitute, and appoint my (relationship of attorney-in-fact to principal), (name of attorney-in-fact), presently of (residence of attorney-in-fact), as my true and lawful attorney-in-fact to act in my name, place and stead, for my use and benefit, and to exercise or perform any act, power, duty, right or obligation whatsoever that I now have or may hereafter acquire relating to any person, matter, transaction or property, real or personal, tangible or intangible, now owned and hereafter acquired by me, including, by way of example and not by way of limitation, the powers set out in this power of attorney. If (s)he cannot or will not so serve, then I appoint my (relationship of substitute attorney-in-fact), (name of substitute attorney-in-fact), presently of (residence of substitute attorney-in-fact), to serve in his/her stead.

Source: *Guardianship and Alternative Legal Interventions: A Compendium for Training and Practice,* The Center for Social Gerontology, Inc.

Article 1—Powers

My attorney-in-fact shall have, by way of illustration and not by way of limitation, the following powers:

Section 1. To ask, demand, sue for, collect and receive each and every sum of money, debt, account, legacy, bequest, interest, dividend, annuity, demand and government benefit (now or hereafter due, owing, or payable) to which I have a claim, and to take any lawful means for the recovery of the same, and to execute and deliver a satisfaction or release, together with the right and power to compromise or compound any claim or demand;

Section 2. To contract for, purchase, receive and take possession of real property, or any interest in or building on real property, and of evidence of title thereto; to lease the same for any term and for any lawful purpose; to sell, exchange, grant or convey the same with or without warranty; and to mortgage, transfer in trust, or otherwise encumber or hypothecate the same to secure payment of a negotiable or non-negotiable note for the performance of any obligation or agreement; it being expressly intended to permit my attorney-in-fact to act on my behalf with respect to all transactions related to my residence at [ ], and any such other real estate as I may own or acquire; it being further intended that my attorney-in-fact may record or cause to be recorded upon public land records any such act or transaction authorized above;

Section 3. To contract for, buy, sell, exchange, transfer, and in any legal manner deal with personal property, tangible or intangible, including goods, wares and merchandise, choses in action and all other property in possession or in action; and to mortgage, transfer in trust, or otherwise encumber or hypothecate the same to secure payment of a negotiable or non-negotiable note or the performance of any obligation or agreement;

Section 4. To borrow or lend money, and to execute and deliver or receive negotiable or non-negotiable notes, with or without security as (s)he shall deem proper;

Section 5. To create, amend, supplement, make additions to, withdraw and receive the income or corpus of, and terminate a trust and to instruct and advise the trustee of any trust of which I may have or will have an interest; to take any action with respect to stock, stock rights, dividends, distributions and bonuses which I, whether as owner or claimant or otherwise, could take; and to compound, compromise, adjust, settle and satisfy any obligation, secured or unsecured, owing by or to me, and to give or accept any property or money whether or not equal to or less in value than the amount owing in payment, settlement or satisfaction thereof;

Section 6. To continue or complete any gifts or gift programs of mine with any of my real estate or personal property to my spouse, any of my children, their spouse, or their descendents, or to any charitable organizations;

Section 7. To prepare, execute and file, by way of illustration and not by limitation, reports, returns, declarations, forms and statements of all and any kinds for tax purposes including, but not limited to, federal, state, local, income, gift, real estate, personal property, business, and intangibles taxes and any other kind of tax whatsoever; to receive any and all information whatsoever bearing upon my obligations to pay taxes; to adjust, settle, pay and compromise any and all claims regarding my tax liabilities; to appear for me and represent me in connection with any tax matter; and to receive any tax refunds due me;

Article II—Scope of Authority

Section 1. This instrument is to be construed and interpreted as a general power of attorney. The enumeration of specific items, acts, rights or powers herein does not limit or restrict and it is not to be construed or interpreted as limiting or restricting the general powers herein granted to my attorney-in-fact.

Section 2. I give and grant to my attorney-in-fact full power and authority to do and perform all and every act and thing whatsoever required, necessary or appropriate, to be determined solely in the discretion of my attorney-in-fact, to be done as fully to all intents and purposes as I might or could do if personally present, hereby ratifying all that my attorney-in-fact shall do or cause to be done by virtue of this power of attorney. The power and authority hereby conferred upon my attorney-in-fact shall be applicable to all matters relating to my financial and business matters, as well as to other matters, as fully as I may decide such matters myself if competent and present.

Section 3. My attorney-in-fact may retain, compensate, and make such use of agents to assist in acting under this power as my attorney-in-fact may deem advisable, and my attorney-in-fact may designate another person as the joint or successor attorney-in-fact, either temporarily or permanently, under this power of attorney if for any reason my attorney-in-fact is unable or unwilling to act individually pursuant to the other provisions of this power of attorney, but my attorney-in-fact has no duty to appoint a joint or successor attorney-in-fact and it would be contrary to my wishes and intent for any person to require that my attorney-in-fact do so or to require that my attorney-in-fact obtain the consent of any other person for any determination which my attorney-in-fact makes.

Section 4. The powers delegated under this power of attorney are separable, so that the invalidity of one or more powers shall not affect any others.

Article III—Revocation

Section 1. This general power of attorney revokes any previous powers of attorney granted by me. This general power of attorney may be voluntarily revoked only by me at any time, either by my written revocation delivered to my attorney-in-fact or by my written revocation entered of record in the deed records of _____ County, _____ (State).

Article IV—Effective Date and Disability

Section 1. Notwithstanding the other provisions of this general power of attorney, the rights, powers, and authorities of my attorney-in-fact shall commence only upon my disability as hereinafter defined and shall remain in full force thereafter until said disability is terminated.

Section 2. Disability shall be defined as a substantial impairment of my ability to manage my business affairs. The inability to manage my business affairs shall mean the inability to know and appreciate the nature and effect of business transactions, notwithstanding a display of poor judgment.

Section 3. For purposes of the exercise of this general power by my attorney-in-fact, my disability shall be conclusively determined by any one of the following:

(a) The filing of a petition in a court of law personally by me to appoint a guardian of my estate or person;

(b) A written declaration of my disability by me to my attorney-in-fact, which declaration shall be attached to this power; or

(c) A written declaration of my disability by my personal physician, _____ (name of physician), and _____ (name of trusted friend or relative),* to me and my attorney-in-fact, which declaration shall be attached to this power.

Section 4. In executing this general durable power of attorney, it is my intent to avoid the necessity of ever having to seek judicial appointment of a guardian of my person and/or for my estate; however, should I ever be adjudged incapacitated or incompetent by a court, I hereby nominate my attorney-in-fact to be appointed as the guardian of my person and/or my estate.

Article V—Indemnification and Ratification of Acts of Attorney-in-Fact

Section 1. I hereby ratify and confirm all that my attorney-in-fact or any successor attorney-in-fact shall lawfully do or cause to be done by virtue of this general power of attorney and the rights and powers granted herein.

The second individual named should be a trusted individual who will have sufficient contact with the principal to be able to make this determination and who is not himself the attorney-in-fact.

Section 2. I hereby bind myself, my heirs, devisees, and personal representatives to indemnify my attorney-in-fact and any other successor attorney-in-fact who shall so act against any and all claims, demands, losses, damages, actions, and causes of action, including expenses, costs, and reasonable attorneys' fees that my attorney at any time may sustain or incur in connection with carrying out the authority granted in this general power of attorney.

Section 3. My death shall not revoke or terminate this agency as to my attorney-in-fact or any successor attorney-in-fact who, without actual knowledge of my death, acts in good faith under this general power of attorney. Any action so taken unless otherwise invalid or unenforcable, shall be binding upon me and my heirs, devisees, and personal representatives. An affidavit, executed by my attorney-in-fact or any successor attorney-in-fact stating that he does not have, at the time of doing an act pursuant to this general power of attorney, actual knowledge of the revocation of termination of this general power of attorney, is, in the absence of fraud, conclusive proof of the nonrevocation or nontermination of the power at that time.

I have signed and delivered this Durable Power of Attorney consisting of _____ pages this _____ day of _____, 19_____.

(name of principal), the Principal named in the foregoing instrument, signed this instrument, on the _____ day of _____, 19_____. At that time, (s)he declared that the instrument reflects his/her will and intent with respect to his/her financial affairs and all other matters contained herein. At the request of (name of principal), in the presence of (name of principal) and in the presence of each other, each of us believing (name of principal) to be now competent, we have signed our names as witnesses.

Witnesses:

_____

_____

_____

State of _____)
) SS.
County of _____)

On the _____ day of _____, 19_____, before me, the undersigned, a Notary Public in and for (jurisdiction of signing), personally appeared (name of principal), known to me to be the person whose name is subscribed to the within instrument, and acknowledged that (s)he executed the same. Witness my hand and official seal.

                        (Seal)   _____
                                   Notary public in and for
                                   (jurisdiction of signing)

My Commission expires _____.
Drafted by:
(Name of attorney
address
telephone number)

Appendix 10
List of Possible Hospital Services

1. Ambulatory surgery services Scheduled surgical services provided to patients who do not remain in the hospital overnight. The surgery may be performed in operating suites also used for inpatient surgery, specially designated surgical suites for ambulatory surgery, or procedure rooms within an ambulatory care facility.

2. Intensive care unit (cardiac care only) Provides patient care of a more specialized nature than the usual medical and surgical care, on the basis of physician's orders and approved nursing care plans. The unit is staffed with specially trained nursing personnel and contains monitoring and specialized support or treatment equipment for patients who, because of heart seizure, open-heart surgery, or other life-threatening conditions, require intensified, comprehensive observation and care. May include myocardial infarction, pulmonary care, and heart transplant units. Beds must be set up and staffed in a unit(s) specifically designated for this service.

3. Intensive care unit (mixed or other) Provides nursing care to adult and/or pediatric patients of a more intensive nature than the usual medical, surgical, pediatric, and/or psychiatric care on the basis of physicians' orders and approved nursing care plans. Included are medical-surgical, pediatric, and psychiatric (isolation) units. These units are staffed with specially trained nursing personnel and contain monitoring and specialized support equipment for patients who, because of shock, trauma, or life-threatening conditions, require intensified, comprehensive observation and care. These units may also include cardiac care when such services are not provided in a distinct cardiac care unit.

4. Open-heart surgery facilities The equipment and staff necessary to perform open-heart surgery.

5. Trauma center Provides emergency and specialized intensive care to critically injured patients.

6. Ultrasound The use of acoustic

Source: American Hospital Association.

waves above the range of 20,000 cycles per second to visualize internal body structures for diagnostic purposes.

7. X-ray radiation therapy The treatment of disease by roentgen rays or other radiant energy, with the exception of radium, cobalt, or radioisotopes.

8. Megavoltage radiation therapy The use of specialized equipment in the supervoltage and megavoltage (above 1 million volts) ranges for deep therapy treatment of cancer. This would include cobalt units, linear accelerators with or without electron beam therapy capability, betatrons, and Van de Graff machines.

9. Radioactive implants The use of radioactive material (radium, cobalt-60, cesium-137, or iridium-192 implants) for the treatment of malignancies.

10. Diagnostic radioisotope facility The use of radioactive isotopes (radiopharmaceuticals), as tracers or indicators, to detect an abnormal condition or disease.

11. Therapeutic radioisotope facility The use of radioactive isotopes (radiopharmaceuticals) for the treatment of malignancies.

12. Histopathology laboratory A laboratory in which tissue specimens are examined by a qualified pathologist.

13. Organ transplant The necessary staff and equipment to perform the surgical removal of a viable human organ, other than a kidney, from a donor, either alive or just deceased, and the surgical grafting of the organ to a suitably evaluated and prepared patient.

14. Blood bank A medical facility with the responsibility for each of the following: blood procurement, drawing, processing, and distribution.

15. Health promotion services Education and/or other supportive services that are planned and coordinated by the hospital and that will assist individuals or groups to adopt healthy behaviors and/or reduce health risks, increase self-care skills, improve management of common minor ailments, use health care services effectively, and/or improve understanding of medical procedures and therapeutic regimens. Includes the following specific activities:

Educational activities.
Written goals and objectives for the patient and/or family related to therapeutic regimens, medical procedures, and self-care; takes place at the hospital.

Community health promotion.
Similar to educational activities, but for individuals in the community not within a place of employment or as a patient.

Worksite health promotion.
Similar to educational activities, but for employees of a company implemented by the hospital and sponsored by their employer.

16. Respiratory therapy services The equipment and staff necessary for the administration of oxygen and certain potent drugs through inhalation or positive pressure.

List of Possible Hospital Services

17. Magnetic resonance imaging (nuclear magnetic resonance) The use of a uniform magnetic field and radio frequencies to study tissue and structure of the body. This procedure enables the visualization of biochemical activity of the cell *in vivo* without the use of ionizing radiation, radioisotopic substances, or high-frequency sound.

18. Self-care unit Provides minimal nursing care to ambulatory patients who must remain hospitalized. Beds must be set up and staffed in a unit specifically designated for this service.

19. Skilled nursing or other long-term care unit Provides physician services and continuous professional nursing supervision to patients who are not in the acute phase of illness and who currently require primarily convalescent rehabilitative and/or restorative services. May include extended care units. Can include, but not restricted to, Medicare/Medicaid certified skilled nursing care. May also include intermediate, residential, or other long-term care units. Beds must be set up and staffed in a unit(s) specifically designated for this service.

20. Hemodialysis Provision of equipment and personnel for the treatment of renal insufficiency, on an inpatient or outpatient basis.

21. Hospice A program providing palliative care, chiefly medical relief of pain and supportive services, to terminally ill patients and assistance to their families in adjusting to the patient's illness and death.

22. Burn care unit Provides more intensive care to severely burned patients than the usual acute nursing care provided in medical and surgical units. Beds must be set up and staffed in a unit specifically designated for this service.

23. Physical therapy services Facilities for the provision of physical therapy services prescribed by physicians and administered by, or under the direction of, a qualified physical therapist.

24. Occupational therapy services Facilities for the provision of occupational therapy services prescribed by physicians and administered by, or under the direction of, a qualified occupational therapist.

25. Rehabilitation inpatient unit Provides coordinated multidisciplinary physical restorative services to inpatients under the direction of a physician knowledgeable and experienced in rehabilitative medicine. Beds must be set up and staffed in a unit specifically designated for this service.

26. Rehabilitation outpatient services Provision of coordinated multidisciplinary physical restorative services to ambulatory patients under the direction of a physician knowledgeable and experienced in rehabilitation medicine.

27. Psychiatric inpatient unit Provides acute care to emotionally disturbed patients, including patients admitted for diagnosis and those admitted for treatment of psychiatric problems, on the basis of physicians' orders and approved nursing care plans. May also include the provision of medical care, nursing services, and supervision to the chronically mentally ill, mentally disordered, or other mentally incompetent persons. Beds must be set up and staffed in a unit(s) specifically designated for this service.

28. Psychiatric outpatient services Hospital services for the diagnosis and treatment of psychiatric outpatients.

29. Psychiatric partial hospitalization program Organized hospital facilities and services for day care and/or night care of psychiatric patients who do not require inpatient care 24 hours a day.

30. Psychiatric emergency services Hospital facilities for the provision of unscheduled outpatient care to psychiatric patients whose conditions are considered to require immediate care. Staff must be available 24 hours a day.

31. Psychiatric consultation-liaison services Provides organized psychiatric consultation/liaison services to non-psychiatric hospital staff and/or departments on psychological aspects of medical care that may be generic or specific to individual patients.

32. Psychiatric education services Provides psychiatric educational services to community agencies and workers such as schools, police, courts, public health nurses, welfare agencies, clergy, and so forth. The purpose is to expand the mental health knowledge and competence of personnel not working in the mental health field and to promote good mental health through improved understanding, attitudes, and behavioral patterns.

33. Women's Center An area set aside for coordinated education and treatment services specifically for and promoted to women as provided by this special unit. Services may or may not include obstetrics but include a range of services other than OB.

34. Organized outpatient department Organized hospital services (or clinics) for the provision of nonemergency medical and/or dental services for ambulatory patients.

35. Emergency department Organized hospital facilities for the provision of unscheduled outpatient services to patients whose conditions are considered to require immediate care. Must be staffed 24 hours a day.

36. Birthing room A hospital-managed combination labor and delivery unit with a homelike setting for mothers and fathers who have completed a specified childbirth course.

37. Family planning services Includes any or all of the following:

Contraceptive care.

A family planning service with full range of fertility control methods including education and counseling on all options of contraception.

Fertility services.

A unit which counsels and educates on infertility problems. Includes laboratory and surgical workup and management on infertility to individuals having problems conceiving children.

List of Possible Hospital Services

Sterilization. A service with capacity to perform total occlusion or ligation, as appropriate, for women and vasectomy for men.

38. Genetic counseling service A service, directed by a qualified physician, equipped with adequate laboratory facilities, to advise parents and prospective parents on potential problems in cases of genetic defects.

39. Extracorporeal shock wave lithotripter (ESWL) A medical device used for treating stones in the kidney or ureter. The device disintegrates kidney stones, noninvasively, through the transmission of acoustic shock waves directed at the stones.

40. Obstetrics unit Provides care to mothers following delivery, on the basis of physicians' orders and approved nursing care plans. Beds must be set up and staffed in a unit specifically designated for this service.

41. Home care program An organized program, administered by the hospital, that provides medical, nursing, other treatment, and social services to patients in their places of residence.

42. Recreational therapy Facilities for the provision of recreational therapy services prescribed by physicians and administered by or under the direction of a qualified recreational therapist.

43. Day hospital Provides diagnostic, treatment, and rehabilitative services to patients who spend the major portion of the day at the hospital but who do not require care for 24 hours a day. More intensive care than provided in an outpatient clinic and of a limited duration.

44. Speech pathology services Personnel available on a routine basis to provide speech therapy for inpatients or outpatients.

45. Hospital auxiliary A volunteer community organization formed to assist the institution in carrying out its purpose and to serve as a link between the institution and the community.

46. Volunteer services department An organized hospital department responsible for coordinating the services of volunteers working within the institution.

47. Patient representative services Organized hospital services providing personnel through whom patients and staff can seek solutions to institutional problems affecting the delivery of high-quality care and services.

48. Alcoholism/chemical dependency inpatient unit Provides medical care and/or rehabilitative services to patients for whom the primary diagnosis is alcoholism or other chemical dependency. Beds must be set up and staffed in a unit specifically designated for this service.

49. Alcoholism/chemical dependency outpatient services Hospital services for the medical care and/or rehabilitative treatment of outpatients for whom the primary diagnosis is alcoholism or other chemical dependency.

50. Geriatric services Includes any or all of the following:

Comprehensive geriatric assessment services.

Services that determine geriatric patients' long-term care service needs. Includes the assessment of medical conditions, functional activities, mental and emotional conditions, individual and family preferences, and financial status.

Geriatric acute care unit.

Provides acute care to elderly patients in specially designed medical and surgical units. These services may have trained staff in geriatrics, architectural adaptations designed to accommodate the decreased sensory perception of older adults, or age 65+ eligibility requirements.

Satellite geriatric clinics.

Clinics or centers which are geographically located at some distance from the hospital and provide health and related services to older adults. Common locations are in senior citizens' centers or senior housing complexes.

51. Neonatal intensive care unit Provides newborn infants with more intensive care than the usual nursing care provided in newborn acute care units, on the basis of physicians' orders and approved nursing care plans. Beds must be set up and staffed in a unit specifically designated for this service.

52. Pediatric inpatient unit Provides acute care to pediatric patients on the basis of physicians' orders and approved nursing care plans. Beds must be set up and staffed in a unit specifically designated for this service.

53. CT scanner Computed tomographic scanners for head and/or whole body scans.

54. Cardiac catheterization laboratory Provides special diagnostic procedures necessary for the care of patients with cardiac conditions. Available procedures include introduction of a catheter into the interior of the heart through a vein or artery or by direct needle puncture.

Reprinted, with permission, from the *American Hospital Association Guide to the Health Care Field,* 1988 edition, © 1988 by the American Hospital Association.

Appendix 11
The American Hospital Association's Patient's Bill of Rights

1. The patient has the right to considerate and respectful care

2. The patient has the right to obtain from his physician complete current information concerning his diagnosis, treatment, and prognosis in terms the patient can be reasonably expected to understand. When it is not medically advisable to give such information to the patient, the information should be made available to an appropriate person in his behalf. He has the right to know, by name, the physician responsible for coordinating his care.

3. The patient has the right to receive from his physician information necessary to give informed consent prior to the start of any procedure and/or treatment. Except in emergencies, such information for informed consent should include but not necessarily be limited to the specific procedure and/or treatment, the medically significant risks involved, and the probable duration of incapacitation. Where medically significant alternatives for care or treatment exist, or when the patient requests information concerning medical alternatives, the patient has the right to such information. The patient also has the right to know the name of the person responsible for procedures and/or treatment.

4. The patient has the right to refuse treatment to the extent permitted by law and to be informed of medical consequences of his action.

5. The patient has the right to every consideration of privacy concerning his own medical care program. Case discussion, consultation, examination and treatment are confidential and should be conducted discreetly. Those not directly involved in his care must have the permission of the patient to be present.

Reprinted with the permission of the American Hospital Association, © 1972.

6. The patient has the right to expect that all communications and records pertaining to his care should be treated as confidential.

7. The patient has the right to expect that within its capacity a hospital must make reasonable response to the request of a patient for services. The hospital must provide evaluation, service and/or referral as indicated by the urgency of the case. When medically permissible, a patient may be transferred to another facility only after he has received complete information and explanation concerning the needs for and alternatives to such a transfer. The institution to which the patient is to be transferred must first have accepted the patient for transfer.

8. The patient has the right to obtain information as to any relationship of his hospital to other health care and education institutions insofar as his care is concerned. The patient has the right to obtain information as to the existence of any professional relationships among individuals, by name, who are treating him.

9. The patient has the right to be advised if the hospital proposes to engage in or perform human experimentation affecting his care or treatment. The patient has the right to refuse to participate in such research projects.

10. The patient has the right to expect reasonable continuity of care. He has the right to know in advance what appointment times and physicians are available and where. The patient has the right to expect that the hospital will provide a mechanism whereby he is informed by his physician or a delegate of the physician of the patient's continuing health care requirements following discharge.

11. The patient has the right to examine and receive an explanation of his bill regardless of source of payment.

12. The patient has a right to know what hospital rules and regulations apply to his conduct as a patient.

Appendix 12
Sample State Bill of Rights for Patients

California Code, Section 70707, Patients' Rights

A. Hospitals and medical staffs shall adopt a written policy on patients' rights.

B. A list of these patients' rights shall be posted in both Spanish and English in appropriate places within the hospital so that such rights may be read by patient. This list shall include but not be limited to the patients' rights to:

1. exercise these rights without regard to sex or cultural, economic, educational, or religious background or the source of payment for care.

2. considerate and respectful care.

3. knowledge of the name of the physician who has primary responsibility for coordinating the care and the names and professional relationships of other physicians and nonphysicians who will see the patient.

4. receive information about the illness, the course of treatment and prospects for recovery in terms that the patient can understand.

5. receive as much information about any proposed treatment or procedure as the patient may need in order to give informed consent or to refuse this course of treatment. Except in emergencies, this information shall include a description of the procedure or treatment, the medically significant risks involved in this treatment, alternative courses of treatment or nontreatment and the risks involved in each and to know the name of the person who will carry out the procedure or treatment.

6. participate actively in decisions regarding medical care. To the extent permitted by law, this includes the right to refuse treatment.

7. full consideration of privacy concerning the medical care program. Case discussion, consultation, examination and treatment are confidential and should be conducted

discreetly. The patient has the right to be advised as to the reason for the presence of any individual.

8. confidential treatment of all communications and records pertaining to the care and the stay in the hospital. Written permission shall be obtained before the medical records can be made available to anyone not directly concerned with the care.

9. reasonable responses to any reasonable requests made for service.

10. leave the hospital even against the advice of physicians.

11. reasonable continuity of care and to know in advance the time and location of appointment as well as the identity of persons providing the care.

12. be advised if hospital/personal physician proposes to engage in or perform human experimentation affecting care or treatment. The patient has the right to refuse to participate in such research projects.

13. be informed of continuing health care requirements following discharge from the hospital.

14. examine and receive an explanation of the bill regardless of source of payment.

15. know which hospital rules and policies apply to the patient's conduct while a patient.

16. have all patients' rights apply to the person who may have legal responsibility to make decisions regarding medical care on behalf of the patient.

C. A procedure shall be established whereby patient complaints are forwarded to the hospital administration for appropriate response.

D. All hospital personnel shall observe these patients' rights.

Appendix 13
Sample Federal Bill of Rights for Patients

Patients' Rights in Veterans Administration Facilities

1. Informed consent: Practitioner performing procedure must inform patient of (a) nature of proposed procedure or treatment; (b) expected benefits; (c) reasonable foreseeable risks, complications, or side effects; (d) reasonable and available alternatives; and (e) anticipated results if nothing done.
2. Treatment with dignity in a humane, safe environment.
3. Privacy with regard to personal needs.
4. Prompt and appropriate treatment for physical or emotional disability.
5. Least restrictive conditions necessary to achieve treatment purposes.
6. Exercise such rights as managing property, entering contractual relationships, executing legal instruments, registering to vote, marrying and divorcing, and holding professional occupational or vehicle operator's licenses.
7. Opportunity to communicate freely with persons outside the facility and to receive visitors.
8. Right to wear own clothing and keep and use personal possessions to extent consistent with safety regulations and rights of other patients.
9. Regular physical exercise, indoors and outdoors.
10. Keep and use own personal possessions and money.
11. Opportunity for religious worship.
12. Interact with others.

Source: Adapted from 38 C.F.R., Sections 17.34 and 17.34a (1985).

13. Freedom from physical restraint or seclusion except where there is substantial risk of imminent harm by the patient to self or others.
14. Freedom from unnecessary or excessive medication.
15. Confidentiality of all information obtained from the patient in the course of treatment.
16. Right to present grievances with respect to infringement of rights.

Appendix 14
An Important Message from Medicare

Your Rights While You Are a Medicare Hospital Patient

- You have the right to receive all the hospital care that is necessary for the proper diagnosis and treatment of your illness or injury. According to Federal law, *your discharge date must be determined solely by your medical needs,* not by "DRGs" or Medicare payments.
- You have the right to be fully informed about decisions affecting your Medicare coverage and payment for your hospital stay and for any post-hospital services.
- You have the right to request a review by a Peer Review Organization of any written Notice of Noncoverage that you receive from the hospital stating that Medicare will no longer pay for your hospital care. Peer Review Organizations (PROs) are groups of doctors who are paid by the Federal Government to review medical necessity, appropriateness and quality of hospital treatment furnished to Medicare patients. The phone number and address of the PRO for your area are:

_____

_____

Talk to Your Doctor about Your Stay in the Hospital

You and your doctor know more about your condition and your health needs than anyone else. Decisions about your medical treatment should be made between you and

Source: Medicare.

your doctor. *If you have any questions about your medical treatment, your need for continued hospital care, your discharge, or your need for possible post-hospital care, don't hesitate to ask your doctor.* The hospital's patient representative or social worker will also help you with your questions and concerns about hospital services.

If You Think You Are Being Asked to Leave the Hospital Too Soon

- Ask a hospital representative for a written notice of explanation immediately, if you have not already received one. This notice is called a "Notice of Noncoverage." You must have this Notice of Noncoverage if you wish to exercise your right to request a review by the PRO.
- The Notice of Noncoverage will state either that your doctor or the PRO agrees with the hospital's decision that Medicare will no longer pay for your hospital care.
  + If the hospital and your doctor agree, the PRO does not review your case before a Notice of Noncoverage is issued. But the PRO will respond to your request for a review of your Notice of Noncoverage and seek your opinion. You cannot be made to pay for your hospital care until the PRO makes its decision, if you request the review by noon of the first work day after you receive the Notice of Noncoverage.
  + If the hospital and your doctor disagree, the hospital may request the PRO to review your case. If it does make such a request, the hospital is required to send you a notice to that effect. In this situation the PRO must agree with the hospital or the hospital cannot issue a Notice of Noncoverage. You may request that the PRO reconsider your case after you receive a Notice of Noncoverage but since the PRO has already reviewed your case once, you may have to pay for *at least one day of hospital care* before the PRO completes this reconsideration.

If you *do not* request a review, *the hospital may bill you* for all the costs of your stay beginning with the third day after you receive the notice of noncoverage. The hospital, however, cannot charge you for care unless it provides you with a notice of noncoverage.

How to Request a Review of the Notice of Noncoverage

- If the Notice of Noncoverage states that your *physician agrees* with the hospital's decision:

How to Request a Review of the Notice of Noncoverage (continued)

+ You must make your request for review to the PRO by *noon of the first work day* after you receive the Notice of Noncoverage by contacting the PRO by phone or in writing.
+ The PRO must ask for your views about your case before making its decision. The PRO will inform you by phone and in writing of its decision on the review.
+ If the PRO agrees with the Notice of Noncoverage, you may be billed for all costs of your stay beginning at noon of the day *after* you receive the PRO's decision.
+ Thus, you will *not* be responsible for the cost of hospital care before you receive the PRO's decision.

- If the Notice of Noncoverage states that the *PRO agrees* with the hospital's decision:
  + You should make your request for reconsideration to the PRO *immediately* upon receipt of the Notice of Noncoverage by contacting the PRO by phone or in writing.
  + The PRO can take up to three working days from receipt of your request to complete the review. The PRO will inform you in writing of its decision on the review.
  + Since the PRO has already reviewed your case once, prior to the issuance of the Notice of Noncoverage, the hospital is permitted to begin billing you for the cost of your stay beginning with the third calendar day after you receive your Notice of Noncoverage *even if the PRO has not completed its review.*
  + Thus, if the PRO continues to agree with the Notice of Noncoverage, *you may have to pay for at least one day of hospital care.*

Note: The process described above is called "immediate review." If you miss the deadline for this immediate review while you are in the hospital, you may still request a review of Medicare's decision to no longer pay for your care at any point during your hospital stay or after you have left the hospital. The Notice of Noncoverage will tell you how to request this review

Post-Hospital Care

When your doctor determines that you no longer need all the specialized services provided in a hospital, but you still require medical care, he or she may discharge you to a skilled nursing facility or home care. The discharge planner at the hospital will help arrange for the services you may need after your discharge. Medicare and supplemental insurance policies have limited coverage for skilled nursing facility care and home health care. Therefore, you should find out which services will or will not be covered and how payment will be made. Consult with your doctor, hospital discharge planner, patient representative and your family in making preparations for care after you leave the hospital. *Don't hesitate to ask questions.*

Acknowledgment of Receipt. My signature only acknowledges my receipt of this Message from (name of hospital) on (date) and does not waive any of my rights to request a review or make me liable for any payment.

———————————————————
Signature of beneficiary or
person acting on behalf of beneficiary

Appendix 15
Guidelines for Hospital Discharge Planning

Introduction

The American Hospital Association believes that coordinated discharge planning functions are essential for hospitals to maintain high-quality patient care. Discharge planning is important because it facilitates appropriate patient and family decision making. In addition, it can also help reduce length of stay and the rate of increase of health care costs.

For most patients, discharge planning is a part of routine patient care. For those patients whose posthospital needs are expected to be complex, special discharge planning services are warranted. These guidelines present general information for organizing services for complex discharge planning.

It is recognized that each hospital has different resources and organizes its services differently to meet specific patient needs. It is further recognized that rapid changes in the hospital environment cause rapid changes in discharge planning. These changes, however, have emphasized the importance of discharge planning, and it is in that context that these guidelines are presented.

Definition

Discharge planning is an interdisciplinary hospitalwide process that should be available to aid patients and their families in developing a feasible posthospital plan of care.

Purposes

The purposes of discharge planning are to ensure the continuity of high-quality patient care, the availability of the hospital's resources for other patients requiring admission,

Reprinted with the permission of the American Hospital Association, © 1984.

and the appropriate utilization of resources. To ensure the continuity of high-quality care, the hospital will:

- Assign responsibility for the coordination of discharge planning
- Identify as early as possible, sometimes before hospital admission, the expected posthospital care needs of patients utilizing admission and preadmission screening and review programs when available
- Develop with patients and their families appropriate discharge care plans
- Assist patients and their families in planning for the supportive environment necessary to provide the patients' posthospital care
- Develop a plan that considers the medical, social, and financial needs of patients

To ensure the availability of hospital resources for subsequent patients with due regard for prospective pricing, the hospital's procedures should be carried out in such a manner as to accomplish timely discharge.

Principles of Discharge Planning

The discharge planning process incorporates a determination of the patient's posthospital care preferences, needs, the patient's capacity for self-care, an assessment of the patient's living conditions, the identification of health or social care resources needed to assure high-quality posthospital care, and the counseling of the patient or family to prepare them for posthospital care. Discharge planning should be carried out in keeping with varying community resources and hospital utilization activities.

Discharge Planning when Multiple Resources Are Required

In addition to discharge instructions for each routine patient discharge plan, the coordination of multiple resources may be required to achieve continued safe and high-quality posthospital care in situations where the patient's needs are complicated.

Essential Elements

The essential elements in accomplishing the hospital's goals for high-quality, cost-effective patient care are:

- *Early Identification of Patients Likely to Need Complex Posthospital Care.* There are certain factors that may indicate a need for early initiation of discharge planning, either before admission or upon admission. Screens for automatic early patient identification are developed for each specialty service by the physician and relevant health care providers and used as guidelines to carry out discharge planning.

- *Planning and Family Education.* With greater emphasis on self-care, patient and family education is critical to successful discharge planning. The coordination of discharge planning must integrate teaching about physical care to facilitate appropriate self-care in the home.
- *Patient/Family Assessment and Counseling.* The psychosocial and physical assessment and counseling of patients and families to determine the full range of needs upon discharge and to prepare them for the posthospital stage of care is a dynamic process. This process includes evaluation of the patient's and the family's strengths and weaknesses; the patient's physical condition; understanding the illness and treatment; the ability to assess the patient's and family's capacities to adapt to changes; and, where necessary, to assist the persons involved to manage in their continued care. Discharge planning and the coordination of posthospital care plans requires an ability to adapt the plans to meet changes in the patient's condition.
- *Plan Development.* The discharge plan development should include the results of the assessment and the self-care instructions, including information from the patient, the family, and all relevant health care professionals. Service needs and options are identified, and the patient and family are helped to understand the consequences of whatever plan they choose to adopt. A supportive climate is critical to facilitate appropriate decision making.
- *Plan Coordination and Implementation.* The hospital achieves high-quality and effective discharge planning through the delegation of specific responsibilities to the principal and specialized disciplines providing care. In order to minimize the potential for fragmented care and to fulfill the need for a central hospital linkage to the community, there should be assigned responsibility for discharge planning coordination for complex cases.
- *Postdischarge Follow-Up.* In complex situations requiring coordinated discharge planning, the plans should ensure follow-up with the patient, the family, and/or community service(s) providing continued care to determine the discharge plan outcome.

Quality Assurance

The quality of the discharge planning system should be monitored through the hospitalwide quality assurance program.

Appendix 16
State Peer Review Organizations

Alabama

Alabama Quality Assurance Foundation
Suite 300
236 Goodwin Crest Drive
Twin Towers East
Birmingham, Alabama 35209
1-800-554-5946
(205) 942-0785

Alaska

Professional Review Organization for
    Washington Alaska Division
Suite 204
700 West 41st Street
Anchorage, Alaska 99503
1-800-445-6941
(907) 562-2252

Arizona

Health Services Advisory Group, Inc.
Suite 157-B
301 E. Bethany Home Road
Phoenix, Arizona 85012
1-800-626-1577
(602) 264-6382

Arkansas

Arkansas Foundation for
    Medical Care, Inc.
P.O. Box 1508
809 Garrison Avenue
Fort Smith, Arkansas 72902
1-800-824-7586
(501) 785-2471

California

California Medical Review, Inc.
Suite 1100
1388 Sutter Street
San Francisco, California 94109
1-800-841-1602
(415) 923-2000

Colorado

Colorado Foundation for Medical Care
Building 2, Suite 400
6825 East Tennessee Avenue
Denver, Colorado 80217
(303) 321-8642

Adapted from *Knowing Your Rights,* American Association of Retired Persons, Washington, D.C.

Connecticut

Connecticut Peer Review Organization
384 Pratt Street
Meriden, Connecticut 06450
1-800-523-8202
(203) 237-2773

Delaware

West Virginia Medical Institute/
   Delaware PRO
Independence Mall
Suite 54
1601 Concord Pike
Wilmington, Delaware 19803
(302) 655-3077

District of Columbia

Delmarva Foundation for Medical Care
Suite 250
650 Pennsylvania Avenue, S.E.
Washington, D.C. 20006
1-800-492-5811
(202) 675-4612

Florida

Professional Foundation for
   Health Care
Suite 100
2907 Bay to Bay Boulevard
Tampa, Florida 33629
1-800-634-6280
(813) 831-6273

Georgia

Georgia Medical Care Foundation/PRO
Suite 1300
4 Executive Park Drive, N.E.
Atlanta, Georgia 30329
1-800-282-2614
(404) 982-0411

Hawaii

Fiscal Intermediary
Hawaii Medical Services Association
P.O. Box 860
Honolulu, Hawaii 96808
(808) 944-2110

Idaho

Professional Review Organization
   for Washington
Idaho Division
Suite 250
815 Park Boulevard
Boise, Idaho 83712
(208) 343-4617

Illinois

Crescent Counties Foundation for
   Medical Care
Suite 240
350 Shuman Boulevard
Naperville, Illinois 60540
(312) 357-8770

Indiana

PEERVIEW, Inc.
Suite 200
501 Congressional Boulevard
Carmel, Indiana 46032
1-800-421-6558
(317) 573-6888

Iowa

Iowa Foundation for Medical Care
Suite 500
3737 Woodland Avenue
West Des Moines, Iowa 50265
1-800-422-2234
(515) 223-2900

State Peer Review Organizations

Kansas

Kansas Foundation for Medical Care
2947 S.W. Wanamaker Drive
Topeka, Kansas 66614
1-800-432-0407
(913) 273-2552

Kentucky

PEERVIEW, Inc.
10300 Linn Station Road
Suite 100
Louisville, Kentucky 40223
1-800-423-6512
(502) 429-0995

Louisiana

Louisiana Health Care Review, Inc.
Suite 200
9357 Interline Avenue
Baton Rouge, Louisiana 70809
1-800-433-4958
(504) 926-6353

Maine

Health Care Review, Inc.
51 Broadway
Bangor, Maine 04401
1-800-541-9888
(207) 945-0244

Maryland

Delmarva Foundation for
  Medical Care, Inc.
341-B N. Aurora Street
Easton, Maryland 21601
1-800-247-9770
(301) 822-0697

Massachusetts

Massachusetts Peer Review
  Organization, Inc.
300 Bear Hill Road
Waltham, Massachusetts 02250
1-800-228-3297
(617) 890-0011

Michigan

Michigan Peer Review Organization
Suite 200
40500 Ann Arbor Road
Plymouth, Michigan 48170
1-800-482-4045
(313) 459-0900

Minnesota

Foundation for Health Care Evaluation
Suite 700
1 Appletree Square
Minneapolis, Minnesota 55420
1-800-888-3423
(612) 854-3306

Mississippi

Mississippi Foundation for
  Medical Care, Inc.
(1900 No. West Street ZIP 39202)
P.O. Box 4665
Jackson, Mississippi 39216
(601) 948-8894

Missouri

Missouri Patient Care Review
  Foundation
311A Ellis Boulevard
Jefferson City, Missouri 65101
1-800-654-1016
(314) 634-4441

Montana

Montana-Wyoming FMC

Montana continued

21 No. Main Placer Center, #201
Helena, Montana 59601
1-800-332-3411
(406) 443-4020

Nebraska

Sunderbruck Corp. of Nebraska
Suite 700 CTU Building
1221 N Street
Lincoln, Nebraska 68508
1-800-422-4812
1-800-624-8617 (after 6:00 P.M.)
(402) 474-7471

Nevada

Nevada Physicians Review
  Organization
Building A, Suite 108
4600 Kietzke Lane
Reno, Nevada 89502
1-800-588-0829
(702) 826-1996

New Hampshire

New Hampshire Foundation for
  Medical Care
P.O. Box 578
110 Locust Street
Dover, New Hampshire 03820
1-800-582-7174
(603) 749-1641

New Jersey

Peer Review Organization of
  New Jersey, Inc., Central Div.
Brier Hill Court, Building J
East Brunswick, New Jersey 08816
(201) 238-5570

New Mexico

New Mexico Medical Review
  Association
Box 9900
707 Broadway, NE
Albuquerque, New Mexico 87119
1-800-432-6824
(505) 842-6236

New York

Empire State Medical, Scientific and
  Educational Foundation
420 Lakeville Road
Lake Success, New York 11042
1-800-331-7767
(516) 437-8134

North Carolina

Medical Review of North Carolina, Inc.
P.O. Box 37309
Suite 200
1011 Schaub Drive
Raleigh, North Carolina 27627
1-800-682-2650
(919) 851-2955

North Dakota

North Dakota Health Care Review, Inc.
301 Mount Vernon Building
900 N. Broadway Avenue
Minot, North Dakota 58701
1-800-472-2902
(701) 852-4231

Ohio

Peer Review Systems, Inc.
Suite 250
3700 Corporate Drive
Columbus, Ohio 43229

1-800-233-7337 (in state)
1-800-237-7337 (out of state)
(614) 895-9900

Oklahoma

Oklahoma Foundation for Peer Review
Suite 400
The Paragon Building
5801 Broadway Extension
Oklahoma City, Oklahoma 73118
(405) 840-2891

Oregon

Oregon Medical Professional Review
 Organization
Suite 300
1220 S.W. Morrison
Portland, Oregon 97205
1-800-452-1250
(503) 243-1151

Pennsylvania

Keystone PRO, Inc.
P.O. Box 618
645 N. 12th Street
Lemoyne, Pennsylvania 17043
1-800-322-1914
(717) 975-9600

Puerto Rico

Puerto Rico Foundation for
 Medical Care, Inc.
Mercantile Plaza Building
Suite 605
Hato Rey, Puerto Rico 00918
(809) 753-6706

Rhode Island

Health Care Review, Inc.

The Weld Building
345 Blackstone Boulevard
Providence, Rhode Island 02906
1-800-662-5028
(401) 331-6661

South Carolina

South Carolina Peer Review
 Organization
1000 Carolina Commerce Center
Fort Mill, South Carolina 29715
1-800-843-0130
(803) 548-8400

South Dakota

South Dakota FMC
1323 South Minnesota Avenue
Sioux Falls, South Dakota 57105
1-800-952-3691
(605) 336-3505

Tennessee

Mid-South Foundation for
 Medical Care, Inc.
Suite 400
6401 Poplar Avenue
Memphis, Tennessee 38119
1-800-873-2273
(901) 682-0381

Texas

Texas Medical Foundation
Suite 200
901 Mopac Expressway, South
Austin, Texas 78746
1-800-252-9216
(512) 329-6610

Utah

Utah PSRO

Utah continued
Suite 200
540 East 5th South
Salt Lake City, Utah 84102
(801) 532-7547

Vermont
New Hampshire FMC
P.O. Box 578
110 Locust Street
Dover, New Hampshire 03820
1-800-582-7174
(603) 749-1641

Virginia
Medical Society of Virginia Review
    Organization
P.O. Box 6569
1904 Byrd Avenue
Room 120
Richmond, Virginia 23230
1-800-533-1745
(804) 289-5320

Washington
Professional Review Organization for
    Washington
Suite 200

2150 N. 107th Street
Seattle, Washington 98133
1-800-233-5439 (residents)
1-800-445-6941 (outside of state)
(206) 364-9700

West Virginia
West Virginia Medical Institute, Inc.
3412 Chesterfield Ave., SE
Charleston, West Virginia 25304
1-800-642-8686
(304) 925-0461

Wisconsin
Wisconsin Peer Review Organization
P.O. Box 1109
2001 West Beltline Highway
Madison, Wisconsin 53713
1-800-362-2320
(608) 274-1940

Wyoming
Montana-Wyoming FMC
Placer Center, #201
21 N. Main Street
Helena, Montana 59601
1-800-826-8978
(406) 443-4020

The Office of Medical Review, Health Standards and Quality Bureau, Meadows East Building, 6325 Security Boulevard, Baltimore, Maryland 21207, (301) 966-6851, can assist individuals who have difficulty reaching any of the offices listed here.

Appendix 17
Model Discharge Notices

Sample Letters Denying Continued Stay

Sample 1: Attending Physician Concurs
(Hospital Letterhead)

Mr. Bert Smith
3 Payne Boulevard
Evanston, Proland 00001

002-59-2300A
(Health Insurance (HI) number)
Dr. Cho
(Attending physician's name)
June 1, 1985
(admission date)

Dear Mr. Smith:

The Nowhere General Hospital has reviewed the medical services you have received for the treatment of the ulcerations of your left leg from June 1, 1985, through June 11, 1985. Your attending physician has been advised and has concurred that beginning June 13, 1985, further treatment of the ulcerations of your left leg could be safely rendered in another setting. You should discuss with your attending physician other arrangements for any further health care you may require.

You will not be responsible for payment of the services which are rendered by this hospital from June 13, 1985, through June 14, 1985, except for payment of deductible, coinsurance, or any convenience services or items normally not covered by Medicare. If you decide to stay in the hospital, you will be responsible for payment of all services

---

Source: Health Care Financing Administration.

provided to you by this hospital except for those services for which you are eligible under Part B beginning June 15, 1985.

The Foundation for Medical Care, Inc. is the Peer Review Organization (PRO) authorized by the Medicare program to review inpatient hospital services provided to Medicare patients, including those services denied by hospitals in the State of Proland.

If you disagree with our decision and you remain in the hospital beginning June 15, 1985, you may request by telephone or in writing an immediate review by the PRO. You make that request through the Hospital or directly to:

_____
(PRO name)

_____
(address, including zip code)

_____
(telephone number)

The PRO will respond to you within 3 working days of receipt of your request. However, if you do not wish an immediate review and you remain in the hospital beginning June 15, 1985, the PRO will automatically review your case. The PRO will send you a formal determination of the medical necessity and appropriateness of your hospitalization and will inform you of your appeal rights. If the PRO determines that you required further inpatient hospital care beyond the point indicated by the hospital, you will be refunded any amount collected by the hospital except for payment of deductible, coinsurance, or any convenience services or items normally not covered by Medicare. However, if the PRO agrees with the hospital's decision, you are still responsible for payment of all services beginning on June 15, 1985, as explained in this notice.

If you are discharged from this hospital on June 15, 1985, you may still request a review within 30 days from the date of this notice to the address specified above.

Sincerely,

_____
(chairperson of Utilization Review Committee)

cc: attending physician

Acknowledgment of Receipt of Notice

This is to acknowledge I received this notice of noncoverage of services from <u>Nowhere Hospital</u> on <u>June 13, 1985</u>.

_____
(signature of beneficiary or person acting on behalf of beneficiary)

_____
(date of receipt)

Sample 2: Attending Physician Concurs
(Hospital Letterhead)

_____ (date of notice)	_____ (Health Insurance [HI] number)
_____ (name of patient)	_____ (attending physician's name)
_____ (address)	_____ (admission date)
_____ (city, state, zip code)	

Dear _____ :

The (hospital name) has reviewed the medical services you have received for (specify services or condition) from (date of admission) through (date of last day reviewed). Your attending physician has been advised and has concurred that beginning (specify date of first noncovered day), further (specify services to be rendered or condition to be treated) (specify: is/are medically unnecessary) or (could be safely rendered in another setting). You should discuss with your attending physician other arrangements for any further health care you may require.

You will not be responsible for payment of the services which are rendered by this hospital from (date of receipt of notice) through (second day after receipt of notice) except for payment of deductible, coinsurance, or any convenience services or items normally not covered by Medicare. If you decide to stay in the hospital, you will be responsible for payment of all services provided to you by this hospital except for those services for which you are eligible for under Part B beginning (third day after receipt of notice.).

The (name of PRO) is the Peer Review Organization (PRO) authorized by the

Medicare program to review inpatient hospital services provided to Medicare patients including those services denied by hospitals in the state of _____.

If you disagree with our decision and you remain in the hospital beginning (date of the third day of receipt of notice), you may request by telephone or in writing an immediate review by the PRO. You may make this request through the hospital or directly to the PRO at:

_____
(PRO name)

_____
(address)

_____
(telephone number)

The PRO will respond to you within 3 working days of receipt of your request. However, if you do not wish an immediate review and remain in the hospital beginning (date of third day after receipt of notice), the PRO will automatically review your case. The PRO will send you a formal determination of the medical necessity and appropriateness of your hospitalization and will inform you of your appeal rights. If the PRO determines that you required further inpatient hospital care beyond the point indicated by the hospital, you will be refunded any amount collected by the hospital except for payment of deductible, coinsurance, or any convenience services or items normally not covered by Medicare. However, if the PRO agrees with the hospital's decision, you are still responsible for payment of all services beginning on (date of third day from receipt of notice) as explained in this notice.

If you are discharged from this hospital on (date of third day of receipt of notice), you may still request a review within 30 days from the date of this notice to the address specified above.

Sincerely,

_____
(chairperson of Utilization Review
Committee, medical staff, hospital
representative, etc.)

cc: attending physician

Model Discharge Notices

Acknowledgment of Receipt of Notice

This is to acknowledge I received this notice of denial of services from (name of hospital) on (date).

_____
(signature of beneficiary or person acting on behalf of beneficiary)

_____
(date of receipt)

Sample 3: PRO Concurs
(Hospital Letterhead)

(date of notice)

_____ (name of patient)	_____ (Health Insurance [HI] number)
_____ (address)	_____ (attending physician's name)
_____ (city, state, zip code)	_____ (admission date)

Dear _____.

The (hospital name) has reviewed the medical services you have received for (specify services or condition) from (date of admission) through date of last day reviewed) and has determined that further hospitalization is not necessary.

The (name of PRO) is the Peer Review Organization (PRO) authorized by the Medicare program to review inpatient hospital services provided to Medicare patients including those services denied by the hospitals in the state of _____. The (name of PRO) has concurred with our decision that beginning (specify date of first noncovered day), further (specify services to be rendered or condition to be treated) (specify: is/are medically unnecessary) or (could be safely rendered in another setting).

We have advised your attending physician of the denial of further inpatient hospital care. You should discuss with your attending physician other arrangements for any further health care you may require.

You will not be responsible for payment of the services which are rendered by this hospital from (date of receipt of notice) through (second day after receipt of notice) except for payment of deductible, coinsurance, or any convenience services or items normally not covered by Medicare. If you decide to stay in the hospital, you will be responsible for payment of all services provided to you by this hospital except for those services for which you are eligible for under Part B beginning (third day after receipt of notice).

If you disagree with our decision and you remain in the hospital beginning (date of third day after receipt of notice), you may request by telephone or in writing an expedited reconsideration. You may make this request through the hospital or to the PRO at:

_____

(PRO name)

_____

(address, including zip code)

_____

(telephone number)

The PRO will respond to you within 3 working days of receipt of your request. The PRO will send to you a formal reconsideration determination of the medical necessity and appropriateness of your hospitalization and will inform you of your appeal rights. If the PRO determines that you required further inpatient hospital care beyond the point indicated by the hospital, you will be refunded any amount collected by the hospital except for payment of deductible, coinsurance, or any convenience services, or items normally not covered by Medicare. However, if the PRO reaffirms the hospital's decision, you are still responsible beginning (date of third day from receipt of notice) as explained in this notice.

If you are discharged from this hospital on (date of third day of receipt of notice), you may still request a reconsideration. Instructions on how to request this reconsideration will be given to you in a notice sent by (name of PRO).

Sincerely

_____

(chairperson of Utilization Review Committee, medical staff, etc.)

_____

(date of receipt)

cc: attending physician

Acknowledgment of Receipt of Notice

This is to acknowledge I received this notice of noncoverage of services from (hospital name) on _____.
                                    (date)

_____
(signature of beneficiary or person acting on behalf of beneficiary)

_____
(date of receipt)

Appendix 18
Medicare Quality Screen

Medicare Generic Screening Criteria

These criteria were developed by the Medicare program. The Medicare Peer Review Organization (PRO) is required to apply these screens to each Medicare case selected for review.

1.* Adequacy of discharge planning
   No documented plan for appropriate follow-up care or discharge planning as necessary, with consideration of physical, emotional, and mental status/needs at the time of discharge.
2. Medical stability of the patient at discharge
   a. Blood pressure on day before or day of discharge
      Systolic—less than 85 or greater than 180
      Diastolic—less than 50 or greater than 110
   b. Temperature on day before or day of discharge greater than 101 degrees oral (rectal 102 degrees).
   c. Pulse less than 50 (or 45 if the patient is on a beta blocker), or greater than 120 within 24 hours of discharge.
   d. Abnormal results of diagnostic services which are not addressed and resolved or where the record does not explain why they are unresolved.
   e. IV fluids or drugs on the day of discharge (*excludes* KVOs [to keep vein open], antibiotics, chemotherapy, or total parenteral nutrition).
   f. Purulent or bloody drainage of postoperative wound within 24 hours prior to discharge.
3. Deaths
   a. During or following elective surgery performed during the current admission.

Source: Medicare.

b. Following return to intensive care unit, coronary care, or special care unit within 24 hours of being transferred out.

c. Other unexpected death.

4*. Nosocomial infections

   a. Temperature elevation greater than two degrees more than 72 hours from admission.

   b. Indication of an infection following an invasive procedure (e.g., suctioning, catheter insertion, tube feedings, surgery, etc.)

5. Surgery

   a. Unscheduled return to surgery within same admission for same condition as previous surgery or to correct operative problem (exclude "staged" procedures).

6. Trauma suffered in the hospital

   a. Unplanned removal or repair of normal organ (i.e., removal or repair not addressed specifically in operative consent).

   b.* Fall with injury or untoward effect (including, but not limited to fracture, dislocation, concussion, laceration, etc.).

   c. Life-threatening complications of anesthesia.

   d. Life-threatening transfusion error or reaction.

   e. Hospital-acquired decubitus ulcer.

   f. Care resulting in (1) *serious* or (2) *life-threatening complications*, not related to admitting signs and symptoms, including, but not limited to the neurological, endocrine, cardiovascular, renal, or respiratory body systems (e.g., resulting in dialysis, unplanned transfer to special care unit, lengthened hospital stay).

   g. Major adverse drug reaction or medication error (1) *with serious potential for harm* or (2) *resulting in special measures to correct* (e.g., intubation, cardiopulmonary resuscitation, gastric lavage) including but not limited to the following:

      1. Incorrect antibiotic ordered by the physician (e.g., inconsistent with diagnostic studies or the patient's history of drug allergy);

      2. No diagnostic studies to confirm which drug is correct to administer (e.g., C & S);

      3. Serum drug levels not performed as needed;

      4. Diagnostic studies or other measures for side effects not performed as needed (e.g., BUN, creatinine, intake and output).

Source: Medicare.

*PRO reviewer is to record the failure of the screen with "B" (exception) but need not refer to physician reviewer.

Appendix 19
State Long Term Care Ombudsman Program Offices

Alabama

Commission on Aging
136 Catoma Street
2nd Floor
Montgomery, Alabama 36130
(205) 261-5743

Alaska

Office of the Older Alaskans
  Ombudsman
3601 C Street, Suite 38
Anchorage, Alaska 99503
(907) 279-2232
(accepts collect calls from older persons)

Arizona

Aging and Adult Administration
P.O. Box 6123-950A
1400 West Washington Street
Phoenix, Arizona 85007
(602) 255-4446

Arkansas

Division of Aging and Adult Services
Arkansas Department of Human Services
1417 Donaghey Plaza South
7th and Main Streets
Little Rock, Arkansas 72201
(501) 682-2441

California

California Department of Aging
1600 K Street
Sacramento, California 95814
(916) 323-6681
1-800-231-4024

Colorado

The Legal Center
455 Sherman Street, Suite 130
Denver, Colorado 80203
(303) 722-0300
1-800-332-6356

Connecticut

Connecticut Department on Aging
175 Main Street
Hartford, Connecticut 06106
(203) 566-7770

Delaware

Division on Aging

Delaware continued
1113 Church Street
Milford, Delaware 19963
(302) 422-1386
1-800-223-9074

District of Columbia
Legal Counsel for the Elderly
1331 H Street, NW
Washington, D.C. 20005
(202) 662-4933

Florida
State LTC Ombudsman Council
Department of Health and
  Rehabilitation Services
1317 Winewood Boulevard, Building 1,
  #308
Tallahassee, Florida 32301
(904) 488-6190

Georgia
Office of Aging
Department of Human Resources
878 Peachtree Street, NE, Room 632
Atlanta, Georgia 30389
(404) 894-5336

Hawaii
Hawaii Executive Office on Aging
335 Merchant Street, Room 241
Honolulu, Hawaii 96813
(808) 548-2593

Idaho
Idaho Office on Aging
State House, Room 114
Boise, Idaho 83720
(208) 334-3833

Illinois
Department on Aging
421 East Capitol Avenue
Springfield, Illinois 62701
(217) 785-3140

Indiana
Indiana Department on Aging and
  Community Services
Capitol Center, 251 N. Illinois
Indianapolis, Indiana 42607-7083
(317) 232-7116
1-800-622-4484

Iowa
Commission on the Aging
Jewett Building, Suite 236
916 Grand Avenue
Des Moines, Iowa 50319
(515) 281-5187

Kansas
Department on Aging
Docking State Office Building, 122-S
915 S.W. Harrison
Topeka, Kansas 66612-1500
1-800-432-3535

Kentucky
Division for Aging Services
Cabinet for Human Resources
CHR Building—6th Floor
275 East Main Street
Frankfort, Kentucky 40601
1-800-372-2991

Louisiana
Governor's Office of Elderly Affairs
P.O. Box 80374
4528 Bennington Avenue

Baton Rouge, Louisiana 70890-3074
(504) 925-1700

Maine

Maine Committee on Aging
State House, Station 127
Augusta, Maine 04333
(207) 289-3658
1-800-452-1912

Maryland

Maryland Office on Aging
301 W. Preston Street
Baltimore, Maryland 21201
(301) 225-1100

Massachusetts

Massachusetts Executive Office of
   Elder Affairs
38 Chauncy Street
Boston, Massachusetts 02111
(617) 727-7273

Michigan

Citizens for Better Care
1627 East Kalamazoo
Lansing, Michigan 48912
(517) 482-1297
1-800-292-7852

Minnesota

Minnesota Board on Aging
Metro Square Building, Suite 204
7th and Robert Streets
St. Paul, Minnesota 55101
(612) 296-7465
1-800-652-9747

Mississippi

Mississippi Council on Aging
301 W. Pearl Street
Jackson, Mississippi 39203-3092
(601) 949-2013

Missouri

Division of Aging
Department of Social Services
P.O. Box 1337
2701 W. Main Street
Jefferson City, Missouri 65102
(314) 751-3082

Montana

Seniors' Office of Legal and
   Ombudsman Services
P.O. Box 232, Capitol Station
Helena, Montana 59620
(406) 444-4204
1-800-332-2272

Nebraska

Department on Aging
P.O. Box 95044
301 Centennial Mall South
Lincoln, Nebraska 68509
(402) 471-2307

Nevada

Division of Aging Services
Department of Human Resources
Kinkead Building, Room 101
505 E. King Street
Carlson City, Nevada 89710
(702) 885-4210

New Hampshire

New Hampshire Division of Elderly and
   Adult Services
6 Hazen Drive
Concord, New Hampshire 03301-6508

New Hampshire continued
(603) 271-4681
1-800-442-5640

New Jersey
Office of the Ombudsman for the Institutionalized Elderly
28 W. State Street, Room 305, CN808
Trenton, New Jersey 08625-0807
(609) 292-8016
1-800-624-4262

New Mexico
State Agency on Aging
LaVilla Rivera Building, 4th Floor
224 E. Palace Avenue
Santa Fe, New Mexico 87501
(505) 827-7640

New York
Office for the Aging
Agency Building #2
Empire State Plaza
Albany, New York 12223
(518) 474-7329
1-800-342-9871

North Carolina
North Carolina Department of Human Resources
Division of Aging
Kirby Building
1985 Umstead Drive
Raleigh, North Carolina 27603
(919) 733-3983

North Dakota
Aging Services Division
Department of Human Services
State Capitol Building

Bismarck, North Dakota 58505
(701) 224-2577
1-800-472-2622

Ohio
Ohio Department on Aging
50 W. Broad Street, 9th Floor
Columbus, Ohio 43466-0501
(614) 466-9927
1-800-282-1206

Oklahoma
Office of Client Advocacy
Department of Human Services
P.O. Box 25352
Oklahoma City, Oklahoma 73125
(405) 521-3731

Oregon
Office of LTC Ombudsman
2475 Lancaster Drive, Building B, #9
Salem, Oregon 97310
(503) 378-6533
1-800-522-2602

Pennsylvania
Department of Aging
Barto Building, 231 State Street
Harrisburg, Pennsylvania 17101
(717) 783-7247

Puerto Rico
Gericulture Commission
Department of Social Services
G.P.O. 11398
Santurce, Puerto Rico 00910
(809) 722-2429

Rhode Island
Rhode Island Department of

Elderly Affairs
79 Washington Street
Providence, Rhode Island 02903
(401) 277-6883

South Carolina
Office of the Governor
Division of Ombudsman and Citizens'
  Services
1205 Pendleton Street
Columbia, South Carolina 29201
(803) 734-0457

South Dakota
Office of Adult Services and Aging
Department of Social Services
Richard F. Kneip Building
700 North Illinois Street
Pierre, South Dakota 57501-2291
(605) 773-3656

Tennessee
Commission on Aging
706 Church Street, Suite 201
Nashville, Tennessee 37219-5573
(615) 741-2056

Texas
Department on Aging
P.O. Box 12786, Capitol Station
1949 IH 35 South
Austin, Texas 78741-3702
(512) 444-2727
1-800-252-9240

Utah
Division of Aging and Adult Services
Department of Social Services
120 North—200 West
Box 45500
Salt Lake City, Utah 84145-0500
(801) 538-3910

Vermont
Vermont Office on Aging
103 South Main Street
Waterbury, Vermont 05676
(802) 241-2400
1-800-642-5119

Virginia
Department for the Aging
10th Floor
700 East Franklin Street
Richmond, Virginia 23219-2327
(804) 225-2271
1-800-552-3402

Washington
Department of Social and
  Health Services
MS OB 44-Y
Olympia, Washington 98504
(206) 586-2258
1-800-562-6028

West Virginia
Commission on Aging
State Capitol Complex
Charleston, West Virginia 25305
(304) 348-3317

Wisconsin
Board on Aging and Long-Term Care
Room 619
819 N. 6th
Milwaukee, Wisconsin 53203-1664
(414) 227-4386
1-800-242-1060

Wyoming
Wyoming State Bar Association
900 8th Street
Wheatland, Wyoming 82201
(307) 322-5553

Appendix 20
State Units on Aging

Alabama

Commission on Aging
State Capitol
Montgomery, Alabama 36130
(205) 261-5743

Alaska

Older Alaskans Commission
Department of Administration
Pouch C-Mail Station 0209
Juneau, Alaska 99811
(907) 465-3250

Arizona

Aging and Adult Administration
Department of Economic Security
1400 W. Washington Street
Phoenix, Arizona 85007
(602) 255-4446

Arkansas

Office of Aging and Adult Services
Department of Social and Rehabilitative
  Services
Donaghey Building, Suite 1428
7th and Main Street
Little Rock, Arkansas 72201
(501) 371-2441

California

Department of Aging
1020 19 Street
Sacramento, California 95814
(916) 322-5290

Colorado

Aging and Adult Services Division
Department of Social Services
1575 Sherman Street, Room 503
Denver, Colorado 80203
(303) 866-3672

Connecticut

Department on Aging
175 Main Street
Hartford, Connecticut 06106
(203) 566-3238

Delaware

Division on Aging
Department of Health and Social Services
1901 N. DuPont Highway
New Castle, Delaware 19720
(302) 421-6791

District of Columbia

Office on Aging

District of Columbia (continued)

1424 K Street, NW, 2nd floor
Washington, DC 20005
(202) 724-5622

Florida

Program Office of Aging and
  Adult Services
Department of Health and
  Rehabilitation Services
1317 Winewood Boulevard
Tallahassee, Florida 32301
(904) 488-8922

Georgia

Office of Aging
878 Peachtree Street, NE, Room 632
Atlanta, Georgia 30309
(404) 894-5333

Hawaii

Executive Office on Aging
Office of the Governor
1149 Bethel Street, Room 307
Honolulu, Hawaii 96813
(808) 548-2593

Idaho

Office on Aging
Room 114—Statehouse
Boise, Idaho 83720
(208) 334-3833

Illinois

Department on Aging
421 East Capitol Avenue
Springfield, Illinois 62706
(217) 785-3356

Indiana

Department of Aging and
  Community Services
115 N. Pennsylvania Street
Suite 1350 Consolidated Building
Indianapolis, Indiana 46204
(317) 232-7006

Iowa

Commission on Aging
Suite 236, Jewett Building
914 Grand Avenue
Des Moines, Iowa 50319
(515) 281-5187

Kansas

Department on Aging
610 W. Tenth
Topeka, Kansas 66612
(913) 296-4986

Kentucky

Division for Aging Services
Department of Human Resources
DHR Building—6th floor
275 E. Main Street
Frankfort, Kentucky 40601
(502) 564-6930

Louisiana

Office of Elderly Affairs
P.O. Box 80374
Baton Rouge, Louisiana 70898
(504) 925-1700

Maine

Bureau of Maine's Elderly
Department of Human Services
State House—Station #11

State Units on Aging

Augusta, Maine 04333
(207) 289-2561

Maryland

Office on Aging
State Office Building
301 W. Preston Street
Baltimore, Maryland 21201
(301) 383-5064

Massachusetts

Department of Elder Affairs
38 Chauncy Street
Boston, Massachusetts 02111
(617) 727-7750

Michigan

Office of Services to the Aging
P.O. Box 30026
Lansing, Michigan 48909
(517) 373-8230

Minnesota

Board on Aging
Metro Square Building, Room 204
Seventh and Robert Street
St. Paul, Minnesota 55101
(612) 296-2544

Mississippi

Council on Aging
802 N. State Street
Executive Building, Suite 301
Jackson, Mississippi 39201
(601) 354-6590

Missouri

Division on Aging
Department of Social Services
Broadway State Office—P.O. Box 570
Jefferson City, Missouri 65101
(314) 751-3082

Montana

Community Services Division
P.O. Box 4210
Helena, Montana 59604
(406) 444-3865

Nebraska

Department on Aging
P.O. Box 95044
301 Centennial Mall South
Lincoln, Nebraska 68509
(402) 471-2306

Nevada

Division on Aging
Department of Human Resources
505 E. King Street
Kinkead Building, Room 101
Carson City, Nevada 89710
(702) 885-4210

New Hampshire

Council on Aging
14 Depot Street
Concord, New Hampshire 03301
(603) 271-2751

New Jersey

Division on Aging
Department of Community Affairs
P.O. Box 2768
363 W. State Street
Trenton, New Jersey 08625
(609) 292-4833

New Mexico

State Agency on Aging
224 E. Palace Avenue, 4th Floor
La Villa Rivera Building
Santa Fe, New Mexico 87501
(505) 827-7640

New York

Office for the Aging
New York State Plaza
Agency Building #2
Albany, New York 12223
(518) 474-5731

North Carolina

Division on Aging
708 Hillsborough Street, Suite 200
Raleigh, North Carolina 27603
(919) 733-3983

North Dakota

Aging Services
Department of Human Services
State Capitol Building
Bismarck, North Dakota 58505
(701) 224-2577

Ohio

Commission on Aging
50 W. Broad Street, 9th floor
Columbus, Ohio 43215
(614) 466-5500

Oklahoma

Special Unit on Aging
Department of Human Services
P.O. Box 25352
Oklahoma City, Oklahoma 73125
(405) 521-2281

Oregon

Senior Services Division
313 Public Service Building
Salem, Oregon 97310
(503) 387-4728

Pennsylvania

Department of Aging
231 State Street
Harrisburg, Pennsylvania 17101-1195
(717) 783-1550

Rhode Island

Department of Elderly Affairs
79 Washington Street
Providence, Rhode Island 02903
(401) 277-2858

South Carolina

Commission on Aging
915 Main Street
Columbia, South Carolina 29201
(803) 758-2576

South Dakota

Office of Adult Services and Aging
700 N. Illinois Street
Kneip Building
Pierre, South Dakota 57501
(605) 773-3656

Tennessee

Commission on Aging
703 Tennessee Building
535 Church Street
Nashville, Tennessee 37219
(615) 741-2056

Texas

Department on Aging
210 Barton Springs Road, 5th floor
P.O. Box 12768, Capitol Station
Austin, Texas 78704
(512) 475-2717

Utah

Division of Aging and Adult Services
Department of Social Services
150 W. North Temple
Box 2500
Salt Lake City, Utah 84102
(801) 533-6422

Vermont

Office on Aging
103 S. Main Street
Waterbury, Vermont 05676
(802) 241-2400

Virginia

Department on Aging
101 N. 14th Street, 18th floor
James Monroe Building
Richmond, Virginia 23219
(804) 225-2271

Washington

Bureau of Aging and Adult Services
Department of Social and
　Health Services, OB-43G
Olympia, Washington 98504
(206) 753-2502

West Virginia

Commission on Aging
Holly Grove—State Capitol
Charleston, West Virginia 25305
(304) 348-3317

Wisconsin

Bureau of Aging
Division of Community Services
One W. Wilson Street
Madison, Wisconsin 53702
(608) 266-2536

Wyoming

Commission on Aging
401 W. 19 Street
Cheyenne, Wyoming 82002
(307) 777-7986

Appendix 21
State Public Guardianship Programs

Statewide Program	Limited Program	No Program
Alaska	Alabama	Arkansas
Arizona	Florida	Colorado
California	Idaho	District of Columbia
Connecticut	Iowa	Indiana
Delaware	Maryland	Kansas
Georgia	Michigan	Louisiana
Hawaii	Minnesota	Massachusetts
Illinois	Missouri	Mississippi
Kentucky	Nevada	Montana
Maine	New York	Nebraska
New Hampshire	North Carolina	New Mexico
New Jersey	North Dakota	Oklahoma
Tennessee	Ohio	Rhode Island
	Oregon	South Carolina
	Pennsylvania	Utah
	South Dakota	Vermont
	Texas	Washington
	Virginia	Wisconsin
	West Virginia	Wyoming

Appendix 22
State Requirements for Personal Status Reports on Wards

Reports Required	Reports Not Required
Alaska	Alabama
California	Arizona
Connecticut	Arkansas
District of Columbia	Colorado
Florida	Delaware
Georgia	Idaho
Hawaii	Illinois
Iowa	Indiana
Kansas	Maine
Kentucky	Massachusetts
Louisiana	Mississippi
Maryland	New Jersey
Michigan	New Mexico
Minnesota	North Carolina
Missouri	North Dakota
Montana	Ohio
Nebraska	Oklahoma
Nevada	Pennsylvania
New Hampshire	Rhode Island
New York	South Dakota
Oregon	Tennessee
South Carolina	Utah

Reports Required	Reports Not Required
Texas	Virginia
Vermont	Washington
Wisconsin	West Virginia
	Wyoming

Appendix 23
State Requirements for Ward Estate Accounting

Not Required	Required Periodically	Required Annually
Maine	Alabama	Alaska
Mississippi	California	Arizona
New Jersey	Connecticut	Arkansas
North Dakota	Delaware	Colorado
Pennsylvania	Illinois	District of Columbia
Utah	Indiana	Florida
	Kentucky	Georgia
	Ohio	Hawaii
	South Dakota	Idaho
		Iowa
		Kansas
		Louisiana
		Maryland
		Massachusetts
		Michigan
		Minnesota
		Missouri
		Montana
		Nebraska
		Nevada
		New Hamshire
		New Mexico

Not Required	Required Periodically	Required Annually
		New York
		North Carolina
		Oklahoma
		Oregon
		Rhode Island
		South Carolina
		Tennessee
		Texas
		Vermont
		Virginia
		Washington
		West Virginia
		Wisconsin
		Wyoming

Appendix 24
State Requirements for Legal Representation of Wards

No Requirements	Court Lawyer Required (1)	Guardian Required Ad Litem (2)	Both 1 and 2 Required	Court Determines, See 3
Arkansas	Connecticut	Alabama	Alaska	California
Nevada	Delaware	Idaho	Arizona	Florida
Ohio	Georgia	Illinois	Colorado	Hawaii
Oklahoma	Iowa	Michigan	District of Columbia	Indiana
Oregon	Kansas	Montana		Maine
Pennsylvania	Kentucky	New Mexico		Massachusetts
South Dakota	Louisiana	North Carolina		Minnesota
Utah	Maryland	North Dakota		Mississippi
Vermont	Missouri	South Carolina		Nebraska
Wyoming	New Hampshire	Tennessee		New York
	New Jersey	Virginia		Rhode Island
		Washington		Texas
		West Virginia		
		Wisconsin		

1. Court-appointed lawyer to represent client's wishes.
2. Guardian Ad Litem, usually a lawyer, who advises court on what would be best for client.
3. Court decides if it wants to appoint a lawyer or guardian ad litem.

Appendix 25

Sample Petition for Appointment of Conservators (Guardians) of the Person and the Property

In re
A.B.C.   Fiduciary No. _____

COMES NOW D.E.C., a resident of Las Cruces, New Mexico ("Petitioner"), and petitions the Court to appoint her as conservator of the person and the property of her natural father, Mr. A.B.C. ("Mr. C.") a resident of _____.

In support thereof, Petitioner states:

1. This court has jurisdiction pursuant to §xxx *et seq.*, of the Code of the _____ ("Code").

2. Mr. C., the proposed ward, resides in _____ at 1434 Maplewood Ct., _____, which residence he owns with the real property thereunder free and clear of encumbrances.

3. Mr. C. was born on _____, in _____ and holds the social security number 123–45–6789. He is now _____ years old.

4. Mr. C. has, within the last 30 days, sustained a major stroke and has been diagnosed as suffering from Alzheimer's Disease. As a result of these debilitating mental and physical conditions, Mr. C. is, in the opinions of his consulting physicians, Dr. _____ and Dr. _____, unable to care for his property, his own personal welfare or health care. (See affidavits attached.) He is, therefore, because of mental weakness not amounting to unsoundness of mind, unable to consent to or participate fully in matters affecting his personal health care or his financial well-being.

5. At present, Mr. C. is being cared for at the _____ Hospital, under the supervision of the physicians above.

6. Petitioner is Mr. C.'s natural daughter and only child. Other known relatives are:
   _____ (sister) ADDRESS
   _____ (brother) ADDRESS
   Said relatives have been contacted by Petitioner and have given their verbal consent to and do not intend to oppose Petitioner's appointment as conservator.

7. The Guardian *ad litem* may also find it useful to contact Delores S. C., former wife of Mr. C. (Office: TELEPHONE NO., home address: _____ for information and documents gathered by Ms. C. and Petitioner to date.

8. Appointment of Petitioner as conservator of the person and the property is clearly in the best interests of her father, Mr. C. She has always demonstrated great love and care for her father, and since his stroke and advancing Alzheimer's Disease, she has taken leave from her husband and employment to travel at her own expense to the jurisdiction. Here she has sat with her father and, with her mother, she has taken what lawful actions she could to assure proper health care for her father and to safeguard his financial well-being while he has been unable to act for himself.

9. If Petitioner's request to be appointed conservator is granted, she intends to file an irrevocable power of attorney for service of process in _____. Moreover, she is aware of the requirements to file inventories and accounts. She is further aware of the need to petition for authorization of expenditures. In addition, Petitioner intends personally to exercise all health care and welfare decisions for Mr. C.

10. If for any reason the Court in its discretion decides not to appoint Petitioner as conservator, Petitioner hereby asks the Court to appoint her mother, Delores S. C., to act as conservator for Mr. C. with all of the duties and responsibilities sought herein. The reason for appointing her include her continuing care for and love of Mr. C., her familiarity with his assets and his needs, her residence in the _____, and the confidence and trust in which she is held by the Petitioner.

11. Petitioner states that, in her opinion, a reasonable estimate of the total assets of Mr. C.'s estate at this time, including his residence, is $_____. The assessed value of his home is approximately $_____. Bank accounts, certificates of deposit, and other personal property comprise the remaining $_____.

Wherefore, the premises considered, the Petitioner prays:

Sample Petition for Appointment of Conservators (Guardians)

(1) that she be appointed as conservator of the person and property of her father, Mr. C., or, in the alternative, to appoint her mother, Delores S. C. so to serve, and

(2) for such other and further relief as the Court may deem just and proper.

Respectfully submitted,

_____

D.E.C.

Verification

)
)SS.
)

I, D.E.C., being first duly sworn, on oath, depose and say that I have read the foregoing petition by me subscribed and that the facts therein stated are true to the best of my knowledge, information and belief.

_____
D.E.C.

Sworn to before me and subscribed in my presence this _____ day of _____, 19_____.

_____
Notary Public

My commission expires:

_____
Attorneys Name
etc.
Counsel for Petitioner

Appendix 26
Sample Conservatorship (Guardianship) Order for the Person and the Property

Superior Court of _____
Probate Division

In re
A.B.C.   Fiduciary No. _____

    Upon consideration of the petition of D.E.C. for the appointment of a conservator of the person and the estate of A.B.C., the Court having heard argument of counsel and the report of the Guardian *ad litem,* and it appearing to the Court that by reason of physical and mental weakness not amounting to unsoundness of mind, A.B.C. needs assistance in caring for himself and his property and that A.B.C.'s best interest would be best served by appointment of a conservator of his estate and of his person, who shall have the charge and management of A.B.C.'s property and person subject to the direction of the Court, it is by the Court this _____ day of _____, 19____.

    ORDERED that D.E.C. be and the same hereby is appointed permanent Conservator of the person and of the estate of A.B.C. upon the execution of a non-resident power of attorney and upon entering into an undertaking with surety approved by the Court in the penal sum of $_____, conditioned upon faithful discharge of trust, and provided that prior to the receipt of any assets in excess of $_____ said conservator shall first petition the Court for additional undertaking as may be required.

Judge

Judge

Copies to:
Attorney for Petitioner: _____
Guardian *ad litem:* _____
Conservator: D.E.C.

Appendix 27
Social Security Payee Application Form

Social Security Payee Application Form

DEPARTMENT OF HEALTH AND HUMAN SERVICES
Social Security Administration

TOE 250

Form Approved
OMB No. 0960-0014

REQUEST TO BE SELECTED AS PAYEE

FOR SSA USE ONLY

Name or Ben. Sym	Program	Date of Birth	Type	Gdn.	Cus	Inst	Nam.

FOR SSA USE ONLY

DISTRICT OFFICE DESIGNATION:

STATE AND COUNTY CODE:

PRINT name of wage earner, self-employed person, eligible SSI beneficiary, Black Lung beneficiary

ENTER SOCIAL SECURITY NUMBER

PRINT name of person or persons for whom you are applying to be payee

ENTER SOCIAL SECURITY NUMBER(S)

PRINT your name (If different from either of the above)

ENTER YOUR SOCIAL SECURITY NUMBER

Answer item 1 ONLY if you are the beneficiary and wish benefits paid directly to you.

1. I request that I be paid directly.
CHECK HERE ☐ and answer only item 5 before completing the signature block on page 4.

I REQUEST THAT THE SOCIAL SECURITY BENEFITS, SPECIAL AGE 72 BENEFITS, SUPPLEMENTAL SECURITY INCOME BENEFITS, OR BLACK LUNG BENEFITS FOR THE PERSON OR PERSONS NAMED ABOVE BE PAID TO ME AS REPRESENTATIVE PAYEE.

2. (a) Are you related by blood or marriage to the person(s) for whom you are filing? ☐ Yes (If "Yes," answer (b) and go on to item 5.) ☐ No (If "No," go on to item 3.)

(b) How are you related? (For example: spouse, child, etc.)

3. (a) Do you represent a bank, social agency, government office or institution? ☐ Yes (If "Yes," answer (b) and go on to item 5.) ☐ No (If "No," go on to item 4.)

(b) Check (✓) below which you represent

☐ BANK (or other financial organization) ☐ SOCIAL AGENCY ☐ PUBLIC OFFICIAL (Representing government office other than social agency or institution) ☐ INSTITUTION (Check one below)

☐ FEDERAL ☐ STATE OR LOCAL ☐ PRIVATE NON-PROFIT ☐ PRIVATE PROPRIETARY If so, is it licensed under State or local law? ☐ Yes ☐ No

4. If you answered "No" to items 2 and 3, what is your relationship to the person(s) for whom you are filing?

5. (a) Is there a legal representative (guardian, conservator, curator, etc.) for the person(s) for whom you are filing? ☐ Yes (If "Yes," answer (b) and (c) below.) ☐ No (If "No," go on to item 6.)

(b) Write the following information about the legal representative(s)

NAME (First name, middle initial, last name)	ADDRESS (include ZIP code)	TELEPHONE NUMBER (include area code)

(c) Briefly explain the circumstances which led the court to appoint a legal representative.

Form SSA-11-BK (6-86)   Page 1

Source: Social Security Administration.

6.	(a) Is the person(s) for whom you are filing living with you or in the institution you represent? ►	☐ Yes *(If "Yes," answer (b) through (f).)*		☐ No *(If "No," go on to item 7.)*

NOTE: If you are the natural or adoptive parent with custody of a minor child or childhood disability beneficiary, or the spouse with custody, or if you are already serving as the beneficiary's payee for SSA, SSI or Black Lung benefits, or if you are the conservator appointed under a voluntary conservatorship, omit the remaining items and go on to page 4.

	(b) Why is he/she living with you? ►	
	(c) Who placed him/her with you? ►	
	(d) When was he/she placed with you? ►	
	(e) How long will he/she be with you? ►	
	(f) If you are not the representative of a financial organization, social agency, government office or institution, does work or other activity take you away from home? ►	☐ Yes ☐ No
	If "Yes," who takes care of the person for whom you are filing when you are away? ►	Name *(First name, middle initial, last name)*

7.	(a) If the person(s) for whom you are filing is not living with you, give the following information:	

NAME OF PERSON(S) NOT LIVING WITH YOU	NAME, ADDRESS AND TELEPHONE NUMBER OF PERSON OR INSTITUTION WITH WHOM HE/SHE IS NOW LIVING. *(Hereafter this person is called the custodian)*	CUSTODIAN'S RELATIONSHIP TO HIM/HER	DATE HE/SHE BEGAN LIVING WITH CUSTODIAN
			Month / Year

(If you are an official or the representative of a financial organization or social agency, or otherwise applying in your professional capacity such as an attorney or accountant, answer (d) and go on to question 8. Otherwise, continue with (b).)

(b) Why isn't he/she living with you or in the institution you represent? ►		
(c) Do you visit the child(ren) or adult not living with you, send him/her clothing or other gifts, write letters, etc.? ►	☐ Yes *(If "Yes," show below how often you do any of those things.)*	☐ No *(If "No," please explain under "Remarks" on page 3 how you will find out about his/her needs.)*

NAME OF PERSON	VISIT	SEND CLOTHING	MAKE OTHER GIFTS	WRITE LETTERS	OTHER *(Describe)*

(d) Do you or any other person or agency give money for his/her support? ►	☐ Yes *(If "Yes," give the following information.)*	☐ No *(If "No," go on to item 8.)*

NAME OF PERSON(S)	PERSON OR AGENCY CONTRIBUTING, ADDRESS AND TELEPHONE NUMBER. SHOW "SELF" IF YOU ARE CONTRIBUTING.	HOW OFTEN CONTRIBUTIONS ARE MADE	AMOUNTS OF EACH CONTRIBUTION	DATE CONTRIBUTIONS BEGAN

Form SSA-11-BK (6-86)   Page 2

Social Security Payee Application Form

Answer item 8 if you are filing on behalf of a child(ren) who is under age 18 and you are not the natural or adoptive parent.

8. (a) Does the child(ren) for whom you are filing have a living natural or adoptive parent? ☐ Yes (If "Yes," answer (b), (c), and (d).) ☐ No (If "No," go on to item 9.)

(b) Give this parent's name, address and telephone number:

NAME OF PARENT — (First name, middle initial, last name)

ADDRESS OF PARENT — (Number and street, city, State, and ZIP code)

TELEPHONE NUMBER (include area code) — ( )

(c) Does this parent show interest in the child(ren)? ☐ Yes ☐ No

EXPLAIN YOUR ANSWER —

(d) Why do you wish to have benefits paid to you instead of to the parent named above? —

Answer item 9 if you are not a relative of the person(s) for whom you are filing.

9. (a) Does the person for whom you are filing have a relative (other than a parent named above)? ☐ Yes (If "Yes," answer (b) and (c).) ☐ No (If "No," go to item 10.)

(b) Give the name, address, and telephone number of this relative, and his/her relationship to the person(s) for whom you are filing.

Name of Relative — (First name, middle initial, last name)

Address of Relative — (Number and street, city, State, and ZIP code)

Telephone Number of Relative (include area code) — ( )

Relative's relationship to person(s) for whom you are filing —

(c) Why do you wish to have benefits paid to you instead of to the relative named above? —

Answer item 10 ONLY if you are not applying in your professional capacity.

10. (a) Are you under age 18? ☐ Yes (If "Yes," show your age.) _____ ☐ No

(b) Are you employed? ☐ Yes ☐ No (If "No," enter below your main source of income.)

Main source of income —

Answer item 11 ONLY if you are a creditor (e.g., a nursing home, landlord).

11. (a) Is the person for whom you are filing indebted to you or your facility for past care or services? ☐ Yes ☐ No
(If "Yes," answer (b) and (c).

(b) Amount of debt | Date(s) debt incurred | (c) Description of care or services provided in connection with this debt

REMARKS: (This space may be used for explaining any answers to the questions. If you need more space, attach a separate sheet.)

Form SSA-11-BK (6-86)

PLEASE READ THE FOLLOWING INFORMATION CAREFULLY BEFORE SIGNING THIS FORM

I UNDERSTAND THAT ALL PAYMENTS MADE TO ME AS REPRESENTATIVE PAYEE MUST BE SPENT FOR THE BENEFICIARY'S PRESENT NEEDS OR (IF NOT PRESENTLY NEEDED) SAVED FOR THE BENEFICIARY'S FUTURE NEEDS AND I AGREE TO USE THE PAYMENTS THAT WAY. I ALSO UNDERSTAND THAT I MAY BE HELD PERSONALLY LIABLE FOR REPAYMENT IF I MISUSE THE PAYMENTS OR IF I AM FOUND AT FAULT WITH RESPECT TO ANY OVERPAYMENT OF BENEFITS. I AGREE TO FILE AN ACCOUNTING REPORT OF THE USE MADE OF THE PAYMENTS WHEN REQUESTED BY THE SOCIAL SECURITY ADMINISTRATION.

I AGREE TO NOTIFY THE SOCIAL SECURITY ADMINISTRATION PROMPTLY WHEN ANY PERSON FOR WHOM I RECEIVE PAYMENTS DIES, LEAVES MY CUSTODY, IS LIVING ALONE OR WITH SOMEONE ELSE AND MOVES ELSEWHERE, OR WHEN I NO LONGER HAVE RESPONSIBILITY FOR SUCH PERSON'S WELFARE AND CARE. I ALSO AGREE TO COMPLY WITH THE CONDITIONS FOR REPORTING CERTAIN EVENTS (AS LISTED ON THE ATTACHED SHEET(S) WHICH I WILL MAINTAIN FOR MY RECORDS) AND FOR RETURNING CHECKS TO WHICH THERE IS NO ENTITLEMENT. WHEN AN ANNUAL REPORT OF EARNINGS IS REQUIRED, I AGREE TO FILE SUCH ANNUAL REPORT.

I ALSO AGREE TO NOTIFY THE SOCIAL SECURITY ADMINISTRATION AS SOON AS I BELIEVE I WILL NO LONGER BE ABLE TO OR WISH TO ACT AS A REPRESENTATIVE PAYEE. (SUCH ADVANCE NOTIFICATION WILL ASSIST IN THE DEVELOPMENT OF AN ALTERNATE PAYEE AND WILL AVOID UNNECESSARY SUSPENSION OF PAYMENTS.)

I know that anyone who makes or causes to be made a false statement or representation of material fact in an application or for use in determining a right to payment under the Social Security Act commits a crime punishable under Federal law by fine, imprisonment or both. I affirm that all information I have given in this document is true.

SIGNATURE OF APPLICANT	Date *(Month, day, year)*
Signature *(First name, middle initial, last name) (Write in ink)* **SIGN HERE** ▶	Telephone Number(s) at which you may be contacted during the day ___ ___ ___ Area Code

Mailing Address *(Number and street, Apt. No., P.O. Box, or Rural Route)*

City and State	ZIP Code	Enter Name of County (if any) in which you now live

Witnesses are required ONLY if this application has been signed by mark (X) above. If signed by mark (X), two witnesses to the signing who know the applicant must sign below, giving their full addresses.

1. Signature of Witness	2. Signature of Witness
Address *(Number and street, City, State, and ZIP Code)*	Address *(Number and street, City, State, and ZIP Code)*

Form SSA-11-BK (6-86)　　　　　Page 4

Appendix 28
Social Security Administration's Order of Preference in Selecting Representative Payee

As a guide in selecting a representative payee, categories of preferred payees have been established. These preferences are flexible. Our primary concern is to select the payee who will best serve the beneficiary's interest. The preferences are:

(1) For beneficiaries 18 years or older, our preference is:

   (a) A legal guardian, spouse (or other relative) who has custody of the beneficiary or who demonstrates strong concern for the personal welfare of the beneficiary;

   (b) A friend who has custody of the beneficiary or demonstrates strong concern for the personal welfare of the beneficiary;

   (c) A public or nonprofit agency or institution having custody of the beneficiary;

   (d) A private institution operated for profit and licensed under State law, which has custody of the beneficiary; and

(2) Persons other than above who are qualified to carry out the responsibilities of a payee and who are able and willing to serve as a payee for a beneficiary; e.g., members of community groups or organizations who volunteer to serve as payee for a beneficiary.

Source: Social Security Administration.

Appendix 29
Social Security Payee Report Form

Social Security Administration Representative Payee Report

We are writing to ask you to complete the enclosed **Representative Payee Report** and return it to us. We must ask you to complete this report when you receive Social Security or Supplemental Security (SSI) payments for another person. We use the facts you give us to make sure that this person's needs are being met. If you receive payments for your spouse or child, you may not have completed this report in the past. A court ruling now requires us to ask you to complete this report once a year.

What You Need To Do

First, please read the instructions below. This is important because **not all questions are self-explanatory**. Then, complete your report and send it to us in the enclosed envelope **within 10 days** from the day you receive it. If you do not return it promptly, we may stop sending checks to you.

General Instructions

To help us process your report and avoid having to recontact you, please follow these instructions.

1. Use black ink or a #2 pencil to complete the report.
2. Keep your numbers and "X's" inside the boxes.
3. Try to make your numbers look like these:

    0 1 2 3 4 5 6 7 8 9

4. Do not use dollar signs.
5. Enter money amounts like this: Show $540.00 as

    DOLLARS   CENTS
    ☐ ☐ , 5 4 0 . 0 0

6. Continue to keep records of how you use the Social Security or SSI money, but do not submit receipts, cancelled checks or any other records with this report. If we need to verify the facts you gave us, we will tell you after we look at your report.

Some Definitions

Benefits—The Social Security (Retirement, Survivors, Disability) and SSI money you receive.

Beneficiary—The person for whom you receive Social Security or SSI benefits.

Custodian—The person with whom the beneficiary lives. If the beneficiary lives alone, he or she is the custodian. A nursing home or institution can also be a custodian.

Report Period—The months for which you must account. This period is shown in the top right corner of the report form.

How To Fill Out The Form

The numbers below match the numbered questions on the report.

1 — Custody of the Beneficiary

Place an "X" in the "YES" box if the beneficiary:

- Lived with you for **some but not all months** in the report period, or
- Lived in an institution or nursing home for **some but not all months** in the report period, or
- Lived alone for **some but not all months** in the report period, or
- Moved from one institution or nursing home to another.

Place an "X" in the "NO" box if the beneficiary lived:

- With the same person during the entire report period, or
- In the same institution or nursing home during the entire report period, or
- Alone during the entire report period.

Do not consider short visits (vacations, weekend or holiday visits) with another person when you answer this question.

2 — Turning Over Payments To Another Person

Place an "X" in the "YES" box if you gave the full amount of the payments to:

- Another person and that person decided how to use the money.
- The beneficiary and he or she decided how to use the money.

Place an "X" in the "NO" box if you:

- Decided how to use the money.
- Told an institution or nursing home how to use the money.

Form SSA-623-F3 (4-88)
Destroy prior editions

Continued on the Reverse ⟶

3 — How You Used The Benefits

Place an "X" in the "YES" box if you used all the benefits you received to pay for the beneficiary's day-to-day needs.

Place an "X" in the "NO" box if you:

- Saved all or part of the benefits.
- Used all or part of the benefits for someone other than the beneficiary or for something other than the beneficiary's current needs.

4 — Personal Needs

In this item include the amount of money you spent on clothing, medical and dental care, education, and recreational items like toys, movies, cameras, radios, and musical instruments. Also include other personal items like stationery, grooming aids, candy and tobacco. **Do not include the money you spent on food and shelter.**

5 — Amounts Left At The End Of The Report Period

If you had no SSI or Social Security money left at the end of the report period, put an "X" in box **5.A.**

If you had SSI or Social Security money left at the end of the period, show how much in box **5.B.** This includes money that you have held from earlier years.

6 — Unused Benefits

If you had Social Security or SSI money left at the end of the report period, be sure to answer items 6.A. and 6.B.

In item **6.A.**, place an "X" in the boxes which show how you are holding the benefits that you have not spent.

In item **6.A.**, place an "X" in the "OTHER" box if:

- The type of account in which you are holding benefits is not shown, or
- You are not holding the money in an account.

In item **6.B.**, place an "X" in the box which describes the title (name) on the account in which you are holding the unused benefits.

If the title of the account in which you are holding the unused benefits is not shown or if you are not holding the money in an account, place an "X" in the "OTHER" box.

Benefits should be held in an account which shows that the money belongs to the beneficiary. If you are not sure whether the account you established does this, you should check with your bank and change the account title if necessary.

7 — Type And Title Of "Other" Account

If you answered "OTHER" in item 6.A., in item **7.A.** describe the type of account or way in which you are holding the unused benefits. For example, U.S. Savings Bonds, Treasury Bills, cash, etc.

If you answered "OTHER" in item 6.B., in item **7.B.** show the title on the account, if there is one. If there is no title on the account, show "NONE."

8 — Signature

You, the payee, must sign your name in this block. If you sign your name by mark ("X"), please have two witnesses sign their names and show the date.

9 — Relationship To The Beneficiary

Show your relationship to the beneficiary. For example, "parent, brother, friend, legal guardian or none." If you represent a bank, institution or agency, show your title.

Your Job As A Representative Payee

As a payee, you must use the Social Security and SSI money you receive for the care and well-being of the beneficiary. You need to be aware of what the beneficiary needs so that you can decide how best to use the money.

You must also tell us about any changes which may affect the checks you receive. You need to tell us if:

- The beneficiary moves, especially if he or she enters or leaves a hospital or institution, marries, goes to work, dies or is adopted.
- You are no longer responsible for the beneficiary.

Your Right To Privacy

We are required by section 205(j) of the Social Security Act to ask you to complete this report. Although the report is voluntary, the law states that as a representative payee, you have a responsibility to complete the report. If you do not return this report to us, we may not be able to continue sending the beneficiary's payments to you.

Sometimes the law requires us to give out the facts on this form without your consent. We must release this information to another person or Government agency if Federal law requires that we do so or to do the research and audits needed to administer or improve our representative payee program. These and other reasons why facts on the Representative Payee Report may be used or given out are explained in the Federal Register. If you would like more information, contact us.

If You Have Any Questions

If you have any questions, you should call, write or visit your local Social Security office. Almost all questions can be answered by phone. If you visit an office, please bring this report with you. This will help us answer your questions.

Social Security Administration Representative Payee Report

FORM APPROVED
OMB NO. 0960-00...

PAYEE'S NAME AND ADDRESS	REPORT PERIOD FROM: TO:	SOCIAL SECURITY NO.		
	BENEFICIARY		PSY	FP
	ID PIC BIC	D	TP	CC
	GS PC	DOC	TYA	
	DOB		MBC	
	CF	FUN	CFL	

Please read the enclosed instructions before completing this form. It will help you answer each question.

YES NO

1. Has the beneficiary's custodian changed during the report period? Please refer to the instructions on page 1 before you answer this question. ☐ ☐

2. Did you turn over the full amount of the payments to another person during the report period (for example, to the beneficiary's custodian or to the beneficiary)? If you answer yes, please explain on the reverse of this page. ☐ ☐

3. Did you use **all** the benefits you received during the report period for the beneficiary? ☐ ☐

4. Show the amount you spent for the beneficiary during the report period on things such as clothing, medical care, education, recreation and personal items. Do not include money you used for food and shelter. → DOLLARS ☐☐,☐☐☐ . CENTS ☐☐

5.
A. If there were NO benefits left at the end of the report period, including money from earlier years, place an "X" here. → ☐

B. If there were benefits left at the end of the report period, including money from earlier years, show the amount you have left here. → DOLLARS ☐☐,☐☐☐ . CENTS ☐☐

6. If you showed an amount in 5.B. above, place an "X" in the boxes below to show how you are holding the remaining money. If you have more than one account, you can mark more than one box in each section.

A. TYPE OF ACCOUNT				**B.** TITLE OR OWNERSHIP		
Checking Account	Savings Account	Collective Savings/ Patients' Fund	Other	Beneficiary's Name by Your Name	Your Name for Beneficiary's Name	Other
☐	☐	☐	☐	☐	☐	☐

7. A. If you answered "OTHER" in 6.A. above, show the type of account or investment in which the benefits are held. → TYPE OF ACCOUNT

7. B. If you answered "OTHER" in 6.B. above, show the title of the account in which the benefits are held. → TITLE OF ACCOUNT

I CERTIFY THAT THE INFORMATION I HAVE GIVEN ON THIS FORM IS TRUE.

8. SIGNATURE OF PAYEE (If signed by mark (X), two witnesses must sign below)   DATE

9. RELATIONSHIP TO BENEFICIARY OR TITLE

10. TELEPHONE NUMBERS (Include area code)
AREA CODE BUSINESS / AREA CODE HOME

WITNESS SIGNATURES ARE REQUIRED ONLY IF THE PAYEE'S SIGNATURE ABOVE HAS BEEN SIGNED BY MARK (X).
SIGNATURE OF WITNESS   DATE   SIGNATURE OF WITNESS   DATE

FORM SSA-623-F3 (4-88)

Appendix 30
Social Security Payee Evaluation Form

Social Security Payee Evaluation Form

327

DEPARTMENT OF HEALTH AND HUMAN SERVICES
SOCIAL SECURITY ADMINISTRATION

Form Approved
OMB No. 0960-0069

REPRESENTATIVE PAYEE EVALUATION REPORT

TP	CC	GS	NAM
TYA	MBA	CF	

BENEFICIARY'S NAME

SOCIAL SECURITY NUMBER
___ ___ ___ / ___ ___ / ___ ___ ___ ___

PAYEE'S NAME

REPORT PERIOD
FROM	TO

PAYEE'S ADDRESS
CITY AND STATE | ZIP CODE | PHONE NUMBER (Include area code)

PART I INFORMATION FROM PAYEE

1. GUARDIANSHIP STATUS

Is legal guardianship now in effect? ☐ YES ☐ NO
If yes, show guardian's name and address below (if other than payee).

GUARDIAN'S NAME | GUARDIAN'S ADDRESS

2. CUSTODY

(a) Did the beneficiary live alone or with someone other than the payee? ☐ YES ☐ NO
If yes, answer 2(b). If no, skip to item 4.

(b) Show below where the beneficiary lived. Show the relationship of the custodian to the beneficiary, the dates of residence and the reason for any change in custody.

NAME	ADDRESS	RELATION-SHIP	DATES OF RESIDENCE	REASON FOR CHANGE

3. DEMONSTRATION OF CONCERN

(a) How did the payee learn of the beneficiary's needs?

(b) Did the payee maintain contact with the beneficiary? If yes, show type of contact (visits, phone, letters) and frequency. If no, explain. ☐ YES ☐ NO

(c) Did the payee provide the beneficiary with funds for personal spending? If yes, show to whom the funds were given (e.g., directly to the beneficiary, the custodian). If no, show why not. ☐ YES ☐ NO

4. USE OF BENEFITS

(a) Did the payee turn over the checks or the full amount of the checks to another party? ☐ YES ☐ NO
If yes, show to whom the funds were given (e.g., the beneficiary, the custodian).

(b) Amount used for beneficiary's care and maintenance. If paid to another party, show to whom.
AMOUNT $ _____ NAME

Form SSA-624-F4 (9-86)

PART I (continued)

4. (cont)

(c) Amount used for beneficiary's clothing. If less than $20, or more than $300, explain. ⟶ Amount $ _____

(d) Amount used for beneficiary's personal spending. If less than $300, explain. ⟶ Amount $ _____

(e) Amount used for other than items (b) through (d) above. (Exclude savings.) Explain. ⟶ Amount $ _____

(f) Total amount of benefits used. ⟶ Total Amount (add (b) through (e) above) $ _____

(g) Did the payee record expenditures (receipts, cancelled checks, etc.)? ⟶ ☐ YES ☐ NO

5. CONSERVED FUNDS

(a) Total amount of conserved funds. Subtract item 4(f) from TYA and add conserved funds from prior years. ⟶ Amount $ _____

(b) How are conserved funds held?
☐ CASH ☐ U.S. SAVING BONDS ☐ OTHER (explain) _____
☐ CHECKING ACCOUNT ☐ SAVINGS ACCOUNT

(c) HOW ARE CONSERVED FUNDS TITLED?

TYPE OF HOLDING	TITLE OR OWNERSHIP	NAME AND ADDRESS OF BANK	ACCOUNT NUMBER

(d) Are the funds mingled with funds of another person(s)?
☐ YES ☐ NO
If yes, answer (e).

(e) Are funds clearly recorded as belonging to the beneficiary?
☐ YES ☐ NO

6. OTHER INCOME

(a) Did the beneficiary have other income which affects the entitlement to or use of Social Security benefits? ⟶ ☐ YES ☐ NO
If yes, answer (b) and (c).

(b) TYPE OF OTHER INCOME
☐ WORKMEN'S COMPENSATION ☐ VA BENEFITS
☐ OTHER (Explain) ☐ PUBLIC ASSISTANCE (Explain)

(c) Is there a payee for other income? ⟶ ☐ YES ☐ NO
If yes, show name and address of payee below.

NAME OF PAYEE	ADDRESS OF PAYEE

7. REMARKS

I certify that the information I provided in Part I above is true.

SIGNATURE	DATE
▶	

Form SSA-624-F4 (9-86)

Social Security Payee Evaluation Form

PART II INFORMATION FROM BENEFICIARY

1. ALL CUSTODY SITUATIONS

(a) Is the beneficiary aware of entitlement to Social Security benefits?
- [ ] YES [ ] NO

(b) Did the beneficiary participate in decisions on expenditures?
- [ ] YES [ ] NO

(c) Did the beneficiary receive funds for personal spending?
- [ ] YES [ ] NO

(d) Were any large purchases made for the beneficiary?
- [ ] YES [ ] NO

(e) Does the beneficiary have any unmet needs?
- [ ] YES [ ] NO
If yes, explain ⟶

EXPLANATION

(f) Did the beneficiary live with someone other than the payee?
- [ ] YES [ ] NO
If yes, answer 2. below.

(g) Did the beneficiary live alone?
- [ ] YES [ ] NO
If yes, answer 2. and 3. below.

2. BENEFICIARY NOT IN PAYEE'S CUSTODY

(a) Did the payee maintain contact with the beneficiary?
- [ ] YES [ ] NO
If yes, show type of contact (visit, phone, letters) and frequency. If no, explain.

(b) Did anyone other than the payee demonstrate concern for the beneficiary?
- [ ] YES [ ] NO
If yes, show who and type and frequency of contacts.

3. BENEFICIARY LIVED ALONE

(a) Was the beneficiary responsible for his/her maintenance expenses? (Rent, utilities)
- [ ] YES [ ] NO

(b) Did the beneficiary purchase his/her food and clothing?
- [ ] YES [ ] NO

4. REMARKS

Form SSA-624-F4 (9-86)

PART III INFORMATION FROM CUSTODIAN

CUSTODIAN'S NAME	ADDRESS	PHONE (Include area code)

1. PAYEE AND CUSTODIAN ARE NOT THE SAME PERSON OR ORGANIZATION

(a) Did the beneficiary live with the custodian during the entire report period? ⟶ ☐ YES ☐ NO
If no, show other custodians if known.

(b) Who would the custodian notify in cases of emergency?

(c) Was a charge made for care and maintenance of the beneficiary? ☐ YES ☐ NO
If yes, show the amount paid by the payee ⟶ Amount $ _____

(d) Did the payee demonstrate personal concern for the beneficiary? ⟶ ☐ YES ☐ NO
If yes, explain below.

FREQUENCY OF VISITS	PROVIDES CLOTHING	GIFTS	OTHER (Specify)
	☐ YES ☐ NO	☐ YES ☐ NO	

(e) Did the payee contribute money for the beneficiary's personal use? If yes, show the amount contributed by the payee. ⟶ ☐ YES ☐ NO
Amount $ _____

(f) Does the custodian hold and control the beneficiary's personal use funds? ⟶ ☐ YES ☐ NO
If yes, answer (g).

(g) Are the beneficiary's funds mingled with funds of other persons? ☐ YES ☐ NO ⟶ If yes, are the funds clearly designated as the beneficiary's? ☐ YES ☐ NO

2. ALL CUSTODIANS

Were any group purchases made? ☐ YES ☐ NO ⟶ If yes, were the purchases approved by SSA? ☐ YES ☐ NO

3. REMARKS

_____
_____
_____
_____
_____

PART IV EVALUATION AND ACTION TAKEN

_____
_____
_____
_____
_____

SIGNATURE AND TITLE	OFFICE	DATE

Form SSA-624-F4 (9-86)

Appendix 31
States with Family Consent Statutes

The family may make health care decisions for
(A) incapacitated adults in:

Arkansas	Excludes patients who are pregnant.
Georgia	
Idaho	
Louisiana	
Maine	
Maryland	
Mississippi	
New Mexico	Patients must be in an irreversible coma.
Utah	

(B) terminally ill and incapacitated adults (including termination of treatment) in:

Arkansas	Excludes patients who are pregnant.
Connecticut	Excludes patients who are pregnant. May not withdraw nutrition or hydration.
Florida	Excludes patients who are pregnant. May not withdraw "sustenance." Doctor can make decisions if no family members are available.
Iowa	May not withdraw "sustenance."
Louisiana	
New Mexico	Patients must be terminally ill and comatose.
North Carolina	Patients must be terminally ill and comatose. Doctor can make decisions if no family members are available.
Oregon	Excludes patients who are pregnant. Patients must be terminally ill and comatose. Doctor decides how much nutrition patients can tolerate. Doctor can make decisions if no family members are available.
Texas	Excludes patients who are pregnant. Doctor can make decisions if no family members are available.
Utah	May not withdraw "sustenance."
Virginia	

Source: B. Mishkin, *A Matter of Choice: Planning Ahead for Health Care Decisions*, Senate Special Committee on Aging, 1986.

Appendix 32
Provisions of Family Consent Laws

	Patient Must Be		Family Members						Consent Not Valid for		
State	Terminally Ill	Comatose	Spouse	Adult Child	Parent	Adult Sibling	Other	Priority Given	Abortion	Sterilization	Mental Health Care
Arkansas			X	X	X	nearest relative	grandparent				
Connecticut[A]											
Florida	X		X	X[C]	X		nearest relative	X			
Georgia			X		X[B]	X[B]	grandparent	X	X		
Idaho			X		X		any competent relative				
Iowa	X		X	X[C]	X	X					
Louisiana			X		X[B]	X[B]	grandparent[B]		X	X	X
Louisiana[1]	X		X	X[C]	X[C]	X[C]	other ascendents or descendents[C]	X			
Maine			X		X		nearest relative				
Maryland			X	X	X	X	grandparent; adult grandchild	X	X	X	X
Mississippi			X	X	X	X	grandparent				
New Mexico	X	or X	X	X	X	X	family members[E]	X			
North Carolina	X	and X	X	X	X	X		X			
Oregon	X	and X	X	X[C]	X	X					
Texas	X		X	X[C]	X		nearest relative	X[D]			
Utah			X	X	X[B]	X[B]	grandparent[B]				
Virginia	X		X	X	X		nearest relative	X			

Source: Adapted from B. Mishkin, *A Matter of Choice: Planning Ahead for Health Care Decisions*, Senate Special Committee on Aging, 1986.

[A] — requires consent of "next of kin," if known
[B] — for minor child
[C] — majority of this class required (if available)
[D] — requires consent of at least two family members, if reasonably available.
[E] — all who can be contacted must agree on what patient would choose
[1] Louisiana has two family consent laws.

Appendix 33
American Medical Association Statement on Withholding or Withdrawing Life-Prolonging Medical Treatment

THE social commitment of the physician is to sustain life and relieve suffering. Where the performance of one duty conflicts with the other, the choice of the patient, or his family or legal representative if the patient is incompetent to act in his own behalf, should prevail. In the absence of the patient's choice or an authorized proxy, the physician must act in the best interest of the patient.

For humane reasons, with informed consent, a physician may do what is medically necessary to alleviate severe pain, or cease or omit treatment to permit a terminally ill patient whose death is imminent to die. However, he should not intentionally cause death. In deciding whether the administration of potentially life-prolonging medical treatment is in the best interest of the patient who is incompetent to act in his own behalf, the physician should determine what the possibility is for extending life under humane and comfortable conditions and what are the prior expressed wishes of the patient and attitudes of the family or those who have responsibility for the custody of the patient.

Even if death is not imminent but a patient's coma is beyond doubt irreversible and there are adequate safeguards to confirm the accuracy of the diagnosis and with the concurrence of those who have responsibility for the care of the patient, it is not unethical to discontinue all means of life-prolonging medical treatment.

Life-prolonging medical treatment includes medication and artificially or technologically supplied respiration, nutrition or hydration. In treating a terminally ill or irreversibly comatose patient, the physician should determine whether the benefits of treatment outweigh its burdens. At all times, the dignity of the patient should be maintained.

Source: *Current Opinions of the Council on Ethical and Judicial Affairs of the American Medical Association,* 1986, with permission.

Appendix 34
Health-Related State Agencies and Organizations (Including Licensure Agencies)

Alabama

Commission on Aging
740 Madison Avenue
Montgomery 36104

Home Health Care Medical Directors Association (1)
P.O. Box 16626
Mobile 36616
(205) 476-0192

Alabama State Hospice Organization (2)
701 Princeton Avenue SW
Birmingham 35211
(205) 592-1738

Alabama Medicaid Agency (3)
2500 Fairlane Drive
Montgomery 36130
(205) 277-2710

---

1. State home care associations
2. State hospice organizations
3. Medicaid assistance offices
4. Self-help clearinghouses
5. Hospital licensure agencies
6. Medical and nursing licensure agencies

State Hospital Licensure Agency (5)
Division of Licensure and Certification
Alabama Department of Public Health
654 State Office Building
Montgomery 36130
(205) 261-5113

Alabama Board of Nursing (6)
One East Building, Suite 203
500 Eastern Boulevard
Montgomery 36117
(205) 261-4060

Alaska

Department of Health and Social Services
Pouch H
Juneau 99811

Office on Aging
Department of Health and Social Services
Pouch H
Juneau 99811

Hospice of Juneau (2)
419 6th Street
Juneau 99802
(907) 586-3414

Division of Medical Assistance (3)
Department of Health and Social Services
PPO Box H-07
Juneau 99811
(907) 586-9496

Health Facilities Licensing and Certification (5)
4041 B Street #101
Anchorage 99503
(907) 561-2171

Alaska Medical Board (6)
Department of Commerce and Economic Development
Division of Occupational Licensing
P.O. Box D-Lic

Juneau 99811
(907) 465-2541

Alaska Medical Board of Nursing (6)
3601 C Street
Suite 722
Anchorage 99503
(907) 561-2878

Arizona

Department of Economic Security
1717 West Jefferson
Phoenix 85007

Bureau on Aging
Department of Economic Security
P.O. Box 6123
Phoenix 85004

Arizona Association for Home Care (1)
3602 East Campbell
Phoenix 85018
(602) 957-0773

Arizona State Hospice Organization (2)
St. Mary's Hospice
1601 West St. Mary's Road
Tucson 85705
(602) 622-5833

Arizona Health Care Cost Containment System (AHCCS) (3)
801 East Jefferson
Phoenix 85034
(602) 234-3655

Office of Health Care Institution Licensure (5)
Arizona Department of Health Services
411 North 24th Street

---

1. State home care associations
2. State hospice organizations
3. Medicaid assistance offices
4. Self-help clearinghouses
5. Hospital licensure agencies
6. Medical and nursing licensure agencies

Phoenix 85008
(602) 220-6407

Arizona Board of Medical Examiners (6)
1990 West Camelback Road
Suite 401
Phoenix 85015
(602) 255-5092

Arizona State Board of Nursing (6)
5050 North 19th Avenue, Suite 103
Phoenix 85015
(602) 255-5092

Arkansas

Department of Human Services
406 National Old Lind Building
Little Rock 72201

Office on Aging and Adult Services
Department of Human Services
7107 West 12th Street
P.O. Box 2179
Little Rock 72203

Arkansas Association for Home Health Agencies (1)
1501 North University, Suite 400
Little Rock 72207
(501) 664-7870

Arkansas State Hospice Organization (2)
P.O. Box 725
Jonesboro 72401
(501) 972-6270

Office of Medical Services (3)
Division of Economic and Medical Services
Arkansas Department of Human Services
P.O. Box 1437
Little Rock 72203
(501) 682-8338

Office of Long-Term Care (3)
Division of Economic and Medical Services

Arkansas Department of Human Services
P.O. Box 1437
Little Rock 72203
(501) 682-8430

Division of Health Facility Services (5)
Arkansas Department of Health—Area 2300
4815 West Markham Street
Little Rock 72205
(501) 681-2201

Arkansas State Board of Nursing (6)
4120 West Markham Street, Suite 308
Little Rock 72205
(501) 371-2751

California

Health and Welfare Agency
926 J Street, Room 917
Sacramento 95814

Department of Aging
Health and Welfare Agency
918 J Street
Sacramento 95814

California Association for Health Services at Home (CAHSAH) (1)
660 J Street, Suite 290
Sacramento 95814
(916) 443-8055

Hospice Organization of Southern California (2)
637 South Lucas
Los Angeles 90017
(818) 788-3295

Northern California Hospice Association (2)
703 Market Street, Suite 550

---

1. State home care associations
2. State hospice organizations
3. Medicaid assistance offices
4. Self-help clearinghouses
5. Hospital licensure agencies
6. Medical and nursing licensure agencies

San Francisco 94103
(415) 543-9393

Medical Care Services (3)
Department of Health Services
714 P Street, Room 1253
Sacramento 95814
(916) 322-5824

Self-Help and Mutual Aid Association (SHAMA) (4)
c/o Alfred Katz
UCLA School of Public Health
405 Hilgard Avenue
Los Angeles 90024
(213) 825-5418

San Diego Self-Help Clearinghouse (4)
1172 Morena Boulevard, P.O. Box 86246
San Diego 92138
(619) 275-2344

San Francisco Self-Help Clearinghouse (4)
Mental Health Association of San Francisco
2398 Fine Street
San Francisco 94115
(415) 921-4401

Licensing and Certification (5)
Department of Health Services
714 P Street, Room 823
Sacramento 95814
(916) 445-3054

California Board of Medical Quality Assurance (6)
1430 Howe Avenue
Sacramento 95825
(916) 920-6411

Board of Registered Nursing (6)
1030 13th Street, Suite 200
Sacramento 95814
(916) 322-3350

Board of Vocational Nurse and Psychiatric Technician Examiners (6)
1020 N Street, Room 406

Sacramento 95814
(916) 445-0793

Colorado

Department of Social Services
1575 Sherman Street
Denver 80203

Division of Services for the Aging
Department of Social Services
1575 Sherman Street
Denver 80203

Colorado Association of Home Health Agencies (1)
7235 South Newport Way
Englewood 80122
(303) 694-4728

Colorado Hospice Coalition (2)
3534 Kirkwood Place
Boulder 80302
(303) 449-7740

Bureau of Medical Services (3)
Department of Social Services
1575 Sherman, 6th floor
Denver 80203
(303) 866-5901

Division of Health Facilities Regulation (5)
Colorado Department of Health
4210 East 11th Avenue
Denver 80220
(303) 331-4930

Colorado Board of Medical Examiners (6)
1525 Sherman Street #132
Denver 80203
(303) 868-2468

---

1. State home care associations
2. State hospice organizations
3. Medicaid assistance offices
4. Self-help clearinghouses
5. Hospital licensure agencies
6. Medical and nursing licensure agencies

Connecticut

Department on Aging
90 Washington Street, Room 312
Hartford 06115

Connecticut Association for Home Care (1)
110 Barnes Road
P.O. Box 90
Wallingford 06492
(203) 265-8931

Hospice Council of Connecticut (2)
461 Atlantic Street
Stamford 06901
(203) 324-2592

Medical Care Administration (3)
Department of Income Maintenance
110 Bartholomew Avenue
Hartford 06106
(203) 566-2934

Hamden Mental Health Center (4)
300 Dixwell Avenue
Hamden 06514
(203) 789-7645

Connecticut Self-Help Mutual Support Network (4)
19 Howe Street
New Haven 06511
(800) 842-1501 or (203) 789-7645

Hospital and Medical Care Division (5)
Connecticut State Department of Health Services
150 Washington Street
Hartford 06106
(203) 566-1073

Department of Health Services
Division of Medical Quality Assurance
Physician Licensure
150 Washington Street
Hartford 06106
(203) 566-7398

Connecticut Board of Examiners for Nursing (6)
Department of Health Services
Division of Medical Quality Assurance
150 Washington Street
Hartford 06106
(203) 566-1032

Delaware

Department of Health and Social Services
Delaware State Hospital, 3rd floor
Administration Building
New Castle 19720

Delaware Hospices, Inc. (2)
3509 Silvergate Road, Suite 109, Talley Building
Wilmington 19810
(302) 478-5707

Medical Services (3)
Department of Health and Social Services
Delaware State Hospital
New Castle 19720
(302) 421-6139

Office of Health Facilities Licensing and Certification (5)
Department of Health and Social Services
3000 Newport Gap Pike
Wilmington 19808
(302) 571-3499

Board of Medical Practice of Delaware (6)
Margaret O'Neill Building, 2nd Floor
Dover 19903
(302) 736-4522

Delaware Board of Nursing (6)
Margaret O'Neill Building, 2nd Floor

---

1. State home care associations
2. State hospice organizations
3. Medicaid assistance offices
4. Self-help clearinghouses
5. Hospital licensure agencies
6. Medical and nursing licensure agencies

Dover 19903
(302) 736-4522

District of Columbia

Office of Aging
Office of the Mayor
1012 14th Street NW, Suite 1106
Washington 20005

Capitol Home Health Association (1)
P.O. Box 70407
Washington 20088
(202) 547-7424

Hospice Care of the District of Columbia (2)
1749 St. Matthews Court NW
Washington 20036
(202) 347-1700

Office of Health Care Financing (3)
D.C. Department of Human Services
1331 H Street NW, Suite 500
Washington 20005
(202) 727-0735

Greater Washington Self-Help Coalition (4)
Mental Health Association of Northern Virginia
100 North Washington Street, Suite 232
Falls Church, VA 22046
(703) 536-4100

Service Facility Regulation Administration (5)
614 H Street NW
Washington 20001
(202) 727-7190

Occupational and Professional Licensing Administration (6)
P.O. Box 37200, Room 904
Washington 20013
(202) 727-7465

Florida

Department of Health and Rehabilitation Services
1323 Winewood Boulevard
Tallahassee 32301

Program Office of Aging and Adult Services
Department of Health and Rehabilitation Services
1323 Winewood Boulevard
Tallahassee 32301

Florida Association of Home Health Agencies (1)
201 South Monroe Street, Suite 201
Tallahassee 32301
(904) 224-4226

Florida Hospices, Inc. (2)
Hospice of Volusia
P.O. Box 1990
Daytona Beach 32724
(904) 254-4237

Department of Health and Rehabilitative Services (3)
1321 Winewood Boulevard
Tallahassee 32301
(904) 488-3560

Office of Licensure and Certification (5)
Department of Health and Rehabilitation Services
27237 Mahan Drive
Tallahassee 32308
(904) 487-2527

Florida Board of Medicine (6)
130 North Monroe Street
Tallahassee 32399
(904) 488-0595

Board of Nursing (6)
111 Coast Line Drive East, Suite 504
Jacksonville 32202
(904) 359-6331

---

1. State home care associations
2. State hospice organizations
3. Medicaid assistance offices
4. Self-help clearinghouses
5. Hospital licensure agencies
6. Medical and nursing licensure agencies

Georgia

Department of Human Resources
618 Ponce de Leon Avenue N.E.
Atlanta 30308

Office of Aging
Department of Human Resources
618 Ponce de Leon Avenue N.E.
Atlanta 30308

Georgia Association of Home Health Agencies (1)
1260 South Omni International
Atlanta 30303
(404) 577-9144

Georgia Hospice Organization (2)
Hospice of the Golden Isles
1326 Union Street
Brunswick 31520
(215) 265-4735

Georgia Department of Medical Assistance (3)
Floyd Veterans Memorial Building
West Tower, 1220C
2 Martin Luther King, Jr., Drive SE
Atlanta 30334
(404) 656-4479

Standards and Licensure Section (5)
Department of Human Resources
878 Peachtree Street NE, Suite 803
Atlanta 30309
(404) 894-5137

Composite State Board of Medical Examiners (6)
166 Pryor Street SW
Atlanta 30303
(404) 656-3913

Georgia Board of Nursing (6)
166 Pryor Street SW
Atlanta 30303
(404) 656-3913

Guam

Department of Public Health and Social Services
Government of Guam
P.O. Box 2816
Agana 96910

Office of Aging
Social Service Administration
Government of Guam
P.O. Box 2816
Agana 96910

Bureau of Health Care Financing (3)
Department of Public Health and Social Services
P.O. Box 96910
Agana 96910

Guam Board of Nurse Examiners (6)
Box 2816
Agana 96910
(671) 734-2783

Hawaii

Executive Office on Aging
Office of the Governor
State of Hawaii
1149 Bethel Street, Room 307
Honolulu 96813

St. Francis Hospital (2)
Maureen Keleher
2230 Liliha Street
Honolulu 96817
(808) 845-1727

---

1. State home care associations
2. State hospice organizations
3. Medicaid assistance offices
4. Self-help clearinghouses
5. Hospital licensure agencies
6. Medical and nursing licensure agencies

Health Care Administration Division (3)
Department of Social Services and Housing
P.O. Box 339
Honolulu 96809
(808) 548-3855

State Health Planning and Development Agency (5)
Medical Health Services Division
Hospital and Medical Facilities
Licensing Department of Health
P.O. Box 3378
Honolulu 96801
(808) 548-2048

Board of Medical Examiners (6)
Department of Commerce and Consumer Affairs
P.O. Box 3469
Honolulu 96809
(808) 548-4392

Board of Nursing (6)
P.O. Box 3469
Honolulu 96801
(808) 548-3086

Idaho

Idaho Office on Aging
Statehouse
Boise 83720

Council of Idaho Hospice Organizations (2)
Hospice Mercy Medical Center
1512 12th Avenue
Nampa 83651
(208) 467-1171, ext. 174

Bureau of Medical Assistance (3)
Department of Health and Welfare
450 West State Street
Statehouse Mail
Boise 83720
(208) 334-5794

Facility Standards Program (5)
Department of Health and Welfare
420 West Washington Street
Boise 83720
(208) 334-4169

Idaho State Board of Medicine (6)
650 West State Street
Boise 83720
(208) 334-2822

Idaho State Board of Nursing (6)
700 West State Street
Boise 83720
(208) 334-3110

Illinois

Department on Aging
2401 West Jefferson
Springfield 62706

Illinois Council of Home Health Services (1)
1619 Ashland Avenue
Evanston 60201
(312) 328-6654

Illinois State Hospice Organization (2)
Hospice of Proviso-Leyden
330 Eastern Avenue
Bellwood 60104
(312) 547-8282

Division of Medical Programs (3)
Illinois Department of Public Aid
628 East Adams

---

1. State home care associations
2. State hospice organizations
3. Medicaid assistance offices
4. Self-help clearinghouses
5. Hospital licensure agencies
6. Medical and nursing licensure agencies

Springfield 62761
(217) 782-2570

Self-Help Center (4)
1600 Dodge Center, Suite S-122
Evanston 60201
(312) 328-0470

Hospital Licensing Section (5)
Division of Health Facilities Standards
Department of Public Health
525 West Jefferson
Springfield 62761
(217) 782-4977

Department of Registration and Education (6)
320 West Washington
Springfield 62786
(217) 785-0800

Indiana

Commission on Aging and Aged
Graphic Arts Building
215 North Senate Avenue
Indianapolis 46202

Indiana Association of Home Health Agencies (1)
P.O. Box 1457
Carmel 46032
(317) 848-2942

Indiana Association of Hospices (2)
2200 Randalea Drive
Fort Wayne 46805
(219) 484-6636, ext. 4183

Assistant Administrator (3)
Medicaid Director
Indiana State Department of Public Welfare
State Office Building, Room 702
Indianapolis 46204
(317) 232-4324

Division of Acute Care Services (5)
Indiana State Board of Health
1330 West Michigan Street
Indianapolis 46206
(317) 633-8488

Health Professions Bureau (6)
Medical Licensing Board of Indiana
P.O. Box 82067
One American Square, Suite 1020
Indianapolis 46282-0004
(317) 232-2960

Indiana State Board of Nursing (6)
Health Professions Bureau
P.O. Box 82067
One American Square, Suite 1020
Indianapolis 46282
(317) 232-2960

Iowa

Commission on Aging
415 West 10th Street
Jewett Building
Des Moines 50319

Iowa Assembly of Home Health Agencies (1)
3000 Southwest 40th Street
Des Moines 50321
(515) 282-6498

Iowa Hospice Organization (2)
205 Loma Street
Waterloo 50701
(319) 273-2702 or 273-2814

---

1. State home care associations
2. State hospice organizations
3. Medicaid assistance offices
4. Self-help clearinghouses
5. Hospital licensure agencies
6. Medical and nursing licensure agencies

Bureau of Medical Services (3)
Department of Human Services
Hoover State Office Building, 5th floor
Des Moines 50319
(515) 281-8794

Division of Health Facilities (5)
Iowa State Department of Inspection and Appeals
Lucas State Office Building
Des Moines 50319
(515) 281-4115

Iowa State Board of Medical Examiners (6)
State Capitol Complex
Executive Hills West
Des Moines 50319
(515) 281-5171

Iowa Board of Nursing (6)
State Capitol Complex
1223 East Court Avenue
Des Moines 50319
(515) 281-3255

Kansas

Department of Aging
Biddle Building
2700 West 6th Street
Topeka 66606

Kansas Association of Home Health Agencies (1)
1526 North Market Street
Wichita 67214
(316) 265-5888

Association of Kansas Hospices (2)
7540 Aberdeen
Prairie Village 66208
(913) 341-5476

Department of Social and Rehabilitation Services (3)
State Office Building
Topeka 66612
(913) 296-3981

Hospital Program (5)
Bureau of Adult and Child Care Facilities
Kansas Department of Health and Environment
Forbes Field, Building 740
Topeka 66620
(913) 296-1240

Kansas State Board of Healing Arts (6)
Landon State Office Building
900 Southwest Jackson, Suite 553
Topeka 66612
(913) 296-7413

Kansas State Board of Nursing (6)
Landon State Office Building
900 Southwest Jackson, Suite 551-S
Topeka 66612
(913) 296-4929

Kentucky

Department for Human Resources
Capital Annex, Room 201
Frankfort 40601

Kentucky Home Health Association (1)
1804 Darien Drive
Lexington 40504
(606) 277-7983

Kentucky Association of Hospices (2)
1105 Nicholasville Road
Lexington 40503
(606) 252-2308

Department of Medicaid Services (3)
Cabinet for Human Resources
275 East Main Street

---

1. State home care associations
2. State hospice organizations
3. Medicaid assistance offices
4. Self-help clearinghouses
5. Hospital licensure agencies
6. Medical and nursing licensure agencies

Frankfort 40621
(502) 564-6535

Division of Licensing and Regulation (5)
Cabinet for Human Resources
Human Resources Building
275 East Main Street, 4th Floor East
Frankfort 40621
(502) 564-2800

Kentucky Board of Nursing (6)
4010 Dupont Circle, Suite 430
Louisville 40207
(502) 897-5143

Louisiana

Health and Human Resources Administration
P.O. Box 44215, Capitol Station
Baton Rouge 70804

Bureau of Aging Services
Division of Human Resources
Health and Human Resources Administration
P.O. Box 44282, Capitol Station
Baton Rouge 70804

Richard N. Murphy Hospice (2)
P.O. Box 111
Hammond 70404
(504) 386-6130

Medical Assistance Division (3)
Department of Health and Human Resources
P.O. Box 94065
Baton Rouge 70804
(504) 342-3956

Division of Licensing and Certification (6)
Louisiana Department of Health and Human Resources
Box 3767
Baton Rouge 70821
(504) 342-5774

Louisiana State Board of Medical Examiners (6)
830 Union Street, Suite 100
New Orleans 70112
(504) 524-6763

Louisiana State Board of Nursing (6)
907 Pere Marquette Building
150 Baronne Street
New Orleans 70112
(504) 568-5464

Louisiana State Board of Practical Nurse Examiners (6)
Tidewater Place
1440 Canal Street, Suite 2010
New Orleans 70112
(504) 568-6480

Maine

Department of Human Services
State House
Augusta 04333

Bureau of Maine's Elderly
Community Services Unit
Department of Human Services
State House
Augusta 04333

Maine Community Health Association (1)
71 Sewall Street
Augusta 04330
(207) 622-3276

Coalition of Maine Hospices (2)
32 Thomas Street

---

1. State home care associations
2. State hospice organizations
3. Medicaid assistance offices
4. Self-help clearinghouses
5. Hospital licensure agencies
6. Medical and nursing licensure agencies

Portland 04102
(207) 774-4417

Department of Human Services (3)
State House, Station 11
Augusta 04333
(207) 289-2674

Division of Licensing and Certification (5)
Department of Human Services
State House, Station 11
Augusta 04333
(207) 289-2606

Board of Registration in Medicine (State of Maine) (6)
RFD 3, Box 461
Waterville 04901
(207) 873-2184

Maine State Board of Nursing (6)
285 Water Street
Augusta 04330
(207) 289-5324

Maryland

Office on Aging
State Office Building
301 West Preston Street
Baltimore 21201

Maryland Association of Home Health Agencies (1)
P.O. Box 1307
Columbia 21044
(301) 964-9698

Maryland State Hospice Network (2)
Sinai Hospital Home Care/Hospice
2401 Belvedere Avenue
Baltimore 21215
(301) 587-5600

Department of Health and Mental Hygiene (3)
201 West Preston Street
Baltimore 21201
(301) 225-6525

Department of Health and Mental Hygiene (5)
201 West Preston Street
Baltimore 21201
(301) 383-6197

Board of Medical Examiners of Maryland (6)
201 West Preston Street
Baltimore 21201
(301) 225-5900

Maryland State Board of Examiners of Nurses (6)
201 West Preston Street
Baltimore 21201
(301) 225-5880

Massachusetts

Department of Elder Affairs
110 Tremont Street
Boston 02108

Massachusetts Association of Community Health Agencies (1)
6 Beacon Street, Suite 915
Boston 02108
(617) 893-4792

Hospice of Lynn (2)
VNA of Lynn
196 Ocean Avenue
Lynn, MA 01902
(617) 598-2454

Department of Public Welfare (3)
180 Tremont Street
Boston 02111
(617) 574-0205

Division of Health Care Quality (5)
Massachusetts Department of Public Health

---

1. State home care associations
2. State hospice organizations
3. Medicaid assistance offices
4. Self-help clearinghouses
5. Hospital licensure agencies
6. Medical and nursing licensure agencies

80 Boylston Street, Room 1125
Boston 02116
(617) 727-5860

Board of Registration in Medicine (6)
Commonwealth of Massachusetts
10 West Street
Boston 02111
(617) 727-3086

Board of Registration in Nursing (6)
100 Cambridge Street, Room 1519
Boston 02202
(617) 727-7393

Michigan

Office of Services to the Aging
300 East Michigan
P.O. Box 30026
Lansing 48909

Michigan Home Health Association (1)
4990 Northwind Drive, Suite 220
East Lansing 48823
(517) 332-1195

Michigan Hospice Organization (2)
1825 Watson Road
Hemlock 48626
(517) 642-8121

Department of Social Services (3)
921 West Holmes
P.O. Box 30037
Lansing 48909
(517) 334-7262

Berrien County Self-Help Clearinghouse (4)
Riverwood Community Mental Health Center
2681 Morton Avenue
St. Joseph 49085
(616) 983-7781

Bureau of Health Facilities (5)
Michigan Department of Public Health
3500 North Logan, Box 30035

Lansing 48909
(517) 335-8500

Michigan Board of Medicine (6)
611 West Ottawa Street, Box 30018
Lansing 48909
(517) 373-6873

Michigan Board of Nursing (6)
Department of Licensing and Regulation, Box 30018
Lansing 48909
(517) 373-6873

Minnesota

Governor's Citizens Council on Aging
Suite 204 Metro Square Building
7th and Robert Streets
St. Paul 55101

Minnesota Assembly of Home and Community Health Nursing Agencies (1)
P.O. Box 300110
Minneapolis 55403
(612) 374-5404

Minnesota Hospice Organization (2)
Metro Medical Center
900 South 8th Street
Minneapolis 55404
(612) 347-4377

Department of Human Services (3)
P.O. Box 43170
St. Paul 55164
(612) 296-2766

Community Care Unit (4)
Wilder Center
919 Lafond Avenue

---

1. State home care associations
2. State hospice organizations
3. Medicaid assistance offices
4. Self-help clearinghouses
5. Hospital licensure agencies
6. Medical and nursing licensure agencies

St. Paul 55104
(612) 642-4060

Health Resources Division (5)
Minnesota Department of Health
717 Delaware Street Southeast
Minneapolis 55440
(612) 623-5440

Minnesota Board of Medical Examiners (6)
2700 University Avenue West, Suite 106
St. Paul 55114
(612) 642-0538

Minnesota Board of Nursing (6)
2700 University Avenue West, Suite 108
St. Paul 55114
(612) 642-0567

Mississippi

Council on Aging
P.O. Box 5136
Fondren Station
510 George Street
Jackson 39216

Mississippi Home Health Association (1)
455 North Lamar Street, Suite 410
Jackson 39202
(601) 353-0015

South Mississippi Home Health (2)
P.O. Box 888
Hattiesburg 39401
(601) 268-1842

Office of the Governor (3)
Robert E. Lee Building, Room 801
239 North Lamar Street
Jackson 39202-1311
(601) 359-6050

Division of Health Facilities Licensure and Certification (5)
Mississippi State Department of Health
2686 Insurance Center Drive

Jackson 39216
(601) 981-6880

Mississippi Board of Nursing (6)
135 Bounds Street
Jackson 39206
(601) 354-7349

Missouri

Department of Social Services
Broadway State Office Building
P.O. Box 570
Jefferson City 65101

Office of Aging
Division of Special Services
Department of Social Services
Broadway State Office Building
P.O. Box 570
Jefferson City 65101

Missouri Association of Home Health Agencies (1)
101 Madison Street
Jefferson City 65101
(314) 634-7772

Missouri Hospice Organization (2)
527 West 39th Street
Kansas City 64111
(816) 531-1200

Department of Social Services (3)
P.O. Box 6500
Jefferson City 65102
(314) 751-6922

Bureau of Hospital Licensing and Certification (5)
Missouri Department of Health

---

1. State home care associations
2. State hospice organizations
3. Medicaid assistance offices
4. Self-help clearinghouses
5. Hospital licensure agencies
6. Medical and nursing licensure agencies

Box 570
Jefferson City 65102
(314) 751-6302

Missouri State Board of Registration for the Healing Arts (6)
Box 4
Jefferson City 65102
(314) 751-2334

Montana

Department of Social and Rehabilitation Services
P.O. Box 1723
Helena 58601

Aging Services Bureau
Department of Social and Rehabilitation Services
P.O. Box 1723
Helena 58601

Montana Hospice Exchange Council (2)
St. Joseph's Mission Mountain Hospice
P.O. Box 1010
Poison 59860
(406) 883-5377

Department of Social and Rehabilitation Services (3)
P.O. Box 4210
Helena 59604
(406) 444-4540

Health Services Division (5)
State Department of Health and Environmental Sciences
Cogswell Building
Helena 59620
(406) 444-2037

Montana State Board of Nursing (6)
1424 9th Avenue
Helena 59620
(406) 444-4279

Nebraska

Commission on Aging
State House Station 94784

P.O. Box 95044
Lincoln 68509

Nebraska Hospice Association, Inc. (2)
1010 East 35 Street
Scotts Bluff 69361
(308) 635-3171 or 632-5549

Department of Social Services (3)
301 Centennial Mall South, 5th Floor
Lincoln 68509
(402) 471-9330

Self-Help Information Services (4)
1601 Euclid Avenue
Lincoln 68502
(402) 476-9668

Division of Licensure and Standards (5)
State Department of Health
301 Centennial Mall South
Lincoln 68509
(402) 471-2946

Bureau of Examining Boards (6)
301 Centennial Mall South
Box 95007
Lincoln 68509
(402) 471-2115

Nevada

Department of Human Resources
505 East King Street, Room 600
Carson City 89710

Division for Aging Services
Department of Human Resources

---

1. State home care associations
2. State hospice organizations
3. Medicaid assistance offices
4. Self-help clearinghouses
5. Hospital licensure agencies
6. Medical and nursing licensure agencies

505 East King Street, Room 600
Carson City 89710

Nathan Adelson Hospice (2)
4141 South Swenson
Las Vegas 89109
(702) 733-0320

Welfare Division, Department of Human Resources (3)
Capitol Complex
2527 North Carson Street
Carson City 89710
(702) 885-4698

Bureau of Regulatory Health Services (5)
Nevada State Division of Health
505 East King Street
Carson City 89710
(702) 885-4475

Nevada State Board of Medical Examiners (6)
P.O. Box 7238
Reno 89510
(702) 329-2559

Nevada State Board of Nursing (6)
1281 Terminal Way, Room 116
Reno 89502
(702) 786-2778

New Hampshire

Council on Aging
P.O. Box 786
14 Depot Street
Concord 03301

Community Health Care Association of New Hampshire (1)
117 Manchester Street
Concord 03301
(603) 225-5597

Hospice Affiliates of New Hampshire (2)
Concord Regional VNA
8 Loudoun Road

Concord 03301
(603) 224-4093

New Hampshire Division of Human Services (3)
Department of Health and Human Services
6 Hazen Drive
Concord 03301-6521
(603) 271-4353

Bureau of Health Facilities Administration (5)
Division of Public Health Services
Health and Human Services Building
6 Hazen Drive
Concord 03301
(603) 271-4592

New Hampshire Board of Registration in Medicine (6)
Health and Welfare Building
6 Hazen Drive
Concord 03301
(603) 271-4502

New Hampshire Board of Nursing Education and Nurse Registration (6)
State Office Park South
101 Pleasant Street
Concord 03301
(603) 271-2323

New Jersey

Division on Aging
Department of Community Affairs
P.O. Box 2768
363 West State Street
Trenton 08625

Home Health Agency Assembly of New Jersey (1)
760 Alexander Road, CN-1

---

1. State home care associations
2. State hospice organizations
3. Medicaid assistance offices
4. Self-help clearinghouses
5. Hospital licensure agencies
6. Medical and nursing licensure agencies

Princeton 08540
(609) 452-9280

New Jersey Hospice Organization (2)
760 Alexander Road
Princeton 08540
(609) 452-9280

Department of Human Services (3)
CN-712 Quakerbridge Plaza
Trenton 08625
(609) 588-2602

Self-Help Clearinghouse of New Jersey (4)
St. Clare's Hospital
Pocono Road
Denville 07834
(800) 452-9790 or (201) 625-6395

Licensing, Certification, and Standards (5)
New Jersey State Department of Health
Division of Health Facilities Evaluation, CN 367
Trenton 08625
(609) 292-5764

State Board of Medical Examiners of New Jersey (6)
28 West State Street
Trenton 08608
(609) 292-4843

New Jersey Board of Nursing (6)
1100 Raymond Boulevard
Newark 07102
(201) 648-2490

New Mexico

Commission on Aging
408 Galisteo-Villagra Building
Santa Fe 87503

Visiting Nurse Services Hospice (2)
P.O. Box 1951
Santa Fe 87501
(505) 471-9201

Department of Human Services (3)
P.O. Box 2348
Santa Fe 87503-2348
(505) 827-4315

Health Services Division, Federal Program Certification Section (5)
Health and Environment Department
1190 St. Francis Drive, Box 968
Santa Fe 87504
(505) 827-2416

New Mexico Board of Medical Examiners (6)
P.O. Box 1388
Santa Fe 87504
(505) 827-9933

State of New Mexico Board of Nursing (6)
4125 Carlisle Northeast
Albuquerque 87107
(505) 841-6524

New York

Office for the Aging
Agency Building
2 Empire State Plaza
Albany 12223

New York City Field Office
Office for the Aging
2 World Trade Center, Room 5036
New York 10047

Home Care Association of New York State (1)
840 James Street
Syracuse 13203
(315) 475-7229

---

1. State home care associations
2. State hospice organizations
3. Medicaid assistance offices
4. Self-help clearinghouses
5. Hospital licensure agencies
6. Medical and nursing licensure agencies

New York State Hospice Association, Inc. (2)
468 Rosedale Avenue
White Plains 10605
(914) 946-7699

Division of Medical Assistance (3)
State Department of Social Services
Ten Eyck Office Building
40 North Pearl Street
Albany 12243
(518) 474-9132

New York City Self-Help Clearinghouse, Inc. (4)
186 Joralemon Street
Brooklyn 11201
(718) 852-4291

Long Island Self-Help Clearinghouse (4)
New York Institute of Technology
6350 Jericho Turnpike
Commack 11725
(516) 499-8800 or 686-7505

Orange County Department of Mental Health (4)
Consultation and Education Department
Harriman Drive, Drawer 471
Goshen 10925
(914) 294-6185

New York City Self-Help Clearinghouse (4)
Graduate School and University Center/CUNY
33 West 42nd Street
New York 10036
(212) 840-7606

Rockland County CMHC (4)
Sanitorium Road
Pomona 10970
(914) 354-0200, ext. 2237

Westchester Self-Help Clearinghouse (4)
Westchester Community College
Academic Arts Building

75 Grasslands Road
Valhalla 10595
(914) 347-3620

Bureau of Project Management (5)
Office of Health Systems Management
Department of Health
Empire State Plaza
Albany 12237
(518) 473-7915

New York State Board for Medicine (6)
Cultural Education Center
Albany 12230
(518) 474-3841

State Board of Nursing (6)
State Education Department
Cultural Education Center, Room 3013
Albany 12230
(518) 474-3843

North Carolina

Department of Human Resources
Albemarle Building
Raleigh 27603

North Carolina Association for Home Care (1)
714 West Johnson Street
Raleigh 27603
(919) 821-3575

Hospice of North Carolina, Inc. (2)
800 St. Mary's Street, Suite 401
Raleigh 27605
(919) 829-9588

---

1. State home care associations
2. State hospice organizations
3. Medicaid assistance offices
4. Self-help clearinghouses
5. Hospital licensure agencies
6. Medical and nursing licensure agencies

Department of Human Resources (3)
1985 Umstead Drive
Raleigh 27603
(919) 733-2060

Division of Facility Services (5)
Department of Human Resources
701 Barbour Drive
Raleigh 27603
(919) 733-2342

North Carolina Board of Medical Examiners (6)
222 North Person Street, Suite 214
Raleigh 27601
(919) 833-5321

North Carolina Board of Nursing (6)
Box 2129
Raleigh 27602
(919) 828-0740

North Dakota

Social Services Board of North Dakota
State Capitol Building
Bismarck 58505

Aging Services
Social Services Board of North Dakota
State Capitol Building
Bismarck 58505

North Dakota Nurse Corps, P.C. (1)
212 North 5th, Greentree Square
Bismarck 58501
(701) 223-1385

St. Joseph's Hospice (2)
7th Avenue West
Dickinson 58601
(701) 225-7200

North Dakota Department of Human Services (3)
State Capitol Building
Bismarck 58505
(701) 224-2321

Health Resources Section (5)
State Department of Health
State Capitol
Bismarck 58505
(701) 224-2352

North Dakota State Board of Medical Examiners (6)
418 East Broadway Avenue, Suite C-10
Bismarck 58501
(701) 223-9485

North Dakota Board of Nursing (6)
Kirkwood Office Tower, Suite 504
Bismarck 58501
(701) 224-2974

Ohio

Commission on Aging
50 West Broad Street
Columbus 43216

Ohio Council of Home Health Agencies (1)
175 South Third Street, Suite 925
Columbus 43215
(614) 461-1960

Ohio Hospice Organization, Inc. (2)
2181 Embury Park Road
Dayton 45414
(513) 278-0060

Medicaid Administration (3)
Department of Human Services
30 East Broad Street, 31st Floor
Columbus 43266-0423
(614) 466-3196

---

1. State home care associations
2. State hospice organizations
3. Medicaid assistance offices
4. Self-help clearinghouses
5. Hospital licensure agencies
6. Medical and nursing licensure agencies

State Medical Board of Ohio (6)
Suite 510, C-10
85 South Front Street
Columbus 43266
(614) 466-3934

State of Ohio Board of Nursing Education and Nurse Registration (6)
65 South Front Street, Room 509
Columbus 43266
(614) 466-3947

Oklahoma

Department of Institutions, Social and Rehabilitative Services
P.O. Box 25352
Oklahoma City 73125

Special Unit on Aging
Department of Institutions, Social and Rehabilitative Services
P.O. Box 25352
Oklahoma City 73125

Oklahoma Hospice Organization (2)
Hospice of Central Oklahoma
4500 North Lincoln
Oklahoma City 73105
(405) 424-7263

Department of Human Services (3)
P.O. Box 25352
Oklahoma City 73125
(405) 557-2540

State Department of Health (5)
1000 Northeast 10th
Oklahoma City 73152
(405) 271-4200

Oklahoma State Board of Medical Examiners (6)
5104 North Francis, Suite C
Oklahoma City 73118
(405) 848-6841

Oklahoma Board of Nurse Registration and Nursing Education (6)
2915 North Classen Boulevard, Suite 624

Oklahoma City 73106
(405) 525-2076

Oregon

Human Resources Department
315 Public Service Building
Salem 97310

Office of Elderly Affairs
Human Resources Department
772 Commercial Street Southeast
Salem 97310

Oregon Association for Home Care (1)
Box 510
Salem 97308
(503) 399-9395

Oregon Council of Hospices (2)
Maryanne Memorial Hospice
P.O. Box 191
Forest Grove 97116
(503) 640-2737

Adult and Family Services Division (3)
Department of Human Resources
203 Public Service Building
Salem 97310
(503) 378-2263

Senior Services Division (3)
Department of Human Resources
313 Public Service Building
Salem 97310
(503) 378-4728

Portland Self-Help Information Service (4)
Regional Research Institute

---

1. State home care associations
2. State hospice organizations
3. Medicaid assistance offices
4. Self-help clearinghouses
5. Hospital licensure agencies
6. Medical and nursing licensure agencies

Portland State University
1912 Southwest 6th
Portland 97207
(503) 222-5555 or 229-4040

Health Facilities Section (5)
Office of Environment and Health Systems
Box 231
Portland 97207
(503) 229-5686

Oregon Board of Medical Examiners (6)
1002 Loyalty Building
317 Southwest Alder Street
Portland 97204
(503) 229-5770

Oregon State Board of Nursing (6)
1400 Southwest 5th, Room 904
Portland 97201
(503) 229-5653

Pennsylvania

Department of Public Welfare
Health and Welfare Building
Harrisburg 17120

Office for the Aging
Department of Public Welfare
Health and Welfare Building, Room 540
P.O. Box 2675
7th and Forster Street
Harrisburg 17120

National Association of Meal Programs (1)
Box 6344
604 West North Avenue
Pittsburgh 15212

Pennsylvania Association of Home Health Agencies (1)
1200 Camp Hill Bypass
P.O. Box 608

Camp Hill 17011
(717) 763-7053

Pennsylvania Hospice Network (2)
South Hills Family Hospice
1000 Bower Hill Road
Pittsburgh 15243
(412) 561-4900

Department of Public Welfare (3)
Room 515
Health and Welfare Building
Harrisburg 17120
(717) 787-1870

Philadelphia Self-Help Clearinghouse (4)
John F. Kennedy, CMHC/MR
112 North Ercad Street, 5th Floor
Philadelphia 19102
(215) 568-0860, ext. 276

Division of Hospitals (5)
Bureau of Quality Assurance
Health and Welfare Building
Harrisburg 17120
(717) 783-8980

Pennsylvania State Board of Medicine (6)
P.O. Box 2649
Harrisburg 17105
(717) 787-2381

State Board of Nursing (6)
Department of State
P.O. Box 2649
Harrisburg 17105
(717) 783-7142

---

1. State home care associations
2. State hospice organizations
3. Medicaid assistance offices
4. Self-help clearinghouses
5. Hospital licensure agencies
6. Medical and nursing licensure agencies

Puerto Rico

Department of Social Services
P.O. Box 11398
Santurce 00910

Gericulture Commission
Department of Social Services
P.O. Box 11398
Santurce 00910

Health Economy Office (3)
Department of Health
P.O. Box 9342
San Juan 00936
(809) 765-9941

Office of Registration and Certification of Professional Health (6)
Call Box 10200
Santurce 00908
(809) 725-7506

Rhode Island

Department of Community Affairs
150 Washington Court
Providence 02903

Division on Aging
Department of Community Affairs
150 Washington Court
Providence 02903

Association of Home Health Agencies of Rhode Island (1)
2845 Post Road
Warwick 02886
(401) 738-8280

Hospice Care of Rhode Island (2)
1400 Pawtucket Avenue
Rumford 02916
(401) 434-4740

Division of Medical Services (3)
Department of Human Services
Aime J. Forand Building

600 New London Avenue
Cranston 02920
(401) 464-3575

Department of Health (5)
75 Davis Street
Providence 02908
(401) 277-2231

Division of Professional Regulation (6)
Rhode Island Department of Health
104 Cannon Building
75 Davis Street
Providence 02908
(401) 277-2827

Samoa

Territorial Administration on Aging
Government of American Samoa
Pago Pago
American Samoa 96799

South Carolina

Commission on Aging
915 Main Street
Columbia 29201

Hospice of Charleston, Inc. (2)
P.O. Box 1125
Charleston 29402
(803) 577-0186

Health and Human Services Finance Commission (3)
P.O. Box 8206
Columbia 29202
(803) 253-6100

---

1. State home care associations
2. State hospice organizations
3. Medicaid assistance offices
4. Self-help clearinghouses
5. Hospital licensure agencies
6. Medical and nursing licensure agencies

Office of Health Licensing (5)
Division of Health Licensing and Certification
South Carolina Department of Health and Environmental Control
2600 Bull Street
Columbia 29201
(803) 734-4680

State Board of Medical Examiners of South Carolina (6)
1315 Blanding Street
Columbia 29201
(803) 734-8901

State Board of Nursing for South Carolina (6)
1777 St. Julian Place, Suite 102
Columbia 29204
(803) 737-6594

South Dakota

Department of Social Services
State Office Building
Illinois Street
Pierre 57501

Office on Aging
Department of Social Services
State Office Building, Illinois Street
Pierre 57501

Department of Social Services (3)
Kneip Building
701 North Illinois Street
Pierre 57501
(605) 773-3495

Licensure and Certification Program (5)
State Department of Health
Joe Foss Building
523 East Capitol
Pierre 57501
(605) 773-3364

South Dakota State Board of Medical and Osteopathic Examiners (5)
1323 Minnesota Avenue

Sioux Falls 57105
(605) 336-1965

Tennessee

Commission on Aging
Room 102 S and P Building
306 Gay Street
Nashville 37201

Tennessee Association for Home Health (1)
4711 Trousdale Drive
Nashville 37220
(615) 331-0463

Tennessee Council for Home Care Services (1)
394 West Main Street
Hendersonville 37075
(615) 822-3094

Hospice of Tennessee (2)
Alive—Hospice of Nashville
1908 21st Avenue South
Nashville 37212
(615) 298-3351

Bureau of Medicaid (3)
Department of Health and Environment
729 Church Street
Nashville 37219
(615) 741-0213

Overlook Mental Health Center (4)
6906 Kingston Pike
Knoxville 36919
(615) 588-9747

Division of Health Care Facilities (5)
Tennessee Department of Health and Environment

---

1. State home care associations
2. State hospice organizations
3. Medicaid assistance offices
4. Self-help clearinghouses
5. Hospital licensure agencies
6. Medical and nursing licensure agencies

283 Plus Park Boulevard
Nashville 37219
(615) 387-6303

Tennessee Board of Medical Examiners (6)
283 Plus Park Boulevard
Nashville 37219
(615) 367-6231

Tennessee Board of Nursing (6)
283 Plus Park Boulevard
Nashville 37219
(615) 367-6232

Texas

Governor's Committee on Aging
Executive Office Building
411 West 13th Street, Floors 4 and 5
Austin 78703

Texas Association of Home Health Agencies (1)
One La Costa Office Building
1016 La Posada Drive, Suite 296
Austin 78752
(512) 459-4303

Texas Hospice Organization, Inc. (2)
2525 Wallingwood #104
Austin 78746
(512) 327-9149

Texas Department of Human Services (3)
P.O. Box 2960, Mail Code 600-W
Austin 78769
(512) 450-3050

Deputy Commissioner for Services to the Aged and Disabled (3)
Department of Human Services
P.O. Box 2960
Austin 78769
(512) 450-3020

Dallas County Self-Help Clearinghouse (4)
Dallas County Mental Health Association
2500 Maple Avenue

Dallas 75206
(214) 748-7825

Tarrant County Self-Help Clearing House (4)
Tarrant County Mental Health Association
904 West 7th Street
Fort Worth 76102
(817) 335-5405

Hospital and Professional Licensure Division (5)
Texas Department of Health
1100 West 49th Street
Austin 78756
(512) 458-7512

Board of Nurse Examiners for the State of Texas (6)
1300 East Anderson Lane
Building C, Suite 225
Austin 78752
(512) 835-4880

Texas Board of Vocational Nurse Examiners (6)
1300 East Anderson Lane
Building C, Suite 285
Austin 78752
(512) 835-2071

Trust Territory of the Pacific

Office of Aging
Community Development Division
Government of the Trust Territory of the Pacific Islands
Saipan, Mariana Islands 96950

Department of Public Health and Environmental Services (3)
Commonwealth of the Northern Mariana Islands
Saipan, CM 96950
(670) 234-8950, ext. 2905

---

1. State home care associations
2. State hospice organizations
3. Medicaid assistance offices
4. Self-help clearinghouses
5. Hospital licensure agencies
6. Medical and nursing licensure agencies

Utah

Department of Social Services
State Capitol Building, Room 221
Salt Lake City 84102

Division of Aging
Department of Social Services
150 West North Temple
Salt Lake City 84102

Utah Hospice Organization, Inc. (2)
1370 South West Temple
Salt Lake City 84115
(801) 627-2504

Division of Health Care Financing (3)
Utah Department of Health
P.O. Box 16580
Salt Lake City 84116-0580
(801) 538-6151

Utah State Department of Health (5)
Bureau of Health Facility Licensure
P.O. Box 16660
Salt Lake City 84116
(801) 538-6152

Division of Occupational and Professional Licensing (6)
P.O. Box 45802
160 East 300 South
Salt Lake City 84145
(801) 530-6628

Vermont

Agency of Human Services
79 River Street
Montpelier 05602

Office on Aging
Agency of Human Services
81 River Street (Heritage 1)
Montpelier 05602

Vermont Assembly of Home Health Agencies (1)
148 Main Street
Montpelier 05602
(802) 229-0579

Vermont Ecumenical Council (2)
Visiting Nurse Association, Inc.
260 College Street
Burlington 15401
(802) 658-1900

Department of Social Welfare (3)
Vermont Agency of Human Services
103 South Main Street
Waterbury 05676
(802) 241-2880

Medical Care Regulation Division (5)
Vermont Department of Health
60 Main Street, P.O. Box 70
Burlington 05402
(802) 863-7272

Vermont State Board of Nursing (6)
26 Terrace Street
Montpelier 05602
(802) 828-2396

Virginia

Office on Aging
830 East Main Street, Suite 950
Richmond 23219

Virginia Association of Hospices (2)
Hospice of North Virginia
4715 North 15th Street

---

1. State home care associations
2. State hospice organizations
3. Medicaid assistance offices
4. Self-help clearinghouses
5. Hospital licensure agencies
6. Medical and nursing licensure agencies

Arlington 22205
(703) 525-7070

Virginia Department of Medical Assistance Services (3)
600 East Broad Street, Suite 1300
Richmond 23219
(804) 786-7933

Division of Licensure and Certification (5)
Virginia Department of Health
109 Governor Street
Richmond 23219
(804) 786-2081

Virginia State Board of Medicine (6)
1601 Rolling Hills Drive
Surry Building, 2nd Floor
Richmond 23229
(804) 662-9908

Virgin Islands

Commission on Aging
P.O. Box 539
Charlotte Amalie Street
Saint Thomas 00801

Bureau of Health Insurance and Medical Assistance (3)
Department of Health
P.O. Box 7309
Government of the Virgin Islands
Charlotte Amalie, St. Thomas 00801
(809) 774-4624 or 773-2150

Virgin Islands Department of Health (6)
Box 7309
St. Thomas 00801
(809) 774-0117

Virgin Islands Board of Nurse Licensure (6)
Knud-Hansen Complex Hospital Ground
St. Thomas 00801
(809) 774-9000 ext. 132

Washington

Department of Social and Health Services
P.O. Box 1788, M.S. 45-2
Olympia 98504

Office on Aging
Department of Social and Health Services
P.O. Box 1788, M.S. 45-2
Olympia 98504

Home Care Association of Washington (1)
P.O. Box 55967
Seattle 98155
(206) 363-3801

Washington Hospice Organization (2)
7814 Greenwood Avenue North
Seattle 98103
(206) 784-9221

Division of Medical Assistance (3)
Department of Social and Health Services
Mail Stop HB-41
Olympia 98504
(206) 753-1777

Health Facilities Survey Section (5)
DSHS Division of Health, ET-31
Olympia 98504
(206) 753-5851

Licensing Division (6)
Box 9649
Olympia 98504
(206) 586-4561

---

1. State home care associations
2. State hospice organizations
3. Medicaid assistance offices
4. Self-help clearinghouses
5. Hospital licensure agencies
6. Medical and nursing licensure agencies

Washington State Board of Nursing (6)
Licensing Division
Box 9649
Olympia 98504
(206) 753-2686

Washington State Board of Practical Nursing (6)
Department of Licensing
Division of Professional Licensing
Box 9649
Olympia 98504
(206) 753-3728

West Virginia

Commission on Aging
State Capitol
Charleston 25305

West Virginia Council of Home Health Agencies (1)
P.O. Box 4227
Star City 26504-4227
(304) 599-9583

Hospice Council of West Virginia (2)
Morgantown Hospice, Inc.
P.O. Box 4222
Morgantown 26505
(304) 598-3424

Bureau Administrator (3)
Bureau of Medical Care
West Virginia Department of Human Services
1900 Washington Street East
Charleston 25305
(304) 348-8990

Health Facilities Licensure and Certification Section (5)
West Virginia Department of Health
1800 Washington Street East
Charleston 25305
(304) 348-0050

West Virginia Board of Medicine
100 Dee Drive, Suite 104

Charleston 25311
(304) 348-2921

West Virginia Board of Examiners for Registered Professional Nurses (6)
Embleton Building
922 Quarrier Street, Suite 309
Charleston 25301
(304) 348-3728

West Virginia Board of Examiners for Licensed Practical Nurses (6)
Embleton Building
922 Quarrier Street, Suite 506
Charleston 25301
(304) 348-3572

Wisconsin

Department of Health and Social Services
State Office Building, Room 700
1 West Wilson Street
Madison 53702

Division on Aging
Department of Health and Social Services
1 West Wilson Street, Room 686
Madison 53702

Wisconsin Homecare Organization (1)
330 East Lakeside Street
Madison 53715
(608) 257-6781

Milwaukee Hospice Home Care (2)
1022 North 9th Street
Milwaukee 53233
(414) 271-3686

Bureau of Health Care Financing (3)
Division of Health

---

1. State home care associations
2. State hospice organizations
3. Medicaid assistance offices
4. Self-help clearinghouses
5. Hospital licensure agencies
6. Medical and nursing licensure agencies

Wisconsin Department of Health and Social Services
One West Wilson Street, Room 244
P.O. Box 309
Madison 53701
(608) 266-2522

Continuing Education in Mental Health (4)
University of Wisconsin Extension
414 Lowell Hall
610 Langden Street
Madison 53706
(608) 263-4432

Mutual Aid Self-Help Association (MASHA) (4)
P.O. Box 09304
Milwaukee 53209
(414) 461-1466

Bureau of Quality Compliance (5)
Division of Health
Department of Health and Social Services
One West Wilson Street, Box 309
Madison 53701
(608) 267-7185

Wisconsin Medical Examining Board (6)
1400 East Washington Avenue
Madison 53702
(608) 266-2811

Bureau of Health Services Professions (6)
Department of Regulation and Licensing
P.O. Box 8935
1400 East Washington Avenue, Room 174
Madison 53708
(608) 266-3735

Wyoming

Department of Health and Social Services
Division of Public Assistance
New State Office Building West, Room 380
Cheyenne 82002

Aging Services
Department of Health and Social Services
Division of Public Assistance and Social Services
New State Office Building West, Room 288
Cheyenne 82002

Sheridan County Hospice, Inc. (2)
2000 Suite 515
Sheridan 82801
(307) 672-3473

Medical Assistance State Program Manager (3)
Department of Health and Social Services
448 Hathaway Building
Cheyenne 82002
(307) 777-7531

Department of Health and Social Services (5)
Division of Health and Medical Facilities
Hathaway Building
Cheyenne 82002
(307) 777-7121

Wyoming Board of Medical Examiners (6)
Hathway Building, 4th Floor
Cheyenne 82002
(307) 777-6463

Wyoming State Board of Nursing (6)
Barrett Building, 4th Floor
2301 Central Avenue
Cheyenne 82002
(307) 777-7601

---

1. State home care associations
2. State hospice organizations
3. Medicaid assistance offices
4. Self-help clearinghouses
5. Hospital licensure agencies
6. Medical and nursing licensure agencies

Appendix 35
National Health Care and Self-Help Groups

THERE are numerous places people can turn to for information on how to get help for the elderly. Many such resources have local offices in towns across the country. The Yellow Pages will list some groups under "Associations" or "Social Service Organizations," or the local public library will have an encyclopedia of associations that lists groups as well. For further information on self-help groups, contact the following.

National

National Self-Help Clearinghouse
33 West 42nd Street
New York, NY 10003
(212) 840-7606

Federal

U.S. Department of Health and Human Services
Administration on Aging
330 Independence Avenue SW
Washington, DC 20201
(202) 245-0724

U.S. Department of Health and Human Services
Health Care Financing Administration
310G Humphrey Building
200 Independence Avenue SW
Washington, DC 20201
(202) 245-6726

U.S. Department of Health and Human Services
Public Health Service
716G Humphrey Building
200 Independence Avenue SW
Washington, DC 20201
(202) 245-7694

U.S. Federal Trade Commission
Correspondence Branch
Pennsylvania Avenue at 6th Street NW
Washington, DC 20580
(202) 523-3567

U.S. Veterans Administration
Department of Medicine and Surgery
810 Vermont Avenue NW
Washington, DC 20420
(202) 389-2596

Professional

Alexander Graham Bell Association for the Deaf
2317 Volta Place
Washington, DC 20007

The Alzheimer's Association
360 North Michigan Avenue
Chicago, IL 60601
(national office; local chapter addresses available on request)

American Affiliation of Visiting Nurse Associations and Services
21 Maryland Plaza, Suite 300
St. Louis, MO 63108
(314) 367-7744

American Association for Continuity of Care
1101 Connecticut Avenue NW, Suite 700
Washington, DC 20024
(202) 857-1194

American Association of Homes for the Aging
1050 17th Street NW
Washington, DC 20036

American Association of Retired Persons
1909 K Street NW
Washington, DC 20049

American Cancer Society
219 East 42nd Street
New York, NY 10021

American Diabetes Association
18 East 48th Street
New York, NY 10017

American Federation of Home Health Agencies
429 N Street SW, Suite S–605
Washington, DC 20024
(202) 554-0526

American Foundation for the Blind
15 West 16th Street
New York, NY 10011

American Geriatrics Society
10 Columbus Circle
New York, NY 10019

American Heart Association
44 East 23rd Street
New York, NY 10010

American Hospital Association
Division of Ambulatory Care
840 North Lake Shore Drive
Chicago, IL 60611
(312) 280-6216

American Lung Association
1740 Broadway
New York, NY 10019

American Nurses Association, Inc.
10 Columbus Circle
New York, NY 10019

American Nursing Home Association
(American Health Care Association)
1025 Connecticut Avenue NW
Washington, DC 20036

American Occupational Therapy Association
251 Park Avenue South
New York, NY 10010

American Parkinson's Disease Association
Room 602, 47 East 50th Street
New York, NY 10022

American Physical Therapy Association
1740 Broadway
New York, NY 10019

American Psychological Association
Division of Adult Development and Aging
1200 17th Street NW
Washington, DC 20036

American Society for Parenteral and Enteral Nutrition
1025 Vermont Avenue NW, Suite 810
Washington, DC 20005
(202) 638-5881

Arthritis Foundation
1212 Avenue of the Americas
New York, NY 10036

Association of Rehabilitation Facilities
5530 Wisconsin Avenue NW
Washington, DC 20015
(information about rehabilitation centers nationwide serving older people)

Cancer Care
One Park Avenue
New York, NY 10016

Council on Accreditation of Services for Families and Children
67 Irving Place
New York, NY 10003
(212) 254-9330

Family Service Association of America
44 East 23rd Street
New York, NY 10010
(212) 674-6100

Gerontological Society
One Dupont Circle NW
Washington, DC 20036

Gray Panthers
3700 Chestnut Street
Philadelphia, PA 19104

Health Insurance Association of America
1850 K Street NW
Washington, DC 20006–2284
(202) 331–1336

Home Health Care Medical Directors Association
P.O. Box 16626
Mobile, AL 36616
(205) 476–0192

Home Health Services and Staffing Association
2101 L Street NW, Suite 800
Washington, DC 20037
(202) 775–4707

Joint Commission on Accreditation of Hospitals
875 North Michigan Avenue
Chicago, IL 60611
(312) 642–6061

National Association for Home Care
519 C Street NE
Washington, DC 20002
(202) 547–7424

National Association for Mental Health
1800 North Kent Street
Arlington, VA 22209

National Association for the Deaf
814 Thayer Avenue
Silver Spring, MD 20910

National Association for the Visually Handicapped
305 East 24th Street
New York, NY 10010

National Association of Hearing and Speech Agencies
814 Thayer Avenue
Silver Spring, MD 20910

National Association of Meal Programs
Box 6344
604 West North Avenue
Pittsburgh, Pa 15212

National Association of Social Workers
1425 H Street NW, Suite 600
Washington, DC 20005

National Citizens' Coalition for Nursing Home Reform
1825 Connecticut Avenue NW, Suite 417
Washington, DC 20009
(202) 797-0657

National Council for Homemakers, Home Health Aide Services
1790 Broadway
New York, NY 10019

National Council of Health Care Services
407 N Street SW
Washington, DC 20024

National Council of Senior Citizens
1511 K Street NW
Washington, DC 20005

National Council on the Aging
600 Maryland Avenue SW
Washington, DC 20024
(information, services, and research on aging; publications on day care and senior centers, retirement housing)

National Federation of Licensed Practical Nurses
250 West 57th Street
New York, NY 10001

National Foundation of Dentistry for the Handicapped
1250 14th Street, Suite 610
Denver, CO 80202
(303) 573-0264

National HomeCaring Council
235 Park Avenue South, 11th Floor
New York, NY 10003
(212) 674-4990

National Hospice Organization
1901 North Fort Myer Drive
Arlington, VA 22209
(703) 243-5900

National Institute of Adult Daycare
600 Maryland Avenue SW, West Wing 100
Washington, DC 20024
(202) 479-1200

National Institute of Neurological and Communicative Disorders and Stroke
Office of Scientific and Health Reports
Building 31, Room 8A-06
National Institutes of Health
Bethesda, MD 20205

National Institute on Aging
Information Office
Building 31, Room 5C-36
National Institutes of Health
Bethesda, MD 20205

National League for Nursing
10 Columbus Circle
New York, NY 10010
(212) 582-1022

National Society for the Prevention of Blindness, Inc.
79 Madison Avenue
New York, NY 10016

Society for the Right to Die
250 West 57th Street
New York, NY 10107

Glossary

ACTIVITIES DIRECTOR. The person in charge of a nursing facility's schedule of activities.

ADMISSION FORMS. Forms to be signed agreeing to enter a hospital and receive the general care provided.

ADULT DAY CARE. Care given during the day to elderly individuals by churches, community centers, and so on; may be part- or full-time.

ADVOCATES. Family members, friends, or professionals employed by hospitals and some state agencies concerned with the patient's condition and willing to ask questions, intercede, or argue on the patient's behalf.

AGENT. The person appointed in a power of attorney to make decisions and handle the affairs of a principal.

AID TO FAMILIES WITH DEPENDENT CHILDREN (AFDC). A social welfare program that gives financial assistance to needy families with children.

ALLOWABLE RESOURCES. The amount of money a state allows individuals to keep and still be eligible for Medicaid (the amount varies from state to state).

ANESTHESIOLOGIST. A doctor trained to give anesthesia.

ATTENDING DOCTOR. The doctor who has primary responsibility for a patient; he or she may also supervise interns and residents working with the patient.

AUTOMATIC BANKING. A service provided by some banks to pay regular bills, such as mortgages or utilities, for persons who can no longer do so themselves.

BENEFICIARY OR RECIPIENT. The person paid money by any entitlement program.

BENEFITS. Money paid to reimburse patients and pay doctors, hospitals, and other health care providers.

BEQUEST. A gift bequeathed after death, in accordance with the will of the deceased person.

BEST-INTERESTS STANDARD. A standard used by a guardian to make decisions based on the best interests of an incompetent or ill individual.

BOARD AND CARE HOMES. A home providing "residential care," "domiciliary care," or "assisted living care." Such a home does not provide medical care, but it does house chronically ill or frail elderly people who require supervision and assistance with things like bathing, grooming, and eating.

BOARD CERTIFICATION IN SURGERY. Certification granted by the American College of Surgeons giving formal recognition that a doctor is capable of performing surgery.

CARDIAC CARE. Care for patients with heart conditions.

CARDIOPULMONARY RESUSCITATION (CPR). A procedure reviving a patient after a heart attack.

CASE MANAGER. The individual whose job it is to manage, plan for, and arrange continuing health care services for ill individuals.

CATEGORICALLY NEEDY. A classification of individuals who qualify for Medicaid based on income and financial resource levels.

CHARGE NURSES, NURSING SUPERVISORS, AND NURSING ADMINISTRATORS. Those who supervise nursing staff.

CLAIM. A bill for medical care or services that a beneficiary wants reimbursed under a entitlement program or an insurance policy.

COINSURANCE. The amount or percentage that patients are required to pay toward Medicare-reimbursed bills.

COMATOSE. Unconscious for a long period; possibly a permanent condition.

COMMUNITY ADVISORY COMMITTEE. A committee, usually made up of concerned and knowledgeable citizens, that works to improve nursing home conditions and hear grievances from patients and their families.

COMPETENCE OR CAPACITY. An individual's ability to think clearly, make rational decisions, and appreciate their consequences.

CONSENT TO TREATMENT FORMS. Forms to be signed consenting to specific surgical or medical treatments.

CONSERVATOR. A person appointed by the court to handle the financial affairs of individuals incapable of doing so for themselves. Also known as the *conservator* (or *guardian*) *of the estate.*

CONTINGENCY FEE. A fee charged by a lawyer only if the case is won; usually the amount is a predetermined percentage of the settlement.

COPAYMENT. Money still owed on a medical bill after Medicare has paid its approved amount.

CUSTODIAL CARE. Nonmedical care for elderly individuals; may include grooming, bathing, and so on.

DEDUCTIBLE. The amount of money an individual pays for medical bills before his or her insurance company begins to pay.

DE FACTO DECISION MAKER. An individual who makes decisions for an incompetent person without any legal authority to do so; also called a *de facto surrogate.*

DE FACTO INCOMPETENT. A description of an individual who is considered incompetent by doctors and family members but who has not been found incompetent by a court.

Glossary

DIAGNOSTIC RELATED GROUPS (DRGs). Groups of Medicare-categorized diseases, each group assigned a specific amount of money to cover the hospital care of patients whose diseases fall into that group.

DIRECT-DEPOSIT BANKING. An arrangement whereby paychecks and Social Security or pension payments are sent directly to a bank.

DISCHARGE PLANNERS OR SOCIAL WORKERS. Persons employed by a hospital to place patients in nursing homes, if necessary, or to arrange for other special services required after patients are discharged from the hospital.

DOCTOR'S PRIVILEGES. A phrase referring to those hospitals in which a doctor is allowed to admit, see, and care for patients.

DONEE. The person who receives gifts or bequests in a will.

DONOR. The person who makes gifts or bequests in a will.

DREAD DISEASE POLICIES. Insurance policies covering only one disease.

DURABLE POWER OF ATTORNEY. A legal document designed to let a principal appoint an agent to make decisions for him or her in the event the principal becomes incompetent.

DURABLE POWER OF ATTORNEY FOR HEALTH CARE. A legal document designed to let a principal appoint an agent to make health care decisions for him or her in the event the principal becomes incompetent.

EARNINGS RECORD. A statement submitted annually by an institutional payee to the Social Security Administration to show how a patient's Social Security benefits are being spent.

EMPLOYEE GROUP HEALTH INSURANCE. A group insurance policy purchased at an individual's place of work that may continue to cover him or her after retirement but that may change in character when the individual reaches age sixty-five.

ENTITLEMENT PROGRAM. Any program that provides financial or other types of assistance to people meeting specific criteria.

EXECUTOR OR EXECUTRIX. The male or female named in a will or otherwise appointed to see that the wishes in a will are carried out.

FAMILY CONSENT STATUTES. Laws in some states that automatically authorize family members to make certain necessary decisions for incompetent individuals; in these states, court appointment of a guardian may be unnecessary.

FAMILY SERVICE AGENCIES. Social service agencies that help families or individuals arrange for and receive care.

FELLOWS. Doctors in the process of being trained in a particular specialty.

FULL GUARDIANSHIP OR PLENARY GUARDIANSHIP. Guardianship arrangements whereby the guardian has the right to make almost all decisions over a ward.

GENERAL PUBLIC ASSISTANCE (GPA). A social welfare program, funded by only some states or communities, that gives financial help to the very needy.

GENERIC SUBSTITUTES. Pharmaceuticals containing the same ingredients as more expensive name brands.

GERIATRIC MENTAL STATE EXAMINATION. An evaluation of a patient's state of mind and/or competency.

GRAY PANTHERS. An activist group of elderly individuals who fight for elder rights.

GUARDIAN. The person appointed by a court to handle the personal (and sometimes financial) affairs of individuals incapable of doing so for themselves. Also known as the *guardian* (or *conservator*) *of the person*.

GUARDIAN *ad litem*. The court-appointed individual authorized to represent a ward in specific matters being heard before the court; this is not to be confused with a lawyer's representation of a client.

GUARDIANSHIP HEARING. A proceeding in which a judge rules on the competency of an individual and may assign him or her a guardian and/or conservator.

HEALTH CARE PROVIDER. Any person or organization providing health care (including doctors, hospitals, home care services, "meals on wheels," and so on).

HEALTH MAINTENANCE ORGANIZATION (HMO). An organization offering a prepaid health insurance plan that provides all acute medical services the policyholder may need.

HEARING. A legal proceeding before a judge.

HOSPICE. A special facility that cares for dying patients or assists them to be cared for in their homes.

HOSPITAL DISCHARGE PLANNER. The hospital employee, usually a social worker or a nurse, who plans for the discharge of patients, notifies patients or family members of the discharge, and prepares a formal discharge plan on request.

IATROGENIC DISEASES OR DISORDERS. Conditions, such as viruses, resulting from medical personnel, treatment, diagnostic procedures, and so on.

INCOMPETENCE OR INCAPACITY. An individual's inability to think clearly, or make rational decisions, and appreciate their consequences.

INDEMNITY. Insurance benefits that pay on specific dollar amounts or a percentage of the costs of care.

INFORMED CONSENT. The state whereby a patient has the necessary information and understanding to agree to or refuse treatment. A patient usually has to sign a form to this effect before treatment is started.

INSTITUTIONAL ETHICS COMMITTEE. A hospital or nursing home committee made up of health care professionals, religious representatives, philosophers, and ethicists; such a committee may be helpful in resolving disputes between family members over treatment decisions.

INSURANCE COVERAGE FORMS. Forms that give a hospital permission to share information on a patient with his or her insurance company.

INTERMEDIATE CARE FACILITY (ICF). A facility providing general and limited medical care for patients who will eventually be able to return home or for those who can no longer care for themselves without supervision.

INTERN. A medical school graduate with one or two years of experience.

INTER VIVOS TRUST. A trust that goes into effect while the grantor is still alive.

INTESTACY LAWS. State laws determining the disposition of assets left by individuals who did not make a will.

INTESTATE. Describes an individual who has died without leaving a will (he or she is said to have died *intestate*).

INVOLUNTARY COMMITMENT. The holding of a person in a hospital or other facility against his or her will for seventy-two hours for psychiatric reasons.

IRREVOCABLE LIVING TRUST. An *inter vivos* trust that cannot be revoked or canceled.

JOINT BANK ACCOUNT. A type of bank account that allows either owner to transact business and sign checks (joint accounts are not available at all banks).

JOINT BANK ACCOUNT WITH RIGHT OF SURVIVORSHIP. A type of joint bank account that guarantees that one owner will receive funds in the event the other owner dies.

JOINT PROPERTY ARRANGEMENTS. Arrangements that permit joint ownership of a house or other assets.

LAETRILE. A controversial anticancer drug, not approved in some states.

LEGAL AID LAWYER. A lawyer who works in a clinic offering low-cost legal services to those in need.

LEGALLY INCOMPETENT. The declaration a court makes about people who are incapable of understanding the consequences of their decisions and who, as a result of this inability, are incapable of handling their affairs.

LICENSED PRACTICAL NURSE (LPN). A nurse who monitors and observes hospital patients and gives care, medication, and treatment on doctors' orders.

LICENSED VOCATIONAL NURSE (LVN). A nurse who monitors and observes hospital patients and gives care, medication, and treatment on doctors' orders.

LIMITED OR PARTIAL GUARDIANSHIP. A guardianship arrangement in which the powers of a guardian are expressly limited by the court and the ward retains some rights.

LIVING WILL. A document that allows individuals to state their medical treatment preferences in advance of their becoming incompetent and unable to speak for themselves.

LONG-TERM CARE. Ongoing care provided by a nursing home or by other residential facilities.

LONG-TERM CARE INSURANCE POLICIES. Health insurance policies to cover the cost of long-term or nursing home care.

LONG TERM CARE OMBUDSMAN PROGRAM (LTCOP). A program, established by the federal Older Americans Act, that helps resolve complaints and protects and defends those elderly whose rights are abused; usually used by the residents of nursing homes. By law, each state is required to have an ombudsman program.

Loss ratio. The minimum level of benefits an insurance company expects to pay out in comparison with money gathered through premiums.

Medically needy. A classification of persons eligible for optional state medically needy Medicaid programs because their medical bills offset their income.

Medicaid. A public assistance program that in certain low-income cases pays for nursing home care.

Medicare. A government insurance program that covers only the costs of medical services (that is, hospital care and doctors' services) for patients over age sixty-five who are suffering from acute illnesses.

"Medigap" or Medicare supplemental insurance policies. Policies sold by private companies to cover the cost of services not covered by Medicare.

Non-routine-treatment decisions. Medical care decisions involving definite changes in treatment for which consent of a guardian or a family member is necessary.

Nosocomial infections. Infections that develop as a result of a patient's hospital stay and are caused by bacteria or viruses.

Nurse anesthetist. A nurse trained in advanced courses to give anesthesia.

Nursing administrators, nursing supervisors, and charge nurses. Individuals who supervise nursing staff.

Nursing assistants, orderlies, and aides. Persons who assist nurses in providing for patients' nonmedical needs.

Nursing home. A health care facility providing residential or long-term care. There are two types: Skilled Nursing Facilities (SNF) and Intermediate Care Facilities (ICF).

Office of the Inspector General. Part of the U.S. Department of Health and Human Services (HHS), an office that reviews cases of misuse of Social Security benefits, among other things.

Ombudsman. The individual working in the state-level office of the Long Term Care Ombudsman Program to investigate and resolve complaints made by or on behalf of older residents of long-term care facilities.

On-site review program. A program in which the Social Security Administration audits state institutions that receive Social Security benefits on behalf of their occupants.

Patient representative or advocate. The individual employed by a hospital or other group to act on behalf of a patient when no family member or friend is available.

Payee or Representative payee. The individual or institution appointed to receive Social Security checks on behalf of an elderly person incapable of handling his or her own finances.

Peer Review Organization (PRO). A group of doctors and nurses who review a patient's case and help determine the patient's length of stay in the hospital.

PETITION. A request that a court begin a hearing or proceeding.

PETITIONER. The individual who files a petition requesting a hearing by a court.

POWER OF ATTORNEY. A written agreement between a principal and an agent, in which the principal authorizes the agent to sign documents and conduct business for him or her. The agreement is valid only if the principal is competent.

PRINCIPAL. The person who appoints someone else to take care of his or her affairs and to make decisions in his or her behalf.

PRIVATE-DUTY NURSING SERVICES. Services in which nurses are hired by a patient to give additional care.

PROBATE COURT. Usually a county or local court that, among other things, handles guardianship petitions.

PROGNOSIS. The probable course of a disease.

PUBLIC GUARDIANSHIP PROGRAM. A state, county, or private organization that acts as a guardian for those incompetent individuals who have no family or friends able to fill that role.

QUALITY SCREEN. A series of questions about a patient's condition that can help determine a patient's physical readiness to leave the hospital. Quality screens are tools that can help identify possible cases of premature hospital discharge.

REGISTERED NURSE (RN). A nurse who coordinates the nursing care of hospital patients.

REPRESENTATIVE PAYEE EVALUATION REPORT. A detailed report requested by the Social Security Administration to help determine whether a payee is handling a beneficiary's checks correctly.

REPRESENTATIVE PAYEE OR PAYEE. An individual or institution appointed to receive Social Security checks on behalf of an elderly person incapable of handling his or her own finances.

REPRESENTATIVE PAYEE REPORT. A short accounting statement completed by a payee or representative payee about once a year, detailing how benefits were spent on behalf of a beneficiary.

RESIDENTS' COUNCIL. A committee usually made up of nursing home facility residents to examine and help resolve residents' problems.

RESPITE CARE. Part-time care offered for elderly individuals or victims of Alzheimer's disease who are living at home; it gives a break, or respite, to family caretakers.

RESPONDENT. The term used for a person during the court process that determines the need for his or her guardianship.

ROUTINE TREATMENT DECISIONS. Relatively minor medical care decisions involving a change of diet or medication, physical exercise, and so on.

SKILLED NURSING FACILITY (SNF). A facility that provides specialized medical care for seriously ill or disabled patients who do not need to be hospitalized.

SOCIAL SECURITY INCOME. A federal supplemental monthly income based on a person's work performance before retirement at age sixty-two.

SOCIAL SECURITY DISABILITY INCOME (SSDI). A government-funded social insurance program that provides assistance to people who, because of their physical or mental disability, are no longer capable of working.

SPECIALISTS OR CONSULTANTS. Doctors who have been trained in a particular specialty.

SPEND DOWN. The process of contrasting individual income and resources against personal medical expenses to qualify for Medicaid.

SPRINGING DURABLE POWER OF ATTORNEY. A type of durable power of attorney that takes effect only if the principal becomes incompetent.

STATUTORY SHORT FORM POWER OF ATTORNEY. A form used by some states to execute a power of attorney.

SUBSTATE OMBUDSMAN PROGRAM. The local office of the state ombudsman, active in investigating and solving the complaints of long-term care facility residents or their spokespersons.

SUPPLEMENTAL MEDICAL INSURANCE (SMI). Insurance provided under Part B of Medicare, requiring a monthly premium to be paid by the consumer for doctor's visits, medical supplies, and equipment.

SUPPLEMENTAL SECURITY INCOME (SSI). A government-funded social welfare program that provides financial aid to poor people over age sixty-five, the blind, and the permanently disabled.

SURROGATE DECISION MAKER. Someone who makes decisions on behalf of people who are unable to do so themselves.

TERMINAL ILLNESS. An illness that cannot be cured and leads to death.

TESTAMENTARY TRUST. A trust that is created within a will and takes effect upon the grantor's death.

THERAPEUTIC PRIVILEGE. A doctor's right to keep the particulars of a patient's record from him or her in the event that the doctor believes such information will harm the patient.

TRUST. An arrangement whereby property is transferred by one person (*grantor* or *settlor*) to benefit himself or herself or someone else. A trust is managed by a *trustee*.

TRUSTEE. The person who manages a trust.

VETERANS' BENEFITS. Benefits available to eligible veterans of foreign wars.

WARD. An individual who is incapable of handling his or her personal and financial affairs and for whom a court has appointed a guardian or conservator.

WILL. A document written by an individual to specify the disposition of his or her money and property after death.

WILL IN PROBATE. The period during which instructions in a will are carried out and bequests are administered.

Additional Reading

1. Wills, Trusts, and Joint Accounts: Using Them Now

There are excellent books and computer software that provide more information on the writing of wills, the establishment of joint tenancies and trusts, and the giving of assets.

Books

Theodore Hughes and David Klein, *A Family Guide to Estate Planning, Funeral Arrangements, and Settling an Estate after Death,* Scribner, New York, 1983.

Alex Soled, *The Essential Guide to Wills, Estates, Trusts, and Death Taxes,* American Association of Retired Persons Books, Chicago, 1988. To order, write AARP Books, Department L078, Scott, Foresman and Company, 1865 Miner Street, Des Plaines, Illinois 60016, or call 1-800-238-2300 to order by credit card.

Software

Willmaker, Nolo Legisoft, Nolo Press, Berkeley, California, 1985.

2. "Medigap" Long-Term Care Insurance Policies

For more information on purchasing Medigap or Medicare supplemental insurance, the following publications might be of interest:

National Association of Insurance Commissioners and Health Care Financing Administration, *Guide to Health Insurance for People with Medicare.* This is available in English and Spanish from state Social Security offices.

Consumer Reports, "Medicare Supplement Insurance," June 1984, p. 347. This includes a policy comparison worksheet and ratings of many policies; it should be available through a public library.

Health Insurance Association of America (HIAA), *How to Use Private Health Insurance with Medicare.* This free book, publication #702, is available from HIAA, 1025 Connecticut Avenue NW, Suite 1200, Washington, D.C. 20036, telephone 1-202-223-7780.

Your Medicare Handbook, U.S. government. This is published annually by the federal government to explain Medicare coverage. It is available from local Social Security offices.

Also see appendix 1 for a reprint of *Medicare,* a pamphlet published by the Social Security Administration.

For more information on purchasing long-term care insurance, the following publications might be of interest:

"Who Can Afford a Nursing Home?" *Consumer Reports,* May 1988, p. 300. This publication should be available through a public library or can be purchased by sending $3.00 for publication #RO77, *Who Can Afford a Nursing Home,* to Reprints, *Consumer Reports,* P.O. Box 53016, Boulder, Colorado 80322. This is highly recommended, as it is an excellent article and includes a checklist for evaluating long-term care policies.

Schaeffer, C., "Insurance for Long Term Care," *Changing Times,* January 1987, pp. 113–118. This publication should be available through a public library.

Health Insurance Association of America (HIAA), *The Consumer's Guide to Long Term Care Insurance.* This free book, publication #1262, is available from HIAA, 1025 Connecticut Avenue NW, Suite 1200, Washington, D.C. 20036, telephone 1-202-223-7780.

Health Insurance Association of America (HIAA), *How to Use Private Insurance with Medicare.* This free book, publication #702, is available from HIAA at the address and phone number listed above.

American Association of Retired Persons (AARP), *Before You Buy: A Guide to Long Term Care Insurance.* This book, stock #D12893, is available free from AARP, Fulfillment Section, 1909 K Street NW, Washington, D.C. 20049. AARP has several publications on long-term care services; for more information, write them at the address listed.

Nancy Chasen, *Policy Wise: The Practical Guide to Insurance Decisions for Older Customers,* American Association for Retired Persons, Chicago, 1988. To order, write AARP Books, Department L078, Scott, Foresman and Company, 1865 Miner Street, Des Plaines, Illinois 60016, or call 1-800-238-2300 to order by credit card.

4. Is a Living Will a Good Idea for You?

Publications

American Association of Retired Persons (AARP), *A Matter of Choice: Planning Ahead for Health Care Decisions.* This very useful publication is available through the AARP by calling (202) 872-4700 or writing American Association of Retired Persons, Special Projects Section, Program Department, 1909 K Street NW, Washington, D.C. 20049.

Taking Charge of the End of Your Life: Proceedings of a Forum on Living Wills and Other Advance Directives, Older Women's League, Washington, D.C., 1985. This publication can be ordered by sending $4.50 to Older Women's League, 1325 G Street NW, Lower Level, Washington, D.C. 20005.

Videos

American Bar Association, Commission on Legal Problems of the Elderly, *In Your Hands: The Tools for Preserving Personal Autonomy,* Modern Talking Picture Service. This 16-minute video, narrated by Helen Hayes, comes with a 31-page program guide and fifty copies of a 12-page viewer's pamphlet. It can be rented for $18 or purchased for $48 from Modern Talking Picture Service, Inc., 5000 Park Street North, St. Petersburg, Florida 33709.

American Bar Association, Commission on Legal Problems of the Elderly, *You're in Control: Older Americans and the Law,* Modern Talking Picture Service. This 19-minute video can be rented for $20 from Modern Talking Picture Service, Inc., 5000 Park Street North, St. Petersburg, Florida 33709.

5. Powers of Attorney and Other Ways to Plan Ahead

Publications

Collin, F., et al., *Drafting the Durable Power of Attorney: A Systems Approach,* RPW Publishing Corporation, Lexington, South Carolina, 1984. Lawyers and local university law libraries should have this book, which is very useful in explaining various kinds of durable power-of-attorney documents.

American Association of Retired Persons (AARP), *A Matter of Choice: Planning Ahead for Health Care Decisions.* This very useful publication is available through the AARP by calling (202) 872-4700 or writing American Association of Retired Persons, Special Projects Section, Program Department, 1909 K Street NW, Washington, D.C. 20049.

Taking Charge of the End of Your Life: Proceedings of a Forum on Living Wills and Other Advance Directives, Older Women's League, Washington, D.C., 1985. This publication can be ordered by sending $4.50 to Older Women's League, 1325 G Street NW, Lower Level, Washington, D.C. 20005.

Videos

American Bar Association, Commission on Legal Problems of the Elderly, *In Your Hands: The Tools for Preserving Personal Autonomy,* Modern Talking Picture Service. This 16½-minute video, narrated by Helen Hayes, comes with a 31-page program guide and fifty copies of a 12-page viewer's pamphlet. It can be rented for $18 or purchased for $48 from Modern Talking Picture Service, Inc., 5000 Park Street North, St. Petersburg, Florida 33709.

American Bar Association, Commission on Legal Problems of the Elderly, *You're in Control: Older Americans and the Law,* Modern Talking Picture Service. This 19-minute video can be rented for $20 from Modern Talking Picture Service, Inc., 5000 Park Street North, St. Petersburg, Florida 33709.

6. Saying Yes to Medical Care: What You Should Know First

American Medical Association's Family Medical Guide, Reader's Digest Association, New York, 1982 (or current edition).

Belsky, M., and Gross, L., *How to Choose and Use Your Doctor,* Arbor House, New York, 1975.

Berman, H., et al., *The Complete Health Care Advisor,* St. Martins/Marek, New York, 1986.

Inlander, C., and Weiner, E., *Take This Book to the Hospital with You: A Consumer Guide to Surviving Your Hospital Stay,* Warner Books, New York, 1987.

Williams, S., *A Consumer's Guide to Health Care Services,* Prentice Hall, New Jersey, 1985.

7. Patients Have Rights, Too

Annas, G., *The Rights of Hospital Patients: The Basic ACLU Guide to a Hospital Patient's Rights,* Avon Books, New York, 1975.

Belsky, M., and Gross, L., *How to Choose and Use Your Doctor,* Arbor House, New York, 1975.

Huttman, B., R.N., *The Patient's Advocate: The Complete Handbook of Patient's Rights,* Viking Press, Penguin, New York, 1981.

Inlander, C., and Weiner, E., *Take This Book to the Hospital with You: A Consumer Guide to Surviving Your Hospital Stay,* Warner Books, New York, 1987.

Maurer, J., M.D., *How to Talk to Your Doctor: Getting Beyond the Medical Mystique,* Simon and Schuster, New York, 1986.

Pinckney, C., and Pinckney, E., *The Patient's Guide to Medical Tests,* 3rd ed., Facts on File Publications, New York, 1986.

Robertson, J., *The Rights of the Critically Ill,* Bantam Books, New York, 1983.

Eugene, Robin, *Medical Care Can Be Dangerous to Your Health,* Harper and Row, New York, 1986.

10. The Medicare/Medicaid Maze

More information on entitlement programs can be found in chapters 2 and 3 and appendix 1 of this book. Other publications that make worthwhile reading are the following:

Office of Technology Assessment, *Losing a Million Minds: Confronting the Tragedy of Alzheimer's Disease and Other Dementias,* Government Printing Office, Washington, D.C., 1987.

Miriam K. Aronson, *Understanding Alzheimer's Disease: What It Is, How to Cope with It, Future Directions,* Alzheimer Disease and Related Disorders Association, Chicago, 1988.

11. Competence and Incompetence: What They Mean

*Annas, G., and Densberger, J., *Competence to Refuse Medical Treatment: Autonomy vs. Paternalism,* Toledo Law Review, vol. 15, 1984.

Brown, R., *Legal Rights of Older Persons,* Avon Press, New York, 1979 (or current edition).

*Kapp, M., *Preventing Malpractice in Long Term Care: Strategies for Risk Management,* Springer, New York, 1987.

14. Limits on Decisions Made for Someone Else

A Matter of Choice: Planning Ahead for Health Care Decisions, American Association of Retired Persons. To purchase a copy, write to AARP, Special Projects Section, Program Department, 1909 K Street NW, Washington, D.C. 20049.

Office of Technology Assessment, *Losing a Million Minds: Confronting the Tragedy of Alzheimer's Disease and Other Dementias,* U.S. Congress, Government Printing Office, Washington, D.C., 1986.

---

*These books may not be of great use to those other than lawyers, health care professionals, or ethicists.

Index

Abuse: in nursing homes, 117; right to be free of, 92–93
Accidents, in hospitals, 79–81
Accounting procedures, for representative payees, 175–176
Administrative law judge (ALJ), Medicare and, 142
Administrator, 4
Adult day care, insurance coverage for, 26
Advocacy, 191–196; community advocacy programs and, 124, 133; influencing a particular problem and, 193–195; media and, 195; political action and, 192–193
Agent(s), 8–9, 181; abuse of power by, 60; power of attorney and, 52, 53, 56–59; substituted judgment and, 187; tasks performed by, 57–59
AHA. *See* American Hospital Association
Air force, living wills and, 49
Alcoholism/chemical dependency inpatient unit, 255
Alcoholism/chemical dependency outpatient services, 255
Aliens, Medicare and, 201–202
ALJ. *See* Administrative law judge
Allowable resources, Medicaid and, 38–39
Alzheimer's disease: competence and, 148; long-term care insurance and, 28, 30
Ambulatory surgery services, 251
American Association of Retired Persons, 105
American College of Surgeons, 74
American Hospital Association (AHA), 105–106; patient's bill of rights of, 83, 257–258
American Medical Association, statement on withholding or withdrawing life-prolonging treatment, 335
Anesthetization, 74

Appeal: of denial for entitlement programs, 138–139, 142, 143; of discharge notice, 107–109
Appeals Council, 140
Application: for Medicaid, 39–40; for nursing home, 41; for representative payee, 313–318
Area agency on aging, 124
Army, living wills and, 49
Artificial feeding and hydration: living wills and, 50; removal of, 50, 185
Assets, sale of, Medicaid and, 40
Assignment, Medicare and, 36
Assisted-living care, 113
Attorney(s): to draw up power of attorney, 52, 54; nursing home care complaints and, 124, 132; power of, 8–9; sources of, 5–6, 36–37, 54, 139, 188
Attorney general, nursing home care complaints and, 132
Attorneys-in-fact, 8–9, 181
Automatic banking services, 11

Banking: automatic, 11; direct-deposit, 10–11; joint accounts and, 11–14; power of attorney and, 60
Bar association, 139
Beneficiary(ies), 6, 137; representative payees and, 171; of trust, 14
Benefits, 137. *See also specific types of insurance*
Bequests, 5
Best-interests standard, 187
Bill of rights. *See* Patient rights
Bill-paying service, 11
Billing problems, in nursing homes, 117
Birthing room, 254
Blood bank, 252
Board and care homes, 113; Medicaid and, 37; regulation of, 130
Burn care unit, 253

Capacity, 159
Cardiac catherization laboratory, 256
Cardiac intensive care unit, 251
Case manager, 137
Catastrophic Coverage Act, 23, 141
Categorically needy, Medicaid and, 38, 142
Certification organizations, nursing home care complaints and, 124
CHAMPUS, 206
CHAMPVA, 206
Children, wills and, 6
Citizen advocacy programs, nursing home care complaints and, 124
Claim, 137
Clinical laboratories, regulation of, 130
Clinical psychology services, 254
Coinsurance: Medicare and, 35–36, 141; medigap insurance and, 21
Commitment, involuntary, 93
Committee, 158
Community advisory committees, nursing home complaints and, 121
Community advocacy programs, nursing home care complaints and, 124, 133
Community health promotion, 252
Competence, 8–9, 147–156, 159; concept of, 150–151; de facto incompetence and surrogates and, 152–153; decisions needing to be made and, 148–150; determining, 51–52, 60, 153–156; geriatric mental status examination and, 155–156; levels of, 151–152; to make specific decisions, 152; policies for evaluating, 154–155; power of attorney and, 53–54; representative payees and, 171–178. *See also* Conservator(s); Conservatorship; Guardian(s); Guardianship; Incompetence
Comprehensive geriatric assessment services, 256
Consent, informed, 87, 162
Conservator(s), 8–9, 181; duties and responsibilities of, 165–166; payment of, 168–169; sample petition for appointment of, 307–309
Conservatorship, 157–159; advantages and disadvantages of, 165; need for, 165; process of petitioning for, 169
Conservatorship order, sample, 311–312
Consumer protection agencies, nursing home care complaints and, 125, 133
Contagious diseases, patient rights and, 96

Contraceptive care, 254
Cost: of guardianship proceeding, 169; of nursing home care, 26, 34; of trusts, 16
Court: competence and, 51; ignored or challenged decisions and, 188; nursing home care complaints and, 125, 132; order of appointment of, 163–164; probate, 5, 159
CT scanner, 256
Curator, 158

Day hospital, 255
De facto surrogates, 153, 181–182
Decision(s): challenged or ignored, 187–188; competence and, 148–150; specific, competence to make, 152; treatment, 183–184
Decision makers: surrogate, 153, 181–182. *See also* Conservators; Guardians; Power of attorney
Decision making: for another, limits on, 179–188; standards for, 187
Decision-making powers, transfer of, 52
Deductibles: under Medicare, 204; medigap insurance and, 21
Dementia, 148
Diagnosis, patient's right to information about, 88
Diagnostic radioisotope facility, 252
Diagnostic Related Groups (DRGs), 78–79, 100–103; impact on hospitals, 101–102; impact on patients, 102–103
Direct-deposit banking, 10–11
Disability: discrimination on basis of, by nursing homes, 117–118; Medicare and, 201
Discharge notice, 106; appealing to Peer Review Organization, 108–109; deciding whether to appeal, 108; losing appeal of, 109; models of, 277–283; responding to, 107
Discharge planning, 102, 104; admission and, 105–106; discharge notice and, 106–110; guidelines for, 267–269
Discrimination: on basis of disability, in nursing homes, 117–118; financial, in nursing homes, 117; racial, in nursing homes, 118
Disease, patient's right to information about, 89
District attorneys, nursing home care complaints and, 131–132
Doctor(s): admitting privileges of, 68; definition of terminally ill and, 45–46; fear of suits by family members, 48–49; finding, 66; giving

power-of-attorney agreement to, 62; hospitalized patients and, 78; informing about living will, 47; Medicare coverage for, 204–205; patients' rights when meeting with, 68–69; referral by, 95; refusal to treat, 95; rights of, 84, 95; selecting, 65–66, 73–74; switching, 69; therapeutic privilege of, 91; what to look for in, 67–69

Doctor-patient relationship: doctor's responsibilities in, 86–87; ending, 95; getting most out of, 70–72; patient's responsibilities in, 85–86; patient's rights in, 68–69, 84–85

Domiciliary care, 113; Medicaid and, 37; veterans and, 42

Dread disease policies, 22

DRGs, *See* Diagnostic Related Groups

Drugs: in nursing homes, 116; prescribed, 72

Durable power of attorney, 48, 54–60, 104, 187; for health care, sample forms for, 235–243; immediate, 54; requirements for creating, 225–226; springing, 8–9, 53–54, 345–349

Duration of services, long-term care insurance and, 29

Dying: process of, 8–9. *See also* Terminally ill patients

Education, in nursing homes, 117

Educational activities, of hospital, 252

Elected officials: approaching, 192–194; nursing home care complaints and, 126, 133

Emergencies: skills for dealing with, 72; what to do in case of, 71

Emergency guardianship, 160

Emergency room, 72–73, 254

Employee group health insurance: Medicare and, 206–207; medigap insurance and, 20

Enrollment period, for Medicare, 202–203

Entitlement programs, 137; denial of eligibility for, 138–139, eligibility for, 138. *See also* Medicaid; Medicare; Social Security Disability Income; Supplemental Security Income

Estate accounting, for wards, state requirements for, 303–304

ESWL. *See* Extracorporeal shock wave lithotripter

Ethics, patient rights and, 96

Exclusions, long-term care insurance and, 28

Executor, 4

Executrix, 4

Extracorporeal shock wave lithotripter (ESWL), 255

Extraordinary care, 44

Fair hearing, Medicaid and, 143

Family(ies): discharge planning and, 103; doctors' fears of suits by, 48–49

Family consent statutes, 182–183; provisions of, 333–334; states with, 331

Family councils, nursing home complaints and, 120–121

Family planning services, 254–255

Federal bill of patient rights, 83, 261–262

Federal health care facilities, living wills and, 49–50

Feeding and hydration: living wills and, 50; removal of, 50, 185

Fertility services, 254

Financial decisions: competence and, 148–149; surrogates and, 186

Financial problems, with nursing homes, 116–117

Financing sources, nursing home care complaints and, 125

First-aid skills, 72

Food: problems with, in nursing homes, 117; removal of, 50, 185

Food stamp program, 137

Fund mismanagement, in nursing homes, 117

General power of attorney, sample form for, 229–233

General Public Assistance (GPA), 137

Genetic counseling service, 255

Geriatric acute care unit, 256

Geriatric mental status examination, 155–156

Geriatric services, of hospital, 256

Gifts, 17; Medicaid and, 40

Government agencies, nursing home care complaints and, 133

GPA. *See* General Public Assistance

Grantor, 14

Gray Panthers, 124

Guardian(s), 8–9, 157–159, 181; appointing, 52; best-interests standard and, 187; duties and responsibilities of, 163–164; payment of, 168–169; sample petition for appointment of, 307–309; substituted judgment and, 187; unethical, 163

Guardian ad litem, 159

Guardianship, 158, 160–164; advantages and disadvantages of, 163; alternatives to, 170; cost of proceeding for, 169; forms of, 158; full versus limited, 160–161; implications of, 160; process of petitioning for, 166–169; programs listed by state, 299; public, 161; sample, 311–312; single-transaction, 161; temporary or emergency, 160; terminating, 169–170; when necessary, 161–162

HCFA. *See* Health Care Financing Administration
Health care: inappropriate, in nursing homes, 116; lack of right to, 94; legal standard of, 79; power of attorney for, 55, 59, 60, 235–243; right to consent or refuse, 94
Health care decisions: competence and, 149–150; types of, 183–184
Health Care Financing Administration (HCFA), 114–115
Health care professionals, 137; competency determination and, 153–154; regulatory and licensure agencies for, 130–131. *See also* Doctor(s)
Health insurance, medigap insurance and, 20
Health Insurance Association of America, toll-free telephone number for, 31
Health maintenance organizations (HMOs), medigap insurance and, 20–21
Health promotion services, 252
Health-related state agencies and organizations, offices of, 317–391
Hearings, 140, 159; fair, Medicaid and, 143
Heirs, 6
Hemodialysis, 253
Histopathology laboratory, 252
HMOs. *See* Health maintenance organizations
Home health care, 255; insurance coverage for, 26; Medicare coverage for, 141, 204, 205; regulation of, 130
Honesty, in doctor-patient relationship, 71
Hospice, 76, 253; Medicare and, 141, 204
Hospital(s): abandonment by, 95; admission to, 75–78, 105–106; complaints about care in, 121; Diagnostic Related Groups and, 101–102; discharge from, 99–110; discharge planning and, 105–106; doctors' admitting privileges and, 68; early discharge from, 99–110; emergency rooms and, 72–73; guardianship petition filed by, 167; length of stay in, 78–79, 100–103; medical records, audits of, 92; Medicare coverage for, 205; mistakes and accidents in, 79–81; patients' right to leave, 93; questions to ask before entering, 74–75; regulatory and licensure agencies for, 130; rights of, 84; selecting, 69–70; services provided by, 251–256; staff of, 77–78; stay in, 78–79; surgery and, 73–74; use of restraints by, 93. *See also* Discharge notice; Discharge planning
Hospital auxiliary, 255
Hospital insurance. *See* Medicare, Part A of
Hospitalization: legal prohibition of refusing, 73; prior, long-term care insurance and, 28–29; reasons for, 73

ICF. *See* Intermediate care facilities
Important Message from Medicare, An, 105, 263–266
Inattention, in nursing homes, 116
Incapacity, 8–9
Incompetence, 8–9, 162; de facto, 152–153; levels of, 151–152; tests of, 162. *See also* Competence; Conservator(s); Conservatorship; Guardian(s); Guardianship
Indemnity benefits, long-term care insurance and, 26
Index for inflation, long-term care insurance and, 26
Indian Health Service, living wills and, 49
Inflation adjustment, long-term care insurance and, 26
Information, patient's right to, 87–91, 94
Information and Referral (I&R) hot line, 37, 54, 139; nursing home care complaints and, 125, 132
Informed consent: competence and, 162; right of, 87
I&R. *See* Information and Referral hot line
Institutions: on-site review of, 176–177. *See also* Hospice; Hospital(s); Nursing home(s)
Insurance: Catastrophic Coverage Act and, 23, 141; discharge date and, 109–110; dread disease policies and, 22; hospital admission and, 77; long-term care, 25–31; medical record reviews and, 92; medigap, 19–25, 26, 109–110; preexisting conditions and, 22; questions or problems with, 31–32; selecting a doctor and, 68. *See also* Medicaid; Medicare
Intensive care unit, cardiac, 251
Inter vivos trust, 14–17

Interested party, living will and, 218
Intermediate Care Facilities (ICF), 34, 113; Medicare and, 36
Intestacy, 7
Involuntary commitment, 93

Joint bank accounts, 11–14
Joint Commission on Accreditation of Health Care Organizations, 69, 70
Joint property arrangements, 11–14; undoing, 13
Joint tenants, 11; in common, 11; with right of survivorship, 11
Judges: administrative law, Medicare and, 142; nursing home care complaints and, 125; judicial review, 140; Medicare and, 142

Kidney failure, Medicare and, 201

Laetrile, lack of right to treatment with, 95
Law(s): family consent, 182–183, 331, 333–334; natural-death, 48, 49; regarding living wills, 217–223. *See also specific laws*
Law enforcement agencies, nursing home care complaints and, 125, 131–132
Lawyers. *See* Attorney(s)
Least restrictive method, of restraint, 92
Legal representation, of wards, state requirements for, 305
Legal services: to draw up power of attorney, 52; ignored or challenged decisions and, 188; living wills and, 47; Medicaid denial and, 40; nursing home care complaints and, 125; sources of, 5–6, 36–37, 54, 139, 188
Legal Services Corporation, 139, 188
Legal Services Corporation Act, 36
Legislative committees, nursing home care complaints and, 126
Licensing agencies: for board and care homes, 130; for clinical laboratories, 130; for health care professionals, 130–131; for home health care agencies, 130; for hospitals, 130; nursing home care complaints and, 124, 129
Life-and-death treatment decisions, 183–184
Life-sustaining procedures, living will and, 218
Living trust, 14–17
Living will, 9–10, 43–50, 180; artificial feeding and hydration and, 50; changing 47–48; contents of, 44; defining terminally ill and, 45–46; effectiveness of, 47; federal health care facilities and, 49–50; limits of, 48–49; power of attorney versus, 48; purpose of, 45; revocation of, 47–48, 218; sample, 215–216; state laws regarding, 46–47, 217–223; suicide and, 44; validity of, 46–47
Long-term care insurance, 25–31; legal requirements for, 29–30; nursing home care and, 35; questions to ask about, 30–31; what to look for in, 27–29; when to purchase, 26–27
Long Term Care Ombudsman Program (LTCOP), 115; discharge planning and, 104; nursing home care complaints and, 124, 126–129; state offices for, 287–291
Long-term care unit, of hospital, 253
Loss ratio, medigap insurance and, 24
LTCOP. *See* Long Term Care Ombudsman Program

Magnetic resonance imaging, 253
Major medical insurance, medigap insurance and, 21
Malpractice, 79
Mandatory recipients, of Medicaid, 142
Media: approaching, 195; nursing home care complaints and, 133
Mediation and arbitration services, nursing home care complaints and, 125, 133
Medicaid, 37–41, 135–136, 142–143; appealing denial of, 40; application for, 39–40; denial of, 40, 116; eligibility for, 37–39, 136; joint bank accounts and, 13; medigap insurance and, 20; nursing home care and, 26, 34, 40–41; selecting a doctor and, 68; trusts and, 16–17
Medical care. *See* Health care
Medical insurance. *See* Medicare, Part B of
Medical problems, with nursing homes, 116
Medical records, 71; patient's rights and, 91–92; release of, 92
Medical tests, patient's right to information about, 88
Medically needy, Medicaid and, 38, 142
Medicare, 135–136, 141–142, 199–207; applying for, 200–201, 202–203; Catastrophic Coverage Act and, 23, 141; coinsurance and, 21; deductibles and, 21; denial of, 36–37, 116; discharge date and, 109–110; eligibility for, 36, 136, 199–200, 201–202; employer group health plans and, 206–207; expenses not covered by, 205; fighting denial of,

Medicare (*continued*)
    36–37; hospital discharge and, 106; *Important Message from Medicare* and, 105, 263–266; intermediary for, 36; new payment system of, 100–103; nursing home care and, 34, 35–37; other health insurance and, 205–206; Part A of, 35, 141–142, 200–201, 203–204; Part B of, 35, 36, 141–142, 201–203, 204–205; premiums for, 35, 202; quality screen and, 285–286; questions about, 36, 207; selecting a doctor and, 68; supplemental insurance and, 19–25, 109–110, 206
Medigap insurance policies, 19–25; cautions regarding 22; discharge date and, 109–110; legal requirements for, 23–24; loss ratio and, 24; nursing home costs and, 26; preexisting conditions and, 24; questions to ask about, 24–25; when to purchase, 20–22
Megavoltage radiation therapy, 252
Mental disorders, long-term care insurance and, 28, 30
Mental status examination, 155–156
Mistakes, in hospitals, 79–81
Money, tools for managing, 10–11

NAIC. *See* National Association of Insurance Commissioners
National Association for Home Care, 106
National Association of Insurance Commissioners (NAIC): long-term care insurance and, 29–30; standards for medigap insurance, 23
National health care and self-help groups, 393–399
National Institutes of Health, living wills and, 49–50
Natural-death legislation, 48, 49
Navy, living wills and, 49
Negligence, in hospitals, 79
Neonatal intensive care unit, 256
Nonroutine treatment decisions, 183
Nontreatment, decision making and, 149
Nuclear magnetic resonance, 253
Nursing assistants, training of, 112–113
Nursing home(s), 113–114; choosing, 114–115; cost of, 26; financial problems and, 116–117; guardianship petition filed by, 167; medical problems and, 116; personal problems and, 117–118; private-pay patients in, 41
Nursing home care, 33–42; application for, 41; complaints about, 41, 118–121; cost of, 34; intermediate care facilities and, 34, 36, 113; long-term care insurance and, 25–31; Long Term Care Ombudsman Program and, 115, 124, 126–129; Medicaid and, 34, 37–41, 142; Medicare and, 34, 35–37; planning ahead for, 42; private-pay patients and, 41; problems with, 111–113, 115–118; regulatory and licensure agencies for, 129; skilled nursing facilities and, 33, 35–36, 113, 141, 203; veteran's benefits and other resources and, 41–42. *See also* Long-term care insurance policies

Obstetrics unit, 255
Occupational therapy services, 253
Older Americans Act, 36, 115, 125, 126, 139, 188
Older Women's League, 124
Ombudsmen. *See* Long Term Care Ombudsman Program
Open-heart surgery, 251
Optional categorically needy, Medicaid and, 142
Order of appointment, 163–164
Organ donation, decisions regarding, 94, 185–186
Organ transplant, 252
Organized outpatient department, 254

Patient(s): Diagnostic Related Groups and, 102–103; discharge planning and, 103; getting the most out of relationship with doctor and, 70–72; private-pay, in nursing homes, 41; qualified, living will and, 218; rights concerning medical records, 71, 91–92; rights when meeting with doctor, 68–69; terminally ill, 45–46, 76. *See also* Doctor(s); Doctor-Patient relationship; Hospital(s); Nursing home care
Patient representatives, 76, 255; discharge planning and, 103; hospital care complaints and, 121
Patient rights, 83–97; American Hospital Association's bill of rights and, 257–258; in doctor-patient relationship, 84–85; doctor's responsibilities and, 86–87; federal bill of rights and, 83, 261–262; *Important Message from Medicare* and, 263; to information, 87–91; informed consent and, 87; lack of absolute nature of, 96–97; leaving the hospital and, 93; making complaints and, 95–96;

medical records and, 91–92; in nursing homes, 118; patient's responsibilities and, 85–86; restraints and abuse and, 92–93; state bill of rights and, 259–260; surgical consent and, 74
Payees. *See* Representative payees
Pediatric inpatient unit, 256
Peer Review Organizations (PROs), 70, 78; hospital discharge and, 102, 103, 106, 108–109; nursing home care complaints and, 124; offices of, 271–276
Persistent vegetative state, 45–46
Personal decisions: competence and, 150; surrogates and, 58–59, 186
Personal money manager, 11
Personal problems, in nursing homes, 117–118
Personal representative, 4
Personal status reports, of wards, state requirements for, 301–302
Petition, 159; competence and, 51; for conservatorship, 169; for guardianship, 161–162, 166–169
Petitioner, 159–160
Physical therapy services, 253
Physician. *See* Doctor(s)
Planning: for nursing home care, 42; reasons for, 8–9. *See also* Discharge planning
Police, nursing home care complaints and, 125, 131
Political action, 192–193
Power of attorney, 8–9, 52–62; automatic ending of, 53; creating, 57–59; discharge planning and, 104; discussing with health care professionals, 62; durable, 8–9, 48, 53–60, 104, 187, 225–226, 235–243; general, sample form for, 229–233; for health care, 55, 235–243; immediate durable, 54; limits on decisions and, 61–62; living wills versus, 48; problems with, 59–60; reasons to use, 55–57; revoking, 52, 54; sample forms for, 227–233, 245–249; springing durable, 8–9, 53–54, 245–249; statutory short form of, 57; using lawyers to draw up, 52, 54
Preexisting conditions: long-term care insurance and, 28; medigap insurance and, 22, 24
Premiums, for Medicare, 35, 202
Preponderance of evidence, guardianship petition and, 168
Principal, power of attorney and, 8–9, 52
Privacy, in nursing home, 117

Private-pay patients, in nursing homes, 41
Probate court, 5, 159
Property: management under power of attorney, 57–58; putting into trusts, 17; tools for managing, 10–11
Protective service agencies, nursing home care complaints and, 125, 133
Proxy, 180
Psychiatric consultation and education services, 254
Psychiatric emergency services, 254
Psychiatric foster and/or home care program, 254
Psychiatric inpatient unit, 253–254
Psychiatric outpatient services, 254
Psychiatric partial hospitalization program, 254
Public guardianship, 161

Qualified patient, living will and, 218
Quality screen: hospital discharge and, 107; 108; Medicare and, 285–286

Radiation therapy: megavoltage, 252; x-ray, 252
Radioactive implants, 252
Radioisotope facility: diagnostic, 252; therapeutic, 252
Real estate, putting into trusts, 17
Recipient, 137
Reconsideration: Medicare and, 142; Social Security Disability Income and, 140
Recreation, in nursing homes, 117
Recreational therapy, 255
Regulatory agencies: for board and care homes, 130; for clinical laboratories, 130; for health care professionals, 130–131; for home health care agencies, 130; for hospitals, 130; nursing home care complaints and, 129
Rehabilitation inpatient unit, 253
Rehabilitation outpatient services, 253
Renewability, of long-term care insurance, 27–28, 30
Representative payees, 11; accounting procedures for, 175–176; application form for, 313–318; evaluation form for, 176, 325–330; guidelines for designating, 172; institutional rules and, 174; misuse of funds by, 175; on-site review of institutions and, 176–177; qualifying as, 172–174; replacing, 177–178; report form for, 321–324; responsibilities of, 174–175; selection of, 319

Research participation, decisions regarding, 149–150, 186
Residents' councils, nursing home complaints and, 120
Resources, allowable, Medicaid and, 38–39
Respiratory therapy services, 252
Respit care, insurance coverage for, 26
Respondent. *See* Ward(s)
Restraints: in nursing homes, 116; right to be free of, 92–93
Rights: of doctors, 84, 95. *See also* Patient rights
Roommates, in nursing homes, 117
Routine treatment decisions, 183

Satellite geriatric clinics, 256
Second opinion, 73
Sedatives, in nursing homes, 116
Self-care unit, 253
Settlor, 14
Single-transaction guardianship, 161
Skilled Nursing Facilities (SNF), 33, 113; long-term care insurance and, 29; Medicare coverage for, 35–36, 141, 203
Skilled nursing unit, of hospital, 253
SNF. *See* Skilled nursing facilities
Social Security, representative payee for, 11, 171–178, 313–319, 321–330
Social Security Disability Income (SSDI), 137, 140
Social Security office, Medicare questions and, 36
Social service agencies: as guardians, 166–167; nursing home care complaints and, 125
Social worker, nursing home complaints and, 120
Society for the Right to Die, 46, 217
Speech pathology services, 255
Spending down, Medicaid and, 38
Springing durable power of attorney, sample form for, 345–349
SSDI. *See* Social Security Disability Income
SSI. *See* Supplemental Security Income
Standard of proof, guardianship petition and, 168
State agencies, health-related, offices of, 317–319
State bill of patient rights, 83
State insurance departments: filing complaints with, 31–32; offices of, 209–214
State Unit on Aging, 37, 54, 124, 139; nursing home care complaints and, 132; offices of, 293–297
Sterilization, 255
Substituted judgment, 57, 187

Suicide: living will and, 44; patient rights and, 96
Supplemental medical insurance, under Medicare, 35, 36, 36
Supplemental Security Income (SSI), 137, 142
Supportive care, 44
Surgery, 73–74; ambulatory, 251; open-heart, 251; patient's right to information about, 90–91; second opinion and, 73
Surrogate decision makers, 51, 181; de facto, 153, 181–182. *See also* Power of attorney

Taxes, gifts and, 17; trusts and, 16, 17; wills and, 5
Temporary guardianship, 160
Terminal condition, living will and, 218
Terminally ill patients: defining, 45–46; facilities for, 76. *See also* Hospice
Testamentary trust, 14
Testator, 14
Theft, in nursing homes, 118
Therapeutic privilege, 91
Therapeutic radioisotope facility, 252
Therapy, in nursing homes, 116
Tissue donation, right to consent or refuse, 94
Transfer(s): of decision-making powers, 52; in nursing homes, 117
Transfer tax, trusts and, 17
Trauma center, 251
Treatment: life-prolonging, American Medical Association statement on withholding or withdrawing, 335; patient's right to information about, 89–90; right to refuse, 94, 95, 96
Treatment decisions: life-and-death, 183–184; routine and nonroutine, 183. *See also* Decision(s); Decision making; Living will
Treatment plan, 71–72
Trust(s), 14–17; advantages and disadvantages of, 16; children and, 6; functioning as wills, 15–16; inter vivos, 14–17; testamentary, 14
Trustee, 14, 16
Trustor, 14

Ultrasound, 251–252
U.S. Department of Health and Human Services; nursing home care complaints and, 41, 125; representative payees and, 177–178
Utilization review, 78

Veterans Administration: health insurance under, 206; living wills and, 49; nursing home care and, 41–42
Visits, choosing nursing home and, 114
Visitors, nursing home care and, 113
Volunteer services department, 255

Waiting periods, long-term care insurance and, 29
Ward(s), 8–9, 158, 160; person and property of, 158; state requirements for estate accounting and, 303–304; state requirements for legal representation of, 305; state requirements for personal status reports on, 301–302. *See also* Conservatorship; Guardianship

Water: living wills and, 50; removal of, 50, 185
Welfare agencies: as guardians, 166–167; nursing home care complaints and, 125
Will(s), 3–7; administering, 4; advantages and disadvantages of, 7; alternatives to, 10–17; dying without, 7; filing, 4; legal services for, 5–6; reasons for omitting, 3–4; state laws regarding, 7; trusts functioning as, 15–16. *See also* Living will
Witnesses: for living wills, 46; for power of attorney, 59
Worksite health promotion, 252

X-ray radiation therapy, 252

About the Advisory Board

WILLIAM BENSON, the consultant and reviewer for chapter 9 ("What to Do if You Have a Problem or Complaint") and the adviser for chapter 15 ("People Will Listen—If You Talk"), is the Staff Director of the Subcommittee on Housing and Consumer Interests, Select Committee on Aging, U.S. House of Representatives. He has also served on the staff of the Senate Special Committee on Aging, was California's state long-term care ombudsman, and managed that state's Advocacy and Civil Rights Office in the Department of Aging. He has also worked on the staff of a federally funded national model project to train and assist advocates to aid the elderly with public entitlement and other legal problems, directed a senior citizens' center, and established and directed a retired senior volunteer program. He has had extensive experience in preparing and providing testimony before legislative and administrative bodies, in drafting and lobbying major legislative initiatives, and in speaking on issues affecting the elderly.

DAVID F. CHAVKIN, the consultant and reviewer for chapter 10 ("The Medicare/Medicaid Maze"), is the Director of Legal Advocacy for the Epilepsy Foundation of America and specializes in representing persons with disabilities. He is a member of the U.S. Advisory Panel on Alzheimer's Disease and has served as directing attorney of the Maryland Disability Law Center, member of the Maryland Governor's Task Force on Alzheimer's Disease, and consultant to the Congressional Office of Technology Assessment for its report on dementia.

JOHN G. FEARS, ESQ., the consultant and reviewer for chapter 13 ("When Social Security Payments Go to Someone Else"), is the Managing Attorney of the Norman Law Center of Legal Aid in Western Oklahoma, which provides civil legal services to low-income individuals. He was the attorney for a landmark beneficiary's case that eventually resulted in the court's requiring all payees to provide annual accountings, to be reviewed by the Social Security Administration. He was also instrumental in working on federal legislation that provided for timely investigation into the backgrounds of prospective payees, as well as increased penalties and fines for the misuse of funds. He has specialized in issues of elder law for more than ten years.

PENELOPE HOMMEL, the consultant and reviewer for chapter 12 ("Guardians and Conservators: When, If, and How"), is the Executive Director of The Center for Social Gerontology (TCSG), a nationally recognized support center in law and aging, in Ann Arbor, Michigan. She developed, with the University of Michigan Law School, a law and aging program for the Institute of Gerontology. She directed a guardianship standards project and is well versed in guardianship issues throughout the country. She was the editor of TCSG's 1986 publication *Guardianship and Its Legal Alternatives* and has conducted countless training programs on protective services issues.

TOM JAZWIECKI, the consultant and reviewer for chapter 3 ("Paying for Nursing Home Care"), is the National Advisor for Long Term Health Care for Ernst and Whinney, the world's leading health care accounting and consulting firm. He is also president of Evergreen Health Care, Inc., a nursing home management corporation, and a member of the Congressional Advisory Panel on Alzheimer's Disease. A former director of the Office of Reimbursement and Financing for the American Health Care Association in Washington, D.C., he was an independent consultant to the California Department on Aging and the California Alzheimer's Task Force. He has written several articles dealing with the financing of long-term care services and recently coauthored a book on long-term care reimbursement.

MARSHALL B. KAPP, ESQ., the consultant and reviewer for chapters 5 ("Powers of Attorney and Other Ways to Plan Ahead"), 11 ("Competence and Incompetence: What They Mean"), and 14 ("Limits on Decisions Made for Someone Else"), is a professor at Wright State University's School of Medicine and at the University of Dayton's School of Law in Ohio. He is the author of numerous articles, reviews, and books on the law and ethics surrounding health care. He has served as a consultant to the Congressional Office of Technology Assessment, the Federal Administration on Aging, the American Hospital Association, and the Retirement Research Foundation. He was a Robert Wood Johnson Faculty Fellow in Health Care Finance and is a Fellow of the Gerontological Society of America.

JOHN LASTER, ESQ., the consultant and reviewer for chapter 1 ("Wills, Trusts, and Joint Accounts: Using Them Now") and the reviewer for chapter 4 ("Is a Living Will a Good Idea for You?"), is a partner at Landsman, Eakes and Laster, a general civil practice firm specializing in estate planning for older people and families in which a member faces long-term illness. A founding member of the National Academy of Elderlaw Attorneys, he has served as chairman of the legal issues section of the Foundation of Thanatology and continues to serve as counsel to the Hospice Council of Metropolitan Washington, Inc. He has taught university courses in estate planning and probate and served as a guest lecturer on legal issues of the elderly for many institutions. He created a popular will-writing workshop in the District of Columbia area and works frequently with the American Bar Association's Commission on Legal Problems of the Elderly.

BARBARA MISHKIN, ESQ., the consultant for chapter 4 ("Is a Living Will a Good Idea for You?"), is an attorney at Hogan and Hartson in Washington, D.C. She is extremely active in many aspects of elder law and is a board member of the Foundation for Critical Care Medicine; Bon Secours Health System, Inc., and the Hebrew Home of Greater Washington. In addition, she is a member of the executive committee on the Legal Counsel for the Elderly; a member of the Committee on Scientific Freedom and Responsibility of the American Association for the Advancement of Science; and a trustee of Mt. Holyoke College. She has published frequently, prepared numerous reports for federal advisory committees, and made many presentations to professional groups involved in elder law and issues.

CYNTHIA E. NORTHROP, ESQ., the consultant and reviewer for chapters 6 ("Saying Yes to Medical Care: What You Should Know First") and 7 ("Patients Have Rights, Too"), is a nurse attorney who specializes in nursing issues in her private law practice in New York City. She also serves as adjunct associate professor on nursing law at Columbia University's Teachers College, Department of Nursing Education. She has taught community health nursing, law, and ethics at various schools of nursing for more than ten years. She is the founder of the American Association of Nurse Attorneys and president of the American Association of Nurse Attorneys Foundation. Ms. Northrop lectures extensively and has published numerous articles on nursing law, as well as an award-winning book on the subject.

SUSAN M. PETTEY, ESQ., M.P.A., the consultant and reviewer for chapter 2 (" 'Medigap' and Long-Term Care Insurance Policies"), Director of Health Policy for the American Association of Homes for the Aging. Previously she was the Deputy Counsel and Associate Director of Government Affairs for the National Association for Home Care. She has also been director of government affairs for the Home Health Services and Staffing Association and a presidential management intern and legislative analyst for the Health Care Financing Administration in the U.S. Department of Health and Human Services. Ms. Pettey has taught graduate courses in health care law and health care financing, as well as many workshops on the legislative and regulatory processes.

DAVID SCHULKE, the consultant and reviewer for chapter 8 ("If the Hospital Tells You to Go Home Too Early"), is a staff member of the Special Senate Committee on Aging. In that capacity, he researched and prepared numerous hearings on problems of quality, access, and cost in Medicare, Medicaid, and Food and Drug Administration programs. Several of these hearings—based on an unprecedented two-year investigation—focused on problems in the quality of care provided under the Medicare prospective payment system for hospitals. As a result of these hearings, the Heinz/Stark Medicare Quality Protection Act of 1986 was enacted by Congress, creating broad new protections for beneficiaries needing acute hospital services. Mr. Schulke has worked for more than ten years in positions overseeing public health policy and focusing on long-term care services and financing.

About the Author

TERESA SCHWAB MYERS is a freelance writer who specializes in issues facing the elderly and in the interaction between medicine and society. She has written extensively on the legal, medical, and ethical issues that confront the elderly and their families; the impact of genetic testing; and medical safety issues. She cowrote *Losing a Million Minds: Confronting the Tragedy of Alzheimer's Disease and Other Dementias* for Congress, and *Caring for an Aging World,* an examination of how different countries approach the universal problem of caring for their sick and elderly individuals. She has lived around the world, and was educated in Africa, Asia, Europe, and the United States.